My Life as a Radical Lawyer

My Life as a Radical Lawyer

William M. Kunstler
with Sheila Isenberg

Birch Lane Press
Published by Carol Publishing Group

A Birch Lane Press Book
Published by Carol Publishing Group
Birch Lane Press is a registered trademark of Carol Communications, Inc.
Editorial Offices: 600 Madison Avenue, New York, N.Y. 10022
Sales and Distribution Offices: 120 Enterprise Avenue, Secaucus, N.J. 07094
In Canada: Canadian Manda Group, P.O. Box 920, Station U, Toronto, Ontario M8Z 5P9
Queries regarding rights and permissions should be addressed to Carol Publishing Group, 600 Madison Avenue, New York, N.Y. 10022

Carol Publishing Group books are available at special discounts for bulk purchases, sales promotion, fund-raising, or educational purposes. Special editions can be created to specifications. For details, contact: Special Sales Department, Carol Publishing Group, 120 Enterprise Avenue, Secaucus, N.J. 07094

Manufactured in the United States of America

10 9 8 7 6 5 4 3 2 1

Library of Congress Cataloging-in-Publication Data

Kunstler, William Moses, 1919–
    My life as a radical lawyer / William Kunstler with Sheila Isenberg.
        p.   cm.
    "A Birch Lane Press book."
    ISBN 1-55972-265-7 (cloth)
    1. Kunstler, William Moses, 1919–   . 2. Lawyers—United States—Biography.   3. Radicals—United States—Biography   I. Isenberg, Sheila.   II. Title.
KF373.K8A35   1994
340'.092—dc20   94-11590
[B]   CIP

To the hundreds of clients I have represented over the years—the real heroes—without whom this book could never have been written.

W.M.K.

I tell you naught for your comfort,
    Yea, naught for your desire,
Save that the sky grows darker yet
    And the sea rises ever higher.
Night shall be thrice night over you
    And heaven an iron cope.
Do you have joy without cause
    And faith without hope.
      —G. K. Chesterton,
       "The Vision of the King"

Nur der verdient sich Freiheit wie das Leben
der täglich sie erobern muss.

Of freedom and of life he only is deserving
Who every day must conquer them anew.
      —Johann Wolfgang von Goethe V,
       "Court of the Palace"

Contents

Part Four: Politically Incorrect

Preface

M<small>Y</small> GENERATION OF WHITE, URBAN, COLLEGE-EDUCATED LIBERALS often heard the name Bill Kunstler during the chaotic and confrontational sixties. He was our darling, the lawyer whose hoarse bass voice and flyaway gray locks graced our television screens night after night during the Chicago Seven trial, who stood shoulder to shoulder with Native Americans, Black Panthers, revolutionaries, and Yippies, whose attention to a case assured defendants that their cause would not go unnoticed.

But times changed, and so did we. My youthful infatuation with the voice of radical law gave way to a feminist's disenchantment with male sexist behavior and pronouncements, including Bill Kunstler's.

Moss grew on my memories of Chicago. Rennie Davis was peddling insurance, Bobby Seale was hawking barbecue sauce, and Jerry Rubin was said to have sold out.

So it was more than a little intriguing to hear the name Bill Kunstler again, years later, and discover that he had remained true and was still giving it all away. The particular case that brought Bill Kunstler back into my life is not important in the context of a great lawyer's story. It involved a country butcher who was also an elected official and who had gotten into a bit of trouble over conflict of interest. For legal help, the butcher called on Kunstler, his neighbor and a man with a solid belief that one should always be there for old friends or old neighbors.

When the case was heard, with the famed attorney defending the butcher, I watched the dramatics from the back row of the Ulster County Courthouse in upstate New York. Kunstler versus the local authorities was the best show in town.

ix

In those days, I was a reporter at a small daily in the Hudson Valley, and after the trial I asked Bill Kunstler for an interview. I had discovered that he spent time each summer in nearby West Shokan, a tiny hamlet in the Catskill Mountains.

Bill was agreeable to the interview—as I was soon to find out, he's agreeable to almost any request put to him by a reporter—and I arrived at his cabin on a morning in late June to find him an amiable and gracious host, offering hot coffee and fresh muffins, and very ready to talk. These qualities, along with his sense of humor, are as fundamental to Bill, it turns out, as his radical politics. We had coffee on an outside deck where Bill needed no prodding from me to discuss his famous cases. At one point, a wasp flew onto his hand, but he just brushed at it and went on talking.

Most people would have taken notice of a wasp. But wasps to Bill are as unimportant as anything else that does not have to do with the law. He doesn't care about what most people care about. He has no relationship with money, is never petty, and is rarely concerned with what he'll earn on a particular case or if he'll be paid at all. Bill's goals are different. They include both an idealistic aspiration to achieve justice for his clients while positively affecting society and a craving for the limelight. He also has a need to win respect, approval, and yes, love for himself.

After Bill and I had talked for a while that day in West Shokan, it was time to take his daughters, Sarah and Emily, then seven and five, to camp. Bill made an ineffectual pass with a hairbrush, then looked at me for help. I brushed their hair; then we drove to the fundamentalist Christian day camp where the girls were enrolled. I thought the camp seemed an odd choice for the children of Bill Kunstler, but he said, "Well, it's right nearby, and they seem to like it. It won't hurt them." He brushed aside the fundamentalists as he had the wasp. The basics can take care of themselves; the energy must be put into the cases and the causes.

Some years later we decided to do this book, and I must say, our early sessions were very tough for me. Somewhat intimidated, I found myself sitting on the caved-in green couch in Bill's office, trying to get him to answer my questions, to focus on his past. In that room, cramped and crowded with files and furniture, he was often distracted, answering the constantly ringing phones, taking press calls, talking to Ron Kuby, his partner, to Sarah and Emily, teenagers now, to his wife, Margie, or taking care of client emergencies.

The office is crammed with photos of Bill with notorious clients, famous friends, and in a place of honor over the fireplace, his favorite, the classic Margaret Bourke-White photograph of a Depression-era breadline with black men and women juxtaposed against a billboard touting the American dream, complete with white nuclear family, dog, and new car.

In the outer room, really a hallway, hemmed in with files, boxes, and an L-shaped desk, sits either Rosa Maria de la Torre, Sue Bailey, or Teresa Gutierrez, the women who rotate days as office secretary because, as they have told me, no one person could handle an average five-day week in that not-at-all-average office.

During our sessions, Bill and I would often walk around the corner for lunch, with him stopping along the way to chat with street people, neighbors, anyone and everyone. Inside the Waverly Coffee Shop, after kibitzing with the waiters while eating his usual lunch—crisp bacon on white bread, washed down with a white-and-black soda—he would talk about Brando, the Berrigans, Gotti, the death penalty, his Supreme Court arguments—whatever the subject was that day.

He talked about H. Rap Brown, Adam Clayton Powell, and Lenny Bruce, of southern bigots and northern racists, of nights in jail cells, of beatings by officers of the law, about lynchings and drive-by shootings, about protests, marches, and demonstrations. He talked about Martin King, Abbie Hoffman, Morty Stavis, and others he loved who are gone.

During the two years that I spent working with Bill, he told me many stories that he couldn't remember clearly. He even told me some that turned out to be untrue. His memories, like all of ours, are composed of what really happened and what he believes happened. Bill's enormous need to be liked led to his occasional portrayal of himself as even more gigantic a figure than he actually is. He is the principal embellisher of his own myth.

Bill has lived through so many intense events that his memories have likely been altered by time and by his desires, hopes, and illusions. Also, he sometimes adheres to a truth that is deeper than a factual one, so if it serves a political purpose to gloss over or fudge a little, Bill does, no doubt about it.

Though this story is told entirely from Bill's point of view and often in language drawn verbatim from our sessions, I have checked key episodes with other sources, finally selecting from the sometimes mutable versions of his storytelling the account that strays the least from the truth.

But while truth telling has been my principal aim in setting about to coax an autobiography from Bill Kunstler, it was not the only goal. Under every question and every narrative digression was the desire not to just know the truth of a famous career but to get to the man behind the colorful veneer; to find the point of intersection between a love of the limelight and the dictates of an integrity and idealism as radical as any the legal profession has known; to find the place where the energy that animates this incredibly loving man intersects with his anger.

Purists are welcome to pick on the factual errors in these pages. Maybe he magnified or omitted, or maybe he simply forgot. But his essence is here. Bill's love of all people, even the ones you and I might wish to avoid, is also here.

In this book, he tells you that he has no fear of dying, for his life has been rich, his work fulfilling, and that he has loved every minute of it. Knowing Bill Kunstler, having spent this time working with him, I believe he speaks the truth.

SHEILA ISENBERG

Author to Reader

F OR MORE THAN THREE DECADES, MY COURSE HAS DEVIATED FROM THE path one might have expected of a graduate of Yale University and Columbia Law School. Beginning with my early civil rights work in 1961, through my defense of political and social activists during the turbulent sixties, to my current caseload of politically unacceptable outcasts, I have worked toward a single goal and followed a single vision.

My vision of America is defined by the original, idealistic principles set forth in the Constitution, that all people are equal and that government has a responsibility to protect our rights and freedoms described in the Bill of Rights. In my legal career, from my defense of the Freedom Riders to Martin Luther King, the Chicago Seven, the Black Panthers, Larry Davis, and El Sayyid Nosair, I have worked steadily to push society in this direction, toward what I view as morally correct rather than socially acceptable.

In 1961, when I agreed to defend several hundred Freedom Riders in Jackson, Mississippi, I saw for the first time the depths to which the government would go to protect the rights of the privileged few. Freedom Riders rode interstate buses throughout the South in an attempt to desegregate bus terminals. Before this time, during the 1950s, individual battles against segregation remained within the borders of the cities and towns in which they began. But the Freedom Riders raised the civil rights movement to a national level by virtue of the publicity they received and because they acted throughout the entire South.

When I saw the brutal battering the Freedom Riders received from white southerners, I aligned with the underdogs. As I be-

xiii

came more and more involved in the southern struggle, I found that I was no longer satisfied practicing conventional law and talking liberal politics. I felt empty inside when I saw black people beaten and bloodied. I had to do what I could to stop their pain because, seeing theirs, my own was unbearable.

Coming from a family that had provided me with a childhood of comfort and security, I felt that in order to validate my life, my time on earth had to count for something. I felt a need to justify the air I breathed, the food I ate, and the water I drank. My defense of Freedom Riders added importance and meaning to my life.

At first, I felt like Lord Bountiful succoring the masses: I would help these poor people, represent them in court, save their lives, help them regain their liberty. But as the years passed, especially after the Chicago Conspiracy Trial, when I learned that the government would stop at nothing to win its case, I became increasingly involved in representing people who could not stand up for themselves. And my view of myself changed. I began to see myself as someone who had a real contribution to make. My constituency was the poor, the uneducated, the powerless, the disfranchised—blacks, Arabs, Native Americans whose lands had been stolen, Italian Americans suspected of "being connected"—anyone whose skin was darker, whose religion was different, who questioned the government. These were the people I represented—whether they were innocent or guilty—because they needed me. They would make my days on earth count. What was it all for, anyway, if I could not make a real difference?

Today I take on mainly cases that I view as political either because the defendants oppose the government in one way or another, because they are members of an oppressed class, or simply because they are society's outcasts. Since I feel most passionate about these cases, they take up most of my time and energy. Usually, the odds against winning them are so high that creating defense strategies provides me with enormous intellectual stimulation. The challenge of outwitting the powerful forces of government prosecutors, with their vast resources, keeps me mentally engaged. Ever since law school, when I held several jobs in addition to attending classes, I have been aware that I need a rather large amount of intellectual stimulation in order not to become bored. My most difficult cases provide me with that.

I also take some cases—very few, possibly too few—simply because they will pay me a healthy fee. These cases pay me enough so that I can represent the major portion of my clientele pro bono, without charge.

Although my caseload is always overfull, I turn down dozens of cases every day either because they are unacceptable to me politically or I find them uninteresting. In early 1994, for example, I chose not to defend a man who allegedly shot and killed Yeshiva students as they rode across the Brooklyn Bridge. My turning down this case had to do with how I viewed the motive behind the shootings and consideration of how it would affect my current caseload. First, there is nothing political about shooting down a bunch of kids. I also felt that the case could seriously harm my representation of defendants in the high-profile, alleged Islamic conspiracy to bomb a number of sites in New York City.

During the years after the Freedom Riders, I began to take on more and more prominent cases and gradually became well known. I loved the excitement of controversial cases. The media attention, in addition to ego gratification, added to my feeling that I was doing important work. During the sixties, I grew close to political leaders of the movement against the Vietnam War and young members of the counterculture who had rejected the values of their parents. I began to understand the Establishment world that had spawned me.

While defending blacks in the South or antiwar activists in the North, I saw the government using criminal tactics in the name of justice. Shocked to discover that justice is rare for those not favored by the system, I witnessed, in case after case, the government systematically destroying individuals who opposed or threatened it.

Today I remain convinced that justice often fails in America. We may tout our democratic principles, claim that we represent the free world, and rush to various corners of the earth to aid fledgling nations in the name of democracy. But can we claim to be the America that was envisioned more than two hundred years ago by the framers of the Constitution and the Bill of Rights when our own justice system is rife with corruption and inequities?

But because I am an unreconstructed optimist, I still seek justice for my clients whenever and wherever I can. In some respects, I see myself as Don Quixote, a good man trying to fight evil who—because he was old and decrepit—sometimes mistook windmills for the real quarry. But he remains a symbol for those of us who fight for our beliefs, even though we may appear foolish to the rest of the world.

So while some people may view me as wildly and indiscriminately tilting at windmills, I see myself as a keeper of the faith, fighting for my own personal vision of America and my own personal goal: That someday, somehow, we will find the hidden path that leads to what we have always outwardly prized but never attained. Equal justice for all.

WILLIAM M. KUNSTLER

Acknowledgments

I WANT TO EXPRESS MY DEEP APPRECIATION TO MY WIFE, MARGARET RATner, my children Sarah and Emily, and my partner and alter ego, Ronald L. Kuby, for their comfort, encouragement, and input. I am grateful also to the daughters of my first marriage, Karin and Jane, their mother, Lotte, my grandchildren, Daniel, Jessica, Andrew, and Christopher, and my sister, Mary, and her husband, Red, as well as the scores of friends, relatives, and colleagues who provided essential details about episodes in my life. My brother, Michael, my first partner, who died much too young, deserves a special tribute for his important role in enabling me to work in the civil rights movement.

I could never have completed this book without the aid of my longtime friend and present collaborator, Sheila Isenberg, who worked with me to create this portrayal of my life and times.

Sheila thanks her husband, Chris Collins, and her daughter, Sunshine Flint, for their love and support; Rebecca Daniels, Judy Fischetti, Kari Mack, Esther Ratner, and Susan Ray for research assistance; Judith Reichler, Gale McGovern, and Jed Horne for editorial guidance; and the many friends, family members, and colleagues of mine who graciously provided factual information, photographs, and other material for this book.

We are both grateful for the efforts of our agent, Richard Curtis, and our lawyer, my longtime friend and colleague, David Lubell, who were instrumental in seeing this project to its completion, as well as those of our editor, Hillel Black, who truly understood our vision of this book.

Some of the attributed quotes reflect the gist rather than the actuality of the conversations in question. Errors and omissions, of which I am certain there are many, are mine, the result of my all too faulty memory. I apologize for each and every one.

W.M.K.

My Life as a Radical Lawyer

CHAPTER ONE

Turning Point: Chicago

You can jail the revolutionary, but you can't jail a revolution!

A SHARP CHICAGO WIND CUT THROUGH ME AS I WALKED UP THE STEPS of the steel-and-glass federal building on Dearborn Street just before 10:00 A.M. on September 24, 1969. Upstairs, on the twenty-third floor, inside the oak-paneled chamber of the U.S. District Court for the Northern District of Illinois, the historic Chicago Conspiracy Trial was about to begin.

The protagonists were eight defendants; a team of government prosecutors; federal judge Julius Jennings Hoffman; my co-counsel, Leonard Weinglass; and me, a fifty-year-old lawyer from New York City.

As I walked into that courtroom and noticed the vast contrast in appearance and demeanor between the defendants and the prosecutors, between our side and the government, I realized what was at stake here: The United States had put the sixties generation on trial. And I was privileged to be one of its defense attorneys.

Americans of every type, age, and political belief would be closely watching what happened in this courtroom, and thousands of young people in the counterculture and antiwar movements would be affected and influenced by the outcome of the case. This trial would be a turning point in America's history, and

3

it was up to me and Len Weinglass to keep the faith—to exonerate the defendants and validate the politics and values of the sixties. I was exhilarated by the challenge of this legal battle but a bit daunted by the responsibility. Only after the Chicago Conspiracy Trial ended would I realize that the national reputation I had gained could be used, forever after, to benefit all of my future clients.

The case was *United States v. Dellinger et al.* and the defendants—Dave Dellinger, Abbie Hoffman, Jerry Rubin, Tom Hayden, Bobby Seale, Rennie Davis, John Froines, and Lee Weiner—had been arrested on charges that the prosecution improvised as the case developed. Old statutes were dredged up and dusted off, and new ones contrived, in order to find criminal indictments that would apply.

Officially, the defendants were charged with conspiracy and with crossing state lines with intent to "incite, organize, promote and encourage" riots at the 1968 Democratic National Convention, in violation of a year-old statute, known colloquially as the Rap Brown Statute. Written into the Civil Rights Act that was signed into law on April 11, 1968, the Rap Brown Statute was passed—illegally, in my opinion—during a time when the administration was particularly disturbed by the rebellions of black residents in Newark, Los Angeles, Detroit, and other cities. By creating an antiriot statute and naming it after Rap Brown, an outspoken black activist, the government attempted to link in the public perception black militants with antiwar protesters, most of whom were white.

The real reason for the arrest of the "Chicago Eight," as the defendants came to be called, is that they represented all aspects of the counterculture of the sixties: irreverent rejection of the Establishment, pacifism, strident militancy, opposition to the war in Vietnam, and rejection of racism. The government's strategy in joining the leaders of the nonviolent antiwar and civil rights movements with militant blacks was to create in the public mind the idea that the burgeoning antiwar movement was an integral part of the Black Power movement.

Contrary to what many in the government believed and stated, the Chicago Eight would have liked to revolutionize America, not destroy it—a goal which they partially attained during the trial. Ironically, this trial contributed more toward radicalizing people than any other single occurrence of the decade. As one of the defendants, Jerry Rubin, said to the judge at the end of the trial: "You are jailing a historical movement. . . . You are jailing your youth . . . for the crime of dreaming, of dreaming of an alternative. You are jailing it for the crime of idealism. . . . You can jail the revolutionary, but you can't jail a revolution."

Convention Week, 1968

It all started on August 25, 1968, a year and a month before the trial, during what came to be called "Convention Week." About ten thousand young people arrived in the Midwest capital to protest the business-as-usual Democratic party as it prepared to nominate Lyndon Johnson's handpicked successor, Hubert H. Humphrey, for the presidency.

The year 1968 had been a brutal one. The assassinations of Martin Luther King and Robert Kennedy. Increasing bitterness between pro- and antiwar Americans. The seemingly endless destruction of human life in Vietnam. A generation gap so wide it seemed no one could bridge it. A developing harshness in the civil rights movement as blacks became more and more frustrated.

The year 1968 also marked the zenith of the sixties' political and social movement for change. More and more young people came to regard the Establishment—the existing social and political order—as a dirty word. These young people created their own culture, the counterculture, which rejected everything the Establishment held dear. They marched and protested to show their opposition to racism and the war in Vietnam. Many began to believe that domestic fascism was a possibility as they witnessed the desperate measures taken by the government to suppress or destroy dissent.

By 1968, 40,000 Americans had died in Vietnam, and 250,000 had been wounded. Thousands of Americans had been prosecuted for resisting the draft. Student protests grew in intensity, and college campuses were the scene of sit-ins, strikes, hostage taking, and campus takeovers. The students' message was: "Hell, no, we won't go!"

The protest at the 1968 Democratic Convention in Chicago was the largest one to date, and many young people believed it would herald the long-anticipated revolution; the old order would fall, and the new system would reign. The counterculture would become the American way of life.

But Chicago Mayor Richard Daley, who had earlier ordered his police force to "shoot to maim and shoot to kill black people on the streets of Chicago," had no patience for the protesters. The kids had come to Chicago for what was billed as a Festival of Life; they planned to protest, march, listen to rock music, and sleep in the city's parks. But under Daley's orders the police beat and clubbed anyone who was out on the streets, including bystanders and reporters, in a classic example of overkill.

The streets ran red with blood as television crews captured the violence of the rampaging police. The young people threw up their arms to protect themselves from blows and chanted, through their tears, through their blood, "The whole world is watching! The whole world is watching!" They believed their ordeal would radicalize the country, that anyone watching police battering unarmed citizens would be forced to comprehend the meaning of government repression.

But the demonstrators were wrong. Even though the Chicago confrontation was one of the most critical moments of the decade, the sight of police beating up the youth of America didn't change anyone's ideology. Those who thought the young people had gone too far did not flinch as they saw heads cracked open. And those of us who believed that the Establishment politicians, barricaded inside the Hilton Hotel, would sacrifice any principle to maintain their power had our worst fears realized. But for most Americans the spectacle of police riots in the streets was simply compelling television.

After Convention Week was over, Ramsey Clark, U.S. attorney general under President Lyndon Johnson, refused to indict any of the protesters. Instead, he brought charges against eight Chicago policemen for interfering with the civil rights of demonstrators.

When Richard Nixon was elected president, however, his attorney general, John Mitchell, was more than willing to indict the protesters. Nixon wanted to come down hard on students, blacks, radicals, hippies, and activists. To set an example, the administration selected eight members of the sixties generation as fall guys and on March 2 indicted them for conspiracy and violating the Rap Brown law.

At about the same time that the Chicago Eight were indicted, Ramsey Clark's police indictments were being blocked by William J. Campbell, chief federal district judge, and Thomas Foran, U.S. Attorney for the Northern District of Illinois. Foran would later prosecute the Chicago Eight. None of the police were convicted. One cop was discharged from the force, and the other seven were only temporarily suspended.

The Chicago Eight

The eight defendants were not targeted because they were members of a cohesive group, although most of them did know each other. This was a planned vendetta against the antiwar movement and the counterculture. As early as October 1968, FBI director J. Edgar Hoover had announced that a group of key political activists would be indicted for conspiring to violate the federal antiriot statute in connection with their actions during Convention Week. Each of the eight men selected by the government for prosecution stood for a particular threat to the country, a threat the government wanted to eliminate.

During Convention Week, seven of the eight defendants had arrived in Chicago to protest the war in Vietnam and the selection of Lyndon Johnson's successor. Abbie Hoffman and Jerry Rubin came to Chicago to create a Festival of Life and a Theater of Disruption. Tom Hayden and Rennie Davis arrived to participate in a large-scale protest against the war, similar to the 1967 March on the Pentagon in which thousands of people protested the bloodbath in Vietnam. Dave Dellinger, working with Tom and Rennie, had opened a MOBE—National Mobilization to End the War in Vietnam—office in Chicago and had planned a loose, unstructured counterconvention in contrast to the undemocratic Democratic Convention. Black Panther party chairman Bobby Seale was in Chicago, briefly, to replace Eldridge Cleaver, another member of the party, as a speaker. Student Lee Weiner and teacher John Froines planned to march and protest.

Abbie Hoffman began his personal struggle against inequality and injustice as a voter registration worker for the Student Nonviolent Coordinating Committee (SNCC). I first met him in 1964 in McComb, Mississippi. As a liberal northern Jewboy, in the argot of southern rednecks, Abbie got beaten up a lot. But he remained in the South, working in the movement, until he opened Liberty House in Greenwich Village, which sold handcrafted items made by Mississippi black women. Later, he started the famous Free Store in the East Village. Since an important part of the counterculture ethic was that all material wealth should be shared, the

Free Store provided various items at no charge to anyone who needed them.

Like me, Abbie's involvement with the sixties began with a first tentative step, a deepening involvement, and finally, a wholehearted commitment. He was the sixties' renegade whose life I might have lived had I been younger. Over the years, there were many times that I wanted to be Abbie instead of myself. His writings reflected his developing philosophy: First, *Revolution for the Hell of It,* then *Woodstock Nation,* and then *Steal This Book.*

As Abbie would tell us in that Chicago courtroom, he was a child of America, a patriot in the two hundred-year tradition of American revolutionaries. He was determined to be free. His thoughts and actions were always original, and he was an emotional man who laughed and cried easily. Once, during the trial, an action of the judge's made him so sad that he was practically in tears. He said to the judge, "You are a *shanda fur de goyim,"* meaning the judge had embarrassed himself, Abbie, and other Jews in front of the non-Jews of the world by his cruel actions.

The press was quite susceptible to Abbie's bag of tricks. During the Chicago trial, for example, when Abbie told reporters he had a supply of powerful aphrodisiacs, they all paid him good money for the "pills." They assumed he had the inside track on illicit drugs and were disappointed to find out these aphrodisiacs were really only simple aspirin.

Abbie played with people's minds. After the Chicago trial, when *Steal This Book* was published, bookstore owners were in a quandary: If they placed it on the shelves, copies would be stolen. But if they didn't carry the book, they might lose sales. This was Abbie's genius: Creating a situation to make people rethink the way they normally did things and inevitably re-evaluate their most basic values.

In April 1967, to point out the meaninglessness of money and to show up the Wall Street players whose lives were motivated by it, Abbie, Jerry, and others caused a national furor when they threw money onto the floor of the New York Stock Exchange. The image of stockbrokers scrambling over each other to grab the dollar bills created a sensation. In Chicago, during Convention Week, the Yippies ran a piglet named Pigasus for president and on national television discussed how favorably he compared to the candidate put up by the Democrats.

Jerry Rubin had an ordinary childhood, with a father who

drove a truck and a mother who stayed at home. His father became an organizer for the Teamsters, but it was more the times in which he grew up than his father's unionism that set Jerry on his path. He went to Berkeley in 1964 and joined various political groups until he became involved in Berkeley's Free Speech Movement, which encouraged not only freedom of speech but acting on one's political beliefs. Later, Jerry became involved with various anti-war groups. Like Abbie, he had an excellent intuitive understanding of how to use the media to get his message across. When he appeared before the House Un-American Activities Committee (HUAC) a couple of years before Chicago, he wore a Revolutionary War uniform. Of course, his regalia received enormous media coverage.

Jerry and Abbie met in New York, and while Jerry directed the October 1967 March on the Pentagon, Abbie organized the Levitation of the Pentagon "to exorcise it of its evil spirits." To ridicule the pomp and pretentiousness of the military, he imagined that the huge Pentagon building could be lifted off the ground using only the power of people's minds. And he convinced many others to join him in the effort.

During the march, Abbie asked me to join a crowd of some thirty thousand people who were in a huge circle about the Pentagon. I agreed because it was a great piece of theater that would dramatize our opposition to the war in Vietnam. As we stood with our hands on the base of the Pentagon, Abbie cried out, "Now, everyone, lift the building!" To this day, many people, fired up with imagination and desire, claim that the building rose several inches in the air.

A few months later, on New Year's Eve, Jerry and Abbie created the Youth International Party, Yippie!—a concept, not an organization—which, for the next two years, created chaos, but always for a political purpose.

Jerry's most outrageous and often quoted statement was when he told the youth of America to murder their mothers and fathers. The remark was shocking, but Rubin spoke as a result of his involvement in Berkeley's Free Speech Movement and meant it figuratively only: By killing your parents' voices inside your head, you could rid yourself of their traditional Establishment values.

Dave Dellinger, at fifty-four, was more than twenty years older than his Chicago codefendants. A lifelong pacifist who had driven an ambulance for the Quakers during the Spanish Civil

War, Dave studied for the ministry after graduating from Yale and spent three years in jail for refusing to comply with the draft during World War II. He believed that nonviolence was the only solution to U.S. militarism and was cochair of the MOBE.

A fourth defendant, Bobby Seale, was the national chairman of the Black Panther Party, whose members believed that the only way to achieve justice for blacks in America was by taking action and by self-defense rather than nonviolence. The organization was created in 1966 by Seale and Huey Newton, who, along with many other blacks, had run out of patience with the slow pace of the southern civil rights movement.

Bobby was in Chicago during Convention Week for one day only and had nothing at all to do with the antiwar protests that took place. His indictment appeared to be an afterthought by the government. He was clearly part of the Chicago Conspiracy Trial only because of the color of his skin; the government needed a representative black defendant, and Bobby took the hit. By the time the trial began a year after Convention Week, Bobby had also been indicted on a Connecticut charge of conspiracy to commit murder. (The case resulted in a hung jury, and the charge was eventually dismissed.) So while the other defendants remained free on bail during the trial, he had to stay in jail.

It was Bobby's mistreatment in that Chicago courtroom that led the rest of us to our most desperate utterances and most rebellious acts. Bobby was abused mercilessly by the prosecution and the judge, but he refused to be humiliated. Bobby's ordeal brought about what we would all remember as the most tragic day of the trial. Bobby was ultimately severed out of the trial, and the case was thereafter referred to as the "Trial of the Chicago Seven."

Defendant Tom Hayden, who drafted the famous Port Huron Statement, which outlined the New Left's political goals, was a founder of Students for a Democratic Society (SDS). SDS, which advocated a political movement that was student-based rather than worker based, eventually grew so large and influential that it had chapters on college campuses all across the country. Defendant Rennie Davis was also a founder of SDS and a leader of the New Left. He had worked for years as a community organizer before that and was the Chicago coordinator of MOBE.

Rounding out the eight were John Froines, a Bard College chemistry professor who had founded the Radical Science Information Service, and Lee Weiner, a doctoral student and instructor at Northwestern University.

The Government's Case

The job of representing Establishment ideology—the voice of the conservative middle class—fell to the federal prosecutors. They prosecuted, and persecuted, the Chicago Eight for their politics during the six long months of the trial. Chief prosecutor U.S. Attorney Thomas Foran was smug: This case was a political plum that would ensure his receiving the Democratic nod to fill a vacancy in the U.S. Senate. The government's number-two man was Assistant U.S. Attorney Richard Schultz, a young, bespectacled, prim-and-proper prosecutor, whom the defendants called "Tricky Dick."

Foran and Schultz tried to present the defendants as Machiavellian plotters of the worst kind: "evil men . . . as evil as they can be . . . [they have an] evil scheme . . . [they are] liars, obscene haters, violent anarchists . . . profligate extremists. . . ." They warned that "no citizen will be safe" if this nefarious group was allowed to go free. They attempted to convince the jury that the defendants and their attorneys were "conspiring to disrupt" that Chicago courtroom in much the same way that the defendants had conspired to disrupt the Democratic National Convention: "You know the other assault they made in this courtroom is an assault on the law itself." Their case was a classic example of government against people.

Frequently, Foran brought the proceedings down to the lowest possible level. Once, he referred to me as "that man," and when I objected and asked him to use my name when he addressed me, he responded: "What I think of calling you I won't say before ladies."

The judge, Julius Jennings Hoffman, had been specially selected to hear the case after Chief Judge Campbell stepped down because of criticism that as Mayor Daley's friend and former partner, he was hardly the proper person to preside over a trial which would consider the propriety of the mayor's actions during Convention Week. Judge Hoffman, a Republican, was known to run a very tight ship and had been given the case because it was believed he would be able to control the eight defendants.

As I look back, Hoffman, a diminutive, cranky man, still fascinates me enormously. We share a German-Jewish origin and the same birthday, July 7. When the trial began, I was fifty and he was seventy-four. Our exchanges were often bitter, but with a humorous undertone, including our ongoing repartee about which of us had the bigger entry in *Who's Who.* (I did, by three lines.)

Right up until his death in 1983, Julie never backed down from the position he held during the trial: The defendants were "terrible"; the trial was "great"; and he was totally in control of the proceedings. In truth, he reminded me more of the Queen in *Alice in Wonderland,* with her cries of "Off with their heads," than of a dignified judicial figure.

Judge Hoffman viewed defendants and defense attorneys as the enemy, and since he believed he represented the lawful authority of the United States, he was certain he was always correct and just. His duty was to put us all in jail for as long as he could. He made absolutely no distinction between clients and lawyers. He demeaned Len's and my professional abilities, treated us with consummate disrespect, and insulted our witnesses. He reviled our politics, lifestyles, and beliefs from the start and never even feigned impartiality. He conducted a personal vendetta against us and was determined to wreck our case and, if he could, our reputations as well.

Months after the trial ended, when the court stenographer sold her tapes, she inadvertently included one she had made in the judge's chambers before the start of the trial. The tape showed that the judge had been listening to *CBS News* in his chambers and heard Walter Cronkite say the Chicago defendants did not expect to be treated fairly by him. When an FBI agent in the room asked him what he was going to do about that prophecy, Hoffman sat up and jeered, "I'll show them how prejudiced I can be!"

But Judge Hoffman was not the prime mover against us. From the beginning, he had been programmed by the government to be suspicious of the defendants. The government wanted him to react emotionally, and he did. So although I hated Julie during the trial, over the years I have come to realize that he was far from the major villain in the case, that once he was selected to be the judge, everything was done to program him to do what Nixon & Company wanted.

I've learned since then that in many high-profile cases, where the government has a large stake in winning, it is not uncommon for FBI agents to be used to influence judges by revealing incriminating or prejudicial details about a defendant or creating such an atmosphere of fear that the judge eventually requests additional protection and more security around the courthouse. The FBI will often create judicial paranoia so that a judge begins a trial already biased against a defendant.

The government took no chances at this trial, we learned later when we obtained documents about the trial through a Freedom of Information Act request. Prior to and during the trial, judge, prosecutors, and FBI agents had colluded and conspired. They conferred daily, infiltrated the defense by taping some of our key legal meetings, and had secret communications with some of the jurors.

By the time the Chicago Conspiracy Trial began, the government may have felt secure, believing that Judge Hoffman would ride roughshod over the defendants' rights and convict them, but what it did not take into account was the popular support among some Americans for the defendants and their lawyers. We became near folk heroes, and to our supporters the evils in the courtroom were being perpetrated by the judge, the prosecutors, and the rest of the government crew cuts.

The Defense

My cocounsel, Len Weinglass, was a bright, quiet, hardworking lawyer who had represented many movement causes and clients in New York and New Jersey. I was a middle-class liberal from Westchester, New York, who had spent Convention Week, 1968, traveling in Europe with my wife and daughters. For the better part of the decade, since 1961, I had worked almost exclusively on southern civil rights cases. Most recently, in the year or two just prior to this case, I found myself changing, along with my clients, rejecting the gentleness of the early civil rights movement and developing a harder, angrier position.

By the time I headed to Chicago in the fall of 1969, I knew that the nonviolent principles of Martin King were giving way, out of necessity, to the militant philosophy of Malcolm X and others like him. Although I had not yet been radicalized, for me the winds of change were definitely in the air.

I was asked to represent the Chicago Eight by Abbie Hoffman and Jerry Rubin, whom I had earlier represented before the House Un-American Activities Committee—a committee of the U.S. House of Representatives which ostensibly routed Communists out of the woodwork but was really an organized witchhunt that destroyed many careers and lives. Abbie and Jerry knew I was far from a radical, even though, along with lawyers Gerald Lefcourt and Arthur Turco, I had initially worked on the defense of the Panther 21, a group of Black Panthers indicted for conspiring to blow up a number of New York City sites, and I had been named East Coast counsel to the Black Panther party.

Abbie and Jerry trusted me to follow their political lead, but most of the Chicago defendants, I found out later, felt uncertain about me. Later, when they discovered that I had voted for Hubert Humphrey in the 1968 presidential election, they were upset that I would vote for a candidate as mainstream as Humphrey, someone who had not repudiated Lyndon Johnson's war policies.

My first act as a Chicago Eight lawyer was to represent Abbie Hoffman, Jerry Rubin, and Dave Dellinger at their New York City arraignments on the Chicago charges, where they entered pleas of not guilty. The other defendants were arraigned in Chicago.

The eight defendants had agreed that Charles Garry would be lead counsel and Lenny and I were to sit second seat to him. Charlie, Bobby Seale's choice, the Black Panther party's general counsel, was often described as "a streetfighter in the courtroom." He was a brilliant lawyer who had created and perfected the aggressive courtroom tactics I would follow in Chicago—and forever after.

Since both the Panther 21 and Chicago Eight cases were heating up and I couldn't decide which case to work on, Gerry Lefcourt and I tossed a coin to determine who would take which one. I got Chicago, and Gerry represented the Panthers. He and the Panther 21 defense team successfully tried what developed into the longest criminal trial in New York's history. All twenty-one defendants, including even those who had jumped bail, were acquitted of every charge.

My fate sealed, I went to Chicago to meet with Len Weinglass, who had been brought onto the defense team by Tom Hayden. Len and I were looking forward to Charlie Garry's leadership in the case, but to our dismay, Charlie suddenly needed gallbladder surgery, and the judge refused to delay the trial the two weeks necessary for his convalescence. This decision was a harbinger of what was to come. Judge Hoffman routinely granted delays, even to lawyers who wanted vacation time. Although we didn't realize it then, by refusing Charlie's request, the judge was letting us know that he would make this trial as difficult for us as he possibly could.

The case now had to go on without Charlie, a great blow for us, although he would in the future joke that his gallbladder had saved him four years' jail time, the sentence I later received for contempt of court. Charlie died in 1991, not long after he suffered a cerebral hemorrhage. When he collapsed, an attendant asked him if he had a headache. A streetfighter until the end, Charlie snapped, "I don't have headaches. I give them!"

With Charlie off the case, Len and I became cocounsel. We were equal partners. I was older and more experienced, but he had the respect of all the defendants and was excellent on details. We worked well together, each of us possessing different strengths. Len was quiet and meticulous, while I was more outspoken and dramatic. In addition to the defendants and their lawyers, the defense committee had attracted volunteers from all over the country. In our communal-style office near the courthouse, the young volunteers did everything from legal work to laundry to obtaining videotapes of Convention Week to be used as evidence.

Any money the defendants or we lawyers earned from speaking engagements went into our treasury. This fund paid rent and bought food, purchased trial transcripts, and paid for subpoenas of tapes, rentals of video equipment, and other trial expenses. Len and I each received $100 a week. This small sum certainly didn't allow me to send any money home to my family, so the burden of supporting my wife and children fell on the law firm I had formed nearly two decades earlier with my younger brother, Michael. He paid the tab for my family throughout the Chicago trial, as he had done for years while I was in the South doing civil rights cases.

One of the major points in the defense's case was that the defendants had spent months trying to secure permits from the City of Chicago but had met with a complete lack of cooperation. This attempt to secure permits showed that none of them had come to Chicago planning to incite a riot. They had all wanted peaceful demonstrations and had tried to secure park permits so that the anticipated thousands of demonstrators could sleep in the city parks. We also tried to prove that the heavy-handed Chicago police had caused whatever violence that occurred, not the protesters.

The Jury

Although the Chicago trial would turn out to be one of the most celebrated trials of our time, the jury was selected in only a few hours. Since, in a federal case, the judge conducts the voir dire, or jury examination, the selection went quickly. Most federal judges ignore the law which allows defense attorneys to share jury examination with them. By cutting out the defense attorneys, judges avoid searching inquiries that might reveal bias against criminal defendants. In Chicago, Judge Hoffman's questioning of potential jurors was wholly inadequate, and when it was over, we knew virtually nothing about the jurors who were selected for this most important trial.

The jury originally consisted of two white men, two black women, and eight white women. They were eventually sequestered and required to live in a hotel for the six months of the trial, isolated from families and friends. After a while, they became strained and tense as a result of their unusual living situation.

These jurors, however, began to demonstrate that they understood that the Chicago defendants were being persecuted as well as prosecuted. The jury was subjected to deceptive practices and prevented from seeing and hearing the entire defense. They also witnessed the defendants' courage and intelligence, the prosecutors' hostility, and the judge's calculated overreaction. In the end, the jury rose above the government's manipulations and demonstrated their humanity.

Our favorite juror was Kristi King; she was young and had a sister who had worked in the VISTA antipoverty program. We believed she would relate to the defendants because of her age and background. A few days after the trial began, however, Foran told the court that threatening letters had been sent to Kristi's family and to another juror. He presented handwritten letters that said, "We are watching you," signed: "The Black Panthers."

We knew the letters were fakes. I thought it was an FBI ploy. The judge ordered the jury out of the courtroom, brought Kristi back alone, and then handed her a letter. He was aware that this was the first time she had seen the letter.

"Now that you've seen this, can you still be a fair juror?" asked Judge Hoffman. After reading the letter, Kristi said that she was afraid, so Hoffman removed her from the jury. I asked for a hearing and the opportunity to have the letters tested, but after first granting my request, the judge thought it over and quickly reversed himself. Undoubtedly, the prosecution convinced him to change his original ruling.

Kristi was replaced by the first alternate, Kay Richards. What we didn't find out until the end of the trial was that Richards's fiancé dispensed patronage for Mayor Daley. Had this been a fair trial, Richards's involvement with a Daley employee would certainly have precluded her from serving on the jury.

In addition to being sequestered, the jurors were driven to the courthouse daily in a van with blacked-out windows so that they couldn't see the defendants' demonstrations in front of the courthouse. Abbie, Jerry, and the others would hold aloft signs saying Free the Jury or The Jury's in Jail.

Before the Trial

Because of Charlie Garry's surgery, Bobby Seale was without legal representation when the trial began. Bobby, who refused to be represented by anyone else, had a certain trust in Charlie that he did not feel toward either me or Len. As a result, he was furious that Judge Hoffman refused to delay the trial for a short time until Charlie could recuperate.

Just before the trial began, Charlie called me from his sickbed and asked me to visit Bobby in jail. I agreed but had to file a notice of appearance stating that I was his lawyer before I could visit him. Normally a mere formality, that notice of appearance would haunt us throughout the trial. Because of it, the judge ruled that I was officially Bobby's lawyer even though Bobby adamantly insisted that his lawyer was Charles Garry. The judge's insistence that I represented Bobby despite the fact that he didn't want me was to skew the whole trial.

Len and I divided up the other seven defendants at random; having two defense attorneys meant two shots at cross-examining prosecution witnesses. I took on Abbie and Jerry because I had known them before and was identified as the Yippie lawyer. I also represented Dave Dellinger because we were contemporaries and had much in common. Len stood up for Tom Hayden, whom he knew, Rennie Davis, John Froines, and Lee Weiner. But our division of clients was casual, and basically we functioned as a unit, doing just about everything collectively.

Sometime before the trial, pretrial motions—to suppress certain statements, exclude wrongfully seized evidence, and have the indictment dismissed for legal insufficiency—were filed on behalf of the eight defendants. Len and I drafted some of the motions. Lawyers Michael Tigar, Michael Kennedy, Dennis Roberts, and Gerry Lefcourt created others.

The Opening Day

When the trial finally began on September 23, I was quite nervous about losing Garry as lead counsel. I also felt unprepared.

I had spent the months prior to this day rushing from trial to trial and had never found the time to study the Chicago case. When I finally scrutinized the government's papers, I saw that their case was a complex, well-orchestrated, and devious plan to convict and imprison the eight defendants. The government's intent in Chicago was to end political dissension by figuratively lynching the sixties generation.

On the very first day, I introduced myself to Judge Hoffman by saying, "That's Kunstler with a K, Your Honor," to clarify my name; many of my more zealous opponents, in both the South and North, had delighted in giving it a pornographic spelling. The judge then ordered all the lawyers who had filed pretrial motions to be brought before him, even though it was never intended that they would handle the trial. He issued bench warrants for Gerry Lefcourt, Michael Tigar, Michael Kennedy, and Dennis Roberts, who, of course, were not in the courtroom.

Federal marshals grabbed Michael Tigar lounging on the deck of the Smothers Brothers' boat docked in Sausalito, California. When I went to the lockup to see him, a deputy marshal said, with a big smile, "We've got a Tigar in our tank." Gerald Lefcourt was also arrested and shared a cell in Chicago's Cook County Jail with Tigar, Bobby Seale, and Jerry Rubin. (Jerry was in jail to complete a brief sentence for his participation in a California demonstration.) Lefcourt recalls that when he complained about the smell of the fish the jail served for dinner, Bobby teased him: "Lefcourt, there's no menu." Then he gave Gerry his portion of chocolate cake.

The other pretrial lawyers, Michael Kennedy and Dennis Roberts, were permitted to come to Chicago on their own, but Hoffman's jailing of Tigar and Lefcourt was so outrageous that two circuit judges went immediately to the jail to set their bail.

Attorney Thomas Sullivan, who would later take Foran's place as the U.S. Attorney for the Northern District of Illinois, represented the pretrial lawyers, arguing that they were not necessarily the lawyers on the case and therefore did not have to appear in court. Judge Hoffman was not persuaded. Finally, a hastily convened appellate panel put the matter to rest by ruling that the pretrial lawyers did not have to obey the judge's order to appear in court.

On the day Sullivan argued, the National Lawyers Guild, an organization of progressive attorneys, held a demonstration which filled the first floor of the courthouse. Chief Judge Campbell made an appearance fully robed and flanked by his law clerks. He threatened to hold all of the demonstrators in contempt if they did not leave the building at once. When they all ignored him, he retreated and flounced into a waiting elevator. None of the demonstrating lawyers was ever held in contempt.

The Chicago Conspiracy Trial began, then, in the midst of these distractions. I made an opening statement which focused on the First Amendment rights of the defendants that were being violated by the charges against them. I said that the First Amendment had been beaten down on the streets of Chicago.

The defendants were furious with me for this opening. They wanted me to talk about Vietnam rather than what was happening to their rights. Innocent men, women, and children were being napalmed while I wasted time yakking about free speech. We decided that during his opening speech in the second half of the trial, Len would make the cogent antiwar statement the defendants had hoped I would make. But when Len's time came, Judge Hoffman cut him off repeatedly, and he was never allowed to explain adequately the defendants' opposition to the war.

It became clear to me after I blew it with my opening statement that these defendants wanted to decide for themselves what happened during their trial. They wanted our legal strategies to reflect their political philosophies. After a time, I began to understand their point of view and act on it. Chicago became a proving ground for the political-legal defense.

The defendants' approach was intellectual, and they were an extremely literate group; the defense table was strewn with dozens and dozens of books (plus clothing, papers, candy wrappers, pens, and other assorted debris). They read when the action in the courtroom was boring. They read to improve their defense; they read to bolster their political positions. Lee Weiner, when he wasn't conducting hand-sign conversations with his girlfriend in the spectators' section, almost always had his head in a book.

The Trial

The prosecution had to prove that the eight defendants had conspired together and had crossed state lines with the intent of causing a riot at the 1968 Democratic National Convention. To that end, from the beginning of its case in October until it concluded on December 8, the prosecution called dozens of witnesses, including a lawyer for the City of Chicago, an assistant to

Mayor Daley, plainclothes police officers, undercover cops, an undercover investigator who grew a beard and long hair so he could pose as Jerry Rubin's bodyguard, paid informants, even a journalist who agreed to spy on the defendants by pretending to be one of them. All of the undercover informant-witnesses had infiltrated various groups of young people during Convention Week by posing as hippies and antiwar activists.

Since many Americans were willing to accept the government at face value, by being charged with acts they had not committed, these eight defendants were sullied and defamed by these false accusations. Underlying the government's case was the real purpose for the entire prosecution: To tie down these eight activists with a lengthy trial so that they would effectively be out of commission and could not do their political work. For the Chicago Eight, the movement stopped for nearly a year. If the system could not destroy the defendants by getting convictions that would stick, at least it could keep them out of circulation for a long time. This was a successful strategy that the government used repeatedly against political leaders and activists.

One example of how seriously the judge and prosecutors took their mandate to convict was that they totally ignored a 1968 Supreme Court ruling, called the Alderman Decision, which ruled that when illegal wiretapping is done by the government, it must turn all tapes over to the defendant. The defendant would then have the right during trial to object to evidence in these illegal wiretaps. Attorney General John Mitchell completely ignored this decision in the Chicago case.

We claimed that the defendants had been tapped illegally after we discovered a listening device manned by FBI agents outside our conference room in the courthouse. Although the government acknowledged that Bobby Seale, Jerry Rubin, Dave Dellinger, Tom Hayden, and Rennie Davis had been illegally tapped, we were given only some of the transcripts. When we argued that we were legally supposed to receive copies of all the tapes, Judge Hoffman decided to hold a hearing on this issue *after* the trial. This meant that the prosecution could use the illegally obtained tapes as evidence.

When the trial first began, our strategy was to demonstrate that the Rap Brown Statute was unconstitutional and violated the First Amendment because it criminalized thought. I believed then, and still do, that conspiracy in this country is too loosely defined. In order to be guilty of conspiracy, it must be proved only that a person has knowledge of the ends of the conspiracy—even though he may not know everyone involved or even what they did. An individual must only know that there is some sort of a group that is going to get together for an illegal reason—even if he never meets with the group—and there must be two overt acts (which may, in themselves, be legal) that in some way further the objectives of the conspiracy.

Called "the darling of the prosecutor's nursery" by the late Supreme Court justice Robert Jackson, conspiracy law is fundamentally wrong because a prosecutor only has to prove that the conspiracy had illegal objectives and that an individual became part of it—even though he may not have known any of the other alleged conspirators or even what it was all about.

What's really wrong with conspiracy law is that it attempts to punish thoughts rather than actions. Conspiracy is too easy for prosecutors; they love to present such cases. Moreover, the word "conspiracy" has a sinister meaning to most people. But its true definition is not at all sinister. In fact, we all wore buttons in Chicago which said We Breathe Together, because conspiracy comes from the Latin *conspirare* (to breathe together).

I soon found that proving the main charge unconstitutional was far less important to the defendants than adhering to their political goals. Their intent was to demonstrate—by their actions and by our words—that the government of the United States acted illegally to repress opposition to its policies. Thus, the trial would become a readily comprehensible political event that would make everyone aware of the government's repression and oppression of minorities, people who opposed the war in Vietnam, and members of the counterculture. The defendants also revealed their personalities and lifestyles to demonstrate exactly what the counterculture was all about.

In addition, in a radical break, the defendants refused to follow the model of courtroom etiquette. Until this trial, courtroom demeanor was rarely breached by political defendants or their attorneys. Chicago was virtually the first time that such defendants spoke back to a judge, talked directly to the jury, acted as if they were sitting in their own homes, and generally were themselves. After all, they had nothing to hide.

Len and I followed the defendants' lead. Every action we took, every statement we made, was an attempt to educate the jury, the audience, and the rest of the world about the politics of the antiwar movement and the counterculture. As a result, the public saw that the defendants and their lawyers were regular people who laughed, cried, and became angry rather than monsters whose primary goal was to burn down the country.

Demonstrations outside the courthouse as well as justified outbursts inside the courtroom were part of an aggressive strategy that I learned from the defendants. We all had closely followed the 1968 trial of Dr. Benjamin Spock, the Reverend William Sloane Coffin, and three others on charges of conspiring to violate the Selective Service Act. These defendants and their attorneys were polite, and the trial was fairly conventional, but they were all convicted. (The convictions were later overturned on appeal.)

In Chicago, we used a new technique. Rather than defending the clients, we decided to put the government on trial. Len and I attacked, fought like dogs, ripping the government's witnesses apart, often with wit and ridicule. The defendants taught us how to show up the government's weaknesses and follies by satirizing and mocking its pompousness.

Abbie often entered the courtroom doing handstands or pole-vaulting over a railing. He blew kisses to the jurors. The defendants refused to stand when the judge entered the courtroom; they talked out loud to themselves and to the witnesses. Sitting around the defense table, they read, ate, joked, laughed, and consulted with their lawyers. But all of these actions, no matter how wacky and spontaneous they appeared, contributed to the defense strategy of putting the government on trial.

Moreover, as a result of these relatively wild and previously untested methods, we fared much better in Chicago than did many other defendants in political trials.

The case for the defense ran for two months, from December 8 until February 9. As witnesses for the defense, we called gurus, entertainers, authors, philosophers, and poets who could testify about the youth culture, the counterculture, the antiwar movement, and the plans and purposes behind the Convention Week protests. One of our most effective witnesses was a British legislator, in Chicago as an impartial visitor, who testified quite articulately about the police brutality she had seen in the streets.

We called poet Allen Ginsberg, whose testimony consisted mainly of one long "Ommmmmm"—a chant used in meditation—as he explained how the chant had calmed frightened protesters when the police began to club heads in Lincoln Park. The chanting upset Judge Hoffman.

"He's just trying to calm us down," I explained.

"I needed no calming down," Hoffman retorted.

Writer Norman Mailer testified for the defense that he saw the police "chasing and chopping up demonstrators with night-sticks." Mailer was with Colorado governor John A. Love, and when the government obtained a corroborating statement from Love, it suppressed it. Although by law the defense is entitled to any evidence the prosecution has, we never heard about Love's statement until almost a decade after the trial.

We called a number of performers, including Phil Ochs, Judy Collins, and Arlo Guthrie, who testified that the Yippies' Festival of Life in Lincoln Park had been peaceful. When Phil Ochs tried to sing "We Ain't Marchin' Anymore," the judge growled, "There will be no songs in a United States District Court." When Judy Collins raised her beautiful soprano voice in song with the opening bars of "Where Have All the Flowers Gone?" a U.S. marshal clapped his hand over her mouth. Arlo Guthrie was also denied the right to sing.

One witness for the defense that we chose not to use was Hugh Hefner, founder of the *Playboy* empire. During Convention Week, Hefner had been walking with the writer William Burroughs and a few others when, for no apparent reason, they were attacked and beaten by police. Since Hefner was attacked even though he had nothing at all to do with the protests, his testimony would have helped prove our charges that the authorities' acts brutalized people indiscriminately during the Convention Week protests. But when we subpoenaed Hefner, he was afraid to testify because Chicago was his home and he wanted to stay on the right side of the police. He offered to buy his way out of our subpoena by donating $10,000 to our defense fund, a sum so high that we quickly accepted it.

Our most important witness was to have been Ramsey Clark, the former attorney general. Near the end of the trial, Tom Hayden and I asked Ramsey to appear as a defense witness, and he flew to Chicago on January 28. We were forced to interview him in a corridor outside the courtroom because we could not get the use of a conference room; then Ramsey had to wait on a bench in that corridor, sitting there for an entire morning while the judge heard arguments about whether he should be allowed to testify. The jury, of course, was not present.

After the afternoon was spent in closed session, with Ramsey telling Judge Hoffman what he planned to say on the stand, the judge ruled that he would not be allowed to testify, relying on some wholly inapplicable federal regulation relating to testimony by former government employees. It was a crushing blow to the defense. As the U.S. attorney general at the time of the protests, Ramsey was informed about government investigations of the demonstrators and knew about the negotiations between demonstrators and city officials regarding park permits and locations for marches and speeches.

He would have been an important witness for us because he would have testified about Mayor Daley's refusal to issue permits to the demonstrators despite Justice Department efforts to have him do so; the arbitrary actions of Chicago officials as he attempted to send his representatives into the negotiations and into the streets to minimize friction; his refusal to authorize any wiretaps of protesters; his presentation of evidence to a grand jury which resulted in the indictments of eight police officers for violating civil rights—not eight demonstrators. He would have also testified that from the time the convention was held in August 1968 until he left office in January 1969, he saw no evidence to support the indictment of any demonstrators.

Ramsey was an outspoken advocate of the government's responsibility to protect rather than prosecute. He believed that the federal government should be acting on behalf of the protesters being punished by authorities in the North, as it had, somewhat half-heartedly, protected protesters in the South during the civil rights days.

The day after Ramsey had cooled his heels and been forced to return home without testifying, our enormous disappointment caused several of the defendants to speak out in the courtroom. They told the jury that the former attorney general had been there but that the judge would not permit him to testify.

None of us, including Ramsey, could get over our shock at the judge's ruling. He had deprived the jury of evidence that was clearly relevant to the issues, evidence it was entitled to hear. It was important for the jury to get a sense of the background behind the charges against the Chicago defendants, and Ramsey would have provided that. It is clear that Judge Hoffman absolutely could not allow the testimony of a defense witness with the status of Ramsey Clark because of the effect he might have had on the jury. In addition, Ramsey was the attorney general who had refused to prosecute protesters and had voiced his opinion that the conspiracy law was unconstitutional.

We had rested our case on a Friday, but on the following

Monday, we petitioned the court to allow Dr. Ralph Abernathy on the stand. Judge Hoffman refused. Ralph, who had been president of the Southern Christian Leadership Conference (SCLC) since Dr. Martin Luther King's death in April 1968, had been in Chicago during Convention Week because he was driving a mule train in the Poor People's March, a plan that had been initiated by Dr. King to highlight the poverty among certain urban blacks. Earlier in the trial, police officers, including a high-ranking commander, testified for the prosecution that Ralph had asked them for protection during the demonstrations. They claimed that, at Ralph's request, the police had escorted the Poor People's mule train through the demonstrators on Michigan Avenue, in front of the Conrad Hilton, to the safety of the police lines.

Ralph was going to testify that the prosecution witnesses had lied. On August 28, 1968, police had forced the mule train to leave the demonstrators and enter police lines. His testimony would include that he saw cops viciously beating people who were standing around peacefully and, finally, that he identified with the demonstrators and their struggle in the streets of Chicago.

When Judge Hoffman refused to allow Ralph to testify, I stood up and said my piece—my rage at this decision and the ruling on Ramsey Clark forced out what I had been holding in for many months:

> Your Honor . . . I think what you have just said is about the most outrageous statement I have ever heard from a bench, and I am going to say my piece right now, and you can hold me in contempt right now if you wish to.
>
> You have violated every principle of fair play when you excluded Ramsey Clark from that witness stand. The *New York Times,* among others, has called it the ultimate outrage in American justice.
>
> . . . I am trembling because I am so outraged. I haven't been able to get this out before, and I am saying it now, and then I want you to put me in jail if you want to. You can do anything you want with me, if you want to, because I feel disgraced to be here.
>
> . . . I have sat here for four and a half months and watched the objections denied and sustained by Your Honor, and I know that this is not a fair trial. I know it in my heart. If I have to lose my license to practice law and if I have to go to jail, I can't think of a better cause to go

to jail for and to lose my license for than to tell Your Honor that you are doing a disservice to the law in saying that we can't have Ralph Abernathy on the stand.

. . . I am going to turn back to my seat with the realization that everything I have learned throughout my life has come to naught, that there is no meaning in this court, and there is no law in this court.

Another very low point in the trial came two days later. The court threatened to revoke Dave Dellinger's bail, without legal argument, because, during a speech he had given in Milwaukee, he had criticized Judge Hoffman.

DELLINGER: Why are you threatening me with revocation of bail for exercising my freedom of speech?
JUDGE HOFFMAN: I will determine what to do if and when speeches of a certain kind and character are brought to my attention. Free speech is not involved here.

I was especially enraged that Hoffman was going to do this without allowing any legal argument. "Your Honor," I said, "is there no decency left here? Can't we just argue the point?" I was cited for contempt, and there was no argument. Dave's bail was revoked.

Comic Relief

Throughout the trial, pranks, jokes, and laughter helped us all and relieved the intensity of this most serious and awful ordeal. Humor became a tactic of the defense team. Abbie and Jerry frequently took the lead on the zany antics, but the other defendants also orchestrated the action. I became something of a comic myself and learned, for the first time, how wit could be used by a trial lawyer to benefit his clients. Many of my comic retorts were a reaction to the judge's sarcasm. I struggled to top him every chance I had, and although I wasn't always successful, my batting average was relatively high.

JUDGE HOFFMAN: This is not a political case.
KUNSTLER: It is quite a political case.
JUDGE HOFFMAN: It is a criminal case.
KUNSTLER: Your Honor, Jesus was accused criminally,

too, and we understand really that was not truly a
criminal case in the sense that it is just an ordinary—
JUDGE HOFFMAN interrupted: I didn't live at that time.
KUNSTLER: Well, I was assuming Your Honor had read
of the incident.

On Bobby Seale's birthday, the defendants had a birthday cake
delivered to him right at the defense table. On the nationwide day
of protest against the Vietnam War, Moratorium Day, all of us in
the defense camp wore black armbands to court, Dave Dellinger
stood and read names of those who had died in Vietnam, and the
defendants unfurled a Vietcong flag on their table. The judge, of
course, ordered the marshals to remove the flag.

At the beginning of the trial, Jerry Rubin wore a wig because
his head had been shaved while he was in California's Santa Rita
Prison serving forty-two days for participating in an antiwar demonstration. Using Jerry's hairlessness as an excuse for a political
prank, the Yippies invited young people all over the country to
mail hair "for Jerry and Julie," to be sent in care of the judge's
courtroom deputy. Judge Hoffman, a dead ringer for Mr. Magoo,
was completely bald. Each morning, one of our rituals was opening our mail to see what the youth of America had sent. After the
Yippies sent out their request for hair, we received packets of it
from all over America and even some from foreign countries.

One morning, I opened what I thought was an envelope of
hair, only to find that it contained an ounce or so of very green
marijuana. I quickly covered it with a newspaper, hoping no one
in the room had noticed. The marijuana sat on the defense table,
with marshals, FBI agents, prosecutors, and deputies all over the
place. I worried about it all day. We were in possession of a controlled illegal substance; if found, it could have sent us all to the
slammer. Near the end of that day's session, I said to Abbie and
Jerry, "Let's get out of here. We'll let the cleaning lady find it.
Maybe she'll throw it away and that will be the end of it."

"Of course not. You can't let good grass be taken by the government or go to waste. Make a motion," ordered my clients.

So I made my first and only marijuana motion. "Your Honor,
there was delivered to us, courtesy of your courtroom deputy, a
supply of cannabis, a controlled substance under the federal code.
I would like your instructions on what to do about it."

"Mr. Kunstler, you're a resolute attorney. I'm sure you'll
know how to dispose of it," replied the judge.

"Your Honor," I promised, "it will be burned tonight."

At that moment, we were in possession of what was very likely the only legal marijuana in the country. It did leave the courtroom, and I can say, with some degree of certainty, that it was burned that night.

The defendants would often burst out laughing at testimony given by prosecution witnesses. They never tried to restrain their natural feelings, which were usually good-humored; they emphasized the comic side of everything. I tried to follow their example in my cross-examination of these witnesses. One police officer testified that he saw a couple making love up in a tree during Convention Week.

"How big was the limb? How high from the ground? Did you arrest them?" I asked him. The whole assertion was such an obvious lie that the defendants cracked up at the story and at my questions. The judge intoned continuously that "laughter has no place in a United States District Court."

There were many funny moments outside the courtroom, too. One day, Abbie, Jerry, and I were invited to lunch by the president of Midas Mufflers at the Standard Club, the most prestigious dining club for Chicago's Jewish business crowd. Judge Hoffman ate there daily, accompanied by two marshals. On the day of our lunch date, we tried to enter the club, but Abbie and Jerry were not properly dressed. The club barber loaned Abbie and Jerry white jackets, and we purchased two ties at a nearby haberdashery.

When we finally entered the dining room, I sat at one table with Dave Dellinger, Jules Feiffer, J. Anthony Lukas, Norman Mailer, and Jason Epstein, and our host. Abbie and Jerry took a table close to the judge, who moved away as soon as he noticed them. When Abbie and Jerry moved, again to a table near him, he moved once more. Then they moved again, and so on. This went on for so long that I don't believe the judge ever ate his lunch that day. Finally, he and his marshals stormed out, and the rest of us enjoyed a delicious meal.

We had a bittersweet kind of fun with the malevolent Mayor Daley when he was called as a witness for the defense. I believed that he would be a wonderful witness for us because I doubted that he could hide from the jury his hostility toward the defendants and his belief that anyone who had the nerve to demonstrate in the streets of Chicago deserved to be beaten up. We also wanted to expose a decision of his that had made police violence inevitable: his refusal to grant permits to the demonstrators who wanted to sleep in Grant and Lincoln parks.

After the noon recess, Abbie took off his jacket in the corridor outside the courtroom, walked up to Daley, and said, "Dick, why don't we settle this here and now—just you and me? The hell with all these lawyers." Daley didn't answer, but he flushed deep red, and his bodyguards closed in around him. It was quite a moment.

When Daley was on the stand, I tried to question him, but the judge wouldn't really allow anything. So I blurted out the now famous Ribicoff question, saying it as fast as I could so the jury would hear it before the judge ordered it removed from the record. A year earlier, during Convention Week, Sen. Abraham Ribicoff of Connecticut had stood at the podium of the Democratic National Convention and condemned the demonstrators' brutal treatment at the hands of the Chicago police. It was reported that Daley, upon hearing Ribicoff, had shouted from his seat on the floor, "Fuck you, you Jew son of a bitch, you lousy motherfucker, go home."

No one was willing to go on the record, but there were those who swore they had read Daley's lips and that he had indeed said that. When I repeated in court what Daley was reported to have shouted at Ribicoff, there was an uproar in the courtroom. The judge struck the question from the record. But the jury had heard it.

Throughout the trial, as Len and I forged ahead with our political-legal strategy, whenever it seemed that we were taking ourselves too seriously, Abbie and Jerry were there to keep us human and, through their antics, neatly set off the actions of a hidebound and malevolent government and a judge who could scarcely hide his animosity toward the defendants.

The Ordeal of Bobby Seale

Bobby Seale was on trial without a lawyer because of Charles Garry's illness. A short time after the trial began, I offered to represent him, since I didn't think he should be without a lawyer. A complex and lengthy debate ensued. Len Weinglass traveled to the West Coast to confer with Charles Garry, Panther leaders, and other lawyers. In the end, I was outvoted. Everyone agreed that Bobby should not allow anyone other than Garry, the lawyer he wanted, to represent him. The political point had to be driven home: A defendant in an American courtroom should be allowed to have his counsel of choice. If Bobby wanted Charlie, the court had a responsibility to wait until Charlie recovered from surgery. But if the court chose not to wait, then Bobby would be tried without the legal counsel guaranteed him by the Sixth Amendment to the Constitution.

If he couldn't have Charlie, then he would represent himself. Bobby's position as the only black defendant—and the only one trying to represent himself—made him the political leader among the Chicago Eight. My suggestion that I represent him was wrong, an error resulting from my political naïveté. At the time, I still believed in the judicial process. I still believed that any evil done in a particular court would be remedied on appeal in a higher court. Since Bobby had made his position clear and preserved the issue for appellate review, I thought he could now proceed with me as his lawyer. Then, if we lost, we would raise the representation issue on appeal. This was the traditional legal strategy, the strategy I still believed in.

But others on the defense team had decided on a stronger tactic. Bobby must inform the jury at every opportunity that he had been denied his lawyer of choice, that this fundamental right had been taken from him by the court. On the surface, Bobby's choice of counsel had been denied because the judge wouldn't adjourn for two weeks until Charlie recuperated—or because I had filed a notice of appearance. In reality, however, the court denied Bobby his counsel because he was a black person caught in a racist legal system. The judge's ruling denied to a black defendant what it allowed for the white defendants.

When Bobby requested that he be allowed to represent himself, his request was denied, and he continuously interrupted the proceedings to state that he wanted to be his own lawyer.

> KUNSTLER: The Constitution says any man that wishes to defend himself may do so.
> JUDGE HOFFMAN: You speak of the Constitution as though it were a document printed yesterday. We know about the Constitution way out here in the Middle West too, Mr. Kunstler. . . . We really do.

Finally, on October 29, after Bobby had interrupted the court time and again with his request to represent himself, came the lowest moment of the trial. Judge Hoffman decided to shut Bobby up. "Take this man out of here and treat him according to law," he ordered. The marshals hauled Bobby out; a short time later, they carried him back in and placed his gagged, chained, and bound body at the defense table. To our horror, he was unable to move or speak, but we could hear him mumble through his gag: "I want my constitutional rights, Judge Hoffman, and you know it. I have a right to defend myself."

To all of us on the defense team, it was reminiscent of slavery and representative of how black people are treated by the American judicial system. It was the moment that the Chicago trial ceased to be a trial and became a classic symbol of government oppression. Bobby's groans and moans agitated the other defendants so much that they lost all remnants of decorum and began to act out and comment aloud. On October 30, there was a tremendous fracas, and the marshals entered the well of the court and attacked the defendants, who fought back—except for Bobby, who was bound and gagged.

> KUNSTLER: Your Honor, are we going to stop this medieval torture . . . ? This is no longer a court of order . . . this is an unholy disgrace to the law that is going on in this courtroom, and I as an American lawyer feel a disgrace.
> FORAN: Created by Mr. Kunstler.
> KUNSTLER: Created by nothing other than what you have done to this man.

Later in this interchange, during which the judge admonished me for pointing at him and for my conduct, I said—and meant it with all my heart—"I just feel so utterly ashamed to be an American lawyer at this time."

On November 5, the judge said he was tired of the disturbance caused by the presence of Bobby Seale and severed his case from the others. (Bobby was never tried on the charges; he had only been accused of conspiracy to cause a riot at the convention. And since the other defendants were ultimately acquitted on this charge, there was no conspiracy charge against Bobby to be tried.)

Bobby's treatment opened my eyes to misuse of power by federal judges. From that moment on, I knew that the judge and the prosecution were my enemies and that the trial was a fake. I knew that the Chicago Eight—now the Chicago Seven—were not being tried for crimes but were being used by the government to belittle and mock the counterculture and antiwar movements and to convince the public that all movement people were destructive criminals.

The Barnyard Epithet

One person in that courtroom needed no convincing about the supposed evils of the counterculture. Already biased against the defendants, Judge Hoffman thought that the youth of America were destroying the country. Almost daily, he violated the rights of the defendants and tried to obstruct their defense. He refused to take any action when we discovered the FBI eavesdropping with a listening device on our lawyer-client meetings, did everything he could to alienate the jury from the defense team, purposely mispronounced Len's last name—calling him Weinstein, Weinberg, Wein-anything except his correct name—and constantly reminded the jury that Len and I were out-of-town shysters from the East Coast who lacked legal skills and abilities.

But as the days passed in that courtroom, which more and more came to resemble a chamber of the Spanish Inquisition, I learned how to handle Judge Hoffman. I began to fight fire with fire, sarcasm with sarcasm. Once, protesting obviously perjured testimony, I said, "It doesn't smell like Chanel Number 5 to me."

"Is that the perfume you use, Mr. Kunstler?" asked the homophobic judge.

"No, I'm a Brut man myself," I responded. The jury laughed, and this time the joke was on Hoffman. Whenever I could, I would take his barbs and digs and turn them against him, using every bit of wit I possessed to offset his hostility.

I now know that the judge was under orders from President Nixon and his cohorts, John Mitchell and Spiro Agnew. Under their direction, the unfolding trial of the Chicago Seven was a precursor of the shortsighted paranoia and poor judgment which would lead to Nixon's downfall a few years later in the Watergate scandal.

The Chicago trial ruined Hoffman's reputation, and he ended up a most unpopular man. For example, students at the Northwestern Law School ripped down a plaque which commemorated a financial donation made by his family. For a long time, I have viewed Hoffman as a pathetic character; he failed utterly in the goals which were set for him by the administration. As a matter of fact, his handling of the trial of the Chicago Seven did more to expose the inequities and prejudices of our unjust judicial system than anything else.

So many of Judge Hoffman's decisions were outrageous, illegal, and just plain unbelievable that after Bobby was severed out, the trial degenerated into a farce. Once, Dave Dellinger lost his temper when he heard lies from a Chicago police official and yelled out, "Bullshit!" (*New York Times* reporter J. Anthony Lukas delicately referred to the word as "a barnyard epithet" in the next morning's edition.) When the marshals stormed the defense table to remove Dave, his thirteen-year-old daughter cried out from the back of the courtroom, "Don't take my father away!" There was bedlam and pandemonium as the marshals began hitting people, including Dave's daughter. I can still hear the pathos in that child's shriek as she saw her father being dragged away.

Celebrity

The celebrity of the Chicago defendants and their lawyers grew with each passing week of the trial. At first, I was simply a solitary lawyer living in a tiny rented apartment that the defense committee leased for me for $100 a month. Every morning, I rode the number 36 bus from my North Side apartment to the courthouse. Once in a while, I managed to get home to Mamaroneck to visit my wife and daughters, or they came to Chicago to stay with me.

For most of the six months I was in Chicago, I was often quite lonely. Len lived with Tom Hayden and the other defendants on the South Side in a large communal apartment. But I had intentionally separated myself because I needed privacy in order to study the daily court transcripts. I also felt the age difference between me and the rest of the defense team, most of whom were at least twenty years younger. Many nights, I struggled with the conflict between my need to be alone and my feelings of loneliness. After each day in court, I would eat dinner by myself and then return to my tiny second-floor walk-up, which consisted of a vestibule, small living room, tiny kitchen, and bedroom. Other nights, I would eat dinner with Len and the defendants, and we'd review the case.

With celebrity came benefits. Some were quite enjoyable, although I'm somewhat ashamed now that I took advantage of them. My marriage suffered as a result of my relationships with these women during this period. When I did refrain from seeing other women, it was because I was afraid of how I might be perceived rather than from any ethical or moral standard; I didn't want the public to get the impression I was a philanderer. I found these women hard to resist. Many times they would actually bang on my door and say, "I'm here to spend the night with you." It was the era of free love, and I participated enthusiastically.

Days were quite different. On our daily lunch break during the trial, I often went off by myself and visited the collection of Impressionist paintings at the Chicago Art Institute. I especially liked the work of Ivan Albright, who painted startling renderings of corpulent women in corsets with their flesh popping out.

Once, when my daughter Jane, then twenty-one, came to visit, I took her to the Chicago Science Museum. As we watched the sharks, I heard a voice in the darkness say, "Boy, they ought to throw the Chicago Eight into this tank!"

Some lunch hours, however, I would writhe in pain with a migraine, an affliction I had suffered for years. I would lie on the conference room floor, my head propped on a pillow, waiting for the pain to stop. It was a personal rule of mine that if a migraine hit me during court, I would not ask for a recess and would wait for the break.

People of all ages liked us, including a group of older Jewish women who regularly attended the trial and always brought us chicken soup in a thermos. One day, I recall that Len and I shared our soup with actor Dustin Hoffman, who briefly worked for the defense committee and shared quarters with Len and Tom Hayden.

We were so popular that many individuals and groups in Chicago feted us and raised funds for us. I remember one party in a posh North Side town house that began quietly but ended with some pretty wild dancing. Abbie whirled around in his underwear, and finally feeling the allure of rock and roll, I stripped off my shirt and danced. I probably made a complete fool of myself that night, but no one seemed to notice or care.

As our celebrity grew, public hostility to the case began to diminish. Whenever we ate at Berghoff's, a large German-American restaurant a few blocks from the courthouse, fellow diners would send over free beer. Celebrity in America seems to override everything, even disapproval. For example, people would come up to me, shake my hand, then say they didn't always agree with me but respected my courage.

The defense team earned money to keep us all going by speaking on college campuses around the country. Abbie and Jerry were most in demand, but the rest of us did our share. Court ended between four-thirty and five every afternoon, and if I had a speaking engagement, I would shoot out the door, and a volunteer from the defense committee would drive me to the airport. A popular destination was California because the two-hour time difference made it possible to do an evening speech there after a day in court in Chicago. After giving the speech, I would fly back to Chicago on the redeye. By 6:00 A.M., I would be in my apartment, where I would wash, change my shirt, and rush back to court.

These speeches were so exhilarating that I was never tired. After I walked on the stage, the audience would stand up and cheer as if I were a superstar. We had an enormous and enthusiastic constituency of young people that kept increasing. I usually spoke extemporaneously, comparing our oppression in the Chicago courtroom to that of people all over America. The denial of our rights in that Chicago courtroom, I would say, is no different from the loss of freedoms being experienced by students and other young people all over the country. I told my audiences that the judicial system, rather than protecting people's rights, was now being used to repress and stifle political expression. If I ran out of things to say about the trial, I would read something written by the Berrigan brothers. They were priests who were passionately committed to the antiwar movement.

Once, I flew in a tiny prop plane to give a speech at the University of Illinois at Champaign-Urbana. From the airport, I was rushed to an auditorium where five thousand people were waiting, then, after my speech, hustled right back to the airport. The next day, I received a night letter from the provost of the university which stated that my life had been threatened. A man said he had a rifle and planned to shoot me as I gave my speech. I was furious that the university never informed me about the threat to my life until I was back in Chicago the next day. Clearly, the administration at Champaign-Urbana didn't give a damn about my life.

Near the end of the trial, Jerry Rubin was scheduled to speak at Berkeley but figured out that the only way he could arrive there on time was to leave the courtroom before the close of that day's session. We sneaked him out by pretending that he had to use the bathroom, and someone drove him to O'Hare Airport. But as fate would have it, a prosecution witness was asked to identify Jerry for the record. When the judge saw that he was not present, he thundered, "Where is he?" After the bathroom was searched, Judge Hoffman found out that the irrepressible Yippie was on his way to O'Hare and ended court early so that Jerry could be intercepted and arrested. Since court had ended early, however, we were able to get Abbie to the airport in time to make the flight and take Jerry's place at Berkeley.

We were celebrities in the trial's hometown, too. Young Chicagoans would form a line around the courthouse at dawn and wait for hours in the freezing cold to get into the best show in town. The line stretched around the courthouse no matter what the weather or time of day. The trial was very much like theater, always entertaining, enlightening, and cathartic. We had a packed house every day, with twenty or thirty folding chairs inside the rail on one side for the press and every seat in the spectators' section filled.

The trial, however, was not about celebrity or theater. The importance of the Chicago Conspiracy Trial in American legal-political history stems from its symbolic value as a sixties morality play.

The Verdict

When the verdicts came in on February 18, 1970, five months after the trial began, they were leaked to FBI director Hoover even before they were announced in the courtroom. Despite the unfair and biased behavior of the prosecutors and judge, the Chicago trial turned out to be a monumental victory for free speech and human rights. After five days of deliberations, the jury acquitted all the defendants of the most serious charge, conspiracy to incite a riot. Lee and John were completely exonerated. Abbie, Jerry, Dave, Rennie, and Tom were each convicted of a single charge, intending to organize, promote, and incite to riot.

By failing to convict the Chicago Seven of conspiracy, the government had lost badly. It had failed in its pernicious goal because of the moral strength of the defendants and the enormous support for them among a large segment of the population. The defendants had earned their own victory by standing up in court and refusing to be silenced. The jury saw them fighting for their political beliefs and witnessed what it was like to be oppressed by the government. Although the defense was belittled and stymied at every turn by prosecutors and judge, although we had a jury that had been handpicked by the government, we prevailed and won rare justice for our clients.

At their sentencing, Abbie, Jerry, Dave, Rennie, and Tom received the maximum penalty, five years and a $5,000 fine.

Contempt

While the jury was deliberating, the judge had his personal revenge. He charged us all with contempt of court, one count for each time he thought one of us had showed disrespect or rudeness. He gave out substantial sentences. Mine, I am proud to say, was the longest. During the trial, the defendants had joked that I would eventually do more time than they would. I laughed, but in the end they were correct, for I was sentenced to four years and thirteen days for twenty-four counts of contempt. (Bobby Seale also received contempt charges for the early part of the trial, before he was severed out; he received a sentence of four years.)

Abbie was sentenced to six days in jail for insulting Judge Hoffman in Yiddish and one day for blowing a kiss to the jurors. Dave got five months for his barnyard epithet. We were all sentenced to prison time for refusing to obey the judge, insulting the judge, berating the prosecutor, protesting the treatment of Bobby Seale, refusing to sit down, and even laughing. The list of our contempts was endless.

When Jerry was sentenced to a total of twenty-five months and twenty-three days for contempt, he gave Judge Hoffman credit for radicalizing enormous numbers of people. The trial's repressive judge had awakened sympathetic responses in people of all ages and all persuasions. "You have done more to destroy the court system in this country than any of us could have done," Jerry said. After Chicago, no one, except the hopelessly myopic, could ever again look at an American courtroom and fully believe that justice would always be done.

Judge Hoffman was particularly venomous with Dave Dellinger, fifty-four at the time, who had refused to bend at all. Before he was to be sentenced, Dave said, "This is a travesty. . . . I am an old man, and I am just speaking feebly and not too well, but I reflect the spirit that will echo—" He was interrupted by the cries of his daughters, along with those from other spectators. Marshals quickly began to drag Dave's daughters and others who had cried out from the courtroom.

I lost my self-control then, ran up to the lectern, and sobbed,

"My life has come to nothing. I am not anything anymore. You have destroyed me and everybody else. Put me in jail now. . . . Come to mine now, Judge, please. I beg you. Come to mine. Do me, too. I don't want to be left out." I was as close to hysteria as I have ever been; I felt the ground under me giving way as the past order of my life was turned inside out and upside down by what was happening in that courtroom.

Judge Hoffman ignored me, and I had to wait. But when it came, as he unloaded my sentence of four years and thirteen days, I felt a coldness in the pit of my stomach. But then the coldness abruptly left me; I had done the right thing. I had stood up to the tyrant, and if the price of that was jail, I was willing to pay for my principles.

I earned a contempt citation for wearing an armband in court on Moratorium Day, October 15, a day dedicated to expression of opposition to the war in Vietnam. After our request that the trial be adjourned for this important day, we had all showed up in court wearing black armbands, including me.

> Foran: Your Honor, that is outrageous. This man is a mouthpiece. Look at him, wearing a band like his clients. . . .
> Kunstler: I am wearing an armband in memoriam to the dead, Your Honor, which is no disgrace in this country. I want him [Foran] admonished. . . . The word "mouthpiece" is a contemptuous term.
> Judge Hoffman: Let the record show I do not admonish the United States Attorney because he was properly representing his client, the United States of America.
> Kunstler: Are you turning down my request after this disgraceful episode?
> Judge Hoffman: I not only turn it down, I ignore it.

I earned another contempt charge for my response to Bobby's being bound and gagged. Another citation came near the end of the trial for my remarks after the judge had refused to allow Ralph Abernathy and Ramsey Clark to testify.

Sentencing

When I was sentenced on my contempt charges, I gave one of the most impassioned orations of my life. I told other lawyers that

if they ever found themselves defending clients who were oppressed by a vindictive and malicious government, they should
do the right thing and not be deterred by the lengthy contempt
sentence I expected to receive.

> I have tried with all my heart faithfully to represent my
> clients in the face of what I consider—and still con-
> sider—repressive and unjust conduct toward them. If I
> have to pay with my liberty for such representation, then
> that is the price of my beliefs and my sensibilities. . . .
> I have the utmost faith that my beloved brethren at the
> bar, young and old alike, will not allow themselves to be
> frightened out of defending the poor, the persecuted, the
> radicals and the militant, the black people, the pacifists,
> and the political pariahs of this, our common land. . . .
> [Other lawyers must] stand firm, remain true to those
> ideals of the law which, even if openly violated here and
> in other places, are true and glorious goals. . . . Never
> desert those principles of equality, justice, and freedom
> without which life has little if any meaning.
> I may not be the greatest lawyer in the world . . . but I
> think that I am at this moment, along with Len
> Weinglass . . . the most privileged. We are being
> sentenced for what we believe in.

When I finished, there was a burst of applause which made me
feel much better. Of course, the judge ordered the marshals to remove those who had applauded. After the contempt sentences
were handed down, we were taken away to the Cook County Jail.
I was released right away, though, because the defense fund put
up my bail of $15,000. My wife and daughters had come to Chi-
cago to support me, and they were waiting for me outside the jail.

Appeal

My former law partner and good friend Arthur Kinoy, ably
assisted by lawyers Doris Peterson and Helene Schwartz, headed
the appellate team on the defendants' criminal convictions. In
less than a year, they wrote a 547-page brief, one of the longest
ever submitted to a federal court. Insisting that none of the defendants had participated in any criminal activity during Convention Week but had instead exercised their rights to the freedoms

guaranteed by the Constitution, we appeared on February 8, 1972, before the Court of Appeals in Chicago. Arthur and Helene led the argument; I also participated. After nine months, we got our decision, and it was a great vindication. All of the single-count criminal convictions of Abbie, Jerry, Dave, Tom, and Rennie had been reversed. The Chicago Seven were now vindicated.

Some lawyers had advised Arthur to "take it easy" and not make the constitutionality of the Rap Brown Statute an issue. He was told by his colleagues at Rutgers Law School to behave like a law professor and not make too much noise. But he and the appellate team wanted to make it very clear that the way the Rap Brown Statute had been used in the Chicago case threatened the rights and liberties of all Americans.

My dear friend the late Morty Stavis was the appeals lawyer on the contempt charges. After two years, that case was heard in the U.S. Court of Appeals for the Seventh Circuit, and again we were victorious. All the contempts received by the seven defendants and Len and myself were reversed. The court ruled that we were entitled to another trial before a different judge.

Arthur, Morty, and their teams proved to the federal appeals court that most of the disruptions in the courtroom had been provoked by the judge and the prosecutors. Both the criminal and the contempt appellate briefs argued that the judge had acted cruelly and irresponsibly, as had the prosecutors, in order to create a chilling effect and frighten people so that they wouldn't participate in the growing antiwar movement or any other progressive movement. We also argued that government illegality had extended beyond the courtroom when our posttrial strategy sessions, held in Len's Newark office, were illegally recorded and the tapes sent to our adversaries. Of course, the court did not rule on that; it was a classic example of the fox judging the fox.

A year after the contempt reversals, I was tried again and convicted on only two contempts, which grew out of my vigorous protestation when the judge would not permit Ralph Abernathy and Ramsey Clark to testify for the defense. Hearings were before District Judge Edward Gignoux, a rather patrician federal judge from Maine. One of my character witnesses, federal judge Robert Mehrige, was asked: "How many times did Mr. Kunstler appear in your court, and has he ever misbehaved?"

Mehrige facetiously replied, "He's here, isn't he? If he had misbehaved in my court, he wouldn't be practicing law for long."

Judge Gignoux did not sentence me to any time on the two

contempts because he thought that everything I had done was instigated by the prosecutors and the judge. He determined that any action taken should be initiated by the New York disciplinary authorities.

In 1974, I was trying a most important case in St. Paul, Minnesota, growing out of the American Indian Movement's occupation of Wounded Knee, S.D., when the Association of the Bar of the City of New York informed me it had decided that some professional action should be taken against me for the contempts. This news came immediately after we had laboriously selected a jury in the trial. Instead of keeping it to myself, I informed the judge, Fred Nichol, in open court that I needed time off in order to get myself a lawyer. He blew up, saying the timing of this Bar Association action would seriously interfere with the trial.

I returned to New York with a transcript of Nichol's remarks. Morty Stavis, again acting as my lawyer, had discovered that the Bar Association technically violated its own procedures in bringing these charges against me. This technical violation was all that was needed by a number of young Turks in the Bar Association who didn't want me charged at all; they raised hell, the charges were withdrawn, and I was never prosecuted.

After Chicago

The repercussions of Chicago continue to this day for me as well as for the others involved. Chicago turned out to be Foran's Waterloo; an immediate consequence was the loss of his promised nomination to the U.S. Senate. Right after the trial ended, a very drunk Foran spoke at a parents' meeting at Loyola High School in Chicago: "The only one [of the Chicago defendants] I didn't think was a fag was Bobby Seale." Foran was probably homophobic, for I recall him muttering "damn fag" after Allen Ginsberg testified during the trial.

Although the U.S. Court of Appeals for the Seventh Circuit found that the judge and prosecutors in the Chicago Conspiracy Trial were directly responsible for the responses of the defendants and their lawyers, these government representatives were never subjected to any official penalties. There were unofficial penalties, of course. The trial meant the practical end of Judge Hoffman's career; his reputation destroyed, he passed into obscurity. Foran and his assistant, Richard Schultz, faded from public memory and afterward never got anywhere in Democratic politics in

Chicago. The residents of that city owe us one for that.

We all know the fate of Nixon, John Mitchell, Spiro Agnew, and that crowd. Many years after the trial, many years after Watergate, the late President Nixon and I were guests on the *CBS Morning News* one day during 1990. I went to the station with Sarah, my next-to-youngest daughter, who was then thirteen. Nixon and I were sitting in chairs next to each other, having makeup dabbed on our faces, when he turned to me and said, "I thought you lived in Chicago."

"No, Mr. Nixon. I live in New York," I said, adding, "How old are you, anyway?"

"I don't know how old I am, but I know I'm having my fiftieth wedding anniversary," said the old dissembler.

Then he turned to Sarah. "Little girl, how old are you?"

"I don't know, either," she answered tartly.

The Lessons of Chicago

Chicago was my personal Rubicon. I had been, first, a traditional attorney handling run-of-the-mill cases and, later, an active civil rights attorney using traditional legal tactics. Just prior to Chicago, lawyers working in civil rights, like myself, enjoyed a long period of eventually winning almost all the cases we took on. At that time, I believed there was essential justice in our justice system—somewhere down the road, even if I couldn't see it at any particular moment.

Although local southern courts almost always enforced segregation laws and convicted civil rights defendants, their decisions were usually reversed at the federal level. So while I knew I would lose in the southern state courts, I expected to win in their federal counterparts. Federal courts knocked down segregation laws and restraints on admissions into public universities and other institutions. All types of statutes that forbade blacks and whites from mingling were destroyed systematically, case by case, in the federal courts.

This was my experience: If a wrong was committed, I thought the courts would vindicate it; if a legal point was right and moral, the courts would sustain it. The way the judiciary functioned in civil rights cases led me to believe that the law was a truly great force for social change. I felt that although there might be aberrations along the way, I could work within the system and eventually achieve essential justice.

But the Chicago case was a dramatic eye-opener that put a tragic twist on everything I had previously believed. In Chicago, in the same type of federal court I had relied on for years, I was suddenly confronted by a tyrannical judge, malicious prosecutors, and lying witnesses. It was the shock of my life. To this day, I have not gotten over it. It taught me the hardest lesson of my life: The judicial system in this country is often unjust and will punish those whom it hates or fears.

Before Chicago, I would not have believed that representatives of my own government would write threatening letters to frighten jurors. That they would present perjured testimony. That they would denigrate and embarrass defense witnesses and lawyers. That they would fabricate evidence. That they would eavesdrop on lawyer-client conferences. But all of this happened in that Chicago courtroom, with the connivance of the presiding judge.

In that crucible on the twenty-third floor of Chicago's federal building, I learned that a courtroom is like a stage. How to use my body and my voice. That the twelve individuals in the jury box were people first and jurors second. I learned to display the side of me jurors could identify with, to be folksy, never arrogant. Chicago taught me that opposition to the Establishment—which is determined to ensure, by fair means or foul, that there is no significant restructuring of the political-social-economic order—does not stand a chance unless it fights as hard as the system.

I learned from Abbie Hoffman and Jerry Rubin that humor can dissipate rancor, win over jurors, and make a political point. Following the defendants' lead, I came to understand that in this case, where the sixties generation was on trial, the only defense possible was one in which we used what the era had taught us. Don't bow down to oppression. Fight fire with fire. Don't give in to oppression; make fun of it. We put the system on trial by mocking it at every turn.

Chicago was my rebirth. I had found my place in the world, knew what I wanted to do with the rest of my life. I would practice movement law and would have a career whose rewards would be something infinitely rarer and far more valuable than money: stimulating cases and an opportunity to write a footnote to history. To this day, the majority of my cases are pro bono—no charge to the client. My riches are what I learn from each case and the delight in my daily courtroom encounters and the memorable people I am so privileged to represent.

Chicago made me feel that I was part of the sixties movement that was rocking and rolling the country off its moorings. I drew great strength from my closeness to the defendants; I belonged and felt cared about, even loved. We were in a great struggle, but we were together. While it may have appeared, on the surface, that I didn't fit in—one counterculture motto was Don't Trust Anyone Over 30—that was only the surface.

The lessons learned in Chicago have stayed with me all these years. "I am going to turn back to my seat with the realization that everything I have learned throughout my life has come to naught," I said to the judge toward the end of the trial. Chicago taught me that a defense lawyer must be a battler rather than a barrister. And it was in Chicago that I first threw down my polite lawyerly behavior and took up the fighter's stance. Today, when I work on a case where there has been oppression and malfeasance on the part of the government, when the prosecutor or the judge behaves unfairly, I remember the lesson of Chicago, and I speak out.

It isn't always the safest course. Over the years, I have often been thrown in jail on contempt charges. As I write this, I have just received notice that an appeals court has voted to publicly censure me for something I said to a judge in 1991. But I am willing, since Chicago, to say whatever has to be said if I feel it is right. As for my public censure, I regard it as a badge of honor.

Because the trial was covered so thoroughly in the media, the image of me as an aging radical with long gray hair askew and glasses perched on my head became familiar to many people. I liked the recognition; actually, I loved it. All the publicity I've received began with this case, and I have been known since as the Chicago Conspiracy lawyer, an image I have tried to use to benefit every client I represent.

During the twenty-five years since this trial, the political and social times, and my clients, have changed. I no longer represent civil rights workers accused of breaching the peace or protesters charged with disorderly conduct. Instead of pacifists like Martin Luther King and antiwar activists like Abbie Hoffman, I stand up for defendants who are not well known and who are often charged with extremely violent felonies. My clients are blacks, Muslims, Latinos, Native Americans, and other minorities who do not have the same moral stature in the eyes of the community as the defendants of the sixties.

These are tougher cases. And while I don't always agree with the politics or principles of my clients, they have in common one characteristic that makes it critical that they be represented by a lawyer who is committed to them: The system has labeled them pariahs, and as such they are treated differently than other defendants. There is no shortage of these unpopular defendants for me to represent: Larry Davis, El Sayyid Nosair, Yusef Salaam, flag burners, an Islamic group charged with conspiring to blow up half of New York City and assassinate public officials.

I use what I learned in Chicago in every defense I undertake, putting myself completely into each case and following it until its end. I appeal, appeal, then appeal again, never resting with a case until it is finally over. No case loses its immediacy with me. Today I am still working for clients whom I've represented for decades. If a case is particularly unpleasant, uncomfortable, or even frightening, I still do my best for the defendant who can't afford to hire a lawyer, who is hated and reviled, who is considered guilty long before trial. I stand up and do what I have to do. It's the only way I know how to live.

PART ONE

The First Forty Years

CHAPTER TWO

Beginnings

Every slap is a boost. It means someone's paying attention.

I_N THINKING ABOUT THE RATHER UNUSUAL NICHE I HAVE CARVED OUT for myself in American jurisprudence, I realize I cannot remember a time when I did not feel within me the desire to resist authority, oppose convention, and champion the underdog. Most likely, I owe these values and ideals to the people who were closest to me during my childhood—my parents and my maternal grandfather. I loved them very deeply, but looking back, I can see they were all somewhat eccentric.

Pa Moe

Moses Joseph Mandelbaum, Pa Moe to me, was not my real grandfather, although it was all the same to me, since he had married my widowed grandmother, Hannah, when my mother was only two. Hannah and Pa Moe were married in Albany in 1898. A short time later, Pa Moe, who was a doctor, moved his new family to New York City, where they lived in a brownstone on West 145th Street that also housed his office.

Pa Moe's upbeat attitude and indomitable spirit excited my child's heart, and I always wanted to be just like him. One of the favorite stories I heard about him revolved around his first days as a doctor in New York. At first, Pa Moe had no patients. In order to impress the neighbors that he was a busy doctor, he would dress up—always impeccable in spats and starched collar—and from time to time, rush out the front door, bag in hand, as if he were off on an emergency. A half hour later, after stopping for coffee, he would return home. He did this several times a day.

On one of these trips, Pa Moe was stopped by a very nervous man who shouted, "Doctor, I hope you have a minute, because there's someone in my house who's sick." Of course, he had a minute; he had all day. After Pa Moe recovered from the shock of being asked to practice medicine on a real patient, he rushed to help—first stopping at home to fill his empty bag with medicines and equipment.

Somehow he survived these early shenanigans, built up a substantial practice, and eventually collaborated with a well-known physician, Chevalier Jackson. As ear, nose, and throat specialists, they were among the first New York City doctors to earn six figures annually. They invented a lung device called a bronchoscope, but for some reason, Pa Moe's contribution went unrecognized, and Jackson was considered the device's inventor.

Urbane, natty, flamboyant, and egocentric, Pa Moe treated all the mayors of New York, from John Hylan to William O'Dwyer, and was a founder of New York City's Mt. Sinai Hospital. He was also the physician for the New York Giants baseball team, and I loved hearing stories about his well-known patients, especially Christy Mathewson, a famous pitcher in the 1920s. Pa Moe died at the age of eighty, penniless because of his losses in the stock market crash of 1929. But to the last day of his life he maintained his spiffy appearance and joie de vivre and always looked prosperous.

Pa Moe also had a reputation as a ladies' man. Rumor in our family had it that he may have fathered a prince. Because he was physician to Mayor John Hylan, Pa Moe was asked to escort Marie of Romania around New York City when she visited here in 1923. The story I heard is that she gave birth to Prince Michael, reportedly the spitting image of Pa Moe, nine months after she returned to Romania.

Besides being a charmer, my grandfather was an inventor who loved to create unusual and whimsical devices. One was a stencil that women could use for drawing on their eyebrows in indelible ink. When he tried out this gadget on my grandmother—whom we called Ma—he drew an eyebrow right in the middle of her forehead.

Ma, who had been a member of Albany's German-Jewish society, often pretended to be hard of hearing, which excused her from listening to Pa Moe's incessant, boastful conversation. In his presence, she was often quiet and a bit withdrawn. Ma was furious at Pa Moe after the eyebrow incident, though, and let him know about it during the many months it took the indelible ink to wear off.

Another contraption he invented was a cartop bed for campers which he tried out on a trip he took with his valet, Peter, and my younger brother, Michael. On the last night of the trip, Pa Moe absentmindedly drove off with Peter beside him in the front seat and Michael asleep in the tent. A wire stretched across the road sliced the tent in half, a bare inch above my brother's sleeping body. It was the last time Pa Moe used this particular invention.

He also devised a gizmo to turn mattresses and demonstrated it at an exposition in New York City. But his only sale was to a notorious brothel madam—Polly Adler—who wanted an easy way to freshen her establishment's much-used beds.

Pa Moe's last great oddball venture was the renovation of a farm he purchased in Carmel, New York. As a joke that only he understood, he built stairs to a nonexistent third floor. He delighted in taking me and my brother and sister up those stairs, seemingly unconcerned that we could have easily fallen off.

His clinic held many fascinations for me. Of particular interest was half a human head which he kept in a jar of formaldehyde. It was sliced down the middle, directly through the nose. When we children misbehaved, we were ordered to look at the head. If we seriously misbehaved, we were forced to touch it. But I was not at all afraid of it and happened to love this punishment.

It is the memory of a lithograph in Pa Moe's office, though, that remains most vivid. I wish I had it today. In the picture, a white-coated doctor, with a stethoscope hanging out of his pocket, is holding a naked young woman in his arms. A skeleton, representing Death, I assume, stands behind them, trying to grab the woman out of the doctor's arms. I could never stop looking at this picture. Of course, as a young boy, I was very interested in the naked woman, but it was the savior image that most drew me— and still does. I loved the notion of being a deliverer, of saving people. Today I often feel, somewhat grandiosely, that my work is the only thing that stands between a victim and the destructive forces of oppression, punishment, or public retribution.

Father

During his earlier and more prosperous years, Pa Moe employed a number of doctors in his clinic, as well as his unmarried sister, Frances, called Big Fanny to distinguish her from his daughter, who was also named Frances and was referred to as Little Fanny. My grandfather hired a young physician named Monroe Bradford Kunstler, hoping for a union between him and Big Fanny. Instead, my father fell in love with Little Fanny.

My parents were married on April 13, 1917, and I was conceived the following year, shortly before my father, a first lieutenant in the Army Medical Corps, went off to fight the Battle of Yonkers during the terrible flu epidemic of that year. I was born at home at seven in the evening on July 7, 1919—so I always think of seven as my lucky number. I have been told that when I emerged, the obstetrician said to my father, "Doctor, you have another lieutenant."

My father and Pa Moe never really got along, no doubt because they were so different. With his wrinkled collars and nicotine-stained fingers, my father was a plodding, sloppy man. Like Pa Moe, he lost most of his money in the stock market crash of 1929, and for this he always blamed his father-in-law, because he had followed his tips.

Eventually, my father left Pa Moe's employ and opened his own practice, first as a general practitioner, then as a proctologist. When I was a child, I told my father that proctology was an undignified profession. Whenever I complained about what he did for a living, he always said: "Don't look down on this work, Bill. It will send you and your brother to college." Father explained that, when he graduated from medical school, there were residency openings in urology, gynecology, and proctology. He was practical and felt that while the other disciplines each covered only half the population, a proctology practice would include everyone.

Our family was quite traditional. We had supper at six o'clock every night, although we often ate without my father. He had his office in a wing of our apartment and often worked late. During a meal, he would sometimes be called away to an emergency. And although I recall feeling resentful about his many absences, I am also often late for my own family supper or not there at all, busy working in my own office, which also is in my house.

Supporting his family was always foremost in my father's mind. Once, when a man was hurt in an accident outside our building, my father treated him and then said, "That will be two dollars." I felt that since this poor man had been hurt through no fault of his own, he should not have to pay for my father's services. I said, "You can't charge him! It was an accident!"

"Bill," said Dad, "you want to go to college, don't you? So I have to charge." At the end of each day, he would peel off the dollar bills he had earned, and my mother would put the cash in boxes marked rent, college, and food. We lived better than most people at that time, but we were hardly wealthy.

Although he was deeply concerned about his responsibility to support his family, my father was always sensitive and compassionate to the poor and was quite willing to accept whatever form of payment his patients were able to make. He was often paid in chickens, turkeys, and other food items during the Depression, for many people simply had no cash. It must have been hard for him to cover all the needs of our family, with its three children: I was the oldest, Michael was three years my junior, and Mary was six years younger. I remember that at one point Mary was attending private school, while I was enrolled in college and Michael was only three years behind me. Even though I worked at college to help out, my father always seemed worried and pressed financially.

I don't recall his ever embracing me, but he was lovable and never tyrannical. Like Pa Moe, though, he was also a bit wacky. Once, at a family dinner many years later, when we all had children of our own, my father thought that my only nephew looked a bit wan. He decided to test the boy's urine. The results horrified him, and he ran into the room where all of us were gathered, exclaiming, "The boy has diabetes, terrible diabetes! His sugar is far over the limit! He has to go on insulin at once!" We were all very upset until we discovered that the child had been told to urinate into a used paper cup containing residue from a sugar-laden soft drink.

My father was always our family doctor, and he helped me out with the debilitating migraines that plagued me throughout most of my life. (They suddenly disappeared when I was sixty.) They were so incapacitating that I would plead with people to shoot me to end the pain. Years later, when I was in the army, I was terrified that I would develop a migraine at a crucial moment. To reassure me, my father developed what the family always called "the Big Pill." I never knew what its ingredients were. But at the first sign of a migraine—an inability to focus or points of light in my peripheral vision—I would take the Big Pill, and it always prevented a full-blown migraine.

My parents usually got along well; I never heard them have a real argument. But they did disagree about their children; my father allowed us to be daring and adventurous, while Mother wanted us safe and sheltered. She had all sorts of rules—we couldn't go out after dark, we couldn't buy cap pistols, we couldn't do anything physically dangerous—about which she was very serious.

My father's cavalier attitude about our safety caused some problems for all of us more than once. One morning, after a huge snowstorm, Michael and I wanted to go sledding at Dead Man's Gulch on Riverside Drive. Now it's quite different, but sixty years ago, it was a wonderful sleigh ride down a magnificent hill. We would get on our sleds on top of the hill and go whizzing down five hundred yards, almost to the railroad tracks along the Hudson River. My mother was dead set against our sledding and said, "Monroe, the boys can't go."

"For God's sake, Fanny, it's vacation time, Christmas. Let them go and have a good time," he argued. He won, and we went sledding, but on one of our runs, my brother fell off, and I slammed into a tree. The sled runner sliced into my kidney. I was brought home bleeding and battered, in agony, and placed on the operating table in my father's office. I never forgot that. As he looked down at me, my father seemed more concerned about what my mother would say than about my condition: "Your mother is going to kill me. She's going to parboil me," he said. She did, of course, because I was quite seriously hurt, urinating blood for weeks and out of school for a month.

Mother

My mother was very proud of her German-Jewish heritage and expected her children to marry within that community; to her, no other marriage would be suitable. My father was not pure German, but I am certain he had no Russian blood in his lineage, because my mother constantly warned me, "Whatever you do, don't marry a Russian." While she was quite pleased with my first wife, Lotte, a German refugee, my mother would no doubt have disapproved of the woman to whom I am married today, Margaret Ratner, a Russian Jew.

My mother was beautiful—tall, willowy, with soft brown

hair. Even when she became heavier as she grew older, she remained attractive. During her middle years, she suffered from spells of depression during which I recall her wailing that she was not pretty and that she didn't want to get out of bed. She, too, had severe migraines, which my father treated with injections of morphine.

Although she was a family-oriented woman who never worked outside the home, my mother was not at all a traditional homemaker. She never rose in the morning until my father brought her breakfast in bed—boiled eggs, toast, and coffee. Imitating him, I have always brought both my wives breakfast in bed. I bring Margie only toast and coffee, though, or just coffee if I'm late, but I am always the earliest one up, and I like doing it.

Mother didn't cook at all except for her delicious one-egg chocolate cake. The housework was done by maids, and the children were overseen by governesses. Except for one Irish maid, most of the work was done by black reformed prostitutes sent to us by Father Divine, the erstwhile spiritual leader, though my mother seemed unaware of their past history. One night, Mother said to some guests, "Did you know that Silas [the maid] once worked in a sporting house in St. Louis?" She thought it was a gambling hall. Silas, embarrassed, ran out of the room, and Father ran after her to comfort her. I don't believe Mother had any understanding of what she had said.

She was snobbish and treated the maids and governesses as if they were her inferiors. Like many Jews then—and today, unfortunately—my parents and their friends referred to blacks as *shvartzes,* not viciously, perhaps, but thoughtlessly. At the time, I knew nothing of the Yiddish word's negative implications.

Many years later, when I had my own children, we took in a Fresh Air child for the summer. She was a black girl named Edith. When she asked my mother, "What should I call you?" my mother told her, "Call me what Karin and Jane do." Yet I could see it made Mother uncomfortable when she took the children to a nearby amusement park and for the entire day was addressed as "Grandma" by each. Several years later, when Karin was dating, some of her young men were black. Mother threatened to jump off the Empire State Building if any of these dates resulted in a marriage. (Years earlier, she had made the same threat in order to force me to return from Spain, where, during the first days of that country's civil war, I volunteered briefly as an ambulance driver in Barcelona.)

I held some of the same snobbish ideas as my mother. When Mary graduated from high school, for example, I was horrified by her desire to attend secretarial school. I felt that no schooling other than a college education had any value.

My mother, although naive about many things, had graduated from Hunter College. As an adult, her focus was mainly on how local and world events affected the Jews. My parents voted for Franklin Delano Roosevelt because they believed his presidency would benefit Jews. But I never heard them criticize his lack of response to the massacre of the Jews then taking place in Europe. Perhaps they could not expand beyond the small sphere of American Jewry.

Like my father and Pa Moe, Mother, too, had eccentricities. She enjoyed all religious rituals and attended Catholic masses as well as Jewish services. She even had her own saint, St. Anthony, to whom she prayed on occasion. Years later, when she died, we found that she had more than enough Catholic medals pinned to her brassiere to weigh her down on her journey.

Despite her ability to embrace different religions, when it came to black people, my mother, and my father as well, displayed stereotypical racist ideas. I often disagreed with them about this. Once, my father called out to another driver who had cut him off: "Nigger!" I was very upset and told him so, but he didn't pay any attention.

As a child, I seemed to be attracted to black people who were not middle class and who were not approved of by my parents. Part of this came from my desire to be unique, to be different from everyone else, to startle my parents and their friends. This need to be different is one that I remember having all my life.

When I was ten, I wrote to a black heavyweight boxer named Sam Langford, who lived in Harlem and was quite ill. I arranged to visit him. When my father heard about this venture, he asked one of his patients, a New York City detective, to scare me so that I would never set foot in Harlem. The detective came to our apartment and told me that I would be mugged and robbed if I ever set foot in that forbidden place. Suitably terrified, I canceled the visit. But I always felt bad about it because I had let Sam Langford down.

As I grew older, I developed a concern for people who seemed to be in a weaker position and who needed my help. I may have been born this way, or I may have imitated my father's compassion toward those who had less, but I can't remember a time when I didn't have these feelings. Mary, my sister, says I was always a pushover.

I remember fighting with my mother about this attitude when I was fifteen. I had a girlfriend, Margaret Hess, who was beautiful, tall, and redheaded but in such poor health that she required frequent hospitalizations. When Mother told me that Margaret's frailty would be burdensome and that I should avoid her, I argued, "Then Margaret's just right for me, because I can take of her when she's sick." Tragically, my mother was right—Margaret died much too young.

Peck's Bad Boy

When I was small, my mother said that each slap she gave me was a boost and was good for me. My childhood was filled with boosts, from both parents, because I was the original Peck's Bad Boy, a D or F student throughout my elementary school years and always rebellious. My father was called to school constantly because of my wrongdoings.

I did the craziest things without being at all aware of what I was doing. One day, I took my brother and sister and some younger children for a stroll on the third rail of the Long Island Railroad. I was nine, my brother was six, Mary was three, and none of us knew what the third rail was. When my father saw us, he cried out, "Oh, my God! Don't move, that can kill you. There's an electric current." Then he yelled, "Everybody jump off!" We all did, pronto.

Another time, I crawled on the roof of our synagogue, Temple Israel, fell through the skylight, and was saved by the grillwork underneath. I swam naked in the Central Park lake and in the Hudson River. As I recall, not a single day went by that I didn't misbehave in some way, large or small. In many ways, I am still that little boy who always must act outrageously so he can remain outside the mainstream.

During my grade-school years, although quite rebellious, I was still a typical boy. I played ball, read, and idolized my heroes, the New York Yankees and Charles Lindbergh. I thought Lindbergh was brave and strong and could not have imagined that one day he would become an archconservative. When the Yankees were in town, they lived at the Concourse Plaza Hotel in the Bronx, which my friends and I would stake out until we caught a glimpse of these great ballplayers: Babe Ruth, Lou Gehrig, Bill

Dickey, Tony Lazzeri, Frank Crosetti. I once had all their auto-
graphs; I wish I still did.

Until I was thirteen, my family lived at 215 West Ninetieth
Street, where I played on a hockey team, the Red Devils, along
with Richard Kuh (who later succeeded Frank Hogan as New
York County district attorney) and Bernard Apfel, among others.
Bernie was my hero. The oldest of the group and a classy dresser,
he wore spiffy light tan knickers with argyle socks and loafers. I
tried to emulate him until the day that he punched me out for
attempting to kiss his cousin—even though I had only done it on
a dare.

In 1932, when I was thirteen, we moved to Central Park West,
where I joined an interracial gang otherwise comprised of blacks
and Hispanics. As the only Jew, I was nicknamed Yiddle. Although I ran with the gang, I never became close friends with any
one boy. We broke windows, stole from penny gum machines,
busted into warehouses, and attacked other kids. I rebelled
against hanging out with the middle-class Jewish kids in the fancy
high-rise apartment house where my family lived, and I reveled in
my gang. There was no reason for it; I simply found the mixed
gang more stimulating and exciting than the other group of kids—
who were all exactly like me.

Cops often visited our apartment to report on me: "Your boy
is going to the penitentiary. He just took a slingshot and put a rock
through a window." One of my gang's favorite targets was a warehouse owner named Goldie, who hated children. We would often
be arrested for shooting pellets through his windows on Amsterdam Avenue. Then I would be released into my father's custody.
Some of the police officers, who were also my father's patients,
told him that I was going straight to hell. With all their predic-
tions, I was uncertain of my final destination. Would it be the pen
or hell?

Both of my parents were afraid that I would never amount to
anything. In an attempt to change my behavior, they would try the
standard punishments, including sending me to bed without
food. Nothing worked. Once, Pa Moe tried to solve the problem by
stipulating that if I wrote daily in a diary he had given me, he
would present me at the end of the year with a twenty-dollar gold
piece. He believed that daily diary writing would instill discipline. But his plan failed. I did not write a single word until a few
days before Christmas, when I scribbled away like crazy, writing
all sorts of nonsense, in order to get the gold piece. At that time,

capitalism still had great influence over me.

I recall my father's rage when he took me to see the Ringling Bros., Barnum & Bailey Circus at the old Madison Square Garden and I slipped away from him and went downstairs to the freak show. Long after the show was over, he found me playing checkers with a midget. Furious that he had missed an important appointment and worried that I was lost in the depths of Madison Square Garden, he gave it to me.

My mother and I had different types of confrontations—more emotional. After she would wallop me, as she often did, I would lie in bed, in the dark, sobbing, waiting for her. Then she would come in, say, "Oh, I didn't mean it. I love you, Billy," and we'd have a dramatic reconciliation. I always managed to get a kiss, too.

Michael

In contrast to my villainy, my brother, Michael, was a paragon of virtue. Most of the time. One day, a neighbor came to our apartment to complain that his radio aerial had been cut. After he told my mother, she assumed I was the culprit and said, "I'll get Billy and have his father give him the whipping of his life."

"It's not Billy. It's Michael," said the neighbor.

My mother was incredulous that my saintly brother had committed this crime. He was so much better behaved that my parents' friends all preferred him and considered me quite nasty. I recall being confused about this, since I didn't regard myself as a bad person. As a child, I viewed my misbehavior as harmless, and I was jealous that everyone favored Michael. I viewed him as a goody-goody and used to beat him up and curse at him whenever I had the opportunity. True to form, he always betrayed me and would repeat to our mother the profanities I had used. She would then whale me for what I had done.

Despite these differences, Michael and I still remained playmates, for we were relatively close in age and shared the same bedroom. As we got older, Michael began to follow me about and, Mary says, idolized me. I don't recall this, but I do know that everything I did, Michael did. I went to DeWitt Clinton High School; he went to Clinton. I went to Yale; he went to Yale. I enlisted in the Signal Corps; he enlisted in the Signal Corps.

Michael and I eventually became rivals, though; neither of us could allow the other to have an accomplishment on his own without it being imitated. Even years later, that sibling rivalry was still a powerful force—for me, at least. Michael enrolled at Columbia Law School after being discharged from the army in 1946, and I remember thinking, I'm not going to let him get away with that. I'll go, too. Which is how I ended up as a lawyer.

I saw a similar rivalry in my own children. When Jane, my second oldest daughter, was accepted at medical school, Karin, the oldest, decided to go to law school. I imagine, based on my own feelings of rivalry with Michael, that Karin thought, If my sister's going to be a doctor, then I'm going to be a lawyer.

Mary

Mary was a different story. She was a sweet younger sister who admired me, looked up to me, and never gave me any trouble at all. She was so much younger than Michael and me that we sort of disregarded her until she was old enough to have friends come over. Even then, we paid attention to her only because her friends provided our first real access to the opposite sex.

Books

One of the things that saved me from being a truly terrible child was that I loved to read. Reading also kept me from being lonely, for despite my gangs, books were really my closest friends. During my childhood, I began a lifetime pattern of not forming very intimate friendships with males, a pattern that continues to this day. I was then, and still am, a solitary person despite my apparent gregariousness.

My love for books also impressed my father and redeemed me to him. The public library at Eighty-third Street and Amsterdam Avenue, a constant source of delight, provided me with a different book each week. Robert Louis Stevenson was my favorite author. I would often begin a new book as I walked home from the library. When I was ten and eleven, I read so much that my father, thinking I looked pale and anemic, would take my hemoglobin count. If the count was low, he would say, "You have to go out and play. Stop reading." I would walk around the block, breathe fresh air, then return home to my book.

I loved reading about pirates, kidnappings, and duels and was always first at the newsstand when the new pulp magazines came out. My favorite was "Doc Savage," the leader of a do-good sextet whose members got into wonderful scrapes, all on the side of truth and justice.

I loved war stories, especially those featuring World War I battles. From the time I could walk, my father took me to the big Decoration Day parades on Riverside Drive, which thrilled me. I played war games with my friends in the Central Park trenches that remained from the construction of the reservoir. I didn't understand what a terrible slaughterhouse World War I really was and thought nothing could be more thrilling than to be a soldier. I even had a prized American helmet that I wore to our mock battles, always guarding it carefully. Although my mother forbade us to buy cap pistols, I managed to have one hidden in my room at all times.

I gulped down one book after another—the Boy Allies, the Hardy Boys, the Rover Boys, and Tom Swift. Once again, my awareness of racism was nil. I didn't understand about the black youth in the Swift books who served as the hero's foil, and enjoyed Amos and Andy, never seeing them as a denigrating portrayal of blacks.

Scholar

When I was fourteen, I started at DeWitt Clinton High School's Manhattan Annex at 717 West End Avenue, which was close enough to my apartment for me to walk to school. From my very first day in high school, I changed completely. I can only explain this change by my realization, as I became older, that I had caused my parents to suffer horribly because of my rebellious misbehavior. I felt remorse and guilt and was determined to make it up to them. I became a scholar. I wanted to prove to my parents that despite my questionable start, I was a good person and could make my mark in the world—even though I wasn't going to do it their way.

As a result of my resolve, my high school career was a triumph, and I was a straight A student for four years. I was a member of the honor society, Arista, wrote poetry, and graduated at the head of my class. It could not have been a more dramatic change.

In addition to academic success, I also qualified for the swimming team. Since I was not an outstanding swimmer, though, I didn't receive a team letter when it was time for seasonal awards and was given only a small patch emblazoned with the words Swim Team. I was so envious of those swimmers who received the big "C," which stood for Clinton High School, that I "appropriated" a letter and had it sewn on my sweater. I so wanted the recognition that I wore the sweater everywhere—except to school—always worried that I would be found out. That little deception has stayed with me all these years.

My parents were proud of me because of my excellent grades in high school and gave me constant reinforcement and approval. Throughout my life, well into adulthood, they were my sounding board; I always sought their approval. When they were dead, many years later, I no longer had anyone to whom I could say, "Look how well I'm doing." Today I have my wife, Margie, and my two youngest daughters, but I have to be careful not to overdo it. They help by reminding me. "All we hear about is Bill, Bill, Bill. We have our own lives to lead," they tell me. So I try not to bring every triumph home, although I don't always succeed.

One of my family's most serious criticisms is that I see events and people mainly in terms of my own relationship to them. For example, they may mention a movie with Robert De Niro and I'll interject, "Oh, I have a contract with him," or, "I represented his wife."

When my mother and father were alive, it was acceptable for me to be the center of the world, to boast about my exploits. I may have transferred my need for approval from them to the world at large, for there is within me a powerful drive to make everyone like me—even love me, the way my parents did.

My parents' hope was that I would become a successful lawyer with a high income who then ran for Congress or some other political office. I don't know how they would react to who I am today, although they approved when I represented Dr. Martin Luther King Jr. in the early 1960s. I think they would have been aghast at my more radical cases during the late 1960s, though, and would have attempted to discourage me—although by that time they had both died. Whatever their feelings about individual cases, or even my politics and life's work, I know that they would have continued to be loving toward me. They always were.

Sex

During the summers, my family rented houses in Rockville Centre, on Long Island, and in later years, in Westbrook, Connecticut. The weeks were quiet, but the weekends brought the excitement of all the fathers driving up from the city, with the mail and fresh baked goods. We children would stand on the road waiting for them to arrive.

Our family also took frequent car trips during the year. We often motored to Mother's hometown of Albany, where we stayed at our Aunt Elka's house. In Albany, I met many girls of German-Jewish background; to my great joy, they were willing to do more petting and kissing than New York girls. Albany was the scene of many necking sessions and where I touched a female breast for the first time. I was thirteen, sitting in a hammock with Barbara, also thirteen, when I reached my hand out to touch, finally, this forbidden fruit. Afterward, knowing nothing about human reproduction, I was terrified that Barbara would become pregnant.

My first real sexual experience was in a graveyard in Westbrook with a girl named Betty Robinson. I was fifteen. It wasn't really intercourse, because I lost all control and ejaculated beforehand. Afterward, I rushed home and washed myself in the ocean with Kirkman's laundry soap, frightened that I would contract an awful disease.

During high school, my sexual gropings continued unabated. When I was sixteen, I enjoyed many necking sessions with my girlfriend Viola Schwartz on her living-room couch. Her parents were merchants and, according to my mother's social snobbishness, not in our class. Maybe they tolerated our necking sessions in their living room because, since my father was a doctor, they thought I was a good catch.

That summer, I had an emergency appendectomy, and Viola was my first visitor when I returned home from New York's Polyclinic Hospital after my surgery. I greeted her by saying, "Vi, take off your clothes and get into bed." Reassured that my father was making hospital calls and the rest of the family was out, she complied. I wore a nightshirt, she was naked, and we began to kiss and hug. Suddenly, the door opened, and my father stood there, looking down on us. He didn't yell or berate us but quietly said to Viola, "You know, you're going to bust his stitches." Then he gave her a lecture on the treatment of postoperative convalescents. He spoke not a single word about the morality of the situation. When Viola recovered her savoir faire, she said, "Doctor, you're absolutely right. If you leave the room, I'll dress and leave Billy alone."

He said nothing else and left. I believe his main concern was that if I popped my stitches, my mother would castigate him unmercifully. After Viola departed, I remained in bed, of course, and my father never mentioned the incident again—either to my mother or to me. It was as if it never happened—except that it ended my relationship with Viola.

Perhaps my most memorable youthful sex took place in Europe during the summer of 1936, when I was seventeen. My grandfather had sent me on a trip to France. There I borrowed a Delage, an old English touring car, from a medical school classmate of my father's, assuring him that I would deliver it to a sanitarium he owned in the Alps. Instead, along with two young friends that I had met on the ship over, I went to Spain. I had read in the *International Herald Tribune* about the outbreak of the Spanish Civil War and was eager to become involved. My friends Richard and Robert Rothman drove the Delage, since I didn't know how to drive, and we headed to Barcelona, where we had heard that Ernest Hemingway was the man to see for volunteer ambulance drivers.

In Barcelona, our car was quickly stripped and converted to an ambulance, its seats ripped out and replaced with stretchers and its top painted with a big red cross. The Rothmans and I never actually went on any ambulance calls. Instead, we whiled away our time making love to Spanish girls on the stretchers. (However, since I really didn't know what I was doing, I don't think I ever really had intercourse with any of them.)

When I contacted my family and told them where I was, my mother threatened to jump off the Empire State Building if I didn't come straight home. So, dutiful son that I was, I took a train to Cherbourg and from there was transported to the *Queen Mary* and sailed for home. I left the Delage with the Rothmans. Later, when my father's classmate saw the damage to his beautiful car, he insisted that my father compensate him for it, which he finally did.

My knowledge about sex was nil other than what I learned from these immature gropings; neither of my parents ever discussed it with me. Once, I found condoms in my father's drawer, which shocked me. I had some vague idea of what they were because years earlier my gang and I saw them floating in the Hudson River whenever we swam in it. We called them Harlem whitefish and would snicker when we saw one. But I never knew what they were. Since I certainly couldn't ask my father, sex remained a great mystery to me throughout my youth.

Yale

In the summer of the Depression year 1937, I had just graduated from high school, and my world had shrunk to two letters: one, a rejection from Columbia; the other, an acceptance by Yale. My father had graduated from Columbia, so I felt awful that I had been rejected. But I rationalized that the admissions people at both universities must have conferred, deciding that Yale was better for me than Columbia. This allowed me to believe that Columbia had not really rejected me.

I was in Westbrook, Connecticut, at my parents' rented summer bungalow on Long Island Sound, and after I read Yale's congratulatory letter, I rowed my boat out into the Sound and sat on a rock called Salt Island, reveling in the knowledge that I had been accepted by a fine college. I was anxious to leave home and take on the challenges of the world, beginning with Yale.

But when my parents drove me to New Haven on September 1, 1937, for the start of my freshman year and I saw their car's rear taillights disappear around the corner, I felt as miserable as I had ever felt in my life. I was eighteen and had never been away from home. Suddenly, here I was, on my own, at one of the country's most prestigious universities, feeling totally unprepared for what lay before me.

I had a choice between living with a roommate selected for me or living alone. I chose to room alone and was placed in Van Sheff, short for Vanderbilt Sheffield, a hoary old freshman dorm off the main campus. For the first couple of weeks, I just locked myself in. I went to class, then returned to my room and worked feverishly on my assignments.

I eventually met other guys in the dorm, including some Jewish students, among them Martin Dash, Philip Silver, and Jacques Isaacs. But I became friendliest with a non-Jew, Shepard Krech, who commuted to New York almost every weekend. I went along each weekend and eventually became as close to him as I did to anyone at Yale. Nevertheless, during my first three years in college I roomed by myself and continued my childhood pattern of not making close friends.

I made the Yale swimming team, did some boxing, and also attempted to play football for my dormitory. During the first scrimmage, I was put in the line as a guard and after a few minutes of play broke my finger. As I walked off the field, I thought, The hell with this. This is not for me. I'll stick to swimming. That way, I won't break anything.

I did well at boxing, though, because I could box left-handed and was able to dodge the right-handers. I was born a lefty but was forced to become ambidextrous at age eleven after I put my left hand through a window, cutting the tendons in my wrist. (I still have no feeling in the middle finger of that hand.) I learned to be right-handed after many hours of tedious practice. My father's suggestion, that I use my right hand to throw a ball against a wall, was especially helpful.

Being the son and grandson of doctors, I had enrolled in a premed course. It was an unspoken assumption in my home that I would become a physician and eventually take over my father's practice. My brother also was supposed to study medicine, but because I was the oldest, there was more pressure on me from both parents to follow in my father's footsteps.

I was not at all happy taking premed at Yale and had only registered for it because of the family's expectations. As a child, my father and grandfather often took me along to observe surgery: One particularly gory operation unhappily remained in my mind for years. I watched Pa Moe perform a mastoidectomy, an obsolete operation today because of the use of antibiotics. But years ago, if one developed an infection in the bone behind the ear, it had to be chopped out with a hammer and chisel. I watched my grandfather whack into his patient, causing blood and pus to spurt out everywhere. I became deathly sick.

My grades reflected my lack of interest in the sciences. I did very poorly in all those courses in contrast to the high grades I received in the humanities. I was beginning to love literature and started contributing to the *Yale Literary Magazine* and the *Yale News*. I began composing Elizabethan and Petrarchan sonnets, writing poetry on an almost daily basis, a habit I continue to this day. (I write several sonnets a week, many for New York City's *Amsterdam News*. My third collection of sonnets, *Hints and Allegations,* was published in 1994.)

I became quite friendly with history professor William Huse Dunham, my adviser, and when he saw the disparity between my science and liberal arts grades, he suggested that I invite my father to meet with him. The two men sat and talked, and Dunham said, "Doctor, this boy is simply not going to be a physician. He's doing poorly in the sciences. He got a D in organic chemistry. He just is not with it. On the other hand, he's getting A-plus in every other subject. I would advise you to let him switch to a nonpremed course."

To my great joy, my father was reasonable, and although he expressed some ambivalence, he told Dunham that I could change my course of study. I was so relieved that I shouted with joy. I then began to live, dropping all the hated science courses and studying only those subjects that I enjoyed: English, history, and French.

After I gave up the sciences, I never received a grade lower than an A, so that even with a D in organic chemistry factored into my average, I made Phi Beta Kappa my senior year.

One of my professors encouraged me to collaborate on a book with another student, William Vincent Stone, who, like me, wrote poetry. Titled *Our Pleasant Vices* from a line in Shakespeare's *King Lear,* our book was a combination of our two poetic voices. My contribution was a number of sonnets. The book was printed, with the assistance of my father's brother, Larry, a trade magazine editor, and we sold it at Yale. A reviewer in the *Yale Literary Magazine* review wrote: "William Kunstler has written the worst and the best poetry in this collection." My collaborator disagreed with only one-half of this appraisal.

When I was at Yale, most of the students were Protestant, just about all of them white, and many evinced disturbing anti-Jewish sentiments. Rooms were decorated with Nazi flags, and Jews were not admitted into certain clubs and societies. A distant cousin of mine, Albert Hessberg, was an outstanding football player for Yale and, because of that, was the first Jew allowed into Skull and Bones, which has since gained fame as President Bush's club. (Bush was a freshman at Yale when I was a senior, but our paths never crossed.)

The message given by anti-Semitic Yalies was that it was not okay to be different. I ended up feeling uncomfortable and sometimes ashamed of being Jewish. At that age, I wanted acceptance more than anything, so while I don't recall ever attending synagogue, I sat through many church services in the company of my poetry collaborator, Bill Stone, a very religious Catholic. Several of the sonnets I wrote for *Our Pleasant Vices* had Christian themes.

I did not date often in college but once had an arranged weekend with Oona O'Neill, Eugene O'Neill's daughter and Charlie Chaplin's future wife. I had become friendly with Eugene O'Neill Jr., my classics instructor during my sophomore year, who arranged the date because he thought his sister and I would suit each other. I was terribly upset when, a short time later, he was found dead in the bathtub with his wrists slashed. His brilliantly sarcastic suicide note said, "Never let it be said that an O'Neill left any vessel filled."

As I began my senior year, Michael entered Yale as a freshman. By this time, I was lonely enough to seek roommates, so I lived with Edward Gravely from Richmond, Virginia, and Gould (Bud) Coleman from Gardner, Massachusetts, in rooms 573 and 574 of Berkeley, a residential college. We had two bedrooms and a sitting room. I shared a bedroom with Ed, who was such a fanatic Confederate that when *Gone With the Wind* opened in New Haven, he went berserk and destroyed our peace for days with piercing rebel yells and hysterical monologues about the Old South.

My father came to visit one night during my senior year at the invitation of my French professor, Dr. Henri Peyre, a wonderful teacher who spoke French better than anyone I had ever heard. First Dad and I went to a football game; then, after a thrilling ride from the Yale Bowl hanging on to a streetcar, we had dinner with Dr. Peyre. When we returned to my dorm, my father and I each took a bedroom, because my roommates had gone home for the weekend.

In the middle of the night, I heard terrible screams and ran into the other room, where I found my father bellowing while a naked and apparently very drunk young woman was trying to climb into bed with him. She had slipped past the campus police, sneaked into the dorm, and, in the darkness, assumed my father was Bud. I switched on the light and saw a sight I will never forget: Dad, in his polka-dot pajamas, shouting that I must withdraw from Yale immediately, while a stark-naked young woman stood beside him, looking stunned.

"You have to be near your home, Billy, where we can keep an eye on you," he yelled. Michael must leave Yale also, he howled. The woman, scared stiff, sobered up quickly, dressed, and ran from the room. I spent hours trying to calm my father and convince him not to force me and Michael to drop out of Yale. But the next morning, as he was about to step onto the train back to New York, he said, "I'm going to make arrangements for you at Columbia."

"Please," I said, "it's ridiculous. She wasn't my girlfriend, anyway." He never carried out this threat, though, and Michael and I remained at Yale.

Years later, my father would wink at me and say, "Bill, I guess I missed one of the great opportunities of my life that night. It was dark, and she wouldn't have known the difference." But then he would add, puritanically, "But how could I do that and live with your mother?"

Other than that near disaster, life went smoothly at Yale. I earned high grades, found great pleasure in literature and poetry, and formed close relationships with several professors, including Prof. Andrew Morehouse, who helped me plan my French major, and Chauncey Brewster Tinker, one of the great scholars in the English Department. I took every course taught by Tinker. He was a perennial bachelor who had a high-pitched voice, a pockmarked nose, and a straitlaced style of dressing. But when he read the poetry or prose of English writers, particularly of the nineteenth century, I was enthralled. We corresponded for years after I graduated from Yale, and his letters later followed me into the army.

During college I began my lifelong love affair with the English poets of the Romantic era—Byron, Shelley, Keats, Wordsworth, and Coleridge. I had read that one of them wrote poetry standing up, so I began to do all my writing while leaning on the mantelpiece. I was totally consumed by English poetry and writers and a few French authors as well, including Pierre Loti, Anatole France, and Molière. I was a French major, and my senior thesis was *"Molière et Médecine."*

I also fell in love with Dylan Thomas and wrote to him after I first read his poetry. I became quite obnoxious and actually began to add stanzas to his poems, mailing his amended poetry to him in Wales. He wrote back, saying that he would be thankful if I didn't finish his poems for him, since that was his prerogative. Many years later, I represented him when Smith College refused to pay his speaker's fee because he had supposedly sexually assaulted a student by putting his hand up her shorts. I met with the president of Smith, a former Yale professor, and was finally able to secure for Thomas $400 of the originally promised $500. He used the money to pay for his transportation back to Wales.

My father paid for Yale, but since I knew it was a struggle, I worked to help out. He paid tuition and gave me five dollars a week allowance, but I earned room and board by doing research for a French professor. I also earned money during the summers by working as a camp counselor, first at Camp Chicopee in Pennsylvania, then at Brant Lake Camp in the Adirondacks. It was at Chicopee, when I was nineteen, that I had my first real sexual experience—with a prostitute from Scranton's red-light district. She was blond and tall, and I went through the usual routine, asking her, "Why are you in a place like this?" She was supporting her daughters, she said. Then she squatted down and washed herself in a basin. Embarrassed, I turned the other way and didn't watch.

"Well, aren't you going to take your clothes off?" she asked.

"Maybe a little later," I said.

"I don't have time, sonny, for a little later. I have other customers out there." I thought she was cold-blooded about it but took off my clothes and did what I was there to do. Afterward, I felt so grown up. As chauvinistic as it sounds, there is no doubt that a young man's first real sexual experience is like a rite of passage.

During my last summer as a camp counselor, in 1941, a group of us chipped in and for thirty-five dollars bought a very old Essex which constantly broke down; we named it Beulah the Bitch. On our night off, we would take Beulah and drive to the races at Saratoga. One night, Beulah broke down in Glens Falls, and with no place to stay and no money, we ended up in jail. The man in the cell next to mine was covered with blood, having just axed his wife to death. He was agitated, raving and screaming all night long. I huddled in the corner, trying to stay out of his reach. I don't think I slept at all.

That was my last carefree summer. I had just graduated from Yale, and it was clear that since America was on the brink of entering World War II, like other guys my age I would soon be in one of the armed services. Summer camp was a fitting finale to the carefree years of childhood and college. Looking ahead to the real possibility of war, I felt quite adult and ready to tackle anything, but, of course, I had no idea what war was really like. My protected and privileged youth had kept me in a comfortable world where few of my needs went unmet. The army and World War II would change all that.

CHAPTER THREE

In the Pacific

William Kunstler . . . plays the part of a thug.

The Army

W HEN THE DRAFT BEGAN IN 1940, I WAS STILL ATTENDING YALE, SO I registered in New Haven, and my father kept track of my number. Even though it had not yet been called when I graduated in June 1941, I decided to enlist. I knew I would be drafted shortly, anyway, and waiting made me nervous. I applied for a commission in the V-12 Naval Officers Program; I thought it might be better to be on a ship during a war than on the ground. During my navy physical I was told that I would be rejected unless I had all my silver and gold fillings replaced with amalgam. Since I really wanted the commission, I went through the painful ordeal of having the fillings replaced. At the next physical, however, I was again rejected by the navy, but this time I was not told why. I suspect the reason was an irregular heartbeat, which my father had diagnosed years earlier, when I was ten. Since then, however, no other doctor has found anything wrong with my heart.

A year earlier, when I was a junior at Yale, my friends William and McGeorge Bundy—who would both become high-level government officials—had suggested we all take an army correspondence course in cryptography. I took the course during my last two years of college and enjoyed it, so when I was rejected by the navy, it seemed only logical for me to continue with cryptography. The way to do this was to join the army as an enlisted man, so I signed up on September 5, 1941, at Fort Monmouth, New

71

Jersey, a Signal Corps post which had a cryptographic school.

When it was time to actually go in, my mother and I drove to Fort Monmouth together. When we arrived, she saw all these characters in blue denim fatigues patrolling the main parade ground, picking up cigarette butts and other debris. "Can they make a Yale man do that?" she asked.

Naively, I assured her, "Of course not, Mother." But a few hours later, I found myself the caretaker of a thirty-six-hole latrine. Because there was no uniform available in my size, I had to wear civvies. I was quite annoyed. I decided not to stay on the base without a proper uniform and went AWOL a few hours after enlistment, creeping out of the camp after dark. I headed for Red Bank, the nearest town, where I rented a room.

I stayed away from the post until Monday, when the uniforms were due to arrive, but on my way back I became worried and imagined that the military police were hunting for me. Quaking, I rejoined my outfit, Company C of the Sixteenth Signal Service Battalion. The top sergeant, who reminded me of Burt Lancaster in *From Here to Eternity,* greeted me.

"Sergeant, I know I've been AWOL," I said. "I know I'm in trouble. I'm willing to confess. I just couldn't stand not looking like everyone else."

To my great surprise, he did not charge me. He had marked me present, so I wasn't ever officially AWOL. Once in uniform, I lost the feeling of being an outsider and from that point on became a gung-ho soldier. Today I can't remember my social security number, but I can still recite my fifty-three-year-old army enlistment number: 12029657.

After two weeks of boot training, I was sent to cryptographic school. Since my time wasn't fully occupied, I decided to try acting in the base production of *Whistling in the Dark,* a comedy which had been tremendously successful on Broadway. I auditioned for, and won, a small part and joined a cast with many excellent performers, including James Whitmore, who later became a well-known Hollywood actor.

The play opened on the evening of December 7, 1941, the day the Japanese attacked Pearl Harbor. Because of the attack, which meant that America would soon be officially at war, no soldiers were allowed off the base, so we played to a full house, about five thousand people. *New York Times* theater critic Brooks Atkinson attended. Although he didn't take much note of my performance, he did mention me, which I found quite exciting: "Everyone in the cast is enormously educated. William Kunstler, a Phi Beta Kappa from Yale, plays the part of a thug."

After Pearl Harbor, I realized I was in not for a simple two-year enlistment but for a long haul and decided it would be best to spend it as an officer rather than as a buck private. In March 1942, I was admitted to officer candidate school at Fort Monmouth and graduated three months later as a second lieutenant in the Signal Corps.

My first orders, to the Second Army Corps in Jacksonville, Florida, were in error. My correct destination should have been the Second Army Headquarters in Memphis, Tennessee, where I eventually ended up. I didn't know about the error, so I went where I was sent. In Jacksonville, I was put in charge of syphilitics and other GIs who were ill and had been shipped back from the Louisiana maneuvers. My job was to oversee them as they unloaded the dirty laundry which arrived daily on railroad cars from the maneuvers area. It was very unpleasant work, and I waited anxiously for my corrected orders.

Finally, I was ordered back to Fort Monmouth, received my correct orders, and became one of two resident signal intelligence officers at Second Army Headquarters in Memphis. I was responsible for keeping cryptographic equipment current, supplying the lower units with their own coding devices, and decoding messages. The Signal Corps was intellectual work and much more to my liking than combat.

None of the messages I decoded seemed to be very urgent, but they had to be decoded right on the spot, because you never knew when a critical message would come in. Once, after I inadvertently destroyed the next month's codes instead of the superseded ones, I was certain I would be court-martialed for my carelessness. Instead, I was given a stiff reprimand by the army's chief signal officer.

One night I was assigned to escort a brigadier general named Benjamin Davis from the railroad station to his hotel. But when we arrived there, the desk clerk refused to give him a room because this was Tennessee and the general was one of the few high-ranking black officers in the army. I called my commander, Gen. Ben Lear, and told him my problem. He said, "Lieutenant, bring General Davis to my house."

This incident made me notice what I had been seeing all along without paying too much attention: the drinking fountains and rest rooms designated Colored Only and White Only, the segregated public facilities, the segregated army. I discussed my observations with the kind, elderly couple who owned the boardinghouse in which I lived, Ma and Pa Frain. They believed that segregation was the natural order of things. Any other way of life would be impossible. "It's good to have the Nigras in their world and us in our world," Pa Frain said.

"The swallows don't fly with the robins," he told me, as if there were really nothing more to say. We talked about segregation often over coffee in the Frains' kitchen, but none of us changed each other's thinking.

Marriage and Family

The years 1942 and 1943 were momentous for me. I married, and my first daughter was born. I had met Lotte Rosenberger six years earlier, in 1936, when she was eleven and I was seventeen. My grandfather sponsored her family when they immigrated here as refugees from Hitler's Germany because they were distantly related to us through my maternal grandmother.

When the Rosenbergers arrived in New York, my family invited them for tea, and I was drawn to Lotte immediately. But I was almost a man, and she was still a child, so I squelched those feelings. According to family myth, the instant my grandmother saw Lotte, she predicted that we would marry. "Fanny," my grandmother is supposed to have said to my mother, "Billy is going to marry that girl." Lotte was still a little girl with long braids at the time, but my grandmother was quite accurate.

After I joined the army, Lotte and I corresponded regularly. By the time she was seventeen and I was twenty-three, I proposed to her in a letter, and she wrote back, "Yes." I went home on leave, and Lotte and I were married on January 14, 1943. She was a most beautiful bride.

Lotte returned with me to the base in Memphis, where we lived in a small front room with a big double bed in the Frains' boardinghouse. The following summer, Lotte, by then almost six months pregnant, accompanied me to my next assignment, the Second Army maneuvers in Lebanon, Tennessee, where we lived in a converted chicken coop on Greenwood Avenue. Our landlady was quite mercenary, not as pleasant as the Frains had been.

I chose an obstetrician for Lotte by looking in the Yale graduate catalog to find a doctor practicing in nearby Nashville. The night Lotte's water broke, I commandeered a truck and driver and rushed her to St. Thomas Hospital in Nashville. I started in to alert the staff, but hearing a sound, I looked behind me and saw the truck—with Lotte in it—rolling slowly backward down the hill. (Nashville is composed of many hills, like Rome.) I ran and jumped into the truck just as the driver put on the brake. Lotte safely delivered our daughter, Karin Fernanda Kunstler, shortly after dawn on October 15, 1943, exactly nine months and one day from our wedding. Karin slept at first in a footlocker on top of a chicken crate in our tiny bedroom.

I was steadily moving up in the army and eventually achieved the rank of major. In the spring of 1944, after I was ordered overseas as part of the new U.S. Eighth Army, it was time to say goodbye to Lotte and Karin, a trembly, teary Lotte and a skinny wretch of an infant. As I traveled by train to the West Coast, the jumping-off point for the Pacific, Lotte drove home to New York City with the wife of another officer, Minthorne Tompkins, their car overloaded with Karin, her car bed, bottles of boiled water for formula, and the Tompkinses' enormous dog. They also had a huge antique revolver in the glove compartment that Min had given them. We were worried about the two women driving alone to New York with a child. I never knew where Min had obtained the gun, but we both felt better about its being in the car, although we knew that it was extremely unlikely that our wives could ever bring themselves to fire it.

Lotte and Karin went to live with my parents while I sailed on the USS *John Pope,* a troop transport, from San Francisco to Hollandia, New Guinea. There we set up our first headquarters as the U.S. Eighth Army. We were now a combat army, no longer a training one. I began my work of decoding ciphers and messages, and since we were not in an immediate battle zone, I felt relatively safe.

Overseas

I stayed in New Guinea until October 20, 1944, when we joined in the invasion of Leyte, marking MacArthur's return to the Philippines. On the ship to Leyte, we were constantly strafed and attacked by Japanese kamikaze planes. Along with the other headquarters personnel, I had to stay below while the sailors and marines above tried to fight off our attackers. From my berth in the belly of the ship, I could do nothing but look out through the portholes. I found having no control, with my life in the hands of others, terribly disturbing. Planes whizzed through the air, anti-aircraft bursts and tracer bullets lit up the sky, and sirens wailed as the battle raged. I spent the entire voyage in a state of muted apprehension.

At Telegrafo, we set up a headquarters, and except for the perpetual nervous tension of most soldiers in a combat zone, all went well. We expected the worst from the enemy, however, because we had all viewed *The Yellow Peril,* a training film that depicted the Japanese as cold-blooded monsters. It was as racist a film as I have ever seen, but I was so young then I didn't know what was racist and what wasn't. We were taught that the Japanese were inhuman monsters who would slaughter us with no mercy. We never perceived them as good soldiers, which they were, or as human as anyone else. We saw them as pure evil.

The night the Japanese supposedly infiltrated our camp, we were absolutely scared out of our minds. I was living in an eight-man tent, and once we got the word, we extinguished our Coleman lanterns, crouched down on the floor behind our footlockers, and drew our .45s. I was petrified, sure that we were about to be massacred. Suddenly, someone in the tent yelled, "They're invading!" and the lights went out. We heard all sorts of noises and sirens. It was hell on earth.

Our radio officer suddenly panicked and fired his gun, hitting the tent pole and causing the heavy tent to crash down on us. I couldn't move or breathe under there; I was suffocating and began to panic myself. Suddenly, someone shouted, "All clear!" and we crawled out, feeling a little ashamed that we had been so frightened. We later learned that the whole thing had been a false alarm.

Shortly after that I had another brush with fear. I drove a jeep to an airstrip at the northeast end of Leyte to pick up some code machines. When a Japanese plane strafed the airstrip, I leaped under the jeep; from there I could see the little dust puffs, each of which marked a bullet hitting the ground. I closed my eyes and hoped hard that no bullets would hit the jeep's gas tank, and none did. Not a single bullet pierced the steel of the jeep.

The jeep still functioned, so I drove back to Telegrafo, noticing many dead Japanese soldiers littering the rice paddies on both sides of the road. The bodies were bloated, with maggots crawling in and out of their mouths. Some were missing legs, arms, and even heads. I later discovered that a common practice of American soldiers was to hack off the heads of dead Japanese, then use them for target practice. The soldiers would place a head on a pole and fire at it until it blew apart. Other American soldiers boiled the meat off the bones of dead Japanese, then carved them into decorative shapes. Thigh bones were the most popular. These souvenirs of war were purchased by other GIs, who would mail them home, a practice that continued until MacArthur put an end to it. The war was marked for me by this type of inhumanity.

Fast Forward

Something happened while I was in Telegrafo that later was to have a profound impact on my life. One night, we heard some-one screaming, in English, and I sent a couple of GIs out to see who was yelling. It was a GI who had been shot by a sniper. The wound was to his femoral artery, so his leg was spurting blood. A medic stopped the flow with a tourniquet, and I sent him to a base hospital. I never heard from him or about him until one day, thirty-two years later, in 1976, when I was living in a tiny studio apartment with my second wife, Margaret Ratner. We were look-ing for a larger place and saw an ad that read: "Greenwich Village triplex for rent."

I called and was asked, when I gave my name, if I had been a major in the Philippines in 1944.

"I sure was," I answered.

"Do you remember the GI that got hit in the leg and whose life you saved? That was me," said Leo Calarco. I certainly hadn't saved his life, merely helped get him to a hospital, but Margie and I needed a new place to live, so I didn't disagree with him. Mr. Calarco generously allowed us to rent his entire house for a very low sum. When he died in 1979, we bought the house from his estate at a very reasonable price and have lived happily in it since. My office is on the ground-floor level.

The way we came to this house reminds me of the saying, When you cast your bread upon the waters, it comes back to you thricefold. I was also especially pleased when I discovered that Harriet Tubman had rented it in 1857 and used it as a stop on the Underground Railroad.

A Touch of Combat

After six months on Leyte, I was sent briefly to Manila. While I was there, I headed alone toward the old part of town, called

Intramuros, which means "between the walls." The Japanese were entrenched in Intramuros and had it encircled with street-cars. We had been told that the Japanese tied young Filipino girls on the outside of the streetcars so that the Americans would not fire on them but I never saw this.

I crawled over a collapsed bridge separating the old city from the new and suddenly saw Japanese and American soldiers firing at each other. I had a .30-caliber carbine with me and, unexpect-edly, wanted to shoot, so I joined a rifle company and found my-self getting into the whole spirit of war. Suddenly, I was face-to-face with the war. I felt no fear at all because I was so caught up in it—adrenaline surging, heart pounding. I could fi-nally understand how soldiers in battle could do what they did. I fired like crazy, aiming at the streetcars.

Then it ended. I ran out of ammo, I was grimy, and I'd had enough of shooting. I walked slowly out of Intramuros, preparing to crawl back over that wrecked bridge toward the new part of Manila. Shocked by my first battle experience, I was not sure I wasn't dreaming when I saw the face of my brother, Michael, before me. I knew his communications ship, the *Blue Ridge,* was in the area, but I never expected to see him this way. We threw our arms around each other and tried to talk, but we were so excited we made no sense.

Finally, we found a Red Cross truck so that we could send a message home. It was right around Mother's Day, 1945. The mes-sage said: "To Mother, with love from Mike and Bill in Manila."

The War Ends

I returned to Telegrafo and, when Manila was finally taken, our army was ordered to take part in Operation Olympic, the inva-sion of Japan. I was really scared, certain that death was waiting for me because of the number of grave-registration teams assigned to the operation. These teams, assigned by mathematical formula, indicated the number of anticipated fatalities. For the invasion of Japan it appeared that a lot were expected, perhaps as high as a million. I'd been lucky so far, but now I prepared to die. Like the other GIs around me, I wrote a will and several letters to be deliv-ered home after my death.

Even after America dropped atom bombs on Hiroshima and Nagasaki in August, Operation Olympic was still on. We were still preparing to die. One night I was sitting on a little camp chair, watching a western, when suddenly—in one of those moments that I can always recall the sound and smell and sight of with perfect clarity—people were shouting and firing guns and yelling the glorious words "The war is over! The war is over!" I felt as if I were floating, flying, my body and spirit lighter than ever, a crushing burden now gone.

We celebrated wildly; then, shortly after the formal surrender ceremonies on the battleship *Missouri,* I was sent to Japan. I was put in charge of Safehand, a program in which classified documents were flown by officer-couriers. Using planes that were formerly bombers and pursuit ships out of Atsugi Airport, I arranged for officers to carry these documents to Burma, Singapore, Hong Kong, India, New Delhi, Chungking, Guam—all over the Far East.

Just before Christmas of 1945, it appeared that I was about to be shipped home soon, so I planned a farewell trip for myself to northern Japan, Korea, Chungking, and New Delhi. I had all the documents ready, was packed and looking forward to the trip, and the plane was set to leave at dawn. But during the night, a lieutenant I knew, Leo Penn, called and begged to go in my place. He was ordered to be shipped home in ten days, and it was his last opportunity to see the exotic Far East. I refused, for I had carefully planned the trip for myself, including in it all the places I longed to see. But finally, just before dawn, Leo wore me down, and I agreed. "All right, take the goddamned trip. I'll take one later," I said.

The plane took off as scheduled, but a short time later, it crashed into a mountain near Sendai, Japan, killing everyone aboard.

When I heard the news, I felt mixed emotions. I felt guilty not only because I had allowed him to go in my place but also because I couldn't escape feeling happy that it wasn't I.

I had to hunt all over Japan for a rabbi to conduct the funeral services for Leo. I succeeded, though, and on a rainy day we drove up the hill toward Tokyo's U.S. Army Cemetery No. 1, with Leo in a plain pine box. I remember that an old Japanese lady threw an orchid on the coffin.

I wrote to Leo's wife in the States and poured out my heart to her, describing all my feelings of guilt in great detail. When I received her answer, it really comforted me, for she made me realize that Leo's death was not my fault, that the trip that led to it was his choice and was part of the risks of life.

Going Home

After that, I refused to fly for a long time, and when I had earned enough points to go home, I returned by ship. The points had piled up quickly because a year earlier, in 1944, I had been awarded a Bronze Star for performing my assigned duties of supplying front-line units with codes. A Bronze Star, like a Purple Heart, gave you five points toward going home. Each six months in the service also earned five points.

I shipped home on the *Takanis Bay,* a small aircraft carrier, a few weeks before Christmas, 1945. I played volleyball, lay on the deck in the sun, relaxed, and thought about the last time I had seen my wife and baby. When I said goodbye to Lotte and Karin a year and a half earlier, my daughter was only nine months old.

The *Takanis Bay* docked in San Francisco on December 19. I hitched a ride on a slow troop train from San Francisco to New York and slept sitting up on a hard seat, a four-day ordeal, but I didn't care. When I arrived at Penn Station, I had a growth of beard, a helmet on my head, and a Nambu pistol in my belt. I carried a Samurai sword and felt like a Bill Maulden cartoon of GI Joe. But Lotte, who met me at the station, didn't seem to mind. We took a taxi to my parents' apartment, and when the elevator doors opened on their floor, Karin was standing there waiting for me. She yelled, "Daddy!" ran, and threw herself in my arms. The elevator operator, Kimball, who had taught me to play chess when I was much younger, cried like a baby as Karin and I hugged. I never forgot that. Tears ran down that man's face. I put my arms around him and cried also.

After

In 1941, shortly before I graduated from college, I applied to Yale Law School. I had no intention of going but knew my parents expected me to become a lawyer, since I had dropped out of premed. I knew I would be spending the next few years in the service, but after Yale Law School accepted me, I had purchased law books and even rented a room. But it had all been a sham, because I knew we would soon be at war. I never told my parents that I had no interest in law.

While I was in the Pacific, I developed a taste for journalism when some of my pieces about my experiences in the army were published by Harry Haines, a family friend and the publisher of the *Paterson Evening News.* I would relive some of my most vivid army experiences by putting them down on paper, and Harry published almost everything I sent him.

During this period, I wrote Lotte about my plan to attend the Columbia School of Journalism after my army stint, then write for a living. She mailed me a catalog from Columbia's journalism school, which arrived in pieces, because she had to cut it up before mailing it. Contrary to the romantic image of hand-knit sweaters and homemade cakes from home arriving overseas to comfort lonely GIs, the truth was that bulky mail never arrived promptly, if at all. We learned this quickly, so all my packages came in bits and pieces.

When I reassembled the dissected Columbia catalog, I read over the list of courses closely and concluded that my instincts had been correct: I did want to be a journalist. I would apply to Columbia as soon as I got home, and I would become a writer.

CHAPTER FOUR

Christ v. Paradise

Do you know another William Kunstler?

Law School

WHEN I RETURNED HOME, I FOUND OUT THAT MICHAEL WAS AT CO-
lumbia Law School. This meant that he had made up the three-
year head start I had on him, at least in terms of school. He was
discharged from the army earlier than I and returned to Yale, graduated, and gained admission to Columbia Law. Furious that my
baby brother was now ahead of me, I dropped my plans to be a
writer, forgot about journalism, and decided to go to law school—
for no other reason than that Michael was going.

I applied to Columbia and, with Michael, joined the entering
class of February 1946. For the next two years, we attended law
classes year-round, including summers, in a special program that
allowed returning war veterans to complete school in two years
rather than the usual three.

College had not been difficult for me, but the first semester in
law school proved very hard. I thought it was because I had problems readjusting to being a student. In the army, I had been a
major with authority and power, engaged in a life-and-death
struggle. The law-school professors treated all of us like little
boys. As vets, we also resented bitterly that our professors had not
soldiered during the war.

The GI Bill of Rights paid for my books and tuition and provided me with a ninety-dollar stipend monthly for living ex-

penses. It helped to ameliorate some of our resentment; at least we were receiving the very tangible gift of a free education.

I was so ambivalent about law school, though, that I didn't put in much effort and received "gentlemen's grades"—I barely passed. I even applied for work as a writer for the *Esso Road News,* a job that entailed traveling around the country writing brief descriptions of major national sites, like Yellowstone Park, for road maps. Motoring was very popular then because the conclusion of the war meant the end of gas rationing and people were eager to be behind the wheel and on the road.

Esso wanted to hire me, but I found that the job offer was like crossing the Rubicon. It forced me to make a very major life choice. If I quit law school, I would have no law degree—and Michael would. I would have hated that, so I turned Esso down and decided to make the best of law school. After that, my grades improved, and I even began to think of myself as a potential lawyer. By the time I graduated, my average was good.

But school was never quite enough for me. To satisfy my urge to write—and to earn extra money—I wrote book reviews for the *Herald Tribune Book Review.* I turned out so many reviews that I was given a pseudonym, David Tilden, so that readers wouldn't know the same person had written more than one review. Eventually, I also reviewed books for *Life* magazine, the *Saturday Review,* the *Atlantic Monthly,* the *New York Times,* the *Chicago Tribune,* the *Boston Herald,* the *New York Sun,* the *Omaha World Herald,* and the *San Francisco Chronicle.*

I also worked as a reader for Paramount's story department. For twenty dollars I would read a book or an article and make a recommendation as to whether it might make a good movie. This job made me feel very important. One of the novels I read was Laura Z. Hobson's *Gentleman's Agreement,* about the evils of anti-Semitism. I thought it was excellent and recommended that it be made into a film. Of course, I'll never know if I had anything to do with it, but *Gentleman's Agreement* became a screen classic.

Michael and I went into business, writing and selling "purples," which were law-course summaries named for the color of the ink used to reproduce them. We would write the purples, then collate them around my parents' dining-room table.

Michael and I were still living at home then. When I was first discharged from the army, I had no savings; my army salary had gone to support Lotte and Karin. We were forced to live as cheaply as possible and shared a bedroom in my parents' large nine-room apartment. Michael had a bedroom, too, and we all used a common bathroom.

After about a year, my extra income enabled me to move my family into an inexpensive apartment in a two-family row house on Twenty-third Street in Astoria, Queens. Since it was right near the Con Ed tanks, we suffered from the constant smell of gas in the air, and there was soot everywhere. Still, it was our home. Other than brief stays in rooming houses while I was in the army, it was the first place of my own in which I had ever lived. Our landlords, Tom and Gertrude Clack, were English and quite wonderful to us. If we were late with the rent, they never said a word, and occasionally they baby-sat for Karin.

During my second and final year of law school, I began to view the law as a powerful force for justice, the only equitable method available to people for correcting wrongs. I was proud that I was very nearly a lawyer and proud of the American legal system. I thought I understood it. I saw its enormous strengths and none of its failings. It was just, fair, treated everyone equally, and was the best system in the world.

Or so I believed then. It took many years, and many legal battles, before I changed my views. But in 1948, at the age of twenty-nine, I felt that the law was the right career for me. My graduating class contained mostly veterans, only three women, and no blacks. Many of my fellow students went on to make history, some good, some bad: Arthur Kinoy, now a law professor, a great lawyer, and someone I have been close to ever since law school; Roy Cohn, who gained notoriety as the evil legal sidekick of Sen. Joseph McCarthy; Jack B. Weinstein and Constance Baker Motley, who became chief judges of federal district courts in Brooklyn and Manhattan, respectively; Jack Greenberg, who succeeded Thurgood Marshall as director-counsel of the NAACP Legal Defense Fund; Marvin E. Frankel, also a federal judge until he resigned to make money in private practice; and David Sive, one of the country's leading environmental lawyers.

Passing the Bar

I was as loath to graduate as I had been reluctant to enter law school. I did not want my school years to end because out in the real world life was tough. I had to study for the bar exam and at the same time support my wife and children; Karin was then seven; Jane, an infant.

My brother enrolled in a bar-review course; he was still single and could afford not to work. But my first step after graduation was to go job hunting. I was hired at R. H. Macy and Company as an executive trainee for seventy-five dollars a week. It was a good salary, and I felt financially stable at last. I even bought a car, a little yellow Ford runabout.

I thought I could study for the bar and at the same time hold down the job at Macy's. Using Michael's bar-review-course textbooks, I would study in the store's cafeteria on my lunch hour. I went through a Macy's executive training program, then met and became friendly with Kenneth Straus, a son of the store's president. I had confided my love of writing to Ken, so one day he made me an interesting offer. He told me that when the *Titanic* went down, one of his relatives was on it. He left behind an unfinished manuscript which was to have been a manual for Macy's department managers. The document had not been touched since the *Titanic* sank in 1912, thirty-six years earlier.

When Ken told me that his father would like me to bring the manual up to date, I agreed and was relieved of all my other duties. The tome I wrote is still, I believe, in use at Macy's.

It took me two tries to pass the bar exam. The first time, I passed the substantive law section but failed procedural law. Michael, to my chagrin, passed both parts and was hired by a small law firm. Although I still felt fleeting ambivalence about actually practicing law, if Michael had passed the bar exam, it was crucial that I pass it, too.

As I awaited the results of the second exam, I was quite anxious. I did not want to fail it again. The day the results were announced, I ran down, bought a paper, and skimmed the list of names for my own. It wasn't there! "Oh, my God, I've failed again," I grieved. Then, realizing that I had looked at the section covering Manhattan, forgetting that I now lived in Queens, I slowly went back over the list. When I saw my name, boy, I gave a war whoop up those stairs to show Lotte. I thrust the paper at her and said, "You are now married to a bona fide lawyer!"

I was exaggerating, of course, because looming ahead was a personal interview with a member of the bar's character committee, Bernard Ferguson. I was not worried about it until I saw the Sunday *New York Times Book Review,* two days before the scheduled interview. It contained a review I had written, and the caption describing me stated I was a member of the New York Bar and a specialist in copyright law.

I prayed that Ferguson had not seen the review. If he had, he would naturally assume I had misrepresented myself. I would be pronounced a man without integrity and would never be able to practice law. When I walked into his office on Tuesday, I waited for the ax to fall, and it did. "Do you know another William Kunstler? I never read book reviews, but on the train from Philadelphia, I picked up the *New York Times Book Review*. I saw there's another William Kunstler who is a lawyer and has written a book review," he said.

"That is I, Mr. Ferguson," I said shakily.

"Did you tell them you were a member of the bar?" he asked.

"No, I never did," I said.

"You have to get an affidavit from the *Book Review* people that you never told them that," Ferguson said. It occurred to me that in my eagerness to write a review, perhaps I had mumbled, "I'm a lawyer" or a similar statement. I imagined every worst-case scenario possible. I went flying over to see the *Book Review* editor, John Hutchens, who most kindly said, "Of course I'll give you an affidavit that you didn't tell us. We assumed it." Quite relieved, I submitted the affidavit and finally was admitted to the New York State Bar on December 15, 1948. I was twenty-nine.

My entire family celebrated. Michael and I were now both officially lawyers, and our sister, Mary, had married a lawyer in Baltimore. We felt we were all on the road to success, something that was quite important to me then. A few months later, Michael and I decided to go into partnership and created the fledgling firm of Kunstler & Kunstler.

Kunstler & Kunstler

We began in a single room at 31 Nassau Street, rented from a group of lawyers who, in turn, leased their suite from the mammoth law firm of Root Ballantine. Our first client was our father, for whom we collected unpaid bills, and occasionally we had a paying client. We hired a secretary, Helen Goldstein, whom we knew was deaf. We never realized just how deaf she was until she had worked for us for a while. Ms. Goldstein sat outside with the other lawyers' secretaries, and Michael and I shared an office.

We took our first interesting case, *Christ v. Paradise,* on a contingency basis; we would get paid only if we won. Our client, Royal Christ, sued the Paradise Taxi Company for damages as a result of injuries he had suffered in an accident. In court, I enjoyed it immensely when the court clerk called out "Christ against Paradise" and the other lawyers present looked up sharply, wondering what this case could possibly be about. Before we actually got into court, we settled in the corridor outside for $1,500, and Michael and I received our first real fee, $500.

We also got some business from Lucien le Lièvre, which means Lucien the Hare. Lucien, a lawyer for Root Ballantine who handled French matters, generously gave us some referrals because I spoke French, having majored in it at Yale. Most of these cases involved trying to spring French nationals who were being held in New York State psychiatric institutions. We were usually successful, since the only requirement for their release was their promise that they would immediately return to France.

During the 1950s, Kunstler & Kunstler handled the ordinary cases which are the foundation of small, private law practices. Because he was excellent at mathematics and details, Michael did background, analysis, real estate closings, and estates. I handled annulments, divorces, and other family-law cases.

One of our first clients was a woman whose estate I still represent. She was recommended to us by James Gifford, associate dean of Columbia Law School, who had a special interest in our class at Columbia. It was the one in which his son would have been enrolled had he survived the war. Dean Gifford called us one day in 1950 and said, "I'm sending you a Mrs. Mae Wightman, who wants a will drawn."

When she arrived, Mrs. Wightman, who was three-quarters blind, had to be steered into the room. We drafted a will and charged her a fee of fifteen dollars, which she never paid. She left everything in trust for her niece, who was then only two and lived with her family in Napa, California. Michael and I were named as executors and trustees. We assumed that Mrs. Wightman had either no money at all or, at most, a few dollars.

In 1950, Lotte and I moved to Portchester—now called Rye Brook—in Westchester County. We were able to buy a house because of a special deal for veterans: no down payment and mortgage payments of only seventy-two dollars a month. Michael, married by this time, bought a house right across the street from us, and he and I commuted together daily to our one-room office.

One morning in July, not too long after we had drawn up Mrs.

Wightman's will, I was playing tennis at a friend's court when Michael ran up and said, "I just got a call from the police. Mrs. Wightman's dead, and they found our business card in her apartment. I'm going there."

What he found was beyond description. Mrs. Wightman's apartment on 116th Street in Manhattan contained not only her decomposing body, which had lain there for three hot, humid days, but a lifetime's accumulation of junk. Mrs. Wightman simply never threw anything away. There were dozens of television sets, cases of unopened wine bottles, and the Braille books she had borrowed from the public library and never returned. Carefully wrapped, half-eaten sandwiches shared space under her bed with leases for land all over the United States and Canada and warehouse receipts from scores of places. After a quick evaluation, we saw that Mrs. Wightman had not been penniless, after all, but had left a sizable estate.

For the next two years, Michael and I traveled all over the country attempting to straighten out the estate, which was incredibly complicated. For example, tracing one warehouse receipt, we wound up in Atlanta, Georgia, in possession of a Civil War uniform and a vintage, fully loaded Colt automatic. Both had belonged to one of her four husbands.

As we investigated, we found more and more deeds to lands with oil and mineral deposits. We also found valuable items of all kinds in warehouses throughout the country. In New Brunswick, one of Canada's Maritime Provinces, during a terrible blizzard, I auctioned off $10,000 worth of furniture that had been left in storage. Michael and I converted all assets into cash, with the estate receiving dividends or rentals from the oil and bauxite lands.

Mrs. Wightman's niece, mentally retarded and now in her forties, has been sent payments over the years through her mother. Since Michael died several years ago, I became the sole trustee, but have tried to transfer my responsibilities to a California successor trustee. As soon as my final accounting is approved by the court, I expect the transfer to take place.

Roy Cohn and Joseph McCarthy

Shortly after I passed the bar exam, I began teaching law at New York Law School. In 1950, I loved the law and loved teaching it. I only recall one negative experience at New York Law School. A student, writing in an exam book, had written my name as "Professor Cuntslaw." I wrote that the name he had given me sounded obscene and that I had subtracted five points from his grade for failure to observe the correct spelling of the professor's name. The student protested quite vigorously to the dean, but my grading was sustained.

When Roy Cohn, one of my former Columbia Law School classmates, asked me to recommend him for a teaching position, I did so because I had no inkling then of what a total snake he was. At the time, I was teaching a course on trusts and estates, and Roy asked me to draft a will for a friend of his. Amazing as it may seem, I prepared a will for Sen. Joseph McCarthy. I was not at all political then and felt privileged to draw up the will of a U.S. senator. At that time, Roy and McCarthy were not yet deeply engaged in the anti-Communist hysteria which would severely damage the country and many individual lives.

When I finished the will, I brought it to McCarthy at Whyte's Chop House in lower Manhattan, where he and Roy were having lunch. Roy and I witnessed it, but it was never probated, because McCarthy later married and, I assume, a new will was executed.

Roy's father, believed to be the conduit for Jewish money to the Bronx Democratic machine, had been a state supreme court judge in the Bronx. People have told me that he used to put Roy, as a young child, up on the bench with him. An only child, doted on by his parents, Roy thought he was God's gift to humankind. He had an enormous desire to be in the spotlight, and being the counsel for Senator McCarthy's infamous Subcommittee on Governmental Operations gave him the limelight he craved.

In later years, because Roy and I were on the opposite sides of all political issues, we became ideological enemies, and he publicly called me every name under the sun. I was urged to sue him but didn't. I never sue, having taken to heart advice given me by Dr. Martin Luther King that one should never retaliate for oneself. Others can speak for you, but don't defend yourself. Roy was truly a vile human being, so despicable that when I heard he died of AIDS, for a moment I felt that perhaps there was a God.

As much as Roy aided McCarthy, his actions also led to McCarthy's downfall. Roy brought in his intimate friend G. David Schine (a camper of mine when I worked at Brant Lake Camp) to serve as an investigator with McCarthy's investigation subcommittee. McCarthy and Cohn tried to keep Schine from being drafted, and when that failed, they attempted to have the army assign him to the committee. When that also failed, they accused the army of holding Schine hostage in order to prevent an investigation of Communists in the army. The dissension between the army and the McCarthy camp eventually led to the famous army-McCarthy hearings, which destroyed McCarthy's credibility and reputation and finally caused his downfall.

Several years ago, I spoke at a college in Appleton, Wisconsin, the town where McCarthy is buried. Afterward, a student asked if I wanted to see his grave, and we drove out to the cemetery, which was on a hill in a most pastoral setting. The senator's grave is a tourist attraction, so I had no trouble locating it. I stood there, looking down on the earthly remains of Joseph Raymond McCarthy, and thought back to Whyte's Chop House and the irony of my having drawn up a will for such a man.

The Rosenbergs

In 1951, when one of the most politicized courtroom cases of the century took place, I was still naive, still not involved in anything outside my small world of family and work. Three people, Ethel and Julius Rosenberg and Morton Sobell, were convicted, under the Espionage Act of 1917, of conspiring to transmit atomic secrets to the USSR during World War II. Julius Rosenberg had a degree in electrical engineering and worked with the U.S. Army Signal Corps. The Rosenbergs were sentenced to death; Morton Sobell, to thirty years. I had been out of law school for three years and should have been well informed about the case, but I wasn't. I may have been attempting to distance myself from it like my parents and many other Jews. "We need this like a hole in the head," my father used to say about the Rosenberg case, implying that Jews did not need such negative publicity. There was enough anti-Semitism in the world.

I was appalled at the death sentences that had been imposed on the Rosenbergs by Irving Kaufman, a new federal judge who had received his appointment because he had helped raise money for Truman's 1948 campaign. While I didn't know then that Kaufman was in cahoots with the prosecution, I did perceive that the sentences were far too harsh. On the night of the Rosenbergs' executions, in 1953, Lotte and I were on the road, driving to Watch Hill, Rhode Island, for a short vacation. When we heard on the car radio the tragic news that Julius and Ethel Rosenberg had been electrocuted at Sing Sing Prison, we stopped the car and began to cry.

A decade later, I became involved with the case—as a result of my big mouth and bigger appetite. During the early 1960s, I was making a small name as a civil rights lawyer and was invited to be a guest on Long John Nebel's popular late-night radio talk show. I went on, looking forward to the absolutely delicious roast beef and turkey sandwiches that were served at 2:00 A.M. to keep everyone going. That night, even though I knew little about the case, I argued against the death penalty but agreed with the convictions of the Rosenbergs and Morton Sobell.

Helen Sobell, Morton Sobell's wife, was also a guest, and she became very upset at what I said. She broke down and told me that I was wrong. Then she asked if I would read the transcript. I read it and decided that Sobell and the Rosenbergs had not only been wrongfully sentenced but had also been wrongly convicted. I next visited Morton Sobell, who was then imprisoned in the U.S. penitentiary in Lewisburg, Pennsylvania, after a long stint in Alcatraz. After I met with him, I was asked by Helen to attempt to have his conviction set aside. Arthur Kinoy, Marshall Perlin, the late Samuel Gruber, and I worked on the motion.

The prosecutors who had convicted the Rosenbergs and Sobell were Roy Cohn and Irving Saypol, both Jewish, and an Irishman, Myles Lane, who must have been added to the team in order to soften the obvious Judas goat allusion. The judge, Irving Kaufman, was also Jewish. Defense attorney Emmanuel Bloch worked on the case with his aged father, Abraham. Manny, who had very little criminal law experience, was running scared because the death penalty was involved.

Ethel Rosenberg's brother, David Greenglass, a machinist assigned to the Manhattan Project, the top-secret government project which developed the atom bomb, was the chief prosecution witness. He told a fanciful tale of meeting with a chemist, Harry Gold, in Albuquerque, New Mexico, and described Gold as a courier from the Soviet spy apparatus in New York.

Greenglass testified that Gold told him, "I come from Julius"—meaning Julius Rosenberg—and then showed him a piece of cardboard cut from a Jell-O package that could be matched to another piece in Greenglass's possession. Then, Greenglass testified, he drew a sketch of the atom bomb for Gold to take back east with him.

While Greenglass did work for the Manhattan Project, I don't believe that he possessed enough knowledge to sketch the bomb itself. When Greenglass was on the stand, the prosecutor held up what was supposed to be a copy of this drawing and then asked, "Is this the sketch of the atom bomb you drew?"

"Yes," Greenglass answered.

This is where the defense for the Rosenbergs made a crucial but understandable error. When Greenglass made this identification of the purported sketch, defense attorney Manny Bloch stood up and said, "We agree it is a sketch of the atom bomb. We agree it should not be shown even to the jury, that it's all secret, that it should be kept under seal." As a result, no member of the trial jury ever saw the drawing, even though the prosecutor said to them during summation, "You heard the defense concede this was a drawing of the atom bomb." The failure on the part of the defense to show the sketch to the jury sealed the Rosenbergs' fate.

Bloch mishandled David Greenglass's sketch in a misguided but well-intentioned attempt to gain the confidence of the jury in a death-penalty case. His strategy was to show them that he would not allow vital government secrets to be revealed. Unfortunately, in doing so, he convinced jurors that the sketch indeed contained the secret of the atom bomb.

Years later, when my cocounsel and I studied the trial transcript, we moved to unseal the evidence so we could actually see the famous sketch. Our motion was granted by District Judge John Cannella, who, along with Kinoy, Gruber, Perlin, and myself, descended into the basement of the U.S. courthouse in Manhattan where the sealed records were kept. It was quite memorable—the judge in his long, flowing black robes leading us into the bowels of the building to unearth this absolutely crucial exhibit.

I actually trembled as we waited to see the famous drawing. The judge withdrew a small item from an envelope, and we finally saw the evidence which had helped send two people to their deaths and another to a long term in prison. It turned out that the drawing was a sketch of a circle, with smaller circles inside it. It was obvious to me, without any expert scientific opinion, that this could not possibly be a sketch of the atom bomb.

We showed this drawing to scientists, including George Kistakowski and several others who had patents on the bombs that were dropped by the United States in 1945 on Hiroshima and Nagasaki. The consensus was that it was no more than a rough copy of material appearing in the available scientific literature, circa 1909. From what I now know about government misconduct, I am firmly convinced that the FBI told Greenglass what to draw and that he merely followed their lead.

In recent years, the published memoirs of Alfred Lilienthal and others within the Atomic Energy Commission have revealed that had the defense not conceded the point but called expert witnesses to refute the allegation that the sketch was of the A-bomb, the government would have dropped the entire prosecution.

In arguing a motion to vacate Sobell's conviction in 1967, Kinoy, I, and the other lawyers said that the original jury had not been given the real facts, that the alleged drawing was not a sketch of the atom bomb, and that Sobell deserved a new trial. Our motion was denied in a ninety-one-page opinion by Judge Edwin Weinfeld, to whom the case was now assigned and who was determined not to reopen it. We also introduced in our motion the fact that Morton Sobell had been illegally seized in Mexico. To that point, the judge responded, "It may be terrible, but once you got him here, you got him here."

I am convinced that had Weinfeld not been Jewish, he would have ruled in Sobell's favor. But I believe he was fearful that he would be charged with following his religion rather than his reason in deciding the matter. This same paralysis—a fear of being identified as a judge following his Jewish affiliation—gripped Circuit Judge Jerome Frank on the day of the Rosenbergs' execution when he refused to join Chief Judge Thomas Swan in granting the doomed couple a stay of execution. A stay could have led to a new legal approach—that the Espionage Act, under which the Rosenbergs were convicted, did not authorize the death penalty during peacetime—that might have prevailed, thus saving the lives of Julius and Ethel.

After much reading and investigation, my own theory is that the Rosenbergs and Sobell were selected as scapegoats by J. Edgar Hoover, then head of the FBI. Hoover was a man who had questionable ethics when it came to garnering glory for himself and the Bureau, a man who saw enemies everywhere and succeeded in infusing much of our country with his paranoid mentality during the 1950s and 1960s.

I believe Hoover was embarrassed because he had been upstaged by the British. A German scientist, Klaus Fuchs, had confessed in England in 1950 that having worked on the atom bomb at Los Alamos, he passed secret information about it to the Russians. Fuchs was sentenced to nine years in prison under the British Official Secrets Act.

Fearing that he and the FBI would appear inept because they had not uncovered Fuchs's espionage, Hoover decided that he needed his own "spies"—scapegoats whose conviction would remove any stigma from the Bureau for not having captured Fuchs. Being an anti-Semite, he selected three Jews to take the fall, fabricated a case against them, and coerced David Greenglass into testifying against his sister by threatening to send both David and his wife, Ruth, to the electric chair if he refused to testify. The result was the terrible tragedy of a brother sending his sister and brother-in-law to their deaths. Today Greenglass lives under an assumed name; he can never show his face again among decent people. Perhaps someday he will partially redeem himself by telling the truth about his role.

Morton Sobell was paroled in 1969 after nineteen years in prison, including the five-year stretch in Alcatraz. He now lives on the West Coast. Because I became involved in Morton's appeal, I traveled all over the country to rouse the public about his case. Every year now, on the anniversary of the Rosenbergs' execution, I speak somewhere, trying to keep the memory of this horrible injustice alive. I want people to always remember the tragic, unnecessary executions of Ethel and Julius Rosenberg that were a result of the self-serving, manipulative, and evil J. Edgar Hoover and the FBI—with the full backing of the U.S. government.

This case was an immense tragedy. Manny Bloch, the defense attorney, had the vivid image of the electric chair constantly in his mind. It was the height of the Cold War, and Bloch, knowing the temper of the times, feared that his clients would be executed. As a result, his defense was weak, and he had no real support; no one thought of questioning the government's prosecution. Today this case would be a cause that would unite multitudes to rise up and protest everything about it, especially the flimsy, phony evidence.

The case was far beyond the reach of Manny Bloch, but I don't blame him. Where were the rest of us Jewish lawyers, myself included? With rare exceptions, we sat around, talking, analyzing, complaining, but doing nothing. Manny's clients stood accused of the most serious kind of espionage, giving the secret of the atom bomb to the Soviet Union, then America's mortal enemy. The Rosenbergs never had a chance.

Introduction to Civil Rights

Because I've always needed a lot of extra stimulation, I did several radio shows during the 1950s. On *The Law on Trial,* over

WMCA, I discussed details of celebrated trials. Later, after the name of the show was changed to *Counterpoint,* I interviewed many interesting people with differing viewpoints on controversial issues, including Eleanor Roosevelt, Alger Hiss, and Malcolm X.

On WEVD (named for socialist Eugene Victor Debs), I discussed momentous trials throughout history on a program called *Famous Trials.* Then Nathan Straus, WMCA's head, created a program called *Justice,* which would dramatize these trials. He hired a repertory company that included talented actors like Telly Savalas, Ruth Chatterton, and Helen Twelvetrees and paid me $200 for each script I wrote. I dramatized the trials of Jesus, John Brown, Sam Sheppard, and others, scribbling away nightly in the attic of my house.

Lotte and I were active in our community. We joined the NAACP and Urban League and worked to get liberals and progressives elected to the local school board. I was a parlor liberal, along with many other middle-class whites in my community, who held meetings, wrote letters, and tried to influence local elections.

My first civil rights case involved Paul Redd, the head of the local NAACP chapter in our town in Westchester. Paul, unable to rent an apartment in Rye because he was black, filed a discrimination suit in which he was represented by Paul Zuber, a lawyer who was famous for bringing the first northern integration suit against the New Rochelle school system. Zuber asked for my assistance on Paul's case, and I agreed. We used an old and perfected technique to determine housing discrimination: shilling. After white applicants determine that a certain apartment is available, a black person is sent in to apply for the same apartment. If he is turned down and told that there is no apartment available, this constitutes evidence of housing discrimination. We did this in Rye and won our case, and Paul and his wife, Oriel, got their apartment.

A fairly important constitutional case was referred to me in 1956 by Rowland Watts, then legal director of the American Civil Liberties Union (ACLU). A black journalist, William Worthy Jr., had had his passport confiscated when he returned home after he had traveled to what was then called Red China to do research for his writing. At the time, a prohibition against travel to China and several other countries appeared on all U.S. passports. The ACLU asked me to represent Worthy in an attempt to recover his passport.

I instituted litigation in the District of Columbia federal court. It was unsuccessful in the short run but brought me into contact with Leonard Boudin, a lawyer who knew more about the legalities surrounding passports than anyone else. I learned a great deal from Leonard, who was a great lawyer and very knowledgeable in constitutional law. I litigated the Worthy case with Leonard's help and active encouragement as well as input from Edward Bennett Williams, a Washington, D.C., lawyer who would later become one of the country's best-known litigators.

Even though we had not won back Bill Worthy's passport, he chose to travel out of the country again, this time to do research on Cuba, another country on the prohibited list. Instead of a passport, Bill used an affidavit of identity, which is a document that unofficially affirms one's citizenship. He attached his picture to the affidavit and had no difficulty entering Cuba. But when he tried to return to the United States, he was arrested at Miami International Airport and charged with "returning to the United States without a valid passport," a most archaic statute. He was convicted in 1961 in Miami; there really was no defense, for Bill had obviously violated the statute.

But the real issue was that the law under which Bill had been convicted was unconstitutional. We made this the crucial issue during trial, but the district judge in Miami ruled against us and validated the statute's constitutionality.

I appealed this decision and argued the case before the U.S. Court of Appeals for the Fifth Circuit in Atlanta in 1961. As I have done in so many courtroom summations and opening statements since that one, I began with a line of poetry to add drama and spirit to my presentation. Before the astonished federal panel, I quoted from "The Lay of the Last Minstrel" by Sir Walter Scott: "Breathes there the man, with soul so dead, / Who never to himself hath said, / This is my own, my native land!" Now that I had their full attention, I argued that a law making it a crime to return to one's country without a "valid passport" was against the Constitution as it had originally been written. Nowhere in that document is it stated that a person can come home to America only if he has in his possession an official paper with a government stamp attesting to his citizenship.

I will always remember this case with special clarity for a number of reasons—not the least of which is that I argued it while suffering from one of the most excruciating migraines I ever had. I could not see clearly and was nauseated and sick, but I forced myself to enter that courtroom to present my argument.

A friend had picked me up at my motel and dropped me at the courthouse, then driven off. As I sat in the spectators' section waiting for my case to be called, trying not to focus on the pain in my head, I suddenly realized that all my files were in the trunk of her car. There I sat: My first constitutional argument. Sick as I could possibly be. And no files.

I staggered to the clerk's office where a young woman kindly gave me copies of all the briefs in the case. I stumbled back into the courtroom and sat down, certain I would never be able to stand when the case was called. When I heard the clerk say, "United States versus Worthy," I got up rather shakily and said to Chief Judge Elbert Tuttle, "Judge, I'm suffering from a terrible migraine. With your permission I'd like to argue sitting down." He said, "Of course," and I sank down at the counsel table. (This was the first of many positive responses I was to receive through the years from this great judge.)

Several months later, the court's decision came down. It invalidated the statute and stated that the government could not make it a crime under the Constitution for an American citizen to return home without a passport. Bill Worthy's conviction was overturned, and from this time on no citizen who returned to the United States without a valid passport could be prosecuted. "This is my own, my native land" must have had some merit in the eyes of the court.

The decision, which made me extremely happy, was momentous for many reasons. By now, I had become involved in the southern civil rights movement, so I was much more cognizant of rights and liberties than when I had first undertaken William Worthy's passport case five years earlier. Also, this was my first experience arguing an issue about which I felt passionate. In trying to prove to a federal circuit court that a law was in violation of the U.S. Constitution, I felt a great sense of responsibility and importance. I was very angry that a journalist, an American citizen, had been restricted in his travel to other countries, then hounded, harassed, and jailed by his own government. I gave long and serious thought to the argument and revised it a dozen times.

This was the first time I had ever invalidated a statute. It confirmed my faith in the justice system. Let the other lawyers draft wills and do real estate closings. I had *changed* the law! I had made a contribution! I felt an enormous thrill and a desire for more of the same.

PART TWO

Call to Action

CHAPTER FIVE

June 15, 1961

*Why don't you shut your goddamned mouth and stay the
hell out of Mississippi!*

Freedom Riders

DURING 1960, STILL NEEDING EXTRA STIMULATION TO SUPPLEMENT MY
law practice, I wrote a book about Caryl Chessman, who had been
executed on May 2 of that year after his conviction as the notorious "Red-Light Bandit." Caryl had been sentenced to death for
violating California's "Little Lindbergh" law, which made it a
capital crime to commit an abduction—even forcing a person,
against his or her will, to move a few feet. Despite the monumental legal efforts of George Davis, a distant cousin of mine, plus my
own small input and the advocacy of thousands of supporters,
including Pope John XXIII, who believed the sentence did not at
all fit the crime, Caryl was put to death in California's gas chamber. Caryl's book, *Cell 2455, Death Row,* written while he was in
prison, had made his cause internationally known, but I was so
incensed by his unjust treatment by the courts that I decided to
write my own book about him.

I worked on it every night as soon as I returned home from my
law office, determined to complete at least two pages a day, a
schedule that I consistently maintained. When my book about
Chessman, *Beyond a Reasonable Doubt?,* was published in June
1961, I traveled to Los Angeles, at the publisher's request, to publicize it. I was in a motel room there when I received an early-
morning call that was to change my life forever.

At 6:00 A.M. on June 15, a ringing telephone woke me out of a sound sleep. The ACLU's Rowland Watts, who had involved me in the William Worthy passport case, which I had been working on since 1956, was calling, asking me to fly to Jackson, Mississippi. He wanted me to assure a group of mostly young people, both blacks and whites, who were riding interstate buses through the South in order to force the integration of segregated bus-station facilities, that the ACLU stood solidly behind them. They called themselves Freedom Riders.

I told Rowland that I needed some time to think about it and would call him back. I sat down on the bed and thought: Ever since the passport case, I had not been much interested in my law practice and had felt faint stirrings within me for more meaningful work, perhaps law on a grander scale. I recalled the words of Justice Oliver Wendell Holmes: "As life is action and passion, it is required of a man that he should share the passion and action of his time, at peril of being judged not to have lived." When Rowland asked me to go South, I was forty-two and decided that when I was old and looked back on my life, I didn't want to discover that I had merely existed.

The Freedom Riders had been organized and sponsored by the Congress for Racial Equality (CORE) to fight the Jim Crow laws that ruled the South. Jim Crow mandated separation of the white and black races in all places of public accommodation: buses, bus terminals, airports, drinking fountains, toilets. CORE was then a respected civil rights organization, quite different from the ersatz counterpart which bears its name today. Freedom Riders began their historic bus rides on May 4, 1961. At every place they stopped, they were harassed, arrested, and brutalized. In Anniston, Alabama, for example, a bus was set afire, and its occupants severely beaten.

Sitting in that motel room, thinking about the opportunity Rowland had given me, my decision came easily. Instead of returning to New York City and resuming my work on the run-of-the-mill cases waiting for me in the practice I shared with Michael, I would fly to Jackson on behalf of Freedom Riders—and perhaps help to save them from being hurt, imprisoned, or even murdered. Within a few minutes, I called Rowland and told him I would be on the next plane.

I arrived in Jackson on the night of June 15. The next morning—Michael's birthday, so I never forget the date—I reported to the office of lawyer Jack H. Young, a former postman who had learned his law in another black attorney's office, there being no law school for anyone not white in Mississippi. "I bring you regards from the American Civil Liberties Union," I said to him.

Jack, the only lawyer for all of the four hundred Freedom Riders who had been arrested in Mississippi, brushed off my niceties. "I don't want regards. I need lawyers here," he said. "Regards are a dime a dozen. Go down to the Greyhound Bus Terminal, because there are going to be arrests when the next bus comes in. Then come back to me and we'll talk."

I understood his abruptness and went immediately to the terminal. Waiting for the busload of Freedom Riders to arrive, I had a hamburger and coffee at the lunch counter. Suddenly, in the middle of a bite, the police ordered me to move because they were clearing the waiting room. As I watched the tense cops, eager reporters, and a jumpy crowd, all of them white, I began to feel nervous myself.

Then the bus pulled in, and five scared but determined-looking young people—three white women, a white man, and a black man—entered the terminal from a rear ramp and sat down at the lunch counter I had just left. Jackson police captain J. L. Ray asked them to leave. When they refused, they were quickly and quietly arrested for breaching the peace and taken to the Hinds County Jail. I did nothing. I truly had no idea what to do, so I walked back to Jack Young's office to consult with him.

In spite of my temporary helplessness, I had learned an important lesson about political action from those five young people who believed so much in what they were doing. They had behaved with dignity and calm despite the fear they must have felt. They sat down at that counter because only by doing so could they desegregate it. All the talking in the world meant nothing; it was the doing, the action, that had meaning.

None of this was completely clear to me that first day, but I did have some inkling of the importance of what was happening as I walked back to Jack Young's office. I knew I had to try to get those five people out of jail, although I had no idea how to go about it. The standard law I had practiced for the last twelve years would not serve me here. I needed new legal techniques.

Jack Young and I prepared a federal writ of habeas corpus—which means "produce the body"—asking the authorities to bring the arrested persons before the court so that a decision could be made. We filed it in the name of Elizabeth Porter Wyckoff, our test defendant. A former professor at Mount Holyoke College, she was the first white female Freedom Rider arrested. In federal court in Biloxi, Mississippi, we argued that under the Commerce Clause of the Constitution, the Riders could not be guilty of breaching the peace simply for sitting together in an integrated fashion on buses or in bus terminals.

During that argument, there was a moment that seemed to presage my future career of fighting for causes and people I believe in while being denounced by those who think I'm dead wrong. A man in the back row of the courtroom stood and bellowed, "Why don't you shut your goddamned mouth and stay the hell out of Mississippi!" It was the first time an angry citizen had told me to get the hell out, but far from the last. I looked him right in the eye, then turned back, and continued my argument. The judge, Sidney Mize, an ardent segregationist, finally ordered this man to sit down.

Mize ruled against our petition, saying we had not exhausted state remedies before applying to the federal courts. While he was technically correct, I knew that even if we had gone to the state courts first, he would have ruled against us because of his obvious bias. I was furious.

A few weeks later, I was even angrier when, during a conversation in his office, which I had naively initiated in the hope that it would help the Riders, Mississippi governor Ross Barnett asked me why I was "mixed up with these troublemakers," then inquired whether I had children.

"Two girls," I replied.

"What would you think if your daughter married a dirty, kinky-headed, field-hand nigger?" asked the governor of Mississippi.

I was dismayed that a man in high political office could be so ignorant and racist. If a governor spoke like this—felt this way—what would I find among the ordinary people in the South? Maybe the civil rights movement was hopeless. Maybe it was the mother of all lost causes. But I tapped into the energy set off by my rage at Barnett, and since the only way I could quiet my feelings of red-hot anger was to act quickly, I called Charles Oldham, national chairman of CORE. "Count me in. If you still want me, I'm available," I told Oldham, who had earlier asked me if I was willing to take Freedom Rider cases on a regular basis.

I wanted to stop Ross Barnett and his kind. As I made this call to Oldham, my heart was pounding with the excitement and challenge. What greater stimulation than to fight for something I believed was right against the greatest odds possible! The civil rights movement was a struggle between the most disfranchised members of our population and the most powerful, the white Establishment. I loved being on the side that, although weaker, was morally right.

The Miracle

The Wyckoff case was the beginning of my involvement in what was called "movement law," the practice of law which considers the political objectives of defendants—the integration goals of the Freedom Riders, for example—most important. In the past, lawyers, myself included, viewed the law as sacred and inviolate. But movement law considered the legal system as something to be used or changed, in order to gain the political objectives of the clients in a particular case. Movement law was created and refined in the South by lawyers like me, and dozens of others, as we rushed from one civil rights crisis to another, inventing legal remedies as we went, with the goal of desegregation before us at all times.

For the next two months I commuted between Jackson and New York while I prepared the cases of the Freedom Riders. Although they were charged with breaching the peace, a misdemeanor according to Mississippi law, they were imprisoned in the state's maximum-security penitentiary at Parchman. The cases were due to come to trial in August.

As I prepared for the trial, I worked closely with many new people—blacks, whites, religious leaders, students, union members, professionals, southerners, northerners. Their concerns were different and seemed more important than those of the people I had known before. My middle-class life in New York and Westchester seemed quite narrow to me now. In the South, I was reborn into a man I liked better, one who contributed to society and tried to make a difference.

I began working with William L. Higgs, a Mississippi-born Harvard Law School graduate, and it was he who later discovered a miracle federal statute. Called the removal statute, it was a Reconstruction-era civil rights law that *forced* the federal courts to accept criminal cases from the state courts when it was alleged that the defendants could not get fair trials in the latter tribunals, and also required them to set bail for defendants.

When I first read that law, I yelled, "Oh, my God!" Under it, a lawyer could secure the release of civil rights workers from jail by simply filing a petition with the federal court and simultaneously presenting the state court with a copy of it. The language of the statute also stated that the federal court *"shall* grant bail"—not "may" or "might." Thus, the miracle statute automatically removed the case from the state's jurisdiction and mandated federal judges to grant bail.

Before I knew about the federal removal statute, I lost almost all my cases, and most Freedom Riders were convicted as charged of breaching the peace. (Although it took four years, on April 26, 1965, the U.S. Supreme Court unanimously reversed the convictions of all the Jackson Freedom Riders.)

Bill Higgs had discovered a brilliant strategy. We needed it desperately to prevent mass arrests from destroying the movement. From this point on, with Bill's assistance, Jack Young and I were successful when we petitioned for the removal of Freedom Rider cases from state to federal court. We began to use the removal statute in cases all over the South. It was the legal lever that made the difference in whether the movement lived or died, the single most important procedural device we lawyers had during the early years of the civil rights movement. After a while, all the other civil rights lawyers would call Bill Higgs or me and ask how to do it, and we gladly shared the information with them.

We used the removal statute to get people out of jail almost as soon as they were arrested. Since the local authorities were unfamiliar with the statute and did not know how to get a case remanded, or sent back, to the state courts, they often floundered, and many cases were never returned to state jurisdiction.

(Several years later, Bill Higgs and I worked with Rep. Robert Kastenmeier of Wisconsin to have a provision concerning the removal of cases to federal courts inserted in the Civil Rights Act of 1964. The addendum stated that defendants whose cases were removed could also appeal if they were eventually remanded to the state courts. Up to that time, only the state authorities had the right to appeal successful removals. After Bill and I testified about it before several committees of Congress, our suggestion was written into the act.)

The federal removal statute was utilized in almost every civil rights case until it was blocked by the Supreme Court in 1965. At that time, the Court ruled that removal to a federal court was only proper if a specific state statute explicitly denied prospective petitioners a fair shake in court. Since no such state laws existed, federal removal became a dead letter—but not before it had served us well in the South.

Although the Freedom Riders suffered personal pain, they completely changed the face of the South and eventually brought about the full integration of interstate bus lines and terminal facilities.

Wyatt Tee Walker

In 1961, right after my first Rider cases in Jackson, Rev. Wyatt Tee Walker, executive director of the Southern Christian Leadership Conference, summoned me to Monroe, North Carolina. Monroe was a small town some thirty miles east of Charlotte and reportedly regional headquarters of the Ku Klux Klan. The lean and dashing reverend had asked me to defend several Freedom Riders who were in jail on charges of rioting, violating the picketing ordinance, resisting arrest, and other charges.

The Riders had been on their way to their home states when they accepted Wyatt's invitation to join forces with local blacks to picket the Union County Courthouse. For several days, the Riders and local blacks marched around the building, its blue neon sign flashing Jesus Saves! They were undaunted by ride-by shootings, beatings by local toughs, and counterdemonstrators whose signs had slogans like It's Open Season on Coons. Finally, the counterdemonstrators attacked the picketers, and after a violent fracas, the police made arrests: Thirteen Freedom Riders and thirty-five other black demonstrators were arrested.

After I arrived in Monroe and met with Wyatt, I strove to have everyone released from jail and their charges dropped so that the Freedom Riders could return home. I worked with the legendary Len Holt, a brilliant and daring civil rights attorney from Richmond, Virginia, whose nickname was "Snake Doctor." Len and I carved out a deal with the prosecutor to drop the charges if the Riders left the community and went home. I remember that Jim Forman, the head of the more militant Student Nonviolent Coordinating Committee (SNCC), thought the arrangement was an unacceptable compromise. At the time, though, I believed that it was the very best deal we could get. I smiled happily at the thirteen Riders as they filed out of the courtroom, heading home, and they smiled back. I packed my briefcase and returned to New York.

Meeting Dr. King

In September 1961, I was invited by Reverend Walker to speak about legal aspects of the Freedom Rider cases at the annual SCLC convention. It was a good chance for me to meet other civil rights lawyers, and Wyatt had arranged a meeting between me and Dr. King. On September 29, Lotte and I flew to Nashville. We were met at the airport and driven to our motel, a Holiday Inn which accepted only white guests. Today I regret that I consented to stay there, but at the time I did not give it a thought. After we dropped off our luggage, Wyatt said, "Dr. King would like to have supper with you," and we were taken to King's motel, the Eldorado, which was for black guests only.

I had no idea what Dr. King looked like. It's startling to think that I had never seen a picture of him, but those were early days, before he gained overwhelming national prominence. He was still a comparative stranger to most Americans, since the country did not yet take the civil rights movement seriously. One of the great tragedies of the movement is how many years it took, how many deaths, injuries, and arrests, before the rest of America paid sufficient attention to it.

As Lotte and I went to meet Dr. King, I expected to see an Old Testament saint with flowing white hair, a cross between Moses and Frederick Douglass. When we joined Martin and his wife, Coretta, in a booth in the motel's coffee shop, I was amazed at his youthful appearance. With close-cropped hair, clipped mustache, slanted eyes, and high cheekbones, Dr. King looked not at all as I had imagined him. After I recovered from my surprise, I was glad he did not have a long white beard or talk in a stentorian voice, that he was pleasant and gentle, a regular man. I felt quite comfortable with him. We chatted as we ate, discussing the Freedom Rider cases and the Monroe confrontations.

Dr. King's most memorable feature was his voice. It was very soft, but rich and full, with a pronounced southern accent. He drew out my name—Biiilll, not Bill. I can still hear that voice, all these years later. I don't think there is a single American who ever heard him—even those who have only heard the speeches on tape or film—who is not affected by the grandeur of that voice. But Dr. King was not oratorical the night we met, just very friendly.

As our meal drew to a close, it was clear there was a purpose behind this casually arranged meeting. Martin wanted additional legal representation from someone like me who was not associated with any organization. He was already well represented by several attorneys, mainly the NAACP's legal arm, called the Inc. Fund. It was a powerful legal organization headed during the civil rights days by Thurgood Marshall, then by Jack Greenberg, a Columbia Law School classmate of mine.

Reverend Walker had told Dr. King that I was a good lawyer who always responded quickly when called, so that night, Dr. King asked me to be his special trial counsel. That title meant, simply, that when he needed me, I would have to be available. I couldn't decide immediately and told him I would sleep on it.

After my meeting with Martin, we all headed to the SCLC convention at the War Memorial Building, which sits on one of the hills of Nashville. Lotte and I arrived at about 8:00 P.M., and to my surprise, I was escorted onto the stage to sit with Martin and several others. I walked up there shaky with excitement.

Martin was to address the group, and I was looking forward to hearing his speech; he was considered a great orator. But first there was to be some entertainment. Harry Belafonte, an early friend of civil rights and a source of money and support for the duration of the movement, was to perform but he was ill and was replaced by the Kingston Trio. They sang "Where Have All the Flowers Gone?" I immediately loved that song, written by legendary songwriter and singer Pete Seeger and so emblematic of the sixties. African folksinger Miriam Makeba also performed.

Martin's speech was a revelation. It took away all my doubts. Suddenly, I knew that the civil rights movement would transcend all obstacles and succeed. He was absolutely electrifying, but it was not the words alone, although his imagery was pure poetry. It was the combination of words and voice, the poetry and the music.

He told the audience, "We can no longer wait, hoping that if we remain quiet and passive, somewhere down the road the white man will recognize the justice of our position and cede to us the same rights that he enjoys. Frederick Douglass reminded us a century ago, 'If there is no struggle, there is no progress.' My brothers and sisters, those words are our marching orders. With God's help and our own perseverance, we must triumph."

My eyes never left his face. I was drawn into the spell he created with words, voice, and certain techniques, like Aristotle's repetition of important phrases three times. Lotte and I walked out into the night, agreeing that Martin King was the greatest orator we had ever heard.

When I left the War Memorial that evening, I was so stirred by the implications of the moment, the drama, and the challenge that I told Lotte, "This is for me. I want more and more of this." I felt as I had in Jackson, only more so. Martin inspired me to work in the movement, to do what I could to right the wrongs I saw around me in the South. The next day, when I went to say goodbye to him at his motel before Lotte and I left for the airport, I said, "I would be very privileged to be your special trial counsel, Dr. King." He smiled, we shook hands, and our bargain was sealed. I remained in this position until Martin's death seven years later.

I hoped that my law practice in New York would continue to support me, that my partner and brother, Michael, would continue to be generous and patient, because I was well aware that I would receive no fees for civil rights work. Only a short time after I returned home to New York with Lotte, I found myself itching to go South again.

Subterfuge and Subversion

Martin called on me a few months later to represent Stanley Levison, a lawyer who was his closest white friend and adviser. Levison, subpoenaed on April 24, 1962, to appear three days later before the Senate Internal Security Subcommittee, was suspected of being a Communist. Of course, I was unaware then that FBI director J. Edgar Hoover, the malevolent master of subterfuge, had been wiretapping Levison's telephone for quite some time. He did this under the pretense of "keeping America safe" from those who had Communist affiliations, ideological leanings toward socialism, or both.

The complete facts about the Levison tapes are still unavailable, but it is true that by bugging his phone, Hoover and the FBI gained intimate knowledge about Martin King, for Martin and Stanley spoke on the phone daily. This allowed Hoover to spy on the plans of the leaders of the civil rights movement. (Later, as is now widely known, Hoover, with the approval of the Kennedy administration, tapped Martin's phone and eavesdropped on his hotel and motel rooms. The rationale given for this subterfuge was Martin's alleged Communist links, but the real reason was his threat to the established order.)

Martin wanted me rather than an Inc. Fund lawyer to represent Levison before the Senate committee. In addition to my not having an affiliation with any group, I was not afraid to represent extremely controversial people. He knew I would not be frightened by the kinds of unpopular cases which might scare off a more organization-minded lawyer. Today I still relish those cases, my taste for controversy having been conceived and nurtured in those heady civil rights days.

Representing Stanley before the Senate Internal Security Subcommittee was frightening; the members of the committee had a reputation for being ferocious, for tearing people apart and destroying them. My legal strategy was quite conventional: I told Stanley to invoke the Fifth Amendment—the right to remain silent—if he was asked any probing questions he didn't want to answer. The committee chair, Sen. James O. Eastland, shouted at Stanley each time he took the Fifth, but we stuck to our plan.

Today I would use a more aggressive tactic against such a vicious Star Chamber—like filing a federal lawsuit—as I, with other lawyers, did against the House Un-American Activities Committee years later. I would have tried to obtain an injunction against the committee on the grounds that its actual purpose in subpoenaing Levison was to inhibit his free speech and attack Dr. King. The committee's real motive was not legitimate investigation but an attempt to cripple the civil rights movement. But in 1962 the times were not yet ripe for this type of lawsuit. And, I must confess, a frontal attack never crossed my mind. It would be years before I learned, in Chicago, to attack the opposition as fiercely as it attacked my client.

Over the years I received many special assignments from Martin and remained loyal to him, although I never joined his inner circle. We shared a lot, however. Martin wrote a foreword to my 1965 book about the civil rights movement, *Deep in My Heart,* and I wrote one for an early edition of his book *Why We Can't Wait.* From the day I first accepted the assignment of special trial counsel until his death, I never turned down calls from Martin and was always honored and thrilled to accept them. As a result of my work in the movement, my name began to appear in the news, and I became respected in what was then the radical arm of the legal profession.

Harry Wachtel, a very successful New York lawyer and Martin's good friend, acted as liaison when I was needed. Martin would call Harry and say, "Send Bill down." Harry would call me, explain the problem, and I would quickly head South. If I didn't hear from Martin for some time, I would muse about Birmingham or Jackson while I was in New York, at Kunstler &

Kunstler, working on a divorce or some other prosaic case.

I filed many federal lawsuits between 1961 and 1968 at Martin's request, and as time went on, we became closer. When I succeeded, along with attorney Constance Baker Motley, in getting an injunction against him dissolved, Martin stood up in the courtroom and said, "Good work, Bill." I had been praised in front of the eyes of the world by the master!

My last act for Martin was in April 1968. I was about to file a federal suit on behalf of striking sanitation workers in Memphis and was planning to meet with Martin to show him the papers. But his tragic, untimely death put an end to all that.

Working in the Movement

During 1961 and 1962, civil rights cases represented only 10 percent of my work, but gradually, to my delight, more and more of my time was spent in the South working on these problems. My share of work at Kunstler & Kunstler diminished proportionately, since movement law was much more attractive to me than drafting wills and trusts, real estate closings, divorces, and all the things a small general law practice entailed.

Even though my brother occasionally grumbled because I didn't earn income for the practice but still drew a weekly paycheck, I couldn't bring myself to do much about it. Whenever he complained, I would put my shoulder to the wheel for a while. But when a civil rights case beckoned, I was off and running.

I was in my forties then, that critical decade when so many people go through major life crises. I wanted to practice meaningful law, and although I didn't realize it at the time, my civil rights work began as a selfish gesture. It gave me a way out of the mundane and petty work of a regular law practice as well as an opportunity to live a more stimulating life.

Wherever I went in the South, I ran into reporters, like Claude Sitton and Ben Franklin of the *New York Times* and CBS's Fred Graham, to whom I was now part of the civil rights movement and an element of the story. I relished being in a historical crusade that people read about or saw on the nightly news. I had within me a longing to rise above the crowd; until the South, I did not realize how strong that desire was.

Throughout my career, I always told my parents about any big case I was working on, and even though I was middle-aged by the early sixties, I still needed their approval. Though they were uncomfortable with some aspects of the civil rights movement, they always said they were proud of me, even if they didn't quite understand everything I did.

By 1963, civil rights began to consume me on every level, and even my family got into it. When Martin wanted to speak in Westchester, Lotte used her talents for organization to put together a successful civil rights fund-raiser at the county auditorium in White Plains with Peter Lawford and Sammy Davis Jr. My oldest daughter, Karin, spent the first half of her sophomore year at the virtually all black Tougaloo Southern Christian College, just outside Jackson, Mississippi. The movement took me away from home very often, though, so that I was practically an absentee father and missed many important family occasions—for example, my second daughter Jane's high school graduation.

I even enjoyed the dangers involved. I was Peck's Bad Boy again, living on the edge, only this time for a good cause. But even I became more careful after Medgar Evers, the NAACP field secretary for Mississippi, was shot and killed in his driveway. I forced myself to become cautious enough to avoid isolated areas and check in by telephone. My family worried about me despite my own relative lack of fear. I received threatening calls and letters, and once, my daughter, Jane, picked up the phone and heard a polite voice say, "Tell your father that all nigger lovers will die."

Have Writ, Will Travel

Northern lawyers were welcomed into their homes by blacks in the South. Living with black families, I found everything quite different from the white middle-class culture in which I had been raised, from the food, furniture, and clothing to the language, values, and religious beliefs.

We movement lawyers in the South called what we did "riding circuit," because we literally rushed from court to court in order to find a sympathetic judge or the right court for a particular case. If we could not get satisfaction in one court, we would get it in another. We would fail in one court, jump in a car, and dash to the next town. I loved the adventure, the demands, the constant change; I never got bored, and I learned about the politics of the law, which judge to see, which one to avoid.

One of the most exciting things about working on the civil rights cases was the real possibility of winning. If we got into the appropriate court, we won. This was because, as former Chief

Judge Elbert Tuttle has said, we were on the right side. The South was so terribly segregated—blacks had curfews, couldn't vote, weren't allowed to serve on juries. Southern politicians relied on inertia and delay to keep segregation in place: One more year of segregated schools. One more year before blacks got the vote.

As cheered as I was by the victories, I knew the movement was still in its early stages. I, too, had just begun my journey. My most important cases were still far, far ahead.

CHAPTER SIX

The Struggle: 1962–63

Hope is all I live on.

Reverend Shuttlesworth

IN THE CIVIL RIGHTS MOVEMENT, FIRST YOU GOT YOUR FEET WET, AND soon you were in over your head. We lawyers shared a feeling of community, and there was no way to be objective and removed from the emotions or the issues. It became a full-time business for me, leaving me little to give to my family back in New York or to the law practice I shared with my brother. It was my crusade, calling and holding me as strongly as any passionate love affair.

Danville. Albany. Birmingham. Lynchburg. Recalling the look and feel of each city or town, I remember the individual struggles, the marches, protests, arrests, and the ugly, bitter hatred of the forces that tried to hold the civil rights movement back.

Birmingham, like most other southern cities, operated under Jim Crow laws. Blacks could not eat in white-only restaurants or sleep in white-only motels. In certain public places—movie theaters and courtrooms, for example—they had to sit in special areas, usually the balcony. In stores, blacks were not permitted to try on clothing, and amusement parks, swimming pools, libraries, and playgrounds were off limits. We had to crush these laws, rip them out of the fabric of southern society.

Martin and other leaders of the movement continued to call on me, and in January 1962, Wyatt Tee Walker asked me to help his friend the Rev. Fred L. Shuttlesworth and overturn his conviction for violating Birmingham's segregation law. Reverend Shuttlesworth was a fiery activist who had been charged with breaching the peace for trying to sit in the white section of a segregated bus. An Alabama state court had found that while Reverend Shuttlesworth and the other blacks with him on that bus had not actually breached the peace, they were still guilty of violating the city's segregation law. After three years of appeals, the U.S. Supreme Court had refused to overturn Shuttlesworth's conviction because of a technicality. I was called in just as Shuttlesworth began serving a ninety-two-day term in the Birmingham City Jail.

Shuttlesworth was a tall and impassioned orator with a rather deep voice who always furrowed his brow when he talked. When he wasn't preaching, he spoke softly and sadly.

Other lawyers had already filed a federal writ of habeas corpus, and it was about to be heard by U.S. district judge Hobart H. Grooms. Because Judge Grooms had previously declared unconstitutional the very segregation statute under which Shuttlesworth had been convicted, I was optimistic that the conviction would be quickly reversed.

The first day in court, when I introduced myself with "I hope that we'll be able to do something for you," Shuttlesworth responded: "Hope is all I live on." It was the hope I had seen in those young Freedom Riders that first day in Jackson, the optimism that seemed to carry the entire movement forward.

When Judge Grooms, to my surprise, dismissed our petition on the grounds that we had not sufficiently exhausted remedies in the state courts, I was upset. But Reverend Shuttlesworth did not lose hope. He said to me as he was taken out of the courtroom and back to jail, "Don't worry. You'll find a way."

With his optimism giving me courage, I planned to draft a petition for what was known as a writ of certiorari, to ask the U.S. Supreme Court to review the case on the grounds that it would be fruitless to seek a remedy in the state courts and that the case contained important questions of law which deserved the high court's immediate attention. I was quite thrilled, thinking that I might get a chance to appear before the highest court of the land. My legal experience in the movement was limited, but I was fast learning the tricks of my new trade and thought I could successfully argue this case.

I was nervous, too, afraid that I might lose my composure,

falter, or be unable to answer a question asked by a justice. The whole legal world sits and judges a lawyer's performance before the Supreme Court. Everyone is watching—the press, other lawyers, the public. But I calmed myself by recalling the many times I had shown, in southern state courts and in federal courts, that I do not falter. I keep going, my style being to continue the argument no matter how nervous or inadequate I feel.

(Whatever anxious feelings I had about this, or any other, court argument diminished whenever I brought to mind a rather raunchy story told me by my director Bill Hamilton, years earlier, when I was doing those WMCA radio shows. Before the debut of his wife, singer Denise Lore, on entertainer Garry Moore's television show, which was watched by some 40 million people, she experienced a bout of mike fright. Moore helped her out by saying, "Denise, all you've got to do is keep in mind that all of those forty million people out there have, at all times, six inches of shit in them." It worked for her, and whenever I needed to, I recalled Moore's crude words of comfort.)

As it turned out, I never had to make the argument. In reviewing the case, I realized that the high court had the power to order the release of persons who were illegally detained. This would require the filing of an original writ of habeas corpus, a much faster route than a review through a writ of certiorari.

When I filed the habeas for Shuttlesworth, it was the first time, to my knowledge, that such a petition had ever been filed in the Supreme Court. Within weeks, I had an answer. Without requiring oral argument the justices converted it into a petition for a writ of certiorari and granted our request. Shuttlesworth was exonerated by a unanimous decision and on February 26, 1962, ordered released from prison on bail. I was back in my office in New York when I heard the news and, thrilled, called Shuttlesworth to tell him.

His reaction only increased the joy I felt about the decision. "Bill," said Shuttlesworth, "I knew the Lord could accomplish many things, but I never truly thought that he had any real influence on the Supreme Court or else the Dred Scott case would have gone the other way. You've made me understand that my faith needed a little builder-upper."

At the same time that the Court ruled on the Shuttlesworth case, it also ruled that no state could mandate segregation of any facilities associated with transportation, like bus-station rest rooms. Reverend Shuttlesworth's case officially ended a year later when Judge Grooms ruled that there was no evidence to support the original conviction.

The NAACP Inc. Fund

For many years, the NAACP, a relatively conservative organization whose mainly middle class members believed that everything could be achieved through court action, dominated the civil rights movement. So the NAACP followed the system's rules but at the same time also initiated legal cases to change them.

In 1955, the NAACP's cautious leadership of civil rights gave way when a woman named Rosa Parks said "No!" to a Montgomery bus driver's command that she move to the back of the bus. Her courageous act was the beginning of the modern civil rights movement. Montgomery's black citizens began a bus boycott, and the movement took a new direction. Protests, boycotts, marches, pray-ins, and other actions took precedence over passivity and patience.

After some months of working in the South, I came to understand the basic division in the movement between the more traditional religious and political leaders and other individuals who had run out of patience and didn't want to wait anymore. Their rallying cry was "Freedom Now!"

Because of its ingrained conservatism, the NAACP was actually late in coming to the active southern struggle of the 1960s. Its earlier battles had been fought mainly in the courtroom, and the organization did not become fully engaged in the southern movement until it was well under way. The legal arm of the NAACP, called the Inc. Fund, while a separate organization, was closely aligned philosophically to its parent group. The lawyers who worked for the Inc. Fund did not advocate protests or demonstrations—even though it was these tactics that ultimately led the movement to succeed. For example, in the early years, the Inc. Fund refused to represent Freedom Riders because it disapproved of "rabble-rousers."

Because of its conservative bent, the Inc. Fund was sometimes a disruptive force in the southern struggle. Inc. Fund lawyers denigrated other lawyers like myself, Arthur Kinoy, and members of the progressive National Lawyers Guild. The Inc. Fund's attorneys attempted to be the only legal representatives for Dr. King and were highly competitive in their attitude toward other lawyers. Dr. King sidestepped this rivalry by using all of us—free agents like myself, Inc. Fund lawyers, and anyone else he needed to win in the courts.

To Dr. King, the pettiness of this infighting was irrelevant; his goal was desegregation, and he had no interest in the minor squabbles that erupted around him among the civil rights leaders and their lawyers. He was a good example to me of how a man can rise above the mundane and set his sights on a single goal without allowing anything to be a distraction. And I have followed his example, to the best of my ability, ever since.

Although many Inc. Fund lawyers were overly cautious, at least one of them rose to true greatness. When Thurgood Marshall, a retired Supreme Court justice, died in 1993 at the age of eighty-four, he had become one of the great figures of twentieth-century law. Marshall had been the first director-counsel of the Inc. Fund and in 1954 argued the momentous *Brown v. Board of Education* case before the Supreme Court. But even he disapproved of more militant desegregation strategies and was suspicious of radical blacks. He once described the Black Muslims as a group "run by a bunch of thugs organized from prison and jails and financed, I'm sure, by some Arab group."

Jack Greenberg became the Inc. Fund's director-counsel, an unpopular move both within and outside the Fund because Greenberg is white, but he was Marshall's chosen heir. Unfortunately, Greenberg grew quite parochial when he took over; he became very protective of the Fund's position and never wanted to allow other lawyers near Dr. King.

Greenberg's pettiness was distressing to me, and I never liked him because of it. Not too long ago, as dean of Columbia College, he demonstrated his continuing narrow-mindedness when he instituted disciplinary proceedings against students who protested the university's plans to raze the Audubon Ballroom. The ballroom was the scene of the 1965 assassination of black activist leader Malcolm X. After a new president was named by the university, Greenberg's actions may well have cost him his job.

Of course, when I first became involved in civil rights, I knew nothing of the internal power struggles and did not understand the tensions. But I learned over time the hard way. I was often criticized by the Inc. Fund for not being prepared and not finishing my cases—their favorite unfounded slurs against me. But whenever the sledding got tough and they ripped into me, I would pull out a letter from Jack Greenberg in which he wrote to me that my habeas in the Shuttlesworth case had been ingenious and offered his congratulations.

Brown v. Board of Education

Thurgood Marshall's place in history is secure because he was a great humanitarian justice. As a young lawyer, he often risked his life in the course of his work for the NAACP. And in 1954, Marshall argued *Brown v. Board of Education.* This historic Supreme Court decision declared that "separate but equal" was unconstitutional, thus ending, on a theoretical basis at least, segregation in the nation's public schools and, by inference, in all public facilities.

Brown gave a kick-start to the nascent civil rights movement, but the strategy behind it summed up the Inc. Fund's dilemma about confronting the constitutionality of racial segregation itself. Determined not to lose in court, the conservatives on the NAACP'S national board forced Marshall to undertake a two-sided course. Racial segregation was unconstitutional, but if Marshall lost on that issue, he could retreat to a backup position—that black schools were not "equal" to white ones under the doctrine of "separate but equal." A half century earlier, in *Plessy v. Ferguson,* the Supreme Court had ruled that it was okay to have segregated facilities as long as they were equal in quality—separate but equal.

In one case in South Carolina, *Briggs v. Clarendon County School Board,* which eventually became part of the complex of cases under the umbrella of *Brown,* Thurgood's adversaries in the lower court tried to force him to adopt one or the other position. Their excellent strategy was to admit, on the record, that Clarendon schools were separate but unequal; this admission took some wind out of Thurgood's sails, obliging him to reexamine the constitutional issue.

Neither the NAACP nor the Inc. Fund wanted to chance a loss, so Thurgood, against his will, was forced to argue that even if racial segregation was *not* unconstitutional, it had already been conceded that Clarendon County's black schools were considerably below the "separate but equal" standard.

My druthers would have been to go right after the real evil, racial segregation, and ignore separate but equal as a legal issue. But Thurgood could not do that, given the NAACP's dual strategy, even after the only judge on his side, J. Waties Waring, desper-

ately attempted to force him to focus only on the unconstitution-
ality of racially segregated schools.

SNCC

The Student Nonviolent Coordinating Committee (SNCC)
was the opposite of the tradition-bound NAACP. Comprised for
the most part of daring young people, SNCC was organized in
1960 as a splinter group of Martin King's Southern Christian
Leadership Conference and was nurtured by the energetic and
dedicated civil rights leader Ella Baker. Several years later, SNCC
broke away from the SCLC and became much more militant and
radical under the leadership of the fiery Stokely Carmichael and
H. Rap Brown.

In the very early 1960s, SNCC was in the forefront of the
movement in Mississippi and Georgia, where fearless young people worked to organize voter registration drives in rural communities. This was hard, dangerous work, and the SNCC people were
often beaten, jailed, and run out of town. But they persisted, and
after their presence in a community had smoothed out the initial
roughness, Dr. King would become involved, receiving most of
the credit and all the publicity.

As a result, there was some internal conflict between Dr.
King's organization and SNCC. Although both groups had the
same goals, their methods were different, and some SNCC workers resented that they were risking their lives while the more sea-
soned preacher-leaders of the SCLC, especially Dr. King, received
the accolades.

Against this backdrop of internal struggles and tensions
evolved the ever-escalating struggle between civil rights leaders
and the administration, especially Robert F. Kennedy, to whom
the political interests of his brother, the president, came first.

I ignored much of the competition, infighting, and politics in
order to concentrate on my court cases. They were difficult, demanding, and presented me with a new challenge almost daily. I
had no time for currying favor with any one group or individual,
no time for back-room politics, no time for anything at all but filing briefs, preparing arguments, consulting with clients, and making court appearances. For me, the civil rights movement was a
war with numerous battles; I fought in as many as I could without
deviating from my objective—to win for my clients, to win for the
movement. I developed a single-mindedness that today enables

me to ignore tempests swirling around me while I focus on my cases.

The Albany Movement

Although the ACLU originally sent me South, it was the Gandhi Society that sent me to Albany, Georgia, then to Birmingham, Alabama, where I had my most profound experiences in the movement. The Gandhi Society for Human Rights was organized in 1962, on the eighth anniversary of the *Brown* decision, by Dr. King and other civil rights leaders in order to teach the principles of Gandhian nonviolence to black southerners. Joseph Curran, then the president of the National Maritime Union, donated $45,000 to the society, as did several other Establishment types, including Dr. Frank Graham, former secretary of the army, activist Cora Weiss, and Andrea Simon, the widow of Simon & Schuster publisher Richard Simon.

Because an important function of the Gandhi Society was to provide immediate, frontline legal assistance, I was named to its board of directors. My first assignment was to provide legal counsel for the Albany Movement, a year-old crusade in that Georgia city whose black citizens had first begun their struggle against rigid segregation laws in December 1961. During 1962, the protests sparked arrests, beatings, and killings. Martin went to Albany to offer his support, along with his chief aide, Dr. Ralph Abernathy, then vice president of the SCLC, and attorney Clarence Jones, another close friend.

Albany's blacks tried to desegregate the city's library, lunch counters, swimming pool, and park. There were mass arrests. When I arrived in Al-benny—as the residents pronounce it—in July 1962, the movement was entering its final months.

I stayed at the home of local physician Dr. William G. Anderson and shared a bedroom with Ralph Abernathy, whose snoring cost me many hours of sleep. "If it gets too loud, Bill," he once told me, "tie a cold washcloth around one of my big toes, and it should stop." No remedy worked more than once or twice, but I eventually became accustomed to the noise and was able to sleep, provided I dozed off before he did.

When I first arrived in Albany, a major crisis arose when an injunction which forbade Martin from making any public speeches was issued by a racist federal judge at the behest of the City of Albany. Neither Martin nor his lawyers were forewarned about the injunction, so that when we finally did hear about it, we panicked. Martin was scheduled to speak that very night at a huge rally, and it was too late to call it off.

"This injunction is completely illegal," I said to Martin, and urged him to speak at the church as planned. The injunction violated his freedom of speech as protected by the First Amendment, I told him. But he felt compelled to obey the injunction because it had been issued by a federal court. "While I might not listen to a state order, Bill, I can't violate this one," he said. Somewhat naively, Martin believed that the federal government was on his side, and he would not do anything he considered illegal against a federal order. I decided then that our only possible course was to find a federal judge who was willing to set aside the injunction.

But first I drove with Martin, Coretta, and several of his aides to the church to determine if people were aware that the speech had been canceled. We looked in a side window and found, to our great joy, that the church was filled to overflowing, with every single seat taken, and that other speakers were inspiring the audience. We all left the area of the church, with Martin enormously exhilarated because the injunction against him was really having no effect on the people's spirits and on the movement.

We got back into the car, and as we began to pull away, a Volkswagen pulled alongside, and the driver said, "Dr. King, there are white men with guns driving a pickup truck who have been heard saying around town they are going to kill you. We advise you to go home, fast."

My stomach muscles contracted, and my heart pounded. Martin's face remained impassive. We drove quickly back to Dr. Anderson's, went inside, and shut all the windows and drew the curtains. Afraid to turn on the lights, we lit a tiny candle in the living room and sat there in the near dark. After a short time, I started pacing, and the others appeared edgy, too. Finally, Martin said, "Let's sing." A young woman walked over to the upright piano and began to play "This Little Light of Mine," and we all began to sing freedom songs like "Don't Turn Me Around." I no longer felt frightened. My overwhelming emotion was joy.

It was a passionate, dramatic moment, the kind that I had learned to live for. We sang for an hour or two, ending with "We Shall Overcome" and a prayer. Then a man came to the door and said the threat had been a false alarm. Someone turned on the lights, and I stood up, stretched my legs, and went up to bed.

The next afternoon, I listened to a fascinating conversation in insurance broker Slater King's backyard. It was a hot, muggy day. Martin and other SCLC leaders, along with James Forman and John Lewis of SNCC, were attempting to settle their differences. SNCC wanted assurance that future movement victories would not all be credited to Dr. King. And he wanted SNCC to receive acknowledgment for its work.

"Dr. King, our grievance is that we risk our lives in a community and then you and SCLC move in and everyone immediately forgets that we were ever there," Jim Forman complained. "We need some sort of arrangement so that our people share the limelight with you. It's important for our own organizing and fundraising that we get the proper recognition for what we do."

Martin agreed, and all the leaders decided that from that point on SNCC and the SCLC would be partners in everything. But the friction never really ended between the two groups; Martin inevitably received the lion's share of attention from the media—and from everyone else, for that matter: He was the moral and spiritual heart of the movement.

That backyard meeting was fascinating. The young people of SNCC did not hold Dr. King in awe and felt free to argue with him about civil rights strategies and policy. Dr. King, Andrew Young, Bernard Lee, and others in the King camp had many heated disagreements with Forman, Lewis, and the SNCC people, but they always worked out their conflicts because their goals were the same.

Early the following morning, C. B. King, a lawyer for the Inc. Fund, and I headed for Macon, Georgia, hoping to persuade federal judge William A. Bootle to set aside the injunction against Martin. After we drove the 116 miles, Judge Bootle let us cool our heels in his chamber's anteroom, refusing even to see us.

I had a crazy idea that we should try Chief Judge Tuttle because he was not a native southerner and always seemed more reasonable about civil rights issues. Over the phone, I said, "Judge, we have a situation here where there's an injunction against free speech. Judge Bootle won't hear us, and Judge Elliot's out of the state."

We drove like hell to Atlanta, went to see Judge Tuttle, and were pleasantly surprised. He listened carefully to us, then said, "I'll give you a hearing in the morning." Meanwhile, C. B. King had called the Inc. Fund from every stop along the road to keep it informed about the case. We went to the office of Don Hollowell, a state senator, and stayed up all night drafting papers. At dawn I discovered that as a result of C. B. King's phone calls, the Inc. Fund had sent down Constance Baker Motley to work on the argument before Judge Tuttle. Connie was then chief assistant to Jack Greenberg, and I assume she was sent to add some more legal power to ensure that the injunction would be voided, as well as to keep the Inc. Fund in the case.

Connie, today a senior federal district judge in New York, asked me and C.B. to arrange for a hairdresser for her when she arrived at 2:00 A.M. We did, and Connie was transported from the airport to the hairdresser's. We filed the papers and by 9:45 A.M. were standing before Judge Tuttle. Martin and his aides were seated in the front row of the courtroom.

Connie, C.B., and I argued that the city must allow Martin to speak without interference—without arresting him—because to do otherwise would be a violation of his freedom of speech. We asked that Judge Elliot's injunction be reversed. As we argued, Martin watched, his face, as always, unreadable.

It was the first time I had argued this type of case. While I was a bit nervous working alongside Connie under Martin's watchful eyes, I stood up tall and did my best despite my inner fears. As Judge Tuttle was concluding his remarks, I felt that we were about to win, so I leaned over and whispered to Connie, "I think we've won."

"Shhh," she said, shutting me up, not the last time I have been quieted in a courtroom.

Judge Tuttle vacated the injunction, and as he explained his reasoning, I understood that we had won because we were in the right, not because we were so brilliant. But a win is a win. I stood up and stuffed papers into my briefcase, preparing to leave the courtroom. Martin, in the spectators' section, was besieged by reporters. As I went up the aisle toward the door, he shouted, "Bill." I stopped and went over to him, and we embraced. He whispered in my ear, "You've done real well. Now it's my turn to go back to Albany and preach my head off. Thanks for all of us." Simple words but, to me, a priceless honor.

I flew back to New York with Connie Motley; we had done our job, and I had paying cases waiting for me at Kunstler & Kunstler. I drove home to Westchester, already aching for the next call South.

Birmingham

In March, I was invited to Harry Belafonte's New York City apartment to meet with Martin and Reverend Shuttlesworth. That night, Martin told us all—actors Ossie Davis, Ruby Dee, Anthony Quinn, and Fredric March, journalists, and others—about Operation C, which stood for Confrontation. Martin wanted to take on the most segregated city in the South: Birmingham, Alabama. Protests were to begin on April 3.

Birmingham had been in the news since Mother's Day, 1961, when a mob brutally attacked Freedom Riders and the police stood by doing nothing. Segregation laws were viciously enforced in Birmingham by police who followed the lead of Public Safety Commissioner Eugene "Bull" Connor, the former chief of police.

The protests began as scheduled, and when Martin's younger brother, the Rev. A. D. King, was arrested, Martin sent me to Birmingham to represent him. I used the federal removal statute for A.D. and the protesters who were jailed along with him and succeeded in getting their cases transferred to federal court, where they were all freed on bail.

It was during the Birmingham protests that, for the first time, I did more than lawyering. One day, walking from the courthouse, I joined a group of marchers. We walked for hours, with our signs held high, singing movement songs, joined in spirit.

I felt revived and renewed. Although I worked on a proposed lawsuit against the city and suggested using the federal removal statute to get more people released from jail, I spent most of my time during the spring of 1963 marching in the streets of Birmingham. I realized that the paperwork and intellectual maneuvers in the courtroom were not the heart of the movement at all, but merely an appendage. Marching and protesting, being out on the streets—that was where the strength of the movement lay, and that would be how it would finally prevail.

The black people of Birmingham wanted desegregation of all public facilities; fair hiring practices; parks and playgrounds reopened (they were closed so they would not have to be desegregated); and the creation of a biracial commission to bring about the desegregation of public schools (in compliance with the 1954 Supreme Court ruling in *Brown*).

Martin came to Birmingham to support the movement, as did Harry Belafonte, Sammy Davis Jr., and Jackie Robinson. Martin was quickly served with an injunction prohibiting protests and meetings and decided he would violate it on Good Friday. That morning, he and Ralph Abernathy were arrested as they began to lead a march through the streets of Birmingham.

From his cell, Martin wrote the famous "Letter from a Birmingham Jail," a response to criticism by white clergymen who had attacked the Birmingham marches as being too radical and had charged King and others with advocating violence. King's answer was smuggled out of his jail cell by Clarence Jones, his close friend and personal aide.

From this moving and impassioned letter, I gained a deeper understanding of how segregation and racism dehumanize the soul. Martin responded to critics, both white and black, who urged him to wait, have patience, and cease the marching and protesting which often led to violence. He wrote:

> I am in Birmingham because injustice is here.
>
> There comes a time when the cup of endurance runs over and men are no longer willing to be plunged into the abyss of despair.
>
> I guess it is easy for those who have never felt the stinging darts of segregation to say, "Wait." When your first name becomes "nigger" and your middle name becomes "boy" . . . and your last name becomes "John" . . . then you will understand why we find it difficult to wait.
>
> One day the South will know that when these disinherited children of God sat down at lunch counters, they were in reality standing up for what is best in the American dream. . . .
>
> . . . in some not too distant tomorrow the radiant stars of love and brotherhood will shine over our great nation with all their scintillating beauty.

Martin's letter moved me profoundly and gave me renewed courage and motivation in my civil rights work. I knew I was on the right path; I went on, with stronger convictions, more intense beliefs, to do this work that I knew now, more than ever, was right for me.

When he was released, Martin called a meeting in his room at Gaston's Motel—the famous room 30 where all the strategy sessions were held—to deal with a peril to the Birmingham operation. Bull Connor had carried out his threat to arrest all demonstrators, and as a result, there simply were not enough adults remaining in the community to march. Spirits were low, perhaps the lowest they had been since the Birmingham crusade had begun only weeks earlier.

There was quite a bit of friction in the room when it looked as if the movement were running out of bodies to fill the jails; Fred Shuttlesworth was angry, and Martin was despondent, fearful that the operation was failing. I was uncomfortable; I could think of no way to help. Suddenly, minister and movement leader James Bevel, a small man with a bald pate and fiery eyes, spoke up.

"Why don't we ask the schoolchildren to start marching? Let's keep them out of school and have them fill the ranks," Bevel suggested. Initially, most of the people in the room were not in favor of this radical idea. It would be too dangerous; children should not be exposed to arrests and beatings, they said. But Bevel persisted. "We're doing what we're doing for the next generation, so why shouldn't the kids join the struggle?"

"Children marching might draw more attention to our protest," I added. Gradually, everyone agreed to Bevel's plan. A message was sent to ministers and other community leaders that parents should keep their children home from school so that the youngsters could pick up the banner and march as their elders had done.

It was this strategy that finally broke the back of the Birmingham power structure. An endless supply of children, large and small, marched, were arrested, and went to jail. These were the children seen on the nightly news being bitten and attacked by police dogs and knocked over by the bruising water gushing from Birmingham's fire hoses.

In May, the country was struck by a news photo which depicted one young boy, fifteen-year-old William Gadsen, his midsection being attacked by a huge German shepherd while his shirt was grabbed by a Birmingham police officer. Although he had actually kicked at the dog when it attacked him, the youth was shown in the classic nonviolent posture, arms at his sides and eyes downcast. The photo caught the interaction between the protesters and the authorities in a way that captured the attention of the country, and quite a few Americans began to understand what was going on in Birmingham. For the very first time, many Americans were awakened to the realities of the civil rights struggle.

When the jails were bursting with Birmingham's black children, they were taken to court, and their charges were dismissed. The students were then all expelled by the Birmingham Board of Education. Two days later, Judge Tuttle ordered them reinstated. The violence and arrests continued until city officials finally agreed to some desegregation measures. They would permit blacks to try on clothing in department stores, and they agreed to desegregate lunch counters and other public facilities.

But other storms were brewing. The entrenched Ku Klux Klan attracted a thousand supporters to a rally at which they vowed to fight the city's leaders as well as the "niggers." Gaston's Motel, where Martin always stayed, was bombed, as was the church parsonage home of A. D. King. Birmingham erupted into chaos, with blacks, whites, police, federal officials, civil rights workers, army troops, and Alabama state troopers in a muddle of confusion, terror, and rage.

Finally, a shaky peace was created after the White House intervened. The bombings and beatings stopped—for a while at least.

Lynchburg

One of the most personally gratifying aspects of my involvement in the civil rights movement is that many people I meet say, "I saw you then," or, "I knew you then." Best of all is when someone says, "I became a lawyer because of you." I hear that often from younger attorneys, and I know that I've had some influence on my times and on young people. Maybe it will ensure that there will always be people around who, even if they don't completely share my beliefs about the law and injustice, at least accept part of them; and maybe there will always be lawyers who have the courage to fight injustice in an arena other than the accepted legal one.

Not too long ago, I ran into a federal judge and a state judge, both black, both recently appointed, who gave me some hope that perhaps there are a few good judges around. I had a case before James Giles, a federal judge for the Eastern District of Pennsylvania, in 1992. When he saw me, he called me up to the bench.

"I knew of you when I was a boy in Lynchburg," he said. "I followed what you did, and it helped influence me to become an attorney." The case Judge Giles was referring to was so dramatic that I can easily understand the effect it would have had on a young person.

In the spring of 1963, Thomas Carlton Wansley, a black youth of seventeen with limited intelligence, was on death row in Virginia. He was convicted of raping and robbing a fifty-nine-year-old white woman. Wansley supposedly had grabbed her and pulled her into the bushes while she was on her way to church, raped her, and robbed her of a bus token as well as her virginity. However, during the trial, the victim could not positively identify Thomas Wansley as her attacker.

When Martin asked me to work with Roanoke lawyer Reuben Lawson on Wansley's appeal, I quickly agreed. The case had characteristics that appealed to me: It was the classic black man charged with raping a white woman. Thomas Wansley would be executed if his conviction stood. I took on the appeal with enthusiasm, determined to save him.

The case was particularly important to me because it was the first time I had lawyered with Arthur Kinoy, a law-school classmate. I asked Arthur to work with me because he had succeeded on a similar death-penalty case in Pritchard, Alabama. He agreed, and we quickly became associates and close friends. We are still friends today.

Len Holt, my cocounsel on earlier cases, soon joined us. It became clear very quickly that our appeal of Wansley's conviction could not be based on what happened at the trial; shockingly, there was no stenographic transcript. We reconstructed the record, however, and had our first success with a stay of execution granted by the Supreme Court of Virginia.

As we continued to work on the appeal, we came under fire by many of Lynchburg's segregationists. Former U.S. senator Carter Glass, a power in national politics and a leader in the city, made certain that his family-owned newspaper regularly labeled me and Arthur Communists and cursed us for defending a convicted rapist. To our surprise and as a result of these attacks, we suddenly became popular with certain other Lynchburg-area residents. Many young women who were students at the leading white colleges—Lynchburg College, Randolph-Macon, and Sweet Briar—joined our defense committee. *Life* magazine, *Newsweek,* and *Time* picked up the story, and as a result of the publicity and the support of our southern belles, we developed a vast support network for Thomas Wansley.

Primarily because of the absence of a trial record, we eventually won the appeal. This win was followed by retrials (one was a hung jury; the other, a conviction on a relatively minor charge), and in the end Wansley was exonerated of the rape charge. Today he lives in Washington, D.C., with his wife and children.

The New KKK

Arthur and I worked so well together on the Wansley case that we agreed he should join my New York City law firm. We became Kunstler, Kunstler & Kinoy, and Arthur and I called ourselves "the new KKK." Often, in a southern courtroom, a judge would look at us and ask, "And who are you?"

One of us would respond, "Oh, we're the KKK," in order to shock, and we always succeeded. Our supporters in the back of the courtroom—blacks were allowed only in the back or in the balcony—would stand up and cheer. Then Arthur would dramatically announce, "We are the new KKK—Kunstler, Kunstler & Kinoy!" (Arthur and I were also nicknamed "the Messiah and the Great K" by Philip Hirschkop, then a Georgetown University law student who clerked for us, but neither of us ever found out which of us was supposed to be the Messiah and which the Great K.)

Arthur and I used the firm as a base for our civil rights work, while Michael did all the private work that brought in the money. This change in the firm's configuration caused me to take stock. For me, everything had changed, so when Michael asked, "When are you ever coming back?" I could not respond.

After I saw the Birmingham hoses wash children down the street, I knew where my future lay. I was committed to the civil rights movement and didn't want to go back to the type of law I had practiced in the past. But when Michael applied pressure and said that I could not stay away and continue to draw money because he would soon have to hire other lawyers to do my work, I knew he was right. And that made me angry. I couldn't tell him off, though, because he was still paying my freight since I had no other income. I felt no guilt, just a sense that what I was doing was correct and important. For a time, we left things as they were. But I knew it was temporary.

Sometime in 1963, I began to realize that local white southern lawyers, with very few exceptions—Charles Morgan in Alabama and Bill Higgs in Mississippi—could not do civil rights work and remain in business. In fact, eventually, even Morgan and Higgs were driven out. Local lawyers were harassed, kicked out of clubs, lost all their cases, were not given court assignments; even their kids were picked on.

We outsiders, the itinerant lawyers, were the only ones who could do civil rights work with no repercussions. There's a wonderful dissent written by Supreme Court justice William O. Douglas in which he describes the traveling lawyer. Most of American history has been punctuated by lawyers who "have writ, will travel," as Douglas wrote. He mentioned Philadelphia attorney Andrew Hamilton, the designer of Independence Hall, relocating temporarily to New York for the famous Zenger case in 1734 and Clarence Darrow running all over the country to do his work.

In the South, the traveling lawyer became very important to the civil rights movement, but unfortunately there weren't enough of us. Many lawyers would come into a situation, work for a while, then go back to their own lives. Black lawyers, locals and imports, were on the scene also, including the totally fearless Len "Snake Doctor" Holt. When he couldn't get a room at the John Marshall Hotel in Richmond because of the color of his skin, he removed his clothes, down to his skivvies, pulled his overcoat over himself, and proceeded to go to sleep in the lobby. The hotel quickly changed its policy and gave him a room.

Danville

In civil rights, everything happened simultaneously. In June 1963, as Birmingham was simmering down, Arthur and I went to Danville, Virginia, a small mill city where the white Establishment was crushing the movement. Since Martin and most of the other movement leaders were in Birmingham, Danville needed organizers. As in Birmingham, I participated on the streets, not just in the courtroom.

Black residents here had desegregated the library, lunch counters, and the public park. But in the late spring of 1963 the remainder of the city was segregated: hospitals, most churches, movie theaters, hotels, restaurants, and—in spite of the 1954 decision in *Brown v. Board of Education*—most public schools. The protests in Danville unleashed police violence the likes of which I had never seen before, not even in Birmingham. One night, the police went berserk, using clubs, fire hoses, nightsticks—any weapon they could grab. They reached under cars with their nightsticks to beat people hiding there. The pregnant wife of a local minister miscarried because she was so badly battered.

In Danville, Arthur and I met with local lawyers who repre-sented the numerous black citizens who had been arrested. I said to Arthur, "I have with me a draft of a petition to remove these cases to the federal courts, an old Reconstruction statute I found out about in Mississippi not too long ago. Let's use it." We all agreed this was the best course, and we filed the petition.

We were heard by federal judge Thomas Jefferson Michie, who was totally unfamiliar with the removal process. When we told him that he was required to release the prisoners on reason-able bail under the removal statute, he said he didn't think the statute included such a provision. He seemed confused, so Arthur went up to the bench, took the index finger of this stubborn and incredulous federal judge, and guided it to the words—"shall grant bail." Michie had apparently not read the statute, because he had denied bail to our clients.

As we returned to our seats at counsel table, I said to Arthur, "I never believed you would have the guts to lift a federal judge's hand the way you did."

"All I did was point him in the right direction," said my col-league, a man small in size but enormous in intellect and courage. Judge Michie had no choice but to sign the bail orders. Arthur and I went to the jail to deliver the orders, and everyone was released.

After this victory, the Danville Movement was revitalized, and the people demonstrated with renewed energy. It was a true people's movement, and although Martin would eventually come to this city to give support, the protests were organized by local people.

Danville was a first for me. I had never before felt so close to the movement. Arthur said he was familiar with this feeling from his union work, but it was new for me, and I loved being part of the action. I spoke in churches and at rallies, whereas earlier, in other places, I'd been on the outside, listening, acting as a lawyer rather than a protester. I was immersed in the movement.

Medgar Evers

Just before the historic summer of 1963, I had spoken with Medgar Evers, the young field secretary for the Mississippi NAACP. Mississippi was, at that time, just about the most violent place in the South: daily murders, beatings, arrests, and bombings of blacks and anyone associated with the civil rights movement. I called Medgar about a federal suit I had initiated in April to prevent Jackson police from arresting peaceful protesters. When I reached him on the phone, he was very down.

"Bill, I'm too upset to even think about legal tactics or strategy. There's so much bad blood in this state that I just know someone's going to get hurt," he said. He added that the FBI was doing nothing at all to help.

On June 12, two days after our phone conversation, Medgar was shot to death in the driveway of his house. A white supremacist, Byron De La Beckwith, was arrested and charged with the murder, but two all-white juries hung, and he wasn't convicted. After many years, the case was reopened, and in 1994, De La Beckwith was finally convicted of the murder of Medgar Evers.

My daughter Karin, who had worked with Medgar when she was a student at Tougaloo, was inconsolable about his death. So when Martin visited New York City next, I arranged for Karin to see him. I hoped he would find the words to bring her out of her depression. I never found out what he said, but apparently it worked, and Karin began to feel somewhat better.

With Medgar's death, the struggle against the enormous odds of Mississippi's entrenched racism died, too. I marched at Medgar's funeral with Martin, comedian-activist Dick Gregory, and others, three abreast behind a police escort. A white-black confrontation began, but through the intervention of John Doar, of the Justice Department's Civil Rights Division, no blood was spilled. My souvenir of this episode was a bruised abdomen—two round marks made from the jab of a deputy sheriff's double-barreled shotgun.

March on Washington

The summer of 1963 ended with the momentous March on Washington on August 28. Ironically, on that same day, W. E. B. Dubois died in Ghana at the age of ninety-five. Dubois, a founder of the NAACP, was a great hero to many despite his having turned away in bitterness from the black struggle in America. I knew nothing of his death, though, as Lotte and I traveled from Westchester to D.C. on a bus, one of hundreds bringing people to the capital from all over the country.

During the long ride, we sang songs of freedom and of the movement, and I was filled with joy and purpose to be part of the first great civil rights March on Washington. We joined the massive crowd along the reflecting pool, with many people stopping to say hello to me, including Martin, Roy Wilkins, and Bayard Rustin.

Martin's speech was the "I have a dream" soliloquy, filled with rich allusions, drama, and poetry. Afterward, as Lotte and I returned to Westchester that night, I knew that my life's work was inextricably bound to Martin and the movement he led. I could not have imagined that in a few short years he would be gone, taking with him much of the hope that civil rights could be won through nonviolence.

It was the most profound speech I had ever heard and moved me as no speech had ever done—before or since. As they have for millions of others, then and now, the words Martin spoke at that historic March on Washington will live forever:

> In a sense, we've come to our nation's capital to cash a check. When the architects of our republic wrote the magnificent words of the Constitution and the Declaration of Independence, they were signing a promissory note to which every American was to fall heir. . . .
>
> I have a dream that one day, down in Alabama, with its vicious racists, with its governor having his lips dripping with words of interposition and nullification, one day right there in Alabama, little black boys and little black girls will be able to join hands with little white boys and little white girls as sisters and brothers. . . .
>
> And when this happens, when we allow freedom to ring, when we let it ring from every village and every hamlet, from every state and every city, we will be able to speed up that day when all of God's children . . . will be able to join hands and sing in the words of the old Negro spiritual: "Free at last. Free at last. Thank God Almighty, we are free at last."

CHAPTER SEVEN

Death of a Dream: 1964–68

We are sick and tired of being sick and tired.

THE DREAM DIDN'T DIE ON SUNDAY, SEPTEMBER 15, 1963, WHEN BIRmingham's Sixteenth Street Baptist Church was bombed, killing four young girls, children actually. But it was hit hard. The violent deaths of Carole Robertson, Denise McNair, Addie Mae Collins, and Cynthia Wesley came only three weeks after Martin's glorious "I have a dream" speech at the March on Washington, only a short time after hard-won victories in Birmingham and other southern cities. People were angry and bitter, tired and disheartened.

There were many, though, who vowed to fight harder, work longer, and dedicate more time and energy to the movement. If these four youngsters were not to have died in vain, I had to use the ammunition of a courtroom fighter—briefs, arguments, case law—to continue what I had begun on June 16, 1961. And in the years following, I did carry on, going wherever I was needed, following some cases for decades, until they were won, dismissed, or hopelessly lost.

St. Augustine

Two decades after my first visit as a young army officer on leave to St. Augustine, Florida, I returned to what is often identified as the oldest city in the United States. It was March 31, 1964, and I had just received another midnight phone call—the kind I was growing to love—requesting me to get down South, fast. Mary Elizabeth Peabody, mother of the governor of Massachusetts and wife of an Episcopalian bishop, and others had been arrested for violating Florida's undesirable visitor and trespass laws.

Mrs. Peabody had tried to integrate a restaurant by having lunch with some black St. Augustine women. She and other members of a Boston-based affiliate of the SCLC were attempting to desegregate St. Augustine at the time a bastion of racism and home of the region's Ku Klux Klan chapter. It operated under the name "Ancient City Gun Club."

One member of the Massachusetts SCLC group, John Harmon, was married to Judge Elbert Tuttle's daughter. The remainder were northern liberals who supported Martin's southern movement, usually by giving fund-raisers. This time, the group, which was committed to direct action, included Yale University chaplain William Sloane Coffin, whose first civil rights arrest was in 1961, during the Freedom Rides.

I called in Tobias Simon, an ACLU lawyer from Miami who had done the William Worthy case with me. We met in St. Augustine and went directly to the jail to visit our clients. We filed removal petitions to bring them all into federal court, and after a hearing, Bryan Simpson, the local federal judge in Jacksonville, ordered everyone released on very reasonable bail. During the hearing, when the single black witness, a fifteen-year-old named Annie Evans, was cross-examined by St. Augustine's counsel, he began to address her as "Annie." All of us at the counsel table immediately jumped up and objected; the Supreme Court had recently ruled that blacks addressed in court by their first names were not required to answer questions. The judge directed the St. Augustine counsel to revise his language, and he then properly addressed the witness as "Miss Evans."

It was a great moment, one of those that I live for in the courtroom. She lit up with a huge smile; the respect automatically given to white witnesses had finally, and rightly, been given to young Annie Evans.

After this incident, civil rights demonstrations in St. Augustine resumed. The marchers, organized by the Reverend Andrew Young, who had succeeded Wyatt Walker as Martin's executive assistant, walked daily to the site of the city's old slave market. Martin was living in a rented house on the beach and, as I recall, was not at home, fortunately, on the day that gunshots destroyed the quiet of the beach and ripped into the walls of his cabin.

After that the local police ordered the marches to cease, so we brought an injunction action against the city officials. Our argument was heard in the Jacksonville federal court, again before Judge Simpson, a tall, stately man who liked to whittle with his penknife while he was on the bench. Our petition, brought in the name of Andrew Young, explained that the marches by black demonstrators had been peaceful and that it was the police and the white counterdemonstrators who caused all the violence.

Judge Simpson was quite interested in the testimony of the St. Johns County sheriff, L. O. Davis, and he questioned him closely on the identity of his "auxiliary deputies." The judge ordered Davis to bring in a list of these deputies and, when he did, pressured him considerably, because at least one of the names on the list was a "convicted felon," in the judge's words.

On June 9, Judge Simpson ordered the city not to interfere with the marches; this meant that the police and the sheriff had no legal authority to stop the daily protest marches. Then all hell broke loose. When blacks attempted to use the St. Augustine beaches, the sand was bloodied as a result of violence instigated by white counterdemonstrators and police.

Although the federal court had previously ordered St. Augustine to integrate, the ingrained racism in that city made it almost impossible for the city's black residents to benefit from the court order. The violence by whites was incredible, and mob rule by bands of Klan members and other thugs wreaked havoc on blacks and those whites who stood by them.

One particularly vicious example occurred on June 18, when Fred Shuttlesworth led a group of blacks and whites to the dining room of the Monson Motel. They were ejected by the manager, who was too busy arguing with them to notice that seven people—two whites and five blacks—were in the motel's pool. The manager responded to this by pouring muriatic acid into the water and calling in police to arrest the swimmers.

The marches in St. Augustine continued; the violence escalated. Finally, the governor of Florida called a temporary truce, and Martin ordered the marchers to cease. "Every thousand-mile journey begins with the first step. This is merely the first step in the long journey toward freedom and justice in St. Augustine," he said. He knew well that St. Augustine would not be desegregated without more bloodshed, but he was willing to wait and see what would happen next.

Only days later, on the Fourth of July, President Johnson signed into law the Civil Rights Act of 1964, providing for the integration of all public accommodations in the United States. This legislation, a direct result of the civil rights protests and demonstrations in the South, helped to end overt segregation in St. Augustine—and everywhere else. By autumn of 1964, the city was integrated.

Mississippi Summer

Recently, I heard that Ben Chaney had returned to his native Mississippi. Ben is the younger brother of James Earl Chaney, martyred, along with Mickey Schwerner and Andy Goodman, during the Mississippi Freedom Summer in 1964, a summer that will never be forgotten by those of us who worked in civil rights. Hearing about Ben Chaney made me think of the triumphs and tragedies of that summer almost three decades ago. I recall it as if it were yesterday.

Arthur Kinoy, Morty Stavis, and I had been appointed general counsel to the Council of Federated Organizations (COFO). COFO, under the leadership of the charismatic and spiritual civil rights leader Bob Moses, organized a voter registration plan for Mississippi during the summer of 1964. One thousand northern college kids would come South to enroll voters. The kids did a wonderful job, enrolling sixty thousand new black voters in Mississippi. But the price paid for this achievement was high. It was paid in human lives.

During the spring of 1964, Lotte and I attended an orientation meeting for parents of the college student volunteers because Karin was to be one of them. At Riverside Church in New York City, an organizer of the Mississippi Freedom Summer told us that there were real dangers involved and that if we wanted to withdraw our kids, now was the time to do it.

A woman leaned over and said to me, "They always say that, and I don't believe it."

Another parent, sitting behind me, looked frightened. "You've had some experience in the South," Robert Goodman said to me. "Is this fellow just an alarmist, or are these kids in any real danger?"

"There's always a chance that someone will be hurt, but I think that everyone will come home safe and sound," I told Goodman.

On June 20, I was at the Western College for Women in Oxford, Ohio, where the students were assembled for a final orientation. I wanted to say goodbye to Karin; also, Arthur, Ben Smith, and I announced at the meeting that we were filing lawsuits in conjunction with the COFO volunteer effort. That day, I met Andrew Goodman and ran into Mickey Schwerner, whom I had met before.

Goodman and Schwerner were on their way to Mississippi; I said goodbye to them, not knowing that I would never see them again. That same night, I heard that Karin might ride to Mississippi with them in Mickey's car, which tragically was soon to be known as the famous blue station wagon.

Two days later, on June 22, Nathan Schwerner called me. "You don't know me, but my son, Mickey, told me to call you if he ever needed a lawyer." Mickey, Andrew Goodman, and James Chaney, a black COFO member, were missing. They had not returned from a June 21 trip to Neshoba County, where they had gone to check out the burning of the Mt. Zion Church, a favorite place for civil rights meetings. They had not called in, either, as all COFO members were supposed to do if they encountered delays.

My first question was: "Anybody else with them?" I thought Karin might have accompanied them. Nat Schwerner told me the three were alone. I had a feeling of relief that my daughter was okay, but I was terrified for the missing trio. After that, the FBI belatedly organized a nationwide search but were unable to find either the boys or the blue station wagon.

When the abandoned vehicle finally was located, it seemed likely that the three young men were dead. Frustrated with the pace of the FBI investigation, Arthur, Ben Smith, and I wanted to file suit to find out what had happened to the three youths. COFO leader Bob Moses agreed with us, and we drafted *COFO v. Rainey* on behalf of COFO, its members and volunteers, Rita Schwerner, Mickey Schwerner's wife, and James Chaney's mother. It was filed against Lawrence A. Rainey, the sheriff of Neshoba County, some of his deputies, the Ku Klux Klan, and several other racist groups. Our purpose was to force a hearing to determine what had happened to Schwerner, Goodman, and Chaney.

With assistance from other lawyers and volunteers, we amassed 100 affidavits which testified to a siege of terror by the hard-core racists of Mississippi. Blacks and northern volunteers had been beaten. Blacks' houses had been burned.

Our lawsuit, so carefully planned with the help of Rita Schwerner, was before local federal judge Sidney Mize, who had earlier displayed his racist bias in the case of James Meredith, the first black student to be admitted, after enormous struggle, to the University of Mississippi, as well as in the case of Freedom Rider Elizabeth Wyckoff. Mize once told me, "As long as I'm on the bench, I'll do everything in my power to keep white and black apart." Mize delayed our lawsuit, then dismissed it on a sheer technicality: The plaintiffs, all black Mississippians, had not appeared in court as ordered.

On the day that Mize dismissed our suit, Sheriff Rainey, who, we were convinced, had organized the murders of Goodman, Schwerner, and Chaney, was arrogant and insolent beyond belief. "I'd like my witness fee if you fellows don't mind," he said, smirking at us. (We had subpoenaed him to appear.) I wanted to strangle him, my feelings of rage and hatred were so strong. We appealed Judge Mize's dismissal of our lawsuit, and it was overturned in December. But by then the bodies had been found. A Klan informant, who had been paid $25,000 by the FBI, revealed that they had been dumped under a dam site outside Philadelphia, Mississippi.

These deaths tore all of us connected with the movement apart. Because Goodman and Schwerner were white volunteers from the North, their murders woke up the country (once again) to the violence occurring in the South.

Everyone connected with the Freedom Summer project was terrified. Over the phone, my mother said, "If anything happens to Karin, I will never, ever, speak to you again!" She insisted that I order Karin home, but, as I tried to explain, this was something I could not, and would not, do; plus, Karin would not have obeyed me, anyway. I didn't tell her that Karin had barely escaped serious harm on at least one occasion. She and Ivanhoe Donaldson, a member of SNCC and COFO, were driving in his car when he saw a bunch of white thugs standing on the roadside. He knew that because he was black and Karin was white, there could be real trouble, so he told her to lie down on the floor in the rear of the car and very possibly saved both their lives. This was not the first time Karin had traveled that way. Medgar Evers had made the same request of her once when she was a student at Tougaloo and was driving somewhere with him.

I was terribly afraid for Karin, and I was also afraid for myself. But I think we both felt the same way. We were doing work that was important, and we simply couldn't stop and live with ourselves. You're scared, but you go on. Despite the terrible effect of the deaths of Chaney, Goodman, and Schwerner on the young volunteers, only one or two left for home. The rest remained throughout the summer and continued to register black voters.

Before the bodies were returned to New York, Arthur, Morty, and I persuaded former Westchester medical examiner Dr. David Spain to fly to Jackson and conduct his own examination. Dr. Spain found that James Chaney had been cruelly beaten, his bones shattered and his body completely broken, before he was shot. It appeared that Mickey and Andrew had not been beaten and had died from gunshot wounds.

On August 9, there was a memorial service for Mickey Schwerner in New York City. I was one of the speakers who were asked to talk about the deaths of the three young men. Two thousand mourners attended. The lives of the dead youths had meaning, we said, because they left behind forty-seven Freedom Schools, sixty thousand newly registered black voters, and all the other college students who remained in Mississippi to continue their work, refusing to be intimidated.

I told the assembly: "Beyond the immediacy of our grief, every one of us feels, in one way or another, that we can look to tomorrow with brighter and clearer eyes, that we can face the morning sun with more faith and courage, that we are stronger and more resolute than ever before because our three friends laid down their lives in the dark of a Mississippi night. We are not afraid because they were not afraid—we will walk hand in hand because they walked hand in hand—we will live together because they died together."

The State of Mississippi never charged anyone for these murders, but eventually seven people were tried by the federal government for violating the civil rights of the three youths. Five men were convicted and sentenced to ten years each. The longest time any of them actually served in prison was six or seven years.

The murderers have been free, now, for two decades. But James Chaney still cannot rest in peace. Andrew Goodman and

At three, with my father, Monroe
Bradford Kunstler

My grandparents—Pa Moe,
M. Joseph Mandelbaum; and
Ma, Hannah Mandelbaum

My mother, Frances Mandelbaum Kunstler

At 16 with my brother Michael, 13, and my sister Mary, 9

My last summer as a camp counselor at Brant Lake. (I'm second from the left in the front row.)

Left. My former wife, Lotte, and I joined hundreds of thousands of demonstrators converging on the Lincoln Memorial during the historic civil rights March on Washington, D.C., August 28, 1963. *(AP/Wide World)*
Right. In the Philippines in 1944, receiving the Bronze Star. I served in the Army from 1941 through 1946, eventually achieving the rank of major.

With my client and close friend, civil rights leader H. Rap Brown, after he was arrested by federal authorities in New York City in February 1968 for allegedly violating a court order that restricted his travel. *(AP/Wide World)*

With anti–Vietnam War activist and pacifist Father Daniel Berrigan in November 1968 after he and eight others, including his brother, Father Philip Berrigan, known as the Catonsville Nine, were sentenced to prison for burning draft records. *(AP/Wide World)*

I was one of the lawyers at the 1969 arraignment of the Chicago Conspiracy defendants who were charged with conspiring and crossing state lines with the intent of causing a riot at the 1968 Democratic National Convention in Chicago. From left to right, lawyer Gerald Lefcourt, former Black Panther member David Brothers, Abbie Hoffman, Dave Dellinger, me, Jerry Rubin, and lawyer Arthur Turco. Abbie, Jerry, and Dave were three of the Chicago 7. *(Courtesy David Brothers)*

Entering the Federal Building during the Chicago trial. *(AP/Wide World)*

Kissed by beat generation poet and guru Allen Ginsberg, whose unusual testimony as a defense witness at the Chicago Conspiracy trial created an uproar in the courtroom. *(AP/Wide World)*

In 1970, I greeted a group of students at a Brooklyn high school with a symbol of 1960s activism: a clenched fist. "Maybe that fist will open some day in brotherhood," I told them. In front is a drawing of Bobby Seale, one of the Chicago Conspiracy defendants, after he was gagged and bound by the court for speaking out. *(AP/Wide World)*

During the 1960s, I was so constantly on the move that my motto was, "Have Writ, Will Travel." Here, I returned from an October 1969 meeting in Paris with the North Vietnamese peace delegation. *(AP/Wide World)*

Marlon Brando and I discuss the imprisonment of American Indian Movement leader Russell Means after the 1973 Second Siege at Wounded Knee in South Dakota. Brando, a champion of Native American rights, supported the Indians' efforts to publicize their plight and the U.S. government's refusal to honor treaties signed long ago. *(Maddy Miller)*

Every year I speak at Kent State in Ohio at ceremonies to memorialize May 4, 1970, the tragic day that National Guardsmen opened fire on college students, killing four and seriously wounding nine. Two of those killed had been taking part in a protest against the Vietnam War. The others had been walking by.
(AP/Wide World)

During the 1971 uprising of inmates at New York's Attica Correctional Facility, I was one of the outside observers invited in by the prisoners to negotiate on their behalf with the authorities. Tragically, we failed, and 39 guards and inmates were massacred by the New York State Police. *(AP/Wide World)*

Citing me for twenty-four counts of contempt of court for my defense of the Chicago 7, the judge sentenced me to four years and thirteen days in prison. *(AP/Wide World)*

Mickey Schwerner are buried in New York, but James lies in Mississippi, where, in 1989, his family erected a monument and enclosed his coffin inside a vault in order to protect it from vandals. In 1992, Ben Chaney founded the James Earl Chaney Foundation, a human and civil rights organization, and moved to Mississippi, where he can live near his brother's grave and watch over it and continue his civil rights work.

That Mississippi Freedom Summer, for me, will always be marked by the tragedy of these deaths. That these young people could be murdered so horribly was a lesson that sobered us all and gave special meaning forever to the COFO project.

Mississippi Challenge

In 1964, the Mississippi Freedom Democratic party (MFDP) was created in an effort to unseat the all-white Mississippi congressional delegation—four Democrats and one Republican. One of its endeavors, known as the Mississippi Challenge, took advantage of a little-known Reconstruction-era statute permitting persons illegally excluded from voting to challenge the elections of members of Congress.

Arthur, Morty, and I attended a meeting of the MFDP leadership, along with representatives from foundations in the North which were contributing money. Joseph Rauh, lawyer for the United Auto Workers and the original attorney for the MFDP, had persuaded some of the northern contributors to threaten that unless the MFDP got rid of their radical lawyers—like Kunstler and Kinoy—they would lose their foundation support.

I was always wary of Joe Rauh, who was far more a politician than an advocate. He represented the liberal wing of the Democratic party more than he did civil rights activists. Rauh was so close to top Democratic leaders that he tried to persuade civil rights leaders not to alienate the Democrats by being too aggressive or militant. At the 1964 Democratic National Convention, Rauh sold out the MFDP for his beloved Democrats.

I condemn him for that, but I'm also a realist and understand that in politics deals have to be made. Some of the agreements made during the civil rights days were a bit dirty, but as they say, politics is the art of compromise. I never wanted to be the one making the deals, so I guess that's why I'm not in politics.

Rauh tried to control the whole show, and when he advised

the black leaders not to be too aggressive, the MFDP's Fannie Lou Hamer came out with her incredible statement: "We are sick and tired of being sick and tired."

Hamer, a powerful, wonderful woman, and the others told the northerners, including Rauh, to go to hell, that they would decide who their lawyers would be, that no one could tell them what to do. Rauh was formally replaced as the group's lawyer by Arthur, Morty, and myself. Using that archaic Reconstruction statute, we began filing our papers.

To make the Mississippi Challenge work, we needed proof that blacks were not being allowed to register to vote. In an incredibly short period of time, Morty persuaded 250 lawyers to come to Mississippi to work; they took depositions in churches, school auditoriums, and every other building that could hold a crowd. In the depositions, hundreds of black Mississippians told about the many methods used by local voting registrars to prevent them from registering.

We then forwarded the depositions to the Speaker of the House of Representatives, who asked the five elected Mississippi representatives (white males, of course) to stand aside until a vote on a motion to exclude them was decided. During the debate on this motion, history was made. For the first time in history, black women were permitted on the floor of the House when Fannie Lou Hamer, Annie Devine, and Victoria Grey—who were the victors in an alternative election held by the MFDP—came in to await the vote on the motion.

The vote was close and unfortunately went against the resolution to unseat the five white men. But in some ways the vote didn't matter: The Mississippi Challenge had confronted the last remaining stronghold of segregation, the ballot box, and had come mighty close to upsetting the system. It was a monumental victory of the spirit.

Fannie Lou Hamer, asked by a reporter if she was seeking equality with the white man, again made one of her remarkable, eloquent comments. "No," she said. "What would I look like fighting for equality with the white man? I don't want to go down that low. I want the true democracy that'll raise me and that white man up . . . raise America up."

The volunteers—young and old, black and white—who participated in the Mississippi Freedom Summer and the Mississippi Challenge had made an enormous contribution to the civil rights movement. In that most backward of states, there were now a few cracks in the seemingly unbreachable wall constructed by a hundred years of Jim Crow segregation. The work would continue—voter registration drives, legal challenges, lawsuits, protests, marches. And I knew that my place would continue to be in the midst of it all. For the next few years, even when I returned north to take up my neglected law practice, my heart was in the South.

Desegregating the Washington, D.C., Schools

Two years after the Mississippi Challenge, I had an opportunity to strike a blow against institutional racism. Many years earlier, shortly after the 1954 *Brown* decision, the Washington, D.C., school board had hired a new superintendent to put in a track system and gerrymander some districts. Their purpose was to ensure that the school system in the nation's capital would remain completely segregated. During 1966 and 1967, I challenged that system in the courts in *Hobson v. Hanson,* a case of which I am most proud.

The late Julius Hobson, a Social Security economist with a daughter in public school in Washington, was a friend of my old running buddy Bill Higgs. Bill had become a resident of D.C. after being driven out of his native Mississippi on trumped-up morals charges. Hobson asked Higgs to represent him in a class-action suit against the Washington, D.C., school system, which discriminated against blacks because its tracking system was based on a white-oriented intelligence test. Higgs filed suit against members of the school board and the federal district judges who had appointed them. Circuit Judge J. Skelly Wright, an integrationist who had been appointed to the bench by President Kennedy, was to preside over the case.

Bill Higgs and I tried the case together. When I first appeared before Judge Wright for a pretrial conference, he warned me of my heavy responsibility. He added that if he felt I wasn't doing a good job, he would replace me with someone more experienced in this type of school case—an Inc. Fund attorney, for example. Happily, he never removed me, and I was on the case for its entire six-month duration.

Higgs and I contended that children attending the Washington, D.C., public schools were unfairly tracked for their entire school career on the basis of a Stanford-Binet IQ test administered to them when they were in the third grade. The test was wholly oriented toward white behavior. I recall that on one page of that test four differently dressed daddies were shown. One wore a bathing suit; a second, a tennis costume; a third, overalls; and a fourth, a business suit. The children were asked to judge, on the basis of the pictures, "Which daddy is going to work?" All the white children answered, "The one in the suit." But many of the black children answered, "The one in overalls." The only correct answer, of course, was "The one in the suit." As a result, many black children did poorly.

The board of education used this test to track the students. Those not on academic tracks were not allowed to take the same courses as college-bound students and were limited to those involving domestic science and automotive maintenance.

One of the most memorable witnesses was psychologist Robert Coles, who testified that blacks imprisoned in the District of Columbia jail at Lorton, Virginia, received a far better education than black children attending public schools in Washington, D.C.

Judge Wright ruled for us: The IQ test would have to be revamped, for it was white-oriented and unfair to black children; busing in some areas was ordered; some of the city's gerrymandering was ended. Although it was impossible to integrate a system that was 93 percent black, the judge did the best he could.

His 150-page opinion was the most gratifying decision of my career. As a result, many black children were now able to take college-track courses. These same students never would have had the chance to become professionals but would have been destined to be mechanics, maids, scrubwomen—honorable work certainly. But all people should have a fair chance to go as far as their abilities can take them.

The school system and board members appealed the decision, represented, as they had been from the beginning, by attorneys from the office of the Washington, D.C., corporation counsel who had unsuccessfully tried to get rid of Judge Wright from the moment of his assignment to the case. They asserted that the judge had earlier written a law review article criticizing segregated schools. However, Wright rebuffed all efforts to oust him. He was determined to strike a heavy blow for color-blind school systems.

The appeal was heard by the entire seven-judge panel of the District of Columbia circuit, which affirmed Wright's decision by a narrow vote of 4–3. Circuit Judge Warren Burger was one of the three who voted to overrule Wright. I will never understand why this did not become a disabling issue when the Senate Judiciary Committee held confirmation hearings on Burger's nomination to the U.S. Supreme Court. I guess the fact that he voted against an opportunity for black kids to get an equal education just wasn't important to the white men who made up the committee.

After 1964

After 1964, there were some more great moments for civil rights. Martin was awarded the Nobel Peace Prize that year. On August 6, 1965, the Voting Rights Act was signed into law. A few months earlier, on April 26, 1965, the U.S. Supreme Court gave the movement a monumental victory in *Dombrowski v. Pfister.*

In this case, the executive director of the Southern Conference Educational Fund, James A. Dombrowski, along with civil rights lawyers Bruce Walzer and Ben Smith, was arrested for violating Louisiana's antisubversive statutes. Arthur and I defended Dombrowski, as well as the two attorneys, after New Orleans police raided his home and removed his organization's files. The documents later turned up in the possession of Senator James O. Eastland, the fanatic chairman of the Senate Internal Security Subcommittee.

Arthur and I asked a three-judge federal court to enjoin the charges against Dombrowski and the others because the antisubversive laws were unconstitutional, violated the First Amendment, and had a chilling effect on public protests. We lost our suit by a vote of 2–1.

We appealed the case to the U.S. Supreme Court, where Arthur argued successfully that Louisiana's Communist control and subversive activities statutes were constitutionally invalid. In its decision, the Court voted to void major sections of these statutes because they unlawfully inhibited freedom of expression. It was a great victory for us and for civil rights.

But we in the movement also suffered many losses and tragedies after 1964. Martin was jailed during the March on Selma only sixty days after he received the Nobel Prize. Northern cities erupted in black rebellions, beginning with Los Angeles's Watts in August 1965.

The Supreme Court's decision in *Palmer v. Thompson* was a great loss both for the movement and for me personally. I don't like losing, especially on issues about which I feel passionate. This was one of those issues. In 1963, Jackson closed its five municipal pools after a federal court order to integrate them. Before that, Jackson had maintained completely segregated pools. It took almost a decade, but the case finally came before the U.S. Supreme Court on November 14, 1970.

Paul Rosen, a Detroit attorney, and I argued before the court that the city's action in closing the pools to avoid an order to integrate them violated both the Thirteenth and Fourteenth amendments and attempted to deny black people their rights. (The Thirteenth declared slavery unconstitutional; the Fourteenth recognized the rights of former slaves to citizenship, due process, and equal protection under the law.)

Rosen maintained that the City of Jackson's position that schools are essential and therefore had to be integrated as ordered, but pools are not, was like "giving black people a little this, and a little that, doling out rights."

I took the position that the Thirteenth Amendment outlawed all remnants of slavery, not slavery alone:

> If the amendment did abolish slavery, truly, and it did establish universal freedom, then our position is that it gives this Court the power, independent of any act of Congress, to abolish any incident of slavery. . . .
>
> I guess the question, Your Honors, comes down to this: What are badges and indicia of slavery?
>
> An indicia of slavery is anything which makes a black man reasonably feel inferior to a white man. It's the opposite of what Mr. Justice Brown said in *Plessy*.* He said, if the black race chooses to put that interpretation upon riding in segregated coaches, that's their lookout, not ours.
>
> But I submit that it is your lookout, our lookout, because this court is really nothing more than an extension of the American personality. . . .
>
> You as a court have just as much responsibility as Congress, just as much responsibility as the Executive, in

*In *Plessy v. Ferguson*, in 1896, the Supreme Court denied the contention of Adolph Plessy, who was one-eighth black and seven-eighths white, that a Louisiana statute compelling racial segregation on railroad cars violated the Fourteenth Amendment. The Court upheld the constitutionality of the Louisiana statute, saying the equal-protection clause of the Fourteenth Amendment did not guarantee social equality. "Separate but equal" was legal if "one race [is judged to] be inferior to the other socially," the court ruled. This ruling formed the basis of the next eighty years of segregation in the Deep South.

wiping out these badges, because unless they are wiped out, no black person can feel secure in the United States, and every black person will begin eventually to build up a rage that is already sufficient enough . . . that he knows in white eyes he is an inferior person.

The Court handed down its decision on June 14, 1971. We lost, 5–4, and Jackson's pools remained closed.

The years after 1965 continued to be difficult ones for civil rights. Many young black civil rights workers lost heart and went off on other quests; some traveled to Africa in search of their roots. SNCC dwindled down to a nonfunctioning group. Perhaps the biggest change of all was that Martin's philosophy of Gandhian nonviolence gave way to the militancy of the Black Power movement.

From my perspective, it appeared that the civil rights movement in the South ended around this time. In theory, the Civil Rights Act of 1964 and the Voting Rights Act of 1965 ended discrimination in all places of public accommodation and provided a method for enfranchising blacks.

I don't recall Martin organizing any real demonstrations in the South between 1965 and 1968. Because of this, some of the more militant black leaders felt that he was an anachronism. But I didn't agree. It's clear from what he said and from his actions that he decided to leave the Deep South and head north, to places like Cicero, Illinois, because he realized the movement had to change. But he didn't do well in the North. What Martin had to offer was peculiarly southern.

Although Martin and I never discussed it, I believe he later felt it had been a mistake to take the movement north, although his original motive, to use his national image to galvanize white liberals, was a valid one. As far as blacks were concerned, however, he really was a regional figure. It just didn't work to tell blacks in the sprawling northern ghettos of Harlem and Watts to turn the other cheek.

The Watts rebellion spread to other cities in the years after 1965. People were angry. Rather than sermons about nonviolence, they wanted to hear Malcolm X and other militants whose themes of rage and black separatism were more appropriate for Newark, L.A., Detroit, Washington, and New York. As early as 1965, Martin knew the future was going to be different, and he tried to plan for it.

Martin

April 4, 1968, was a very sorry day for those who worked with Martin King, for those who loved him, and for everyone who hoped for racial equality and harmony. On that day, he was assassinated.

Two weeks earlier, on March 18, he had gone to Memphis to support a nearly all black union of sanitation workers who were striking for benefits and increased wages. He led a march there on March 28, left town, then returned to the troubled city on April 3. He checked into room 306 at the Lorraine Motor Inn, which was for blacks only. Martin had asked me to prepare a legal action on behalf of the strikers, and I was in the middle of this task when he was murdered.

He was on the balcony outside his room, leaning on the railing, when, at 6:00 P.M., a single shot rang out; he collapsed with a fist-sized hole in his neck. I can never forget the picture of Andrew Young standing near Martin's body, his right arm outstretched and his index finger pointing toward the source of that single awful shot—a rooftop across the way where the assassin, James Earl Ray, was hiding.

There is no question in my mind that James Earl Ray fired the fatal shot. He pleaded guilty in 1969 and was sentenced to a ninety-nine-year term but has since claimed he was set up. But I believe the assassination was actually the result of the vendetta that the Establishment had waged for years against Martin.

Several years before he was killed, Martin had been publicly denounced as "the biggest liar in America" by FBI chief J. Edgar Hoover. The FBI tapped his phone, bugged his bedroom, did everything possible to create the illusion that Martin was an enemy of America. Even to this day, there are people trying to discredit him with allegations of a plagiarized doctoral dissertation and extramarital affairs. A truly great black leader like Martin could not be tolerated, so he had to be eliminated.

The hostile atmosphere surrounding Martin in 1968 was the perfect backdrop for an act of madness. It took only one maniac to end the life of this great, great man, whose visionary dream was shared by millions and who was the very soul of the civil rights movement.

Martin died young, at the height of his powers. He will be forever young, forever the spirit of the movement that caused fundamental and immutable changes in this country's social and political structure. In death, Martin was apotheosized, and his murder had a galvanizing effect on the civil rights movement.

The night of his assassination, Lotte and I were at home, in the comfort and security of our house in Westchester, watching a televised benefit for Tougaloo. Suddenly, someone stepped from behind the curtain and said, "The concert will be canceled because Dr. King has just died in Memphis." To hear the breath come out of the audience! The "Oh, no!" uttered by almost every person in that large room! That's what I remember. I don't remember anything as well as the grief and horror on those hundreds of black and white faces, as if their very hearts had been cut out.

I walked with the others at Martin's funeral. I have long thought that it was a little artificial. His body was hauled on a mule cart despite the fact that he was a sophisticated, urbane man with a Ph.D., rather than a backwoodsman. Martin came from a family of successful preachers, including his brother, A.D., and his father, Daddy King. He attended the best schools—Crozer Theological Seminary, Morehouse College, Boston University—and his wife, Coretta, graduated from Spelman College, which was then a mecca for young black women from wealthy families.

Martin's funeral seemed to be an attempt to gild the lily; he did not come from the soil. As a matter of fact, I was with him when he picked his first cotton in a field near Camilla, Georgia. Wearing a sharkskin suit and patent leather shoes, using one hand, he gently plucked a boll off a cotton plant.

The other extreme is the brick-and-stone mausoleum in Atlanta, complete with eternal flame, where Martin is buried. I don't like shrines. Martin was a man like other men, and he played his role and did what he had to do. It's myopic to create a shrine at which people kneel and pray, although I do understand the human urge to create an illusion of perpetuity by constructing elaborate tombs for notable corpses.

About seven years ago, I visited Martin's gravesite, along with my daughters from my second marriage, Sarah and Emily. I was a bit appalled, especially after I saw souvenirs for sale and discovered that some American corporations—many lacking good civil rights records—had contributed financially to the mausoleum. Mule cart and mausoleum are both false to Martin's memory. He would have opted for an ordinary hearse and grave, I think. If you're going to bury a man from a mule cart, how can you then build a multi-million-dollar mausoleum? It doesn't ring true. Better a simple resting place like Malcolm X's in Ferncliffe Cemetery in Westchester or John Brown's in the Adirondack Mountains of New York.

I would have let Martin sleep where he was first buried, on the campus of Morehouse College.

CHAPTER EIGHT

Dallas

Don't ask what took place in my mind. I don't know.

President Kennedy Assassinated

ALTHOUGH I DIDN'T LIKE JOHN F. KENNEDY—A VERY UNPOPULAR OPIN-ion which has gotten me into considerable trouble over the years—I was stunned and horrified by his assassination in Dallas on November 22, 1963. Like everyone else, I remember exactly where I was and what I was doing when I heard the news. I was in an elevator with Arthur and Michael, returning to our office from lunch. I didn't cry, but I felt awe and amazement, then a sense of tragedy. We were living in a time when a president of the United States could be assassinated! It was hard to comprehend; it was just that overwhelming. Something was very wrong in this country.

I became directly, and quite briefly, involved in the case immediately after Lee Harvey Oswald was charged with the assassination. Two days after his arrest, Oswald was still without legal representation, and Melvin Wulf, then the ACLU's legal director, asked me if I would consider defending him. Oswald had requested an ACLU lawyer, since his first choice, John Abt, the attorney for the Communist party in the United States, had refused to take him on.

I agreed to represent Oswald and immediately headed for the airport. I wanted to get to him fast to let him know someone was willing to defend him and to stop the authorities from interrogating him further. If anyone ever needed a good lawyer, it was Oswald; he didn't stand a chance unless he was defended very powerfully. I believed I could do it and planned to use the team approach, which Arthur Kinoy had taught me was necessary for complex cases. In keeping with my political values, I wanted to be Oswald's defense attorney because I believed he would get short shrift in Texas; his rights were certain to be violated. And I was not at all convinced that Oswald was, in fact, the president's murderer. Of course, I also was influenced by the fact that this was the crime of the century and there would be a highly publicized trial.

Before heading for Dallas, I called Lotte to say goodbye. She told me that Oswald had been shot dead only moments earlier with the whole country watching. His killer, a squat man in a fedora and a dark suit, had entered Dallas City Hall and killed Oswald right in front of reporters and camera crews. I was probably one of the few people in the country not watching television that day, so I missed that historic televised shooting.

Oswald's murderer, Jack Ruby, was defended by Melvin Belli and prosecuted by Dallas district attorney Henry Wade. Wade was furious at Jack for shooting Oswald and felt cheated out of the immortality he would have gained as the man who prosecuted President Kennedy's assassin. As a result, he threw the book at the hapless Ruby, who was convicted and became the most notorious death-row inmate in the country. I don't know how much immortality Henry Wade sought, but his name eventually got into the history books (although not in a very positive light) for being the Wade of *Roe v. Wade,* the Supreme Court's historic 1973 decision which upheld a woman's constitutional right to abortion. I can identify with Wade's desire for glory a bit, though: It would really have been something to be the attorney who defended Oswald.

Jack Ruby

About two years later, Martin and I were in La Guardia Airport on our way to Atlanta when a middle-aged man rushed up to us. Given the Kennedy assassination and the threats that had been made against Martin, we sort of surrounded Martin in a protective phalanx, but the man turned out to be Earl Ruby, Jack's brother.

Earl looked at Martin and pleaded, "Can we have Bill?" He wanted me to join an appellate team working to have Jack's conviction and death sentence overturned. Martin said, "Sure," and then glanced at me. Although I was up to my ears in civil rights cases, I couldn't turn this down. It was an important death-penalty case. Besides, Martin had said, "Do it." So I agreed to join the appellate team, and Earl Ruby handed me a check for $2,500 right then and there.

A week after that meeting, I went to Dallas to confer with the other attorneys and to meet Jack, who was then under very close watch at the Dallas County Jail. But when I arrived, the residents of that city were less than welcoming. Kunstler, Go Home! read the pickets carried by hundreds of people demonstrating at the Dallas airport. I assume they had heard or read that I was joining Jack's team of lawyers. They called me a Communist, urged me to return to New York, and handed out copies of a speech made by Rep. William Tuck of Virginia on the floor of Congress the previous year. In February 1964, Tuck had sailed into me in connection with the Wansley rape case in Lynchburg, Virginia, and said: "A character by the name of William Kunstler . . . posing as a respectable professor of law" had power enough to "impede the processes of justice."

Okay, so Dallas didn't want me, but after all, I was not trying to be popular; I was there to help save the life of Jack Ruby.

Death is the punishment for premeditated murder in Texas, so we appellate lawyers worked to have his conviction reversed so that he could be tried for murder without malice, similar to manslaughter in my home state of New York; the penalty for this carried a maximum sentence of five years. Jack's appellate team consisted of Sol Dann, from Detroit; one of Jack's original defense lawyers, Phil Burleson, from Texas; ACLU lawyer Sam Houston Clinton, also from Texas; Elmer Gertz, from Chicago; and myself.

Although Gertz would later characterize me as the anchorman at the appellate argument, there was a Texas lawyer, Joe Tonahill, who did everything in his power to keep me out of the Ruby case. Tonahill was part of the original defense team and was so dead set against my helping in the appeal that he tried to prove that Jack was not mentally competent to pick his own counsel. Jack wanted me in and Tonahill out, so we worked toward eliminating him. It was a lengthy, tedious struggle, but we eventually succeeded.

The Appeal

In early 1966, Jack's original trial judge, Joseph Brown, set a date for a preliminary hearing on his mental ability to select appellate counsel. At the same time, the appellate team moved to have Brown disqualify himself because he was under contract to write a book about the case before it was concluded—a most unethical involvement for a sitting judge. Predictably, Brown denied our motion that he disqualify himself and set Jack's sanity hearing for March 29.

At that point, I suggested we utilize my favorite technique of petitioning to have the case transferred from state to federal court under the Civil Rights Removal Act. The other lawyers concurred, and we filed the petition with the local federal court. Then the state moved to remand the matter back to state court. At the hearing on the state's motion, Jack Ruby told Judge T. Whitfield Davidson, of the U.S. district court: "I guess it was my destiny to kill [Oswald]. If I had been three seconds later, I would never have met this person. I guess God was against me. Don't ask what took place in my mind. I don't know."

That was the key to Jack: He never knew why he did what he did, never understood what motivated him to enter the stream of history and change its course.

Judge Davidson sent the case back to state court, but he suggested that Brown should not be the presiding judge. We then turned to the U.S. Court of Appeals for the Fifth Circuit, asking for a stay of the sanity hearing until we could appeal Davidson's ruling. That stay was denied, but Chief Judge Tuttle also strongly hinted that Brown should be removed.

Finally, Montague County judge Louis Holland was assigned to decide whether Brown should be disqualified and which lawyers would represent Jack. Holland ruled that since Jack had not yet been found insane, he could choose his own lawyers. This meant that Tonahill was out of the picture, although he later participated in the appellate argument as a friend of the court. Judge Brown withdrew from the case, based, I think, on our obtaining a copy of a letter he had written to his publisher. In it, he wrote, "We are coming along nicely. We have approximately 90 pages complete. . . ." This letter proved our contention that the judge could not possibly remain impartial on a case he was writing about for commercial purposes.

After more legal wrangling, our team prepared for our most important argument before the highest state tribunal for criminal cases, the Texas Court of Criminal Appeals. The case was heard in the summer of 1966. We argued that Jack's conviction should be overturned because the evidence used to convict him of murder with malice should not have been admissible. This evidence was what he reportedly said to a police sergeant some minutes after he shot Oswald: "I'm glad I got the son of a bitch."

Under Texas law, statements made by a defendant during the res gestae—during the commission of the crime, in the heat of the moment—are allowed into evidence. But statements made after the crime, after the res gestae, and without a lawyer present, cannot be used as evidence. Using these statements as evidence violates the rule that a defendant has a constitutional right to have a lawyer present when he is making a statement about a crime. This worthwhile rule predated the historic 1966 Supreme Court *Miranda* decision. That decision mandated that suspects be informed of a series of constitutional rights—their "Miranda rights"—before any police interrogation can begin.

The statement reportedly made by Jack after the shooting should not have been allowed in as evidence, I said vehemently during our argument before the court. While I talked, I inadvertently used as a pointer one of the exhibits—the gun with which Ruby had shot Oswald, a .38-caliber, six-shot Colt Cobra. (Earl Ruby sold that gun at auction in 1991 for $220,000.) Chief Judge Morrison stopped me. "Mr. Kunstler, that weapon has already killed one man, and we don't want it to kill any more. Please put it down and continue your argument without it." I dropped the gun as if it had suddenly become molten iron.

The court's decision was handed down on October 5, 1966, and Jack's conviction was overturned. He would be tried again, this time on the lesser charge of murder without malice. The court also stated that Judge Brown should have allowed a change of venue, since Dallas was probably the worst place in the country for Jack Ruby to get a fair trial. Accordingly, Wichita Falls, some ninety miles northwest of Dallas, was selected as the place for the new trial.

For the Jews

At this point, Jack was technically a free man until a second trial could be arranged. It was a great victory, because he certainly had never schemed to kill Lee Harvey Oswald. Jack's was the act of a madman, perhaps, but not one who planned. There is a Yiddish word for someone like him—meshugana. He came from a family with mental problems, and many of his close relatives were emotionally unstable.

Jack, the fifth child in a family of eight children, was born on either March 25 or March 19, 1911, depending on which records you believe. The family moved often and was abandoned by the father when Jack was eleven. Jack's childhood was marked by truancy, behavior problems in school, and a brain injury that resulted in psychomotor epilepsy. He was placed in a foster home in 1923. During his late teens and early twenties, he lived either alone or with a boyfriend. As a young adult, he was a hustler and a ticket scalper, a tough guy who often got into fights.

On the more positive side, he was active in a union and started a novelty business with some family members. Jack joined the army and was discharged after three years with a good record. But his growing violent outbursts and extreme sensitivity, almost paranoia, about anti-Semitism left those who knew him concerned about his mental stability. In the late 1940s, Jack moved to Dallas to be near his sister Eva. There he owned and operated a couple of small-time strip joints, the Carousel Club and the Vegas Club.

When Jack told me he had killed Oswald "for the Jews," I believed him. On each of the three occasions we talked, he said, "Bill, I did this so they wouldn't implicate Jews." Lee Harvey Oswald had belonged to Fair Play for Cuba, an organization with a number of Jewish members. Because of this association of Oswald's, Jack's convoluted thinking led him to believe that the Kennedy assassination would be linked to Jews. During our last visit, he handed me a note in which he reiterated his desire to protect American Jews from a pogrom that could occur because of anger over the assassination. He also told me, "I wanted to save Mrs. Kennedy from being put through the ordeal of a trial, and that's why I did this thing."

Some conspiracy theorists claim that Jack had close ties to the FBI, but I think he was much too unstable for that. Jack Ruby, one of the most confusing and confused people I ever met, could not have had a responsible part in a conspiracy. His murder of Oswald was clearly an act of individual insanity. Based on what I know of Jack's personality and the actions he took on the day he killed Oswald, it's clear that he acted alone, on impulse, with no premeditation. One proof that Jack shot impetuously is that he left his beloved dachshund, Sheba, locked in his car when he made his fateful trip down the ramp into the basement of Dallas City Hall. He planned to return to that dog.

Maybe he thought he would become a hero. He certainly never dreamed that he would be convicted and receive the death penalty. On the evening of the Kennedy assassination, Jack had taken sandwiches and coffee to the police working overtime at city hall, a perfectly normal thing for him to do. He was friendly with many of the officers. In order to keep his clubs running smoothly, Jack curried favor with the Dallas police by being a tout, a flunky, perhaps an informer. The police also were aware that Jack carried a legal handgun.

Jack was on the street as the police prepared to transport Oswald only because he had gone to a Western Union office in order to send money to one of his Carousel Club dancers who lived in neighboring Fort Worth. The dancer had called Jack, said she was broke, and asked him to wire her rent money. The only Western Union office in Dallas open that Sunday happened to be just down the street from city hall, where Oswald was being temporarily held.

When Jack left the Western Union office—the official stamp on the money order shows 11:17 A.M.—he saw a crowd outside the city hall basement and a Dallas County Jail van backed into the ramp leading into the basement. He correctly assumed Oswald was about to be transferred to the county jail, even though the authorities had stated publicly that the move was to take place at 10:00 A.M. He walked past the van and down the ramp and entered the basement just as Oswald was being led toward the vehicle's rear door. Jack pulled out his gun, went up close to Oswald's left side, and fired. Capt. Will Fritz, head of Dallas homicide, yelled, "Jack, you crazy son of a bitch!" as Oswald fell. The time was 11:21 A.M.

Many assassination experts are convinced that Jack was part of the complex conspiracy to kill Kennedy. For example, the late Jim Garrison, who was a New Orleans prosecutor, believed that the CIA and the military-industrial complex wanted the president out of the way and thought that Jack, with some ties to organized crime, the FBI, and the CIA, killed Oswald in order to keep the conspiracy a secret. All of Garrison's theories about Jack Ruby are backed up by pseudo facts that can be easily disproved. I certainly believe that CIA goons plot and carry out assassinations, but I just don't see Jack as part of those schemes. Many details of the Kennedy assassination and its aftermath are unclear, true. But it seemed incredible to me then, and still does, that if enormously powerful networks like the military-industrial complex and the CIA were behind the Kennedy murder, they would trust even the smallest link in the plot to the likes of a Jack Ruby. He was missing too much and was not someone who could be trusted with a responsibility that important. Jack Ruby was lucky if he remembered the Dallas cops' sandwich order. Besides, after he was sentenced to death, he was the type of man who certainly would have traded any conspiracy information for his life.

Jack, legally innocent while he awaited a second trial, became ill with cancer. He died of a blood clot in the lungs on January 3, 1967. Conspiracy theorists, like Mark Lane, might assume that Jack was poisoned. I don't agree.

The American public remains enormously curious about what may yet prove to be the most bungled murder mystery in our history. If all of the sealed government files on the assassination are eventually opened to historians and researchers, we may yet discover the truth. More likely, we won't. If it turns out that Jack Ruby did play a part in a conspiracy, I will be very much surprised.

The Kennedys

The Kennedy administration has been remembered, over the years, as one of benevolence and wisdom. But while it appeared that all was well, the Kennedy brothers were dangerous and deceptive men. Although he promised civil rights legislation, Jack Kennedy did not actually offer any until Birmingham blew up, two years after he took office. He allowed many civil rights workers to die, especially in Mississippi, by failing to protect them. Both Kennedys approved of the wiretapping of Martin Luther King. J. Edgar Hoover should not take the sole blame for that. The White House gave him the authority to tap Martin's phones and wire his hotel bedrooms. I have been told that President Kennedy used to play those tapes as entertainment for certain of his guests. He didn't like Dr. King at all, for Martin was causing trouble for the administration, with disruption and dissension erupting all over the South.

When he ordered the first combat troops into Vietnam, Kennedy violated an international agreement that only military advisers would be sent there. His actions ultimately led to the deaths of more than fifty-eight thousand Americans and untold numbers of Vietnamese.

Today I can say these things without being considered totally intemperate because so much information has been revealed about Jack Kennedy's relationship with the Mafia, plans to murder Castro, and alleged affair with Marilyn Monroe. But the Kennedys' real immorality has to do with their lack of ethics as political leaders rather than their sexual exploits. This failing was more dangerous in them than in other politicians because the Kennedys pretended to be so righteous. After the Kennedys, we had Johnson, Nixon, Reagan, and Bush. Nixon, who actually deserved credit for ending the war in Vietnam and for opening up China, was easily attacked because his political motives were so obvious and his deceits so clear. Reagan was a stupid man who was easily led by the nose. All of these later presidents were easier to attack than Kennedy because they lacked the Kennedy mix of intelligence and charisma.

It is possible that any president becomes a danger because of the enormous power he holds. Lord Acton's theory that power corrupts is one I always remember when I see these political leaders in action. But the Kennedys, with their semblance of a royal family, gave us one of the most dangerous presidents we have ever had. Had the Kennedy brothers lived, they might have successfully carried out their plot to kill Castro. And a president who employs mobsters to murder another country's head of state is straying far from the moral line.

In the end, however, John Kennedy's death placed him beyond criticism. Like Martin, he was sanctified in death.

PART THREE

The Sixties: Decade of Change

■   ■   ■

T HE SIXTIES WAS MY TIME OF TRANSFORMATION. DURING THIS PERIOD and into the 1970s, I changed from a liberal into a radical and tried to "be here now," in the words of sixties cultural icon Richard Alpert. Life was to be lived fully, in the present, because the past was over and gone and the future was not yet here. Nothing lost its immediacy for me then, nor does it today. Because of the wrenching and overwhelming effect of the sixties, I still live very much in the moment, racing from case to case, from cause to cause, not worrying or reflecting about what happened yesterday or what might happen tomorrow.

During the latter part of the sixties, having discovered in middle age the joys of freedom from convention and a commitment to a political philosophy that was stronger than fear, I metamorphosed into the person I am today. As the movement expanded from civil rights to Black Power, from protest to militant dissent, I took on almost all political cases that came my way. From the mid-1960s on, I represented pacifists like Dave Dellinger and the Berrigans, rebels like Lenny Bruce, revolutionaries like H. Rap Brown, counterculture heroes like Abbie Hoffman—all the while still working on civil rights cases in the South. I have no idea how I did it all, but today I still conduct my life at the frenetic tempo I came to love during the sixties.

The decade between 1965 and 1975 saw the unraveling of my marriage, the breakup of the law partnership with my brother, Michael, and the end of my relatively quiet family life in Westchester.

I became completely committed to the struggles of my clients and, through that commitment, to the political movement itself. I worked only on political cases and traveled anywhere, on a moment's notice, whenever I was called. Although my marriage tottered on for another few years, it was worn thin by my lengthy absences from home and, I must confess, by my liaisons with other women.

The sixties didn't begin in 1960 or end in 1970, but was a span of time as unlimited as a hippie's dress code. It was an era

165

unlike any other, not merely ten years in American history but a political and social upheaval created by people who believed in individual rights, peace, love, and concern for others. The sixties generation expressed itself in many different ways, from rhetoric to revolt, from the nonviolence of Martin King to the militancy of the Weathermen.

Most members of this generation were so young that the movement appeared, at times, to be a revolution by America's youth against the traditional, stodgy ways of their parents. And although I was even older than some of the kids' parents, I became caught up in it as much as anyone.

We had plenty of enemies to fight and to unite us: the oppression of minorities and anyone else who was different; institutional segregation; racism; a Big Daddy government; and an unjust, unpopular war. Drugs opened our minds. Rock, jazz, and soul music gave us our rhythm. In the sixties, for the first time, people asserted their rights and freedoms even if they weren't white or male or rich, even if they didn't follow the established ways. Civil rights, the sexual revolution, the women's movement, gay and lesbian rights—things will never be the same again, to my great satisfaction, because of what occurred during those years.

The sixties evolved slowly, spiraling up and out from the subterranean lifestyle of black hipsters in the 1930s and 1940s, from the complacent affluence of the 1950s, from the southern civil rights movement. The leaders of the sixties came from these earlier movements and showed up, one at a time, here and there, in the South or at antiwar protests.

The sixties seduced me, and I felt as if my entire life had led me to this time and place, to this work. After the earlier part of the decade, when I worked primarily on southern civil rights cases, I saw a gradual enlargement of the movement until its theme became not just peaceful integration but radical change. Change, by any means necessary, in the words of Malcolm X. Change was the rallying cry of the New Left, the counterculture, radicals, hippies, Yippies, Weathermen.

The years, and the cases, whizzed by as I ran from courtroom to courtroom, city to city, state to state. Between 1965 and 1975, I don't think there was a significant political case in this country in which I wasn't, in some way, involved. And I had the time of my life.

CHAPTER NINE

Rebels

Have you ever shot up?

1965
Lenny Bruce

BY THE MID-1960S, THE ESTABLISHMENT HAD BEGUN TO REALIZE THAT the counterculture, comprised of activists, radicals, dissidents, and militants in the civil rights, antiwar, and New Left movements, would not go away. The government, acting for the Establishment, decided to neutralize counterculture leaders with a variety of devices. Many were arrested, prosecuted, and jailed; others had their reputations and personal lives ruined through smear campaigns; and some were assassinated. A large number of sixties people were tied up with costly, protracted legal struggles that prevented them from doing anything else. Some fought legal battle after legal battle; as soon as one case was over, they would be arrested on other charges, and the battle would begin again.

My experience with Lenny Bruce—often described as a stand-up comic but really one of the greatest political satirists of our time—was the first time I saw in action the government's use of the might and power of the criminal justice system to crush dissent. Establishment minions complained that Lenny's nightclub routines were smutty and lewd, immoral and indecent, and that the government had a responsibility to stop them. His brilliant and unconventional humor had riled the Establishment so much that the authorities busted him for indecency, obscenity, and a whole range of trumped-up charges that would be impossible to bring today.

At the end of 1965, I was one of Lenny's appeals lawyers, working to overturn his various convictions on obscenity charges. By this time his legal battles had taken over his life. On Christmas Eve he walked into the office I shared with my brother at 511 Fifth Avenue just as I was about to go down the hall to a Christmas party. Lenny, dressed in his traditional long white coat and sneakers, with his usual disregard for time, holidays, and convention, said it was urgent he talk to me and suggested that the party could wait.

That snowy evening, he talked about the effect of drugs on his sense of humor and point of view. "Bill, you can never understand what it means to shoot up unless you've done it," he said. Then he asked, "Have you ever shot up?"

When I told him I hadn't, he said, "Let's go into the men's room down the hall." Like a lunatic, I agreed, and we walked down the hall to the bathroom. Lenny tied rubber tubing around my left arm just above the bend of my elbow. Then he put a needle into my arm and injected me. At first, I felt absolutely nothing, so I went, as planned, to the Christmas party, leaving Lenny in the men's room. It was the last time I ever saw him.

Shortly after I arrived at the party, I collapsed. Someone carried me to my office, put me on a couch, and called my wife; I was completely unconscious. Lotte drove down from Westchester and took me home. I was totally out of it and vomited for quite a long time the following morning. I was capable of locomotion but was sick as a dog. If it was ever possible for me to become addicted to heavy drugs, the possibility vanished that evening.

Lotte berated me, saying that I had shown incredible immaturity and poor judgment. At the time, I suppose I wanted Lenny to think I was a regular guy and that I understood all about shooting up heroin. But when Lenny OD'd in Hollywood eight months later, on August 3, and was found dead on a bathroom floor with his arms wrapped around a toilet, I saw at once the utter recklessness of what I had done—and vowed never again to be so careless.

I believe Lenny OD'd deliberately. Six years earlier, he was at the height of his career. But after the government's persecution, he became so obsessed with his legal struggles that he lost his perspective and brilliant sense of humor. He was a ruined man. The government hounded Lenny until his single-minded drive to vindicate himself took precedence over everything else. Fighting the government is appropriate, but Lenny's manic fixation destroyed him.

I remember one of Lenny's criminal trials particularly because the prosecutor, Richard Kuh, and I had lived in the same building and belonged to the same hockey club when we were children. During that trial, Lenny's obscenity charge was based on testimony that he had simulated masturbation onstage using a broomstick and had then touched his crotch suggestively. Cross-examining a detective who had seen the performance, Kuh asked, "How near were you to Mr. Crotch when you saw him touch his Bruce?" We all thought of many new uses for the word Bruce after this. Even Lenny laughed.

I was fortunate to have seen many of Lenny's performances, and my favorite was his routine about Moses, Jesus, and the pope. Moses and Jesus are at the back door of the Vatican, clamoring to get in. At the same time, the pope scurries around hiding the Vatican loot and ordering the Swiss Guards to help him get the place to look like a poor man's refuge rather than an opulent palace.

Lenny's witty irreverence disturbed many people, but those of us who rejected authority, institutions, and convention loved him. In the end, I guess the other side won, because they took Lenny from us, piece by piece.

(Thirty years after Lenny's death, I played a lawyer defending rock star Jim Morrison on obscenity charges in *The Doors,* directed by Oliver Stone. With Oliver's approval, I changed my lines to include some of the actual language from one of Lenny's trials. I was not a hit, though. One reviewer wrote, "That old movie star William Kunstler as Morrison's defense attorney . . . plays himself. As usual, he's unbelievable.")

Lenny's death might have been prevented, for many overdoses are caused by the dangerous substances used to cut the drugs rather than the drugs themselves. I strongly advocate legalizing the most common drugs, like marijuana, cocaine, and heroin, as they have done in England and now in Holland and Germany, among other countries. New York's draconian Rockefeller drug laws and other similarly inappropriate statutes should be taken off the books. Penalties for use of almost all drugs should be eliminated, and drug addiction should be treated for what it is, a social and medical problem and not a crime.

I would not legalize some of the hallucinogens and amphetamines, which can have very serious effects on the body and mind. But marijuana? The well-known medical benefits of marijuana for some AIDS and cancer patients make criminal prosecution for its possession ridiculous. And heroin has no effects—except that it is

addictive. I know a surgeon who performs the most delicate operations—reattaching fingers and similar types of surgery—who has
been addicted to heroin for most of his life. Since he's a doctor, he
can get clean heroin. But Lenny Bruce, like most junkies, had to
buy his on the street.

Compare marijuana, cocaine, tobacco, and scotch and tell me
why two of these items are legal and two are not. Cocaine was for
years an ingredient in that all-American drink Coca-Cola. This
was possible because drugs have been illegal in the United States
only since 1909, when the Harrison Act was passed. I am not advocating cocaine use, but when compared to alcohol, which stul-
tifies, I question why cocaine is illegal and liquor legal. But I
know the answer: money. Control of our drug laws is in the hands
of those individuals who make money from drugs being illegal
and liquor and tobacco legal. These people have the full cooperation of the government. In order to protect us from the ill effects of
dangerous substances, it engages in misguided efforts to fight a
"war against drugs" at the same time that it subsidizes the phar-
maceutical companies and supports the influential tobacco and
liquor industries.

1966
HUAC

I was working in the South on civil rights cases when a resus-
citated relic from the McCarthy era, the evil House Un-American
Activities Committee (HUAC), reappeared in the government's arsenal of weapons against the movement. HUAC scheduled hearings to investigate alleged subversive and Communist elements in
the nascent antiwar movement. Shortly after Jerry Rubin made a
dramatic visit to Capitol Hill garbed in a Revolutionary War uniform, he and Abbie Hoffman were subpoenaed to appear before
HUAC, as were several other organizers of protests against the
Vietnam War.

John Pemberton, then the energetic ACLU director, organized
a team of lawyers to stop the hearings. We brought a lawsuit to
enjoin the committee from convening in which we accused it of
acting only to punish expression of First Amendment views. We
were ecstatic when a district court judge issued an injunction for-
bidding the hearing. It was the first time in the history of the
United States that a congressional committee had been stopped!
All hell broke loose. HUAC members were furious not only at

movement people but also at their own lawyers.

Of course, the government moved immediately to have the injunction overturned. After a three-judge appellate panel met in a nighttime emergency session and hastily set aside the injunction, HUAC was allowed to hold its hearing the following morning, August 17, 1966.

Along with Arthur Kinoy and six other lawyers, I appeared at the hearing to represent Abbie, Jerry, Walter Darwin Teague III, a supporter of medical aid to North Vietnam, and the others. During the hearing, I objected when the committee called a witness to testify about Teague, who was supposed to be "friendly"—on the side of the defendants—but who was really "hostile"—against the defendants. The committee's own rules stated that hostile testimony must first be given in executive session rather than in open session. I also objected to the fact that we, as Teague's attorneys, would not be able to cross-examine this witness because he was deemed a friendly witness; defense attorneys can only cross-examine hostile witnesses.

Rep. Joe R. Pool of Texas, chairman of the Anti-Vietnam War Activities Subcommittee of HUAC, overruled each of my objections, but Arthur continued to argue. Pool became angry and yelled at Arthur to sit down. Arthur continued arguing. Pool again yelled at him to sit. Then the marshals moved in to grab Arthur, and I shouted, "Take your hands off this man. He's a member of the bar."

Arthur, who weighed only about 100 pounds soaking wet and stood five feet two inches tall, yelled, "I am an attorney-at-law, and I will not be removed from this hearing." He was lifted off the ground by three federal marshals and dragged from the room, struggling and shouting, "Let the record show—Don't touch a lawyer!"

"Throw us all out," I shouted. "Mr. Kinoy is my colleague, a professor of law at Rutgers University, and a member of the bar of New York." I insisted that the members of the committee bring Arthur back and apologize to him. They refused. I said I was withdrawing because of the committee's treatment of Arthur and did so. I was quickly joined by the other lawyers.

Arthur was eventually charged with disorderly conduct and using loud and boisterous language during a congressional hearing. The incident generated enormous national publicity and probably contributed more to the collapse of HUAC than any other single occurrence. I appeared as Arthur's lawyer in the District of Columbia court the day after his arrest, but when it became clear that I would have to testify as a witness, Morty Stavis took over the defense. It was a nonjury proceeding, and after two days, Judge Harold Greene found Arthur guilty of disorderly conduct. More than a thousand lawyers protested and filed briefs on Arthur's behalf. NYU Law School professor Anthony Amsterdam, a leading civil rights attorney, successfully argued the appeal, and two years later, Arthur's conviction was unanimously reversed.

1966
Black Panthers

Founded in Oakland, California, in 1966 by Huey Newton, Bobby Seale, and others, the Black Panther Party for Self Defense quickly became the leader of the militant Black Power movement. The Panthers believed that blacks had the right to bear arms and to use them, if necessary, to defend themselves against unjustified police attacks. With their berets, leather jackets, guns, rage, and rhetoric, the group scared the hell out of white America.

I met Leonard Bernstein for the first time in 1966 at a fundraising party for the Black Panthers given by his wife, actress Felicia Montealegre. I was invited because at the time I was serving as general counsel for the Panthers' East Coast division. The party, a frantic scene with people collecting money and making speeches, was the subject of writer Tom Wolfe's snotty but entertaining *New York* magazine piece "Radical Chic." Although we never became great friends, I always liked and respected Lenny. He was also the only man I knew who kissed me on the lips whenever we met. I'm a hugger, but Lenny always kissed. Years later, I found out that the Bernstein family's initial support for the Black Panthers had been undermined by certain actions taken by the FBI, including the Bureau's creation and circulation of a blatantly anti-Semitic coloring book which was made to look like a Panther publication.

1966
Harlem Six

The summers seemed longer and hotter during the incendiary sixties, and in Harlem especially, tensions were high between police and young blacks. James Baldwin, a gifted writer with an extraordinary social consciousness, drew me into two cases that arose directly out of the turmoil of these summers. In 1964, a group of young kids who came to be called the Harlem Six had formed a club and flew gray homing pigeons from the roof of a tenement. When several young blacks robbed a clothing store on 125th Street, stabbing the white owner to death and seriously injuring her husband, the kids in the pigeon club were charged.

Their arrest was based on the testimony of a young man named Robert Barnes, who claimed to be a member of the group. As the chief witness for the prosecution, he said he had pretended to go along with the robbery that was planned by the others but had not participated in the murder.

Before the trial began, Jimmy Baldwin joined with the Charter Group for a Pledge of Conscience, a group of New York City white liberals who had organized around this case, and attempted to help them get acquitted. When the six were convicted in 1965, Jimmy enlisted my help on the appeal, which was argued before New York's highest court by attorney John Silverberg in 1968. The seven-judge panel threw out the convictions of the Harlem Six, since they had been tried together and convicted on the evidence of a statement made by one of them.

The court's decision was based on a Supreme Court ruling known as the Bruton Rule. If defendants are tried together and one has given a statement implicating the others, the prosecution cannot use that statement against the others because, unless the confessor decides to take the stand, the other defendants' lawyers would have no chance to conduct a cross-examination of him. In a criminal trial, a defendant can elect not to testify. It is up to the prosecution to prove its case independent of the testimony of an accused.

The defendants were slated for a new trial, and along with several attorneys, I applied to the assignment judge, Gerald Culkin, to be one of their court-appointed lawyers. Culkin turned down our request with the astonishing statement, "These boys wouldn't know a good lawyer from a good watermelon." Forever after, he was known everywhere as the Watermelon Judge. We filed a disciplinary complaint against him, but nothing ever came of it. And the lawyers that he did appoint were taken directly from the patronage list of those who were due political favors.

In the second trial of the Harlem Six, now reduced to four, the jury hung, 11–1 for conviction. By this time the defendants were in their twenties. For their third trial, we again applied to be their lawyers. This time, we were appointed. One codefendant, Robert

Rice, had a different lawyer who was appointed, according to courthouse gossip, by Judge Culkin because she was his mistress and they were enjoying each other's favors in chambers. Rice, whose statement to the police had brought the Bruton Rule into play, was later tried separately and convicted. Another, David Hamm, had pleaded guilty to manslaughter after his mother had a nervous breakdown. Conrad Lynn, Lewis Steel, Legal Aid attorney Edward Leopold, and I represented the remaining four.

We tried the case to a fare-thee-well in front of Joseph Martinis, an acting Supreme Court justice, but the jury again hung, this time 7–5 for acquittal.

The defendants were about to be tried for a fourth time when I received a postcard from chief prosecution witness Robert Barnes, who was in prison on an unrelated charge. He asked me to visit him, and when I did, he said that he had lied originally because the police pressured him and that everything he had said implicating the Harlem Six in the murder and robbery was false.

Lewis Steel and I obtained detailed affidavits from Barnes and submitted them to the court, moving to have the case dismissed because of prosecutorial misconduct. The state then permitted the defendants to plead to manslaughter and be immediately released. I wanted to try the case rather than plead because I am certain that we would have won, but the four by this time had had more than enough of prison. The case had already dragged on for almost a decade; it was now 1972. *The Torture of Mothers* by Truman Nelson describes how the mothers of the four defendants stuck together throughout their sons' ordeal, which I believe is what ultimately helped to liberate these young men.

1966
Harlem Five

Jimmy Baldwin also involved me with the Harlem Five, a group of black youths arrested in 1966 for conspiring to steal arms from a local armory and blow up bridges linking Manhattan to the other boroughs. Then, according to the charges, this group was going to take over Manhattan, a preposterous accusation and completely untrue. There may have been some outrageous talk, but that was the extent of it.

The Harlem Five case resulted in a couple of convictions on minor gun charges, but everything else was dropped because no jury would believe such a tall tale. These were five young kids;

how could anyone believe they would try to take over Manhattan? I believed the entire case was part of a plan to arouse the public so that it would be willing to tolerate police brutality during the racial rebellions expected that summer, the summer of 1966. Black people had been rebelling in cities all over the country, and the NYPD wanted the public to accept it when they came down hard on black citizens in New York City.

Jimmy Baldwin and I stayed friendly over the years, and in the mid-1980s, he again involved me in a case, the wrongful conviction of Wayne Williams as the so-called Atlanta Child Murderer. When Jimmy died in 1987, I was defending accused cop shooter Larry Davis, but I was able to get permission to be excused from the trial so I could attend the funeral. He was buried from the Cathedral of St. John the Divine in New York City with eloquent eulogies by Amiri Baraka, once known as Le Roi Jones, another of my clients, and Toni Morrison.

1966–67
Stokely and Rap

During 1966 and 1967, I met two men who would always be important in my life, Stokely Carmichael and H. Rap Brown. Both quickly fell victim to the government's methodical destruction of dissent through borderline lawful, though unjust, means—repeated arrests, prolonged court battles, never-ending legal entanglements. These tactics deprived both Stokely and Rap of significant time and energy. Each man handled the harassment differently; Stokely eventually left the country, while Rap fought it out for years, then quietly retreated to a different way of life.

I met Stokely first. He was fascinating and charismatic, with burning, piercing eyes. He was enormously eloquent, and I was very fond of him. A native of Trinidad who spoke with a slight trace of a West Indian accent, Stokely was a field secretary for SNCC. In 1966, shortly after he became chairman of SNCC, he picked me up at the airport in Birmingham and we drove to Selma, where he and other SNCC members conferred with me about legal matters, including a possible lawsuit against the segregationist Democratic party in Alabama.

Stokely, who had been doing voter registration for SNCC since 1964, created the black panther symbol in response to the white rooster used by the Democrats. And it was Stokely whom I first heard use the term "Black Power"—during a march in Mississippi on June 10, 1966. Adam Clayton Powell later claimed that he had coined the expression, but if Stokely didn't invent it, he certainly made it popular.

During 1966 and 1967, Stokely traveled all over the world, sparking controversy wherever he spoke. On June 20, 1966, he startled an audience at Nashville's Vanderbilt University with fiery statements like "The only way these honkies and honky lovers can understand is when they're met by resistance." After Stokely was arrested that day, he said about the police, "If their armed aggression continues, we will resist by any means necessary."

I went to Nashville in the summer of 1966 on behalf of the newly formed Center for Constitutional Rights (CCR) to help several Vanderbilt University students who had been arrested during the uprising that followed Stokely's June 20 speech. Arthur Kinoy, Morton Stavis, and I, along with Louisiana lawyer Ben Smith, had formed this tax-exempt organization, initially using donations we had received from Ethel Clyde, a wealthy nonagenarian living on New York City's Fifth Avenue. From time to time, she would hand Arthur and me a check and say, "Use this for your civil rights cases." So we did, first calling the organization the Law Center for Constitutional Rights and later removing "Law" from the name. The center still thrives today, taking on dozens and dozens of important cases.

Working with local counsel, I brought an injunction action in federal court and tried to have the Tennessee statutes under which the Nashville students were held declared unconstitutional. In those days, if you attacked the validity of state statutes, such a tribunal would be automatically convened.

While in Nashville, I lived at the home of Rev. James Woodruff. I was introduced to marijuana there. Both because there was a lot of it around and because I didn't want to look like Mr. Fuddy-Duddy, I smoked my share. Actually, in that house, even if I hadn't inhaled, it would have made no difference. The smoke was so intense that you would get stoned just walking up the stairs to your bedroom.

We eventually lost our lawsuit to have the Tennessee statutes declared unconstitutional. But we did manage, through testimony, to dramatize the grievances against segregation that had been articulated by Stokely. Winning would have been preferable, of course, but win or lose, the case served as an organizing and rallying tool.

Stokely was later indicted in Georgia under an old sedition statute that carried the death penalty and had been last used in the 1930s against the notorious black Communist organizer Angelo Herndon. The statute, a carryover from the antebellum days, made it a crime, punishable by death, to make a speech that threatened insurrection against the state. We asked a federal panel to invalidate the statute, arguing that it conflicted with the First Amendment and could be used to punish words rather than actions.

My cocounsel, Howard Moore, ran out of gas at one point during his argument. When Judge Tuttle asked him a question, he said, "Bill, you answer that." I was flabbergasted to be thrown into an argument that I wasn't prepared to make. In any event, the judges knocked out the Angelo Herndon statute, and Stokely was exonerated.

In early 1967, Stokely resigned as chairman of SNCC. During the following summer, he became prime minister of the California-based Black Panther party. But he quit the Panthers a year later, critical of their willingness to work with white allies, and moved to Guinea, West Africa, where he still lives.

In Nashville, before Stokely left SNCC, he introduced me to his successor, Hubert Geroid "Rap" Brown, a tall, gangly fellow. "People will be happy to have me back when they hear him speak," Stokely said. Rap was only twenty-three when he took over the leadership of SNCC and was soon well on his way to becoming one of the most hated and feared men in America. His speeches reflected his rage at the treatment of African-Americans, and he threatened nothing less than a civil war to achieve freedom for his brothers and sisters. "If America don't come around, we going to burn it down," he thundered, and white America shook. He was very much influenced by Malcolm X.

Rap's most famous statement is the often-quoted "Violence is necessary. It is as American as cherry pie."

Many of Rap's speeches were provocative, designed to rouse and unite his fellow black citizens and terrify their white oppressors: "America doesn't rule the world with love. It rules with guns, tanks, missiles, bombs. . . . When America fights a nonviolent war, I'll become nonviolent. But I ain't gon' hold my breath waiting. . . . I preach a response to violence. Meet violence with violence."

Over time, Rap was deluged with state and federal charges in a no-holds-barred attempt by the government to stop him. Among other things, FBI agents, police, and other law enforcement agents tried to kill him several times. Rap was first arrested in Cambridge, Maryland, in July 1967. The authorities claimed that a speech he made at a rally organized by black leaders in Maryland's Dorchester County was inflammatory and that he had urged his audience to burn the town down. This accusation eventually led to the passage of the Rap Brown Statute, the federal law that was the basis of the 1969 indictments against the Chicago Eight. It made it illegal for anyone to cross state lines with the intention of inciting a riot.

When a thirteen-state alarm was issued for Rap by the Maryland authorities, he called me for advice, and I told him to give himself up. As he boarded a plane in Virginia to go to Maryland to turn himself in, he was arrested and thrown in jail. I got him released, pleading for his freedom by stressing his clean record and his First Amendment right to free speech. It was fortunate for our case that the government prosecutors were insistent in their belief that if Rap were free, he would travel and make incendiary speeches. Robert Mehrige, the presiding federal judge, had a real commitment to free speech, and in large part because of the prosecutors' overzealousness and paranoia, he released Rap on his own recognizance. We quickly left Richmond and flew back to New York, where we were met at the airport by a jubilant band of SNCC members.

From this time on, Rap was constantly followed by government agents and police. In September, he was arrested again after he allegedly carried a semiautomatic carbine onto a plane from New York to his native Louisiana. During the flight, he supposedly asked a flight attendant to hold the gun for him. When he returned to New York, he was arrested and charged by the feds with transporting a weapon across state lines while under a Maryland felony indictment.

Rap's bail hearing took place before District Judge Thomas Murphy. Murphy was a former New York City police commissioner and the prosecutor in the celebrated 1949 perjury trial of Alger Hiss, a State Department official alleged to have turned over classified information to the Soviet Union. The courtroom was jammed with Rap's supporters; their vocal enthusiasm thoroughly intimidated Judge Murphy. After listening to political activist and feminist Florynce Kennedy and me plead for low bail and a government prosecutor argue for an astronomical figure, the judge abruptly left the courtroom, never to return that day. Instead, one of his law clerks handed me an order, setting bail at a reasonable $15,000. Flo and I mounted the vacant bench and, in unison, read the order aloud. The audience broke into frenzied cheering, and in less than an hour, Jeffrey Glenn, a wealthy, progressive lawyer, posted bail.

Rap was then arraigned in New Orleans, where a judge restricted his travel to the Southern District of New York—which consists of Manhattan, the Bronx, and a few counties north of the city—and to necessary court appearances in Louisiana. Rap was tried on the federal weapons charge in Louisiana before District Judge Lansing Mitchell, who, from the start, appeared very prejudiced against him. During the trial, I pulled a flashy stunt after a stewardess testified that when she saw Rap on the plane to New Orleans, he had with him a gun case that looked as if it contained a rifle. I surreptitiously removed the gun, then stretched out the empty case so that it appeared to still contain the weapon. During cross, I asked the stewardess, "Are you certain that this is what you saw on the plane?"

"Yes," she answered.

"And you're sure that it had a gun in it, right?"

When she said, "Yes," I tossed the empty case at her and it sort of buckled in the middle. She gasped, as did many others in the courtroom. During my summation, I told the jury that things are not always what they seem, that there was no real proof Rap had the gun in the case while he was en route to Louisiana.

Rap was found not guilty of transporting the gun from New York to Louisiana but convicted of transporting it on the return trip. Without bothering to wait for the usual presentence report from the probation department, Mitchell gave Rap the heaviest sentence possible: five years in jail and a fine of $45,000. Then, in order to get Rap out of Louisiana as fast as he could, he continued his bail, pending the outcome of the inevitable appeal.

In February 1968, Rap traveled to California to meet me; I was at a "Free Huey" rally at the Oakland Auditorium. (Panther founder Huey Newton was in prison for killing an Oakland police officer.) The morning after Rap returned to New York, he was arrested for violating the terms of his bond—he had traveled outside the limited area of Louisiana and the Southern District of New York—even though he explained that he had gone to California to consult with his attorney about his Cambridge, Maryland, case.

When I landed in New York from California, I was given a police escort to the federal court in Manhattan. There I explained that Rap had come to Oakland to consult me about the Cambridge prosecution, and the judge reinstated his bail. A few months later, in May, Rap resigned as chairman of SNCC. Like Lenny Bruce, Huey Newton, the Chicago defendants, and so many others, he had no time or energy to do any organizing; it all went into fighting his legal cases.

In 1969, when Rap wrote his autobiography, *Die, Nigger, Die,* SNCC changed its name from Nonviolent to National and again elected him chairman.

A year later, in March 1970, along with Newark attorney Carl Broge, I was preparing for trial in Rap's Maryland case and staying in a motel near Bel Air. The case had been moved there from Cambridge because of prejudice in that community. Rap was not around; he was staying as far as possible from the court proceedings. One night, a car with two men in it was blown to bits a few blocks from where we were staying. When I saw the accident scene, with half a human brain slowly sliding down a stop sign, I was very much afraid that Rap was dead. One victim turned out to be Ralph Featherstone, a SNCC member and former schoolteacher from Chicago, someone I had liked very much. Another SNCC member, William "Che" Payne, was also killed.

Although there were suspicious tire tracks near the explosion site that were never explained, the authorities insisted that the two victims had been killed while transporting a bomb.

The day after these killings, a bomb seriously damaged the Cambridge courthouse. The next morning, the Bel Air judge asked us to accompany him to a garage where the remains of the bombed car had been assembled. "If you think I'm going to subject my county to any more such violence," he told Broge and me, "you've got another think coming." He then put the case on a back burner, where it has simmered ever since.

While all this was going on, Rap went underground for about a year and was on the FBI's 10 Most Wanted List, one of the Bureau's public relations creations. He never contacted me. When I next saw him, in October 1971, he was lying in a New York hospital bed, nearly dead, after being shot by police. The police claimed that Rap and three members of the Black Liberators of St. Louis, allegedly an armed street gang, had held up twenty-five customers in the Red Carpet Lounge on West Eighty-fifth Street in Manhattan. Rap's codefendants told me they were not committing an ordinary robbery but wanted to rip off a drug dealer there who had been selling drugs to students at nearby predominantly black Brandeis High School.

Although many people believed Rap and his cohorts were guilty of armed robbery, I did not. I think the whole incident evolved from idealistic convictions and attempts to stop the exploitation of black children. Each of Rap's codefendants told me exactly the same story. Based on my long association with Rap, I was convinced, and remain so to this day, that he was not a venal criminal.

When I saw him in the hospital, he pretended he didn't know me and said, "Who is this man?" He was trying to keep his identity secret. In early 1973, Howard Moore and I defended Rap in this case on charges of armed robbery and the attempted murder of a police officer. (The prosecutor, Jack Litman, later became a defense attorney whose roster of clients included Robert Chambers, the "Preppie Murderer.") Rap was convicted of the other charges, but the jury hung on the charge of attempted murder, and no effort was ever made by the state to retry him.

Rap served three years in prison, 1973–76, for the New York conviction and during that time became a Sunni Muslim and changed his name to Jamil Abdullah Al-Amin. His health was bad due to the after-effects of the gunshot wound, but after a number of operations, he was eventually strong enough to play on the Greenhaven Correctional Facility football team. Once, I watched the cons against the police at the Hofstra University stadium, and I recall that the end of the football field had a wide-open gate. I had an image of Rap running out of the stadium as he went to catch a pass and going underground again. But, of course, he didn't.

The reversal of his New Orleans conviction was due to a lucky accident. Rap and I had written an article for *University Review* during slow moments in the New York trial which told how the authorities had been after him since the late 1960s. A colonel, just retired from the Marine Corps and newly admitted to the Louisiana bar as a patent lawyer, happened to read the article and sent me a postcard.

Oh, my God, we've got something here! I thought when I read the card. At a meeting of the Louisiana Bar Association in Biloxi, Mississippi, the colonel had overheard the judge in the gun case, Lansing Mitchell, say: "I've got to keep my health, because I'm gonna try the Rap Brown case and I wanna get that nigger."

I immediately brought a proceeding in Louisiana to get rid of Rap's five-year sentence, pointing out that the judge had been prejudiced. There was a marvelous hearing, one of the best I've ever had, in which Mitchell, on the stand, would not say unequivocally that he had not made that incriminating statement. Instead, he made a very weak denial: "I don't think I would have said that." Although the hearing judge concluded that Mitchell had indeed said these words, he still did not set aside Rap's convictions.

The Court of Appeals for the Fifth Circuit, after argument by Elizabeth Schneider, one of the CCR's young attorneys, finally did set the verdict aside, ruling that Judge Mitchell's expressed prejudice made the trial presumptively unfair. The government never attempted to retry the case.

One of my happiest memories was Rap's wedding to Lynne Doswell, now known as Karima, at my house in Westchester. A Unitarian minister from the White Plains Community Church conducted a beautiful ceremony inside the house while, outside, New York City cops patrolled the block in the old green-and-whites. Murphy Bell, a Baton Rouge lawyer and my cocounsel in the Louisiana gun case, brought a wedding cake baked by Rap's mother. It was slightly lopsided from being on a plane but nevertheless was as beautiful as the wedding, and quite edible.

Today Jamil and Karima, who is now a law school graduate, have two boys and live in Atlanta, where Jamil runs a grocery store in the Muslim community. Every time I'm in Atlanta, I visit with him and eat pickles; he's got the best kosher dills I have ever tasted.

Rap, once six and a half feet of burning rage—"If you give me a gun, I just might shoot Lady Bird"—is now the imam, or spiritual leader, of his community. He is working to raise funds for construction of a mosque, and knowing Rap and his religious fervor, this mosque will surely be built.

Through the late 1960s and the 1970s, Rap and I spent so much time together and grew so tight that he is my closest friend from those days. There is probably no one I love more among men than H. Rap Brown; with him, I broke my old childhood pattern of remaining a bit of a loner and not forming intimate friendships. I think he shares my feeling, because he never fails to call me when he's in New York, even if he has nothing much to say except "How's the family?"

Rap and I were in Memphis a couple of years ago for the dedication of the National Civil Rights Museum at the site of the old Lorraine Motor Inn where Martin was assassinated. The occasion provided an emotional reunion for many of us, black and white, who had participated in the movement. When I got up on the podium to introduce Rap, I tried to speak, but I totally broke down and could not continue. He stood up, put an arm around me, and led me back to my seat. "I'm a sentimental fool," I whispered.

He whispered back, "No, you're an old friend."

CHAPTER TEN

Renegades

I just can't understand why they did this to me.

1967
Adam Clayton Powell

THE GOVERNMENT USED SUBTLER TACTICS TO DESTROY REP. ADAM Clayton Powell than it did with rebels like Lenny Bruce or Rap Brown. In his day, Adam had more real power than any black person in America had ever achieved in this country. He served in Congress for twenty-two years, and in addition to this enormous seniority, he was the chair of the important and powerful House Labor and Education Committee.

The entrenched power structure had to be shrewd to oust a man as popular as Adam. A campaign of whispered innuendos was initiated which eventually became the open slander that brought about the end of his career—and his life.

I first met Adam after he had been elected to his eleventh term. He was immensely popular and won solidly in each election in his Eighteenth Congressional District in Harlem. But after the election of November 1966, his fellow congressmen would not allow him to take the oath of office for the term beginning January 1967. The charges against him—including alleged phony travel expenses, alleged illegal payments to his wife, and his rather wild and unconventional lifestyle—made him unfit to sit in Congress, according to his colleagues in the House of Representatives.

Adam's aide Charles Stone invited me to Washington to discuss this exclusion. Arthur Kinoy and I went there together and were ushered into the "presence." In his sumptuous office, Adam asked us to help and said, "Do something. How do we fight them? We gotta fight it." Then he handed us a $2,500 check and left. Along with lawyers Herbert Reid, Frank Reeves, and Jean Camper Cahn, Arthur and I litigated Congress's refusal to allow Adam to take his oath.

During the course of the case, I visited Adam in Harlem and in Bimini, where he had a second home. In both places, he could always be found at his favorite tavern, playing dominoes and drinking what seemed to me a strange combination, scotch and milk, which he loved. In Harlem, he spent his time at the Red Rooster on Seventh Avenue, now Adam Clayton Powell Boulevard. (Once black leaders are safely dead, streets, schools, or projects are named after them.) In Bimini, Adam often took me out on his runabout, *Adam's Fancy,* where I was reminded by the presence of oxygen tanks on board that he had a serious heart condition.

Adam was always his own man, even arrogant, for he had grown used to having things his own way for many years. He could have passed as white but chose to be a black man and strongly identified with his race. During his lifetime, he had several wives, numerous lovers, and many children.

An example of his arrogance was his refusal to participate at all in a New York legal case, just prior to his problems with Congress, that was brought against him by a woman named Esther James. She sued Adam for libel after he had allegedly described her as a "bag woman"—a distributor of illegal funds. She won the lawsuit and was awarded a sizable judgment, but Adam erred by ignoring the entire case and not showing up in court for any of the legal proceedings.

In our efforts to have Adam reinstated in Congress, we represented him first, and unsuccessfully, at the House Judiciary Committee hearings that followed his exclusion. Then we filed a lawsuit based on our argument that Adam met all three of the qualifications necessary to be a congressman—citizenship, a minimum age of twenty-five, and residency in the appropriate district. At trial, we argued that while Congress might have the power to expel a member, it had no authority to prevent an elected individual from taking the oath of office.

We were unsuccessful and were headed to the U.S. Supreme Court when Arthur became suddenly ill with tachycardia, a rapid heartbeat. Without the benefit of his help, I drafted a certiorari petition which had to be filed with the Supreme Court within ninety days. (If the court were to grant certiorari, it would mean that four or more of the justices believed the lower court decision merited review.) I wasted precious days trying to convince the board of trustees of the Abyssinian Baptist Church, where Adam was the lead minister, to pay the huge printing bill. Because of delays, I didn't receive the final printed copies of the petition until late in the afternoon on the very last day for filing. Forty copies had to be filed before midnight, so I called Henry Williams, who is now a judge but was then Adam's personal lawyer, and asked for help.

"I'm wiped out here, Henry," I said. "I've got the petition. Can you go down and file it in Washington? The ninetieth day is up at midnight tonight." Somehow we got him on the last shuttle to Washington. He landed in the capital at about 11:00 P.M. and raced in the pouring rain to the Supreme Court building. The guard on duty stamped in the petition just minutes before midnight.

Lo and behold, the Supreme Court granted the petition, took the case, and set April 21, 1969, as the date for the argument. Our assertion that Congress had violated the Constitution when it would not allow Adam to take his oath of office had apparently interested at least four members of the high court. By this time, Arthur was fully recovered, and our team decided that he should make the argument, along with Herbert Reid, who later became dean of the Howard University Law School. I was not overjoyed. It's always a thrill to argue before the Supreme Court, and I would have loved to do it. But I have no regrets. With Adam sitting in the courtroom, watching and listening closely, Arthur and Herb did an outstanding job.

Arthur and I have completely different styles. He is a syllogistic arguer, moving from the minor to the major premise. Because he is small, with a booming voice and a histrionic manner, he represents the little guy fighting the forces of evil, which is usually a most persuasive image. In contrast, I am more folksy, use more humor, and don't often become heated and angry. In this case, although there is no doubt that I wanted to make the argument, Arthur was clearly the best man.

Two months later, in *Powell v. McCormick,* the Supreme Court validated our argument that Adam had been unconstitutionally denied his seat in the House. Although Adam was thrilled with the victory, it was soon evident that it came much too late for him. He never recovered from the psychological blows he suffered from the treachery of his fellow congressmen. Although we had won in the Supreme Court, Adam never returned to Congress. Before the next general election, Charles Rangel, sensing that Adam was vulnerable, ran successfully against him in the Democratic primary and today still occupies his seat. (Ironically, Adam Clayton Powell IV, one of Adam's sons, is contemplating challenging Rangel for the Democratic nomination at the next primary election.)

At about the same time, Adam's live-in lover, a former beauty queen, ran away with the captain of his boat. I had just given Adam a funny book called *Sex after Sixty,* but after she ran off, the book did not seem very humorous. Losing this woman must have been the final blow, because Adam died a short time later. His heart, broken by his colleagues in Congress, with whom he had worked for a generation, finally gave out. I last saw him lying in his coffin in the Abyssinian Baptist Church. As I filed by, I could not resist saying, "Goodbye, Congressman Powell." A woman behind me in line said through her sobs, "He'll always be my congressman."

Adam may have had organic physical ailments, but he would have lived a lot longer had he not been so devastated over what had happened to him. For months before his death, he would say wearily: "I just can't understand why they did this to me." He thought Claude Pepper of Florida and many other colleagues had betrayed him. And he could never understand this betrayal, for they were accusing him of acts they also had committed.

Despite his years of service and his seniority, safe seat, and committee chairmanship, Adam was destroyed in the end because he was, to his enemies, a nigger with too much power. Black leaders who begin to rise to prominence are either killed, destroyed by criminal charges, or ruined by gossip and innuendo. Think of Marcus Garvey, Martin Luther King, Medgar Evers, and Malcolm X. If a black political figure manages to gain significant clout, the Establishment will go after him and knock him out of the ring. In Adam's case, those in authority saw to it that his faults were magnified so that he could be eliminated.

For the last twenty years, this country has been experiencing what I call a second post-Reconstruction period. During the first post-Reconstruction period, the dominant white community eliminated every black official who had been elected or appointed in the Deep South during the few years immediately following the

Civil War. One hundred years later, even after the struggles of the civil rights movement and the passage of the Voting Rights Act of 1965, only 2 percent of elected and appointed officials are black. But 40 percent of indicted politicians are black.

Since blacks are the largest minority, the Establishment must make certain they never become organized under a single leader; that would threaten the existing order of power. This is an undeniable part of American history: No black leader has ever survived who had the potential to unite the national black community.

1968
The Berrigans

During the late 1960s, the antiwar movement took up more and more of my time, replacing my civil rights cases. I represented many clients who were arrested for actions that attempted to push the United States to end the war in Vietnam. One of the most charismatic antiwar leaders, Father Daniel Berrigan, first called me from prison in 1968 and asked me to join a team of lawyers who were defending his group, the Catonsville Nine, against charges of destroying government property.

On May 17, 1968, along with seven other Catholic antiwar protesters, Dan and his brother, Philip, entered a draft board in Catonsville, Maryland, removed five hundred files of young men who were classified 1-A, and set them afire in a nearby parking lot. They used homemade napalm as fuel to protest the napalm bombs then being dropped by the United States in Vietnam. They held hands and prayed and waited to be arrested as the fire burned.

Since the government property they destroyed had a value of more than $100, the crime was classified as a federal felony. I worked on a defense team along with local lawyer Harold Buchman, William J. Cunningham, a Jesuit attorney, and Cornell law professor Harrop A. Freeman.

While the Catonsville Nine were awaiting trial and discussing trial tactics, I learned more about the power and meaning of political conviction and the subjugation of legal maneuvers to such convictions. Dan told me right off, "We don't want a jury trial because we don't want to participate in the selection of a jury. That would make it look as if we think the legal system is legitimate."

"We've got to have a jury," I insisted. "A jury gives us an

audience and will also educate America because it represents the public."

"We don't want a jury." Dan was adamant.

"Maybe," I said, "we can work out something, because, as a lawyer, I feel that it makes a better trial with a jury. That way, you're not putting it all in the hands of a judge. You're going to lose, anyway, because you burnt the draft records, and you never hid that fact."

This was before Chicago, before I was radicalized, so I still viewed myself as a legal Lord Bountiful, the great savior delivering the poor struggling masses. I was the professional, I thought, and the clients were babes in the legal woods who should follow my advice.

Some years earlier, in Wordsworth Chapel on the campus of Tougaloo, when I met Freedom Riders who were due in court the next day, I told them to dress neatly, be quiet, and listen to the proceedings. I would never do that today. Now I believe that people should wear what they damn well please and not cater to the system. And that lawyers should be guided by their clients' politics, not by their own legal agenda.

Emotionally, I wanted to be the star in all my cases, but during the sixties I learned that I had to listen to movement people and tailor my actions to their needs. Arthur Kinoy once told me a story about Lenin, who, before the Bolshevik Revolution, was informed that the person operating the mimeograph machine was a tsarist spy. "Well, how is he at mimeographing?" Lenin asked. "He's excellent," was the answer. "Well," Lenin said, "watch him and keep him working." I feel that way now, that a lawyer is just another worker who serves a function—no more, no less, important than that of the Russian at the mimeograph machine.

If the Catonsville Nine case had occurred after the Chicago trial, I would have agreed with Dan Berrigan completely when he said no jury. But in the spring of 1968, I was still the good liberal lawyer, believing in the justice system and insisting that its rules be followed.

Although I was used to handing out legal advice, not taking it, Dan and I eventually hammered out a compromise. We would have a jury, but the defense would not participate in selecting it and would make no challenges to any member. Any challenges would be those exercised by the prosecution; we would sit mute, accepting all jurors who ended up in the box.

From this interchange with Dan Berrigan, a man whose principles were rock solid, I learned that I couldn't have it all my way and that a reasonable alternative could be worked out if it met the political necessity of the client.

For the duration of the Catonsville Nine trial, in the autumn of 1969, I stayed in Baltimore with my sister, Mary, and her family. Every night, the Catonsville supporters had either a rally or a teach-in, and I usually participated. Because of who the defendants were, I looked forward to an insightful and moving experience in the courtroom; in the end, it far exceeded my expectations. The nine—including priests, nuns, missionaries, an artist, a nurse, and George Mische, who had worked with the Alliance for Progress in Central America—were marvelous in court, sitting together on a bench and testifying most eloquently. They told about their lives before they burned the draft records, including those who had been in Guatemala helping the people against the ruling military dictatorship. From them I learned about "liberation theology," a more progressive strand of the Catholic Church which challenges the offical, traditional church doctrine.

Daniel, a Jesuit priest, is poetic, with a great sense of drama and a warm, lovely speaking voice. Philip Berrigan, a Josephite priest, was more robust and had already been convicted for pouring chicken blood on files at a Baltimore draft board. Phil was not as lyrical in speech or outlook as Dan but he was equally committed to pacifism. Philip was later excommunicated from the church when he married former nun Elizabeth McAlister.

During the trial, after Dan's testimony, he turned to the judge and said, "Your Honor, I would like to recite the Lord's Prayer." The judge was startled, clearly didn't know what to do, and asked the U.S. attorney, "What is the government's position on this?"

To his eternal credit, Steven Sachs, the prosecutor, said, "The government has no objection, Your Honor, and would join in the prayer." As Dan began reciting the prayer, many in the audience stood, some holding lighted candles. The judge stood. The lawyers stood. We recited the Lord's Prayer, probably the first time it was ever said in an American courtroom. It was one of the most stirring moments of courtroom drama I have ever experienced.

Before the jury began its deliberations, we lawyers asked the judge to include in his instructions to the panel that it should acquit the Catonsville Nine if it found the defendants had acted according to their consciences and without intent to commit a crime in the normal sense. In essence, we requested that the jury be allowed to put conscience above the law. The judge refused.

He also admonished me when I told him I intended to use part of Andrew Hamilton's summation in the famous 1735 John Peter Zenger case. Zenger, publisher of the *New York Journal,* a Colonial newspaper, had been charged with libeling New York's royal governor, Sir William Cosby, by publishing statements that the governor had grabbed most of the Mohawk Valley for himself. Zenger admitted printing the statements about the governor but insisted they were not libelous because they were true. Hamilton argued brilliantly, urging the jurors to use their consciences in their decision.

Hamilton said:

> The power is in your hands, gentlemen, to safeguard our liberties. If you should be of the opinion that there is no falsehood in Mr. Zenger's papers, you will, nay, you ought, to say so. . . . [You must] support liberty, the only bulwark against lawless power. Nature and the laws of our country have given us a right—the liberty—both of exposing arbitrary power . . . by speaking and writing truth.

Zenger was acquitted. Unlike our current libel laws, which are civil in nature and require dismissal if the statement is true, libel was a criminal charge under the operative law of that time, and the only consideration was whether a statement impugned a public official, whether or not it was true. From the moment Zenger was acquitted, freedom of the press became an accepted concept in the thirteen colonies. That was more than a half century before the First Amendment was enacted.

It was important that the Catonsville Nine jury be permitted to vote their consciences. When the judge threatened to hold me in contempt for quoting from Hamilton's summation, I was sufficiently intimidated to change my statement. I would like to believe that later in my career I would have had a different reaction and fearlessly followed through on my plan. However, prior to Chicago, I had not yet adopted the attitude that lawyers must take chances with their liberty, and with their licenses, to advance their client's political views.

Ever since Chicago, I have tried to follow what was formerly Canon 15 of the Canons of Professional Ethics for lawyers: "No fear of judicial disfavor or public unpopularity should restrain him [the lawyer] from the full discharge of his duty." That I hold this belief and no longer allow anything to frighten me out of performing as a fully committed defense attorney, neither the anger of a judge nor the disapproval of the public, is partially why I have difficulties with some judges and am very unpopular in certain quarters.

At any rate, back in the autumn of 1969, I improvised and gave what I thought was an adequate summation, telling the jury that Dan and Phil and the rest of the Nine had first tried other means to stop the slaughter in Vietnam, including petitions, marches, letters to the editor, and electoral politics, but nothing had worked. They then had burned the draft records in order to make the world take notice, thinking that the destruction of little bits of paper in Catonsville, Maryland, might prevent the destruction of human life in Vietnam.

We lost, and the Nine were convicted and sentenced to prison terms. We appealed, claiming that we had the right to raise the conscience issue and let the jury know they were empowered to nullify the law. One great concept in both British and American law is that juries can override the law, since they are supposedly the conscience of the community. In fact, in several state courts, including Maryland, the jury is informed that it may act as judge, both of law and fact, so that if it doesn't like the law, it can disregard it. But this case was being tried in a federal court where that concept did not pertain.

During the appeal, I argued that the jury, acting as the conscience of the American people, should be able to say: Yes, they burned the draft records. Yes, the draft records are government property. Yes, under ordinary circumstances, it's a crime to destroy government property with a value of more than $100. But we think that under the circumstances what the Nine did was right and that we should not apply that law.

The circuit court of appeals wrote a lengthy opinion praising the defendants but denied my application, stating that juries could not nullify the law even in cases where they thought they were dealing with good people who had the best of intentions.

The Catonsville Nine were ordered to prison, but Dan, Phil, and a nurse, Mary Moylan, went into hiding instead. The FBI captured Dan at a friend's home on Block Island. Phil sought refuge in St. Gregory the Great, a Manhattan church, after Father Harry Brown, a strong supporter of his, offered him sanctuary. The church, in my old neighborhood on Ninety-first Street, was where my mother, at her ecumenical best, had once obtained her St. Anthony medals.

When the FBI tried to barge into the church, Father Brown stood before them, crucifix in hand, and said, "I have given this man sanctuary, and you cannot enter."

Sanctuary, of course, is a medieval concept and not recognized by American law, so the FBI agents disregarded the whole thing and went in after Phil. Both Phil and Dan each served three years, most of it at the Danbury Federal Correctional Institution in Connecticut, where I went to see them regularly. When Jessica and Daniel Philip Goldman were born—Karin's twins, my first grandchildren—I took them to the prison and held them up to a window for Dan and Phil to bless. I was very sorry that the Berrigans later were punished by prison authorities for this blessing because of a rule that imprisoned priests could not perform religious services. Today I am most pleased that two of my grandchildren were graced by the benediction of these marvelous men and that my oldest grandson bears both their names.

1969
Fred Hampton

As peaceful civil rights action turned militant, even the Student National Coordinating Committee fell into disarray, and eventually the Black Panthers became the voice for blacks seeking change. And with their slogan All Power to the People, the Panthers eventually came to represent the change advocated by all progressive people in the sixties, not blacks alone. After Rap's tenure as its head, SNCC all but merged with the Panthers, a group as different in ideology from Martin's Southern Christian Leadership Conference as possible.

Police harassment of black radicals and revolutionaries, especially the Panthers, escalated. Panthers were arrested, tried, convicted, and jailed despite the brilliant strategy created by their chief counsel, Charles Garry. In this strategy, used first at Huey Newton's 1967 trial for shooting a police officer, Charlie attacked rather than defended. He charged that law enforcement was homicidal and the criminal justice system so infected with racism that blacks could not get a fair trial. It was a tactic that I used in my own Panther cases—and, of course, in Chicago.

On December 4, 1969, while the Chicago trial was on, the charismatic head of the Illinois Panther party, Fred Hampton, and another Panther, Mark Clark, were assassinated by Chicago police officers and FBI agents. Fred, drugged by an infiltrator, was shot to death while he slept. He was twenty years old. The authorities tried to hide the truth from the public and even created a false videotaped version of the incident. The official version was that a routine warrant to search a Panther hangout on Chicago's West Side had backfired and when the authorities tried to enter, they were met with a barrage of gunfire.

Officers and agents claimed they had only fired in self-defense. But this was a complete lie. The cover-up was exposed when forensic expert Herbert Leon MacDonell proved conclusively that except for one, all of the hundred or so bullets recovered from the scene had been fired by law enforcement officers.

MacDonell, whose testimony was critical to the case against the authorities, did not share the politics of the Panthers, but he had an open mind. In a later book about his work, MacDonell and coauthor Alfred Allan Lewis wrote:

> Mr. MacDonell had no more sympathy for the aims and practices of the Black Panther Party than the FBI, but there was one fundamental point on which he differed with the agency: What the evidence revealed must never be concealed, no matter whom it vindicated.

The charges against surviving Panthers were dismissed, and the Hampton family eventually received a substantial cash settlement. I had known Fred Hampton well; he was a very courageous man whose loss to the movement and to his family was immeasurable. He was another casualty in the government's ongoing war against dissent.

1969
Abbie Hoffman

Unlike Lenny Bruce, Fred Hampton, and countless other renegades and rebels, Abbie Hoffman survived the sixties. I met him first in the South in the late 1960s and then represented him in 1966 before the House Un-American Activities Committee. I came to know him well during the Chicago trial, when we spent five months together. Abbie was a complicated and brilliant iconoclast whose ideas and actions brought spirit and zest to the movement. His method of fighting the Establishment, the war in

Vietnam, the government's repression of dissent, was to tweak noses, make fun, and wreak havoc through humor.

After the HUAC hearing, I met and worked with Abbie at various other sixties events, including the levitation of the Pentagon in 1967. Then, a month before the Chicago trial began, in August 1969, Abbie invited me to the Woodstock Music and Arts Festival in upstate New York. "Come see how the flower children live," he said. "I don't think you're too old to play at being young for a few days." Of course, I went, even though, at fifty, I was older than just about everyone there.

When I arrived, I went first to a tent that Abbie had set up for festivalgoers who had taken too many drugs and needed medical and psychological treatment. "Billy, remember that you're a lawyer and don't take off all of your clothes," Abbie told me. "I would also advise you, if you're going to smoke grass or drop acid, to do it in the tent and not out in the open. You're too big a fish for the narcs to overlook."

At Woodstock, no one could avoid getting stoned; the marijuana fumes were so intense you could get high just walking through the crowds. Most of the time, I stayed near Abbie's tent, listening to music and talking. He and I smoked a little grass, and some of the other people who were there dropped acid. I didn't, because a few years earlier, I had tried it and found the absolute loss of boundaries within my consciousness frightening.

Abbie talked about how wonderful it was that half a million people had traveled to Yasgur's Farm, where the festival was held, to hear Janis Joplin, Jimi Hendrix, Richie Havens, and the other talented performers and to make a public declaration of love for each other. The mythic and symbolic Woodstock Nation was born at this festival, the spiritual home of all free spirits like Abbie Hoffman. Forever after, he would describe himself as a child of Woodstock.

At some point during the festival, I became extremely aware of my age: I was a lover of opera and Rodgers and Hammerstein–style musicals, not rock and roll. Although I listened to the music along with the rest of that vast audience, I wasn't completely with it and realized that no matter how I tried, I simply could not identify fully with these young people. But I enjoyed the experience—at least until the thunderstorm came. As the earth turned into mud, I decided that it was time for me to go home.

Abbie and I remained close during the years after Woodstock. When we saw each other, we would share laughter and wonderful conversation. In 1974, he was arrested for selling cocaine to an undercover agent. He had obviously been set up, as were so many other counterculture and antiwar leaders of the day, in order to get him out of circulation. But Abbie fooled the government; he loved to fool the government. Instead of getting caught up—like Rap, Stokely, and so many others—in a lengthy court battle, Abbie went underground and remained there for six long years. During that time, using the symbolic alias Barry Freed, he became a community organizer in upstate New York, working to prevent the construction of a dam on the St. Lawrence River. While he was underground, he called me often but never said his name over the phone. I always knew it was Abbie, though, as soon as he said, "Hello, Billy." Other than my parents, he was the only person I ever knew who always called me Billy.

Sometimes we would meet for lunch in a Greenwich Village restaurant and have a wonderful time, even with the specter of Abbie's fugitive status hanging over us. "If they catch me while I'm with you," he'd say, "at least I'll have a lawyer from the git-go. I'll swear that I just happened to run into you and that we didn't plan it. If they don't believe that malarkey, then you'll just have to do your lawyer thing, and we'll hope for the best."

When Abbie decided to surface and face the cocaine-selling charge, he did it on nationwide television in keeping with his love of publicity. He appeared in an interview with Barbara Walters on September 3, 1980. He turned himself in, pleaded guilty to one count of sale of cocaine to an undercover agent, and served a brief sentence, most of it at a drug treatment center in New York. After his release, he continued organizing, mainly against the Central Intelligence Agency's being allowed to recruit on college campuses. He also did some stand-up comedy and was in demand as a guest speaker at many colleges.

He called me often, from wherever he was, and told me he was homesick for New York. "Billy, I want to move back to the Village," he would say. "Try to get me a cheap apartment, East or West Village. I don't feel right not being where the action is. Please, please, try your damnedest to find me a place for low bucks, with a nice view." I never could find an inexpensive enough place for him.

During the late 1980s, Abbie lived in a converted poultry coop in Pennsylvania, writing books and articles and continuing his work against the CIA, and opposing the pollution of the Delaware River. The place had pet llamas, and Abbie used to ride one that he had named "Fernando Llama." Once, when I visited him, I tried to ride Fernando, but he refused to be mounted and spit at me.

On April 12, 1989, Abbie was found dead in that converted coop. He had taken an overdose of barbiturates, which some of his friends linked to a manic-depressive disorder from which he suffered. The coroner's report said it was suicide, but it's also possible that Abbie's work protesting the CIA's presence on college campuses provoked enough anger to endanger his life. Although some, including Dave Dellinger, believe this scenario is most probable, in the absence of any concrete evidence to the contrary, I accept that it was an accidental death due to an overdose.

Abbie had been very depressed. Writer William Styron, who wrote about his own experiences with depression, said that Abbie most likely did not intend to kill himself; that's why he left no suicide note. What he intended to do, what he tried to do by taking all those pills, was to stop the pain. Anyone that depressed, according to Styron, will do anything to end the hurting, including taking drug after drug after drug.

Abbie was just fifty-two when he died. I miss his jokes, warmth, wit, and irreverence. I miss the intimacy we shared, like the New Year's Eve during the Chicago Conspiracy Trial when he cooked a chicken—he loved to cook—and we had a couple of glasses of wine, laughed a lot, and fell asleep by eleven. I miss the rush of excitement and happiness I felt whenever I heard his raspy, gravelly voice saying, "Hello, Billy." During the Chicago trial, Abbie described himself as "a child of America." Despite his sophisticated political savvy, underneath the veneer of a man who was so anti-Establishment that he named one of his sons amerika, there was another Abbie. This Abbie's essential innocence was shown in his strong, everlasting faith that the world could indeed be made a better place. Abbie may be dead and buried, in the literal sense of those words, but to me he is, and will always be, as he once wrote, "anywhere and everywhere."

CHAPTER ELEVEN

Death and
Destruction

Now Vietnam and Kent State are one!

1969
The Weathermen

Bᴙ 1968 ᴀɴᴅ 1969, ᴛʜᴇ ᴘᴏʟɪᴛɪᴄᴀʟ ᴀɴᴅ ꜱᴏᴄɪᴀʟ ᴍᴏᴠᴇᴍᴇɴᴛ ᴡʜɪᴄʜ ʜᴀᴅ its origins in the southern civil rights struggles of the 1950s had changed its goals and methods. The antiwar movement appeared to take precedence temporarily over civil rights, and the youthful antiwar leaders, who had begun by sticking flowers in the gun barrels of soldiers, now themselves became increasingly militant.

The end of 1969 and the beginning of 1970 brought a reign of terror. The government was even more paranoid and brutal in its attacks on young political leaders, and the rhetoric of violence became a reality. As the government became more vicious, political actions became more militant. What had been a movement became a revolution, and with that change the demise of the sixties was in the air.

Students for a Democratic Society (SDS), whose Port Huron Statement had inspired the antiwar movement, divided into different factions. The most aggressive group called itself "the Weathermen." Taking their name from the Bob Dylan lyric "You don't need a weatherman to know which way the wind blows," the Weathermen were to the SDS what the Black Panthers were to SNCC—a radicalized, combative version of the earlier group. The

198

Weathermen were going to change the system not by nonviolence or burning draft cards but with bombs, guns, death, and destruction.

Protests became rebellions, and marches turned into uprisings. Where once Martin Luther King and his followers knelt stoically as they were beaten and arrested, the Weathermen and other revolutionary groups thought there was a better, quicker way to achieve change. Bombings and other violent acts were not uncommon.

While I thought some of the violence was too extreme and counterproductive, I certainly understood the frustration and anger that generated it. And I admired the Weathermen's dedication to a world without racism and oppression and their willingness to jeopardize themselves to attain it. The government's crushing repression of dissent, its cruel and unjust tactics, had created in many a belief that fascism in America was a real possibility.

On October 8, 1969, the second anniversary of the death of Che Guevara, one year after Convention Week and two weeks after the start of the Chicago Conspiracy Trial, the Weathermen erupted in Chicago in the "Days of Rage." Unlike the chaotic protests a year earlier at the Democratic National Convention, Days of Rage was a military-style maneuver, planned and executed to be a revolutionary act. But the promise of the first half of 1969 died in the streets of Chicago when Days of Rage degenerated into sporadic property damage. Not even the Weathermen, with all their commitment and intensity, could organize the rebellious youth of America.

For all the media and public attention they received, the Weathermen were actually a very small group who shared passionate political beliefs and a commitment to changing the system. They traveled from college to college, gathering support, establishing bases, and, of course, attracting the attention of the FBI.

On March 6, 1970, three Weathermen died when bombs inside a town house on West Eleventh Street in Greenwich Village accidentally detonated. Two Weathermen fled from the scene: Kathy Boudin, the child of my old friend, progressive attorney Leonard Boudin, and Cathlyn Wilkerson, daughter of the building's owner. The night of the explosion, Dustin Hoffman, who lived next door, stood in the street in his pajamas and robe, afraid that his house was going to collapse. I wondered if the movement could withstand the fallout from this tragic explosion.

A month before this blast, most of the Weathermen had gone underground as a political statement. Calling themselves the Weather Underground, they had decided to remove themselves physically from the daily life of America and carry out the revolution from hiding places, as fugitives. They maintained communication with people like Abbie Hoffman, other movement leaders, and, occasionally, me. A go-between would contact me and direct me to a designated safe house where they would ask me eagerly for information about what was going on in legal circles and with my clients and about the political scene in general.

I enjoyed the cloak-and-dagger aspects of meeting clandestinely with people the government was eager to find and prosecute. The danger also appealed to me because I was always a little uncomfortable with the fact that lawyers took no risks, while our clients took many. Meeting with the Weather Underground gave me a chance to demonstrate that I was ready, willing, and able to take some chances; it increased the camaraderie we felt with each other.

On one occasion, I received directions to drive in a rented car to a Long Island diner, sit at the counter, and order a hamburger. I did so, and within minutes there was a woman on either side of me. "Hello, Bill. We are everywhere," murmured the one disguised in a shapeless dress and red wig. All three of us got into my car, and they directed me to a modest frame house where I met other members of the group. After an hour or so of talk, I left and drove home.

The Weather Underground remained in hiding for years, but by now I believe they are all above ground.

1970
Kent State

What heralded the end of the sixties for some people was the approaching conclusion to the Vietnam War. Nixon seemed determined to pull out of Vietnam; it was tearing his administration apart. Also, the Tet offensive had indicated that the North Vietnamese had sufficient resources and that the south could never win, no matter what the extent of American involvement. After Tet, most people who were opposed to the war knew it was only a matter of time. Even though I hoped it was true, I was still uncertain, given the bellicose announcements constantly emanating from the Pentagon.

For others, the sixties ended with the tragic slaughter of four students at Kent State, a sizable university in Ohio. Nixon had sent American troops into Cambodia, ostensibly to find out whether the Cambodian government was providing shelter for the Vietcong, and this expansion of the hated Vietnam War into a new theater caused college campuses all over the country to erupt in protest, including Kent State.

On May 4, 1970—three months after the end of the Chicago trial—antiwar demonstrators at Kent State were fired upon by National Guardsmen from a vantage point on a hilltop, Blanket Hill. They killed two boys and two girls and wounded nine other people, including one who became paralyzed from the waist down. Of the students killed, two had been demonstrating against the war; the other two were just walking by.

Twenty-four years later, as I watched the funeral of Richard Nixon, the man directly responsible for the Kent State massacre, I was nauseated by the latter-day praise for this murderer and crook. The young blood spilled on Blanket Hill and in Southeast Asia is his only proper epitaph.

After the Kent State murders, more than three hundred college campuses shut down to express their solidarity with students and faculty at the Ohio university as well as their rage at what the government had done. Nixon was so frightened by these protests that he emerged, late one night, from his White House lair to meet with student leaders at the Lincoln Memorial and explain his actions. Eventually, he was forced to withdraw the troops from Cambodia because it seemed that America was on the brink of outright civil war.

Like most Americans, I received the news of the senseless carnage at Kent State with an aching heart. The startling photograph of a young woman screaming in agony as she knelt by one of the victims came to symbolize not only the four deaths but the sinkhole our country had become. Death and destruction were here, too, not just across the ocean. Vietnam and Kent State became synonymous. The war had finally come home.

I was invited to speak at a rally organized to memorialize the dead and provide support for the wounded as well as for the entire Kent State population, which was in shock. I was not allowed on campus, though, because the administration wanted to keep "outside agitators" away, so the meeting was held in the Kove, a college hangout in town. The Kove was wall-to-wall students that day as I talked about the politics behind the shootings. I said that a frightened and paranoid government had chosen to suppress dissent with guns and bullets. Up to that point, the government had quietly been killing only leaders of the movement, such as Fred Hampton. The next step, I said, was sending the National Guard out to shoot all movement people, counterculture people, and hippies.

I promised the Kent State audience that day that if any of them, students or faculty, were charged with crimes of any sort, I would help to organize a legal team to defend them.

Later on, when a grand jury indicted twenty-four Kent State students and one faculty member on riot and related charges, I helped to organize a legal team, which included Ramsey Clark, David Scribner, William Allison, Benjamin Schearer, and several other progressive attorneys. After the first person was acquitted, the rest of the indictments were eventually dropped because the prosecution belatedly recognized that there was no substance to the charges and that they had been instituted only to protect the state from civil suits.

Several years after the massacre, along with Terry Gilbert and a number of other Cleveland lawyers, I filed a federal lawsuit to stop the university from building a gymnasium on Blanket Hill. We argued that the site should be declared a national historic landmark by the federal government and asked the court to enjoin the construction of the gym so that Blanket Hill could remain intact. District judge Thomas Lambros was initially sympathetic to our arguments but in the end ruled that a federal court had no jurisdiction to prevent construction because a site *might* be declared a national landmark. So the gym was built, and I believe it is a travesty that an edifice so prosaic now occupies what is, for many of us, hallowed ground.

One of the most exciting moments in the fight to save Blanket Hill occurred just as the first bulldozers rolled onto the campus. Chic Canfora, one of the students originally indicted and the sister of Alan, who was wounded on May 4, called my office in New York to plead for help. I dictated an emergency motion to her to stop the bulldozers. She took it down in shorthand and then typed it up at a Kent law office. She then rushed to Judge Lambros who, minutes before the court closed, issued an order stopping construction. While our victory was short-lived, it provided the momentum for continued protests against the building of the gym. Almost every year, at the invitation of the May Fourth Task Force, a group organized to preserve the memory of the tragedy, I speak at Kent State on the anniversary of the massacre. On one occasion, Dean Kahler, the student who was paralyzed as a result of his injuries, was onstage alongside Ron Kovic, author of *Born on the Fourth of July*. Ron, a former marine who became an antiwar activist, is also paralyzed from the waist down, the result of his war injuries in Vietnam. After Ron's emotional speech, he wheeled over to Dean, hugged him, and cried out, "Now Vietnam and Kent State are one!" In the audience, people sobbed and shouted, echoing Ron's words: "Vietnam and Kent State—one!"

Directly after the bloodbath at Kent State, I spoke about it often, including in a May 1970 speech before hundreds of Westchester County high school students. From a flatbed truck, I explained that the college students at Kent State had been killed and injured because of their opposition to the unjust war America was fighting in Vietnam. I reminded the high school audience that black college students had recently been shot down by police in Orangeburg, South Carolina, and in Jackson, Mississippi, and that those murders should not be overshadowed by Kent State.

People were dying not only on college campuses and in Vietnam but in the South and in urban ghettos, I said. "The four white lives at Kent State were part of a train of murder and violence that goes back to the lynchings in the South."

I urged my young audience to protest all of these cruel murders by refusing to go to school. "Students should shut every institution of learning in the U.S. Strike every institution . . . do one unequivocal act of faith: Refuse to go to school until there is a unilateral cease-fire. There is no time to waste."

I have no idea how many of these youngsters I may have influenced. But I was very angry. The death and destruction of these last years of the sixties had taken their toll. I became more and more affected by the senseless waste of life all around me, at Kent State, in Jackson and Orangeburg, in Vietnam, in the northern ghettos.

The seeds of my current work were planted during these years as I saw blacks mistreated by the justice system and radicals—black and white—hounded, harassed, even murdered by the government. At the end of the decade and into the 1970s, my practice consisted primarily of political cases. I defended activists and protesters like the Chicago Seven, but also others whom

I believed were victims of the government, of society's racist attitudes, of overt or covert discrimination. Today these are still my
cases, still the clients that I stand up for.

Fame

After Chicago, I thought the publicity would soon die down
and I would sink into relative obscurity. But that was not to be. I
took on client after client in important political cases, and my
name was constantly in the news.

Often my work brought me famous clients. For example, Ber-
trand Russell telephoned me from Stockholm about what he perceived to be an invasion of his privacy by Honeywell, the giant
war matériel firm. At the height of the Vietnam War, Honeywell
had placed an ad for engineers in the *New York Times* which featured three pen-and-ink sketches of noted scientists, including
the dates of each man's birth and death. One sketch was of Lord
Russell, who was very much alive. In addition to this error,
Honeywell had exploited his face and name without permission.

After I negotiated with Honeywell, the company agreed to a
financial settlement, which I promptly sent to Lord Russell. He
wrote me that he was grateful for my help and intended to contrib-
ute the settlement money to one of his peace tribunals; these were
mock trials in which the legality of major political events—like
the Vietnam War—was litigated. He also promised to send me
plane tickets to Stockholm so I could attend the tribunal. Unfortunately, he died before any of this occurred, so I never met him.

Years later, in the 1970s, I had a fleeting relationship with
John Lennon and Yoko Ono when they lived near me on Bank
Street in Greenwich Village. I occasionally went to their apartment, shared a pizza, and talked about John's legal problems—he
had been convicted of marijuana possession in England and so
was threatened with deportation by the United States—the civil
rights movement, and politics in general.

John had contacted me in the early 1970s when I was working
on a murder case in St. Croix, in the U.S. Virgin Islands, with
Margaret Ratner, who would later become my second wife. He
requested that we fly to nearby Trinidad to help a friend of his,
Michael X. Malik, who had been convicted of a murder he hadn't
committed and was about to be hanged.

As Margie and I found out, Malik, who had become radicalized as a result of his meeting Malcolm X in London, was framed

by Eric Williams, the island's prime minister. Williams was afraid that Malik had returned to his native Trinidad to organize a revolution. Margie and I went to Trinidad to retain appellate counsel for Malik and helped organize worldwide opposition to his death sentence. We also went to London, at John Lennon's request, to attempt to get a stay of execution from Queen Elizabeth II. We were unsuccessful; Malik was eventually hanged at the island's Royal Gaol.

1970
White Panthers and Watergate

Only weeks after the Chicago trial ended, Len Weinglass and I went to Detroit to work on a fascinating case involving the White Panthers, Ann Arbor, Detroit-based political revolutionaries and antiwar activists who modeled themselves after the Black Panther party. This case would turn out to have historic consequences. In *U.S. v. Plamondon, Forest and Sinclair,* three men, Lawrence Plamondon, Jack Forest, and John Sinclair, were charged with being leaders of the White Panther party and conspiring to bomb the CIA building in Ann Arbor. The case was assigned to Judge Damon Keith, who today sits on the U.S. Court of Appeals for the Sixth Circuit.

Damon Keith, a black judge who many believe should have received the Supreme Court nomination instead of Clarence Thomas, was wonderful to us and even joked that he would let his hair grow long for the trial. While this trial had the same potential for disruption as the Chicago trial, Judge Keith, the marshals, and other court personnel were well trained, disciplined, and intelligent, so there was absolutely no disorder.

In Chicago, where Judge Hoffman turned off and didn't want to deal with anything and the marshals in the courtroom were often confrontational, the defendants reacted accordingly. But the White Panther case was very different. I am often asked how judges can stop disruptive trials. One answer is to have more judges like Damon Keith. On the first day of trial, he called the prosecutors and defense lawyers into his chambers for a conference; he served, as I recall, very delicious buns and coffee. He broadly hinted to Len and me that he did not expect this trial to be similar to Chicago. We assured him that unless we had the same type of provocations that permeated the Chicago trial, we didn't expect any difficulties.

Pretrial hearings were held to determine if the defendants, who were part of the counterculture, could get a fair trial with a jury composed primarily of older people. In order to get new jurors, we would have to prove that the defendants' class was being denied representation in the jury pool. We called Allen Ginsberg as a witness to demonstrate that the counterculture represented a separate and distinct class: they were young, and they were at odds with the values of the Establishment. Then we called Julian Bond, a former SNCC member and Georgia legislator. Before I could question him, Judge Keith interrupted. "Let me ask you this. You're a black man. Would you prefer to be tried by twelve black jurors over the age of forty or by twelve white jurors under twenty-five?"

Without hesitating, Bond supported our contention that the counterculture represented a separate class when he told the judge that the ages of the jurors would be more important to him than their race. "I would rather be tried by twelve white jurors under twenty-five than twelve black jurors over the age of forty," he said.

The judge reserved decision on our motion for a new jury pool; I think he was actually considering bringing in younger people. But then the issue of wiretaps surfaced, and everything changed. The key evidence against Plamondon, Forest, and Sinclair was contained in tape recordings made of conversations they allegedly had with employees of the Cuban embassy. Before Len and I went to Detroit for the trial, we had moved to suppress these tapes on the grounds that they had been made without a legal warrant. In front of Judge Keith, we engaged in oral argument about whether the tapes could be introduced as evidence.

Under what it called the national security exemption to the Fourth Amendment, the government claimed it could tap phones without a legal warrant if it was done in the interest of national security. Now, the Fourth Amendment mandates that all searches be "reasonable" ones, so Len and I strongly disagreed with any exemption that would violate our clients' Fourth Amendment rights.

Judge Keith issued a marvelous ruling: The tapes could not be introduced as evidence because the government's national security exemption simply did not exist. There was no such exemption, he said. In 1971, the government petitioned the Sixth Circuit of the U.S. Court of Appeals, claiming that the national security

One of my favorite photos, taken in 1985. I am in the garden of my Greenwich Village house surrounded by my four daughters: Karin, then 41, has her arm around me; Sarah, on my lap, was 9; and Jane, then 34, is on the arm of the chair with 7-year-old Emily behind her. *(Maddy Miller)*

Emily, Sarah, and I are out for a jaunt on a lovely spring day. *(Maddy Miller)*

Enjoying a sunny day with my wife, Margaret Ratner. My first marriage ended in the early 1970s. Margie and I were married in 1975.

In December 1973, Jerry Rubin *(left)* and I were jubilant after defendants and lawyers in the Chicago case were cleared of all contempt charges because of the great work done by my close friend and lawyer, Morty Stavis *(right)*, on our appeals. *(AP/Wide World)*

At a powwow in South Dakota, attempting a traditional Native American dance. *(Maddy Miller)*

In 1980, black leaders, including Stokely Carmichael *(left)* and H. Rap Brown *(right)*, called for a congressional investigation into the FBI's illegal COINTELPRO operation. For at least two decades, this "counterintelligence" program infiltrated and disrupted political movements, destroyed many black leaders' reputations and ability to lead, and even caused the murders of some of them. *(AP/Wide World)*

Jerry Rubin **Abbie Hoffman** **William Kunstler**

Almost two decades after the Chicago trial, some of the defendants and I posed with actors who played us in an HBO version of the case. From left to right are Jerry Rubin, Abbie Hoffman, me, and Dave Dellinger. Behind us are the actors who played Jerry and Abbie, the producer, the actor who played Bobby Seale, and, in a white jacket, Bobby himself. *(AP/Wide World)*

In 1985, the progressive National Lawyers Guild threw a dinner in my honor. Sparkler in hand, I celebrated the birthday of Harry Belafonte, an old friend and ardent supporter of civil rights and other political movements. *(Maddy Miller)*

Jubilant, I celebrate the December 1991 acquittal of my client, El Sayyid Nosair, who had been charged with assassinating Rabbi Meir Kahane. Nosair has now been targeted by the government as a leader of the 1993 alleged Islamic conspiracy to bomb several New York City sites and assassinate some political leaders. The defendants in this conspiracy case, which is alleged to be connected to the World Trade Center bombing, go to trial in the autumn of 1994. *(AP/Wide World)*

Fists raised, principal defendant Gregory Joey Johnson and I marched victoriously down the steps of the U.S. Supreme Court Building in March 1989 after I argued that the right to burn the American flag as an act of protest was protected under the First Amendment. This argument and a similar one in 1990 were both successful, with the highest court ruling in our favor. *(Andrew Gordon)*

The only time I've been a judge: With director-producer Spike Lee, I pose in robes and slicked-down hair for my role in his 1992 film *Malcolm X. (David Lee)*

During the 1988 trial of Larry Davis for attempted murder of nine police officers during a shootout, Lynne Stewart and I successfully argued that Larry had been set up and had shot in self-defense after police busted into his sister's apartment, guns blazing. Larry was acquitted and I became Public Enemy No. 1 to the NYPD. *(AP/Wide World)*

A working lunch with my partner and alter ego, Ron Kuby. (*Ari Mintz*/New York Newsday)

The odd couple: John Gotti and I hugged outside the courtroom where he was tried and convicted in 1992 of murder and racketeering. I had filed a motion for him, contending that his Sixth Amendment rights were violated when the court refused to allow him his counsel of choice. (*WNBC-TV, courtesy of the* Daily News)

At my desk in the basement office of my Greenwich Village house. *(Ricardo Betancourt)*

exemption was valid and that Judge Keith should permit the wiretaps to be introduced into evidence.

The case now became known as *U.S. v. U.S. District Court,* with the U.S. government the petitioner and Judge Keith the respondent. Arguments on this case were scheduled in Cincinnati before the U.S. Court of Appeals for the Sixth Circuit. I arranged to split the brief that had to be written to back up our arguments with a young Detroit lawyer, Buck Davis. I would write my portion in New York, and Buck would write his part in Detroit. Our point was, in the main, that the Fourth Amendment's stricture that a warrant for wiretapping must be issued by a court could not be dispensed with by claiming there was a national security exemption to that requirement.

We planned to meet in Cincinnati for the argument; it was scheduled for 2:00 P.M. on a freezing cold day in the winter of 1971. I flew to Cincinnati and heard my name paged when I landed. When I picked up a courtesy phone, I found out that Buck had crashed on an icy road somewhere in the middle of Ohio and was in the hospital. He had lost an ear, which, at that moment, was being sewn back onto his head. I needed Buck's half of the brief, so I rented a car and, ignoring the weather, drove the ninety or so miles to the hospital at full speed. As Buck was wheeled out of the operating room, with his ear back on and surgeons assuring me he'd be fine, I asked, "Buck, where is your half of the brief?"

"In the car . . . on the Interstate," he said, semiconscious and unable to give me an exact location. A police officer in the hospital waiting room gave me more specific directions. I jumped in my car and drove to where Buck's car was supposed to be, and sure enough, the copies of his half of the brief were under the overturned vehicle, half-buried in the snow. I grabbed whatever looked salvageable, threw it in my rented car, and drove at top speed back to Cincinnati. I arrived only thirty minutes before the argument was scheduled to begin.

I noticed a tailor shop near the hotel where I was to meet Herman Schwartz, a professor at the University of Buffalo Law School who was going to argue the case for the ACLU. I raced into the shop with the soaking wet pages of the brief in my hand. The tailor very kindly put five or six pages at a time on his huge steam machine and pressed them until they dried. I stapled the pages together and raced to the courthouse. As I ran up the steps at two o'clock, I saw Chief Circuit Judge Harry Phillips, who was to be one of the judges on our panel. I handed him the still-warm pages and said, "Here's a hot brief for you, Judge Phillips!"

To my great joy, the panel sustained Judge Keith's original decision, that there was no national security exemption to the Fourth Amendment warrant requirement. The panel ruled 2–1 that not "one written phrase" in the Constitution supported the Justice Department and that the government's wiretapping without warrants of groups it considered "radical" violated the Constitution.

The only step the Justice Department could take then was to apply to the U.S. Supreme Court, which it did. Our team for the Supreme Court argument consisted of myself, Arthur Kinoy, William Bender, a former staff lawyer at the Center for Constitutional Rights, and others. When it came time to decide who would actually make the argument, I assumed that I would because I had argued the case in both the court of appeals and the district court. But the group felt that Arthur should do it. He had done a great deal of work on the Supreme Court brief and had considerable experience in arguing before the high court.

At the time, this decision wounded my ego substantially, and I walked around for days with a burning sensation in the pit of my stomach. Eventually, however, I came to realize that we would do best with Arthur and his strenuous, articulate, and committed method. He argued the case, and we won handily, 8–0, with Justice Rehnquist abstaining. To decide otherwise would have gutted the Fourth Amendment and returned us to the days of King George III's infamous writs of assistance.

Rehnquist, today chief justice, abstained from the vote because he had been instrumental in framing the national security exemption when he was a deputy attorney general under Nixon. On June 19, 1972, we received the Supreme Court ruling in our favor: Warrantless searches or telephone taps could not be sustained by claiming a national security exemption. It was a monumental victory. The ruling was direct: "The danger to political dissent is acute where the Government attempts to act under so vague a concept. . . ."

The case against Plamondon, Forest, and Sinclair was dismissed and never went to trial because the government could not use the evidence that it claimed was on those tapes. This great victory resulted from our use of the tactics that Len and I had learned in Chicago: Attack the government even while the government is attacking the defendants.

Rather ironically, the lawyer who argued for the government against us in both the court of appeals and the Supreme Court, Robert C. Mardian, was later indicted for illegal wiretapping in the Watergate scandal.

But, more important, I am certain that the timing of the activities which brought about the Watergate scandal was directly linked to the wiretapping decision in *U.S. v. U.S. District Court.* I believe that Rehnquist, a very loyal Nixon follower, leaked the Supreme Court's decision to the president before it was officially released on Monday, June 19.

As we know all too well, three weeks earlier, on May 28, the Committee to Re-Elect the President, appropriately nicknamed CREEP, had bugged the Watergate office of Larry O'Brien, chairman of the Democratic National Committee. Bugs were installed in O'Brien's phone, without a warrant, under the national security exemption—the Democratic party was supposed to be a danger to national security.

Once Nixon knew of the impending decision in *U.S. v. U.S. District Court,* he decided to remove the bugs because there could no longer be the slightest justification for them if they were ever discovered. So, on Friday, June 16, the Miami-based Plumbers, the group that had installed the bugs, were ordered to remove them. In the early-morning hours of June 17, Frank Willis, a black security guard at the Watergate, saw something suspicious at the Democratic National Committee headquarters, investigated, and found people inside the office attempting to debug O'Brien's telephone. The break-in eventually led to Nixon's downfall.

Now, while I can't claim to have had a major role in toppling an American president, I do believe that the decision in *U.S. v. U.S. District Court* played an important part. Also, there was proof here, in my mind, that Rehnquist had leaked the Supreme Court decision on wiretapping to Nixon and was therefore not trustworthy. Fourteen years later, in 1986, I had a wonderful time before the Senate Judiciary Committee expressing my opposition to President Reagan's nomination of Rehnquist as chief justice of the Supreme Court. I had three minutes to make my denunciation of this reprehensible man and used my allotted time to discuss the wiretapping case and what I believed to be its connection to Watergate.

When he was an assistant attorney general under Nixon, I said Rehnquist "advised the President that it was perfectly all right to wiretap without a warrant whenever the President decided to do so; that he had the inherent power to violate the Fourth Amendment."

I added that nothing could be more unconstitutional than the national security exemption concept that Rehnquist had "both formulated and advocated" in order to wiretap domestic groups and individuals without a warrant. I also reminded the committee members of the Supreme Court decision of June 19, 1972, in which Rehnquist abstained, that invalidated the national security exemption.

"I think that you have a justice here," I said, "who does not understand the Constitution and will destroy, if he can, the written Constitution. . . . A man who will tell the president of the United States that he has the power to tap anybody's phone without a warrant, without judicial authority, is not fit to sit as an associate justice, much less the chief justice, of the U.S. Supreme Court."

Then I described the probable connection between the date of the Watergate break-in, June 16–17, and the release of the Supreme Court decision on wiretapping three days later. Armed with advance knowledge from Rehnquist that removed any claim of legitimacy to bugging the Democratic National Committee headquarters, Nixon arranged for the removal of the bugs. The arrest of the people hired to do this led, of course, to Watergate and Nixon's resignation, I told the committee. It was also my conviction that the famous missing eighteen minutes on Nixon secretary Rose Mary Woods's tape of June 22 implicated Rehnquist in leaking the impending wiretap decision.

When the chairman of the Senate Judiciary Committee told me my time was up, I said, "I just ended. Perfect." Never let them have the last word.

But after what I believed were some astounding revelations, none of the committee members, except Sen. Edward Kennedy, seemed the least bit interested in my theory. Rehnquist was confirmed as chief justice, but I felt satisfied that I had done my piece in opposing him. Every bit helps, even if it doesn't appear at the time that it's effective. My hope is that someday my condemnation of Rehnquist will be taken out, dusted off, and used in connection with a decision he makes on a wiretapping issue.

1971
Ben Chaney

Directly after the White Panther trial, I accepted the lead counsel spot in a murder case in West Palm Beach, Florida. Ben Chaney, sixteen, the younger brother of James Chaney, one of the three civil rights workers murdered during the Mississippi Freedom Summer, had been charged with aiding and abetting in the murders of two Florida Atlantic University women students. This was the first of many similar cases I would take on during the next two decades. A young black man like Ben Chaney did not stand a chance of obtaining a fair trial because of the racism inherent in the criminal justice system. Over the years, I have represented many clients whose membership in a minority makes them, in my opinion, political defendants.

Ben had been living in New York since his brother's murder in 1964 because some well-meaning northern liberals thought it best to remove him from his native Mississippi and enroll him in private school in New York City. At the exclusive Walden School, Ben was suddenly among white overachievers; it was the wrong place for him. People had good intentions, but the teenaged Ben was completely miserable there, away from family and friends and thrust into an unfamiliar world. When a former marine, who had been discharged because of emotional problems, came along and convinced Ben to run away from school, he jumped at the chance.

The ex-marine took Ben and another youth, Martin, both fourteen, on a crazy journey through the South. He was a homicidal maniac: At least five people were killed during the trip. An insurance salesman in Fort Lauderdale was murdered. Two women students were shot. The former marine then headed north with Ben and Martin but stopped in South Carolina to rob a roadside fireworks stand. There he killed another person and was killed himself during the shootout. Martin and Ben were tried for the roadside homicide; Martin was convicted, and Ben was acquitted and returned to Florida to stand trial for the murders of the two coeds.

In Florida, the only evidence against Ben was a statement he made to Florida police officers who had traveled to South Carolina to interview him when he was in custody there. They were black officers, specifically selected to get Ben to talk. On the strength of the statements he made to these officers, Ben was charged with felony murder in the Florida case; this meant that he didn't actually commit the crime but was involved in some way.

Mrs. Fannie Lee Chaney, Ben's mother, knew me from the civil rights movement and asked me to represent her son. Ben, too, wanted me because, as he said not too long ago, I was "fire." I asked Alcee Hastings, a local attorney and Florida legislator, to work with me.

Ben's prosecutor was David Bloodworth. (Twenty years later, Bloodworth would be the state's attorney in Palm Beach County when William Kennedy Smith was tried for rape. By supervising the Kennedy prosecution but not handling the case himself, Bloodworth played both ends: He would get credit for indicting a Kennedy, but he wouldn't offend his affluent constituency by being personally involved in the trial itself.)

I was excused from Ben's pretrial proceedings for a few days in September 1971 to go to the Attica Correctional Facility, a maximum-security institution in upstate New York where inmates had taken many hostages and were in control of one of the prison's four yards. When I returned, the trial resumed.

Ben's trial began in early 1972 with our motions to suppress the statements he had made to the police on the grounds that he was suffering from schizophrenia. Our psychiatrist testified to that contention, but the judge overruled us, and Ben's statements eventually went into evidence. We never really had a chance after that. We concentrated on his youth, his spotless record, and his tragic adolescence.

During the trial, I had some difficulty with David Bloodworth. He alleged that I violated the gag order—an order not to discuss a case publicly—issued by the judge, when I gave a speech at Atlanta University. Bloodworth attempted to bring me up on charges. During the hearing on these charges, I called the prosecutor to the stand, and his testimony discredited his own allegations against me. It was a victory; the judge ruled that I did not violate the gag order.

During my summation, I remember that the courthouse was packed with what seemed to be every lawyer in Palm Beach County. I walked around the courtroom in tears as I talked about the life Ben had endured since his brother's murder.

We failed, and Ben was convicted, probably because he was black and the victims were white. One study has shown that in capital cases, when the victim is Caucasian, a black defendant has an 80 percent greater chance of being sentenced to death than when the victim is of any other race. In noncapital prosecutions, the rate of convictions is even more lopsided when white victims are involved.

Ben Chaney served thirteen years in prison.

CHAPTER TWELVE

Attica: The Worst of Deceptions

I can't go back to my classroom and teach justice.

WHEN I FIRST SAW THE GREAT, GRIM PRISON BUILDINGS OF ATTICA, THE trees were just starting their annual transformation from green to gold and red. The rising began in the early hours of September 9, 1971, a quiet, ordinary autumn morning. But moments later there was nothing normal any longer as scores of angry, frustrated men crashed through a flimsy barrier and took control of a prison yard. For the next four days the insurrection at the Attica Correctional Facility in upstate New York, thirty miles to the east of Buffalo, commanded the attention of the nation.

Then, on September 13, at 9:43 A.M., without adequate warning, certainly without an acknowledgment that the men inside—inmates and guards alike—had any essential value or humanity, the prison yard was attacked by the armies of the law. When the brief, bloody massacre was over, the body count was thirty-nine, and scores of people lay seriously injured.

The insurrection of 1,281 inmates at Attica was inspired by the prison system's inhumane treatment of those it housed. The inmates revolted for better medical care, translators for Hispanic inmates, more black and Latino guards, better educational programs, and better food, including special diets for Muslim inmates. They wanted the guards to accept them as human beings, even though they were imprisoned. They were also expressing their grief and anger over the August 21 killing of political revolutionary George Jackson, shot while supposedly trying to escape from California's San Quentin prison.

At the time of the rebellion, Attica held twenty-two hundred men, even though it was built to house only sixteen hundred. The inmates were 54 percent black and 9 percent Puerto Rican, with their keepers almost all young white males from nearby rural counties. Attica was a ticking bomb in September 1971, a bomb that exploded, causing fallout for more than two decades on the political and social landscape of New York State.

Thursday: Day One

When the Attica takeover occurred, I was in sunny, peaceful West Palm Beach. While arguing a motion for Ben Chaney, I was handed a telegram which informed me of the Attica rebellion and requested my presence. The inmates wanted me there right away. The judge on the Chaney case allowed me to leave. "You go. That's important," he said when he learned that fifty hostages had been taken.

I knew some of the Attica inmates from a similar uprising the year before at the Auburn Correctional Facility, also in upstate New York. There, inmates who had been denied permission to hold a Black Solidarity Day engaged in a sit-down protest after taking several guards as hostages. Although the prison's administrators assured the inmates that those who led the action would not be punished, they never kept their word. All of the Auburn leaders were beaten, then shipped to Attica and put in the hole—solitary confinement.

That prison officials had lied at Auburn played a key role in the Attica tragedy and caused the rebelling inmates to suspect a similar betrayal. Their distrust was compounded when, right after the Attica takeover, New York governor Nelson A. Rockefeller ignored requests that he personally assure inmates there would be no reprisals. These requests were made by inmates, hostages, prison officials, and a group of observers, including me. Rockefeller's silence understandably caused the inmates to fear repercussions, and that fear inevitably overshadowed any negotiation attempts.

Arthur O. Eve and Herman Schwartz were at Attica almost from the very beginning of the crisis. Eve, a New York State assemblyman, was a prison-reform advocate, and Schwartz was a law professor at the State University of New York in Buffalo and an appellate attorney for some of the inmates. They asked the state to call in the other observers the inmates wanted. The observers were to act as witnesses to what was happening as well as advocates and negotiators.

Initially, I thought I could be useful at Attica as an intermediary. The takeover also appealed to my sense of the dramatic. My reasons for becoming involved in any case or situation were all here: Attica was high stakes, in lives and in political importance, and it was high profile.

Friday: Day Two

Before I left Florida, I called Lotte at home in Westchester and asked her to come with me to Attica. I thought she would worry less if she was there, and truthfully, I felt better with her along; I'd never been involved in anything as potentially dangerous as this, and her presence gave me a sense of comfort. I met her at La Guardia Airport, and we flew on to Buffalo together. Herman Schwartz picked us up at about 10:00 P.M.; then we dropped Lotte at a motel in Batavia and drove to the prison. When we arrived, I heard a harsh voice calling from outside the prison gates, "Nigger lover!"

The group of observers I joined was a mixed bag: Eve; Schwartz; Tom Wicker, associate editor of the *New York Times;* Lewis Steel, radical lawyer and vice president of the National Lawyers Guild; New York State senators John Dunne and Robert Garcia; the Reverend Wyatt Tee Walker, who was then urban affairs adviser to Governor Rockefeller; Clarence Jones, Martin King's former aide and then publisher of the *Amsterdam News;* Herman Badillo, a U.S. congressman; Thomas Soto, a Latino representative of the Prisoner Solidarity Committee; plus other officials, reporters, ministers, community organizers, and prison advocates as well as representatives of ethnic and prisoners' groups.

Some of the observers came to Attica on their own initiative. The inmates had requested me, Jones, Wicker, and Soto; Black Panther chairman Bobby Seale; David Anderson of the Rochester Urban League; Muslim minister Louis Farrakhan (who never showed up); reporters Richard Roth and James Ingram; Kenneth Jackson, Mel Rivers, and David Rothenberg of the Fortune Society, a group of former inmates; and Juan Ortiz and José Paris, members of the Young Lords, a Puerto Rican group modeled after the Black Panthers.

Many of the observers, uncomfortable with the violence barely beneath the surface at the prison, did not believe any deal could be cut. I distrusted most of what the authorities said, too, but hoped an agreement could be reached. Both sides had so much to lose if they could not come to an understanding.

Individually, the observers had different interests and attitudes. For example, Wyatt Tee Walker became angry the second day and left, blasting me for agitating the inmates. But I didn't take his outburst personally, since he was there to represent Governor Rockefeller. Others left for a variety of reasons. Although those that remained were a very disparate bunch, we agreed on one thing: No one wanted to see a bloodbath in that yard.

Shortly before midnight that night, a group of us headed for D-yard, where the hostages were being held. Prison guards took us to a tunnel that led to Times Square, an intersection where the passageways that connected the four cell blocks met. Halfway to Times Square, we were turned over to the inmates' security force, many of whom hid their faces with towels or other coverings.

A large makeshift wooden table in front of the cell-block wall where we sat served as the center of operations for the inmates. Nearby, the hostages were being held under the protection of a phalanx of Black Muslims. The entire area was brightly illuminated by the lights of a Buffalo television crew. Inmate leaders organized the area and kept order and discipline; they had rules for eating, sleeping, and cleaning up and had organized a racially integrated security force and even some sort of medical care for those prisoners suffering from emotional shock.

Sam Melville, one of the few white inmates, walked over to me and introduced himself, saying we had many mutual friends. Sam was a young revolutionary who had been convicted of firebombing a New York bank; he had changed his name to express his love for the great writer Herman Melville. Although neither of us knew it at the time, Sam had only three more days on this earth.

Attica was one of the most important events of my life. Twelve hundred inmates were holding fifty hostages, surrounded by armies of state police. It was my nature to romanticize the situation, and I saw it as a moment where the disfranchised and unempowered had seized power and control most dramatically from the prison guards, who represented the twisted authoritarian control of government gone bad.

The inmates asked the observers to speak. When I stood up, many of the men applauded and cheered. I felt that these men, society's outcasts, were my people, my constituents. I felt close to them and believed they had asked me to come to Attica as their representative. I wanted to demonstrate that I was with them completely and that I recognized the significance of this moment. I wanted them to know I was not just another lawyer with a briefcase saying, "I'll do the best I can." I wanted them to know that I was willing to go to the wire for them.

I told the inmates that Huey Newton or Bobby Seale would come to Attica. I wanted to convince them that they were not without outside support. "We are your brothers," I said.

One of the men, Brother Herb, said: "Brother Bill, will you be our lawyer? Will you represent the brothers as only you can?" When his request was put to a vote, the inmates shouted their approval. I was thrilled and honored and from that moment on served as the inmates' counsel, along with Jerry Rosenberg, a jailhouse lawyer well known in New York prison circles as Jerry the Jew.

Then someone asked me about the injunction that Herman Schwartz had obtained from a federal court promising that there would be no retaliation against the inmates if they surrendered. I felt compelled to tell them the truth. "The injunction is nothing. It's not worth the paper it's written on." It was dangerous for the inmates to rely on a worthless piece of paper. One of the prisoners, Flip Crowley, followed my remarks with an emotional and eloquent speech: "If we cannot live as people, then we will at least try to die like men."

He recalled the Chicago Conspiracy Trial and asked about my jail sentence for contempt: "Brother Kunstler, what did they do with you in court?"

"The same thing they did with you, brother!" I cried out, completely overcome. We hugged each other, and a bond was sealed.

Saturday, Day Three

I had called Charles Garry, the Black Panthers' attorney, shortly after I arrived at Attica, asking him to come there with Bobby Seale. The two men arrived on the evening of the third day, September 11. That was the day we observers compiled the twenty-eight points, a list of inmate demands that state officials

said they were willing to concede. It was also the day that Corrections Officer William E. Quinn died from injuries he had received
during the September 9 Times Square melee. Quinn had been the
officer on duty at the Times Square junction when the gate broke
open and the inmates rushed in; in the ensuing fracas, three
guards were beaten, including Quinn.

As a member of the observers' six-man executive committee,
I drafted the twenty-eight points, based on input from the other
observers and notes from conversations with inmate leaders and
prison officials. In addition to their other points, the inmates
wanted amnesty for physical injuries they had allegedly caused to
guards. Since we knew that such amnesty would never be
granted, it was not included in the twenty-eight points. I suspected, from the beginning, that this demand might well be key,
particularly after Quinn's death.

After Bobby Seale arrived, I asked him to explain to the
twelve hundred men that they must accept the twenty-eight
points or we, the observers, were certain there would be terrible
bloodshed. Bobby had enormous influence because of his position with the Black Panthers and also because of his stance during
the Chicago trial. If he had said to the inmates, "The twenty-eight
points are great and the Panther party recommends you accept
them," it might have had some effect. But Bobby wouldn't do it.

"I'll take these twenty-eight points to the Central Committee
of the Panther Party in Oakland. We'll get an answer back to you
as to what we think about them," Bobby told the men. It was a
hopeless approach. These twelve hundred inmates were teetering
on the edge of a cataclysmic precipice. Bobby said he would deal
with their problem through an administrative process, but there
was no time for this route with a massacre imminent. The inmates
booed him after he spoke.

When we went over the events later, Bobby told me that he
had not grasped the nature of the crisis. He hadn't realized that he
should have circumvented the usual processes of the Black Panther party. He was there as an individual, not as a Panther official,
and should have taken a stand and said, "Yes, accept the twenty-
eight points." Because I had recommended that the twenty-eight
points be accepted and desperately wanted Bobby's voice to join
mine, I was bitterly disappointed.

Bobby Seale had fallen victim to a phenomenon that I saw in
many black organizations, whether it was the Blackstone Rangers
in Chicago or the Panthers. These organizations enacted complex

rules and regulations so that they wouldn't become what they thought Dr. King was—a one-man show. The Black Panther party was a collective, and Bobby had his marching orders to report back to the Central Committee first, before he made a recommendation to the Attica inmates. But Attica was not an ordinary situation. Decisions at Attica could not wait for consideration by the Panther party collective. Attica was a war zone, and the end battle was imminent.

Clarence Jones read the twenty-eight points to the inmates while I was outside talking to Bobby. When I came back in, the inmates had ripped up the list, causing Tom Wicker to comment: "They're gonna kill us all." Frank "Big Black" Smith, one of the inmates in charge of security (and today a private investigator in New York), said, "There's going to be real trouble here. The men are in terrible shape. They're angry, bitter, frustrated."

When I got up to the table, the atmosphere was thick with fear on both sides; some of the observers were certain we were going to be killed. After Jones recommended that the twenty-eight points be accepted, the men went wild, shouting and jeering. Someone asked, "What does Kunstler think about it?" I took the microphone. I was scared, sensing their mood, and my first thought was to say something soothing. I wanted to tell them they were right to reject the twenty-eight points, to say, "You're all correct. You're perfectly right about it. To hell with them."

But when I began speaking, I realized I had to tell them the truth, not the political ideal that I had perhaps intended to communicate. I thought, My God, knowing in my heart that they are not going to get amnesty for Quinn or for physical injury of guards, I must talk to them honestly.

I said that the only reason we were pushing the twenty-eight points is that we wanted our brothers to stay alive and this was the best they were going to get. "We don't want people to die. You can turn it down, though. You have an absolute right to do that, but I wouldn't be fair to you if I didn't tell you what the consequences might be." Putting aside any remaining middle-class faith I might have had in the system, I told them the hard facts, that they would never get amnesty for the death of Quinn and the injuries to the other guards.

Everyone, inmates and observers, had been stretched so tight that the air was filled with high-wire tension. But as soon as I spoke, it was as if someone had deflated a balloon. *Pshhhhh!* The anxiety level was greatly reduced. "This [the twenty-eight points] is the best I can do, and I recommend that you accept it. I'm your lawyer, and I recommend that you accept the state's response and let the hostages go," I said. Then there was a quiet hush over the place. And the atmosphere began to clear, as after a thunderstorm, very quickly. Wicker leaned over and said, "Bill, you've saved all our lives."

What happened, I think, is that the prisoners knew we had not betrayed them, had not joined with the prison authorities, that we were not their enemies. Hopefully, they understood that we cared about them and that what we said was out of friendship and loyalty to them and their cause rather than an attempt to induce them to surrender to the institution. Of all the speeches I made inside the prison, that was the one that came most from my heart.

Earlier, the observers had discussed who would tell the inmates of the death of Officer Quinn. I had volunteered. "I'm their attorney. I'll tell them." No one was very comfortable about telling them. We knew that all it would have taken to launch a full-scale riot would be just one guy going off, one person doing something crazy. However, although it was risky, I felt that the men had a right to know that William Quinn had died.

Despite later criticism of my statement, I don't think it was a mistake to tell them. The men had their radios tuned to the news and knew what was going on. It was only a matter of time until news of Quinn's death hit the airwaves. They would have realized then there could be no amnesty. Not with a guard dead. No matter what. They knew the system well enough to realize there would be no quarter given to men who were held responsible for killing a prison guard.

Maybe they would have surrendered on that third night, thinking they would get full amnesty, if they never found out about Quinn. But if I hadn't told them about Quinn, they might have accepted a deal under false circumstances, and I could not have lived with such a deception. They deserved to know the truth before making their decisions.

Whatever doubts I have about what I said come from the end-game of Attica. If I had anticipated the bestiality of the authorities, perhaps I would not have told them about Quinn in order to save lives. At the time, however, I could not have anticipated what was going to happen.

Sunday, Day Four

On Sunday morning, a woman eating breakfast in a diner near the prison became hysterical at the sight of a black man sitting near her: It was Assemblyman Arthur Eve. This hysteria was a reflection of the level of anxiety in the entire community, not only inside the walls of Attica but among all the people who lived and worked nearby.

In the prison, the atmosphere continued to be terribly tense. None of the observers had left the prison for more than brief periods of time. Some nights, we stayed there all night, and food was delivered to us by prison officials. I wore the same suit the whole time I was there and washed out socks and underwear when I could get back to my motel room, where Lotte was waiting. Each time we entered or left the building, we had to walk through a gauntlet of jeering troopers and corrections officers. State troopers were bivouacked at the prison, turning it into an armed camp.

During the entire four days, the prison was surrounded by the husbands, wives, children, and parents of the hostages, as well as the news media. Inside the prison, I felt as if I were watching a huge bomb that could be set off by anything or anyone at any second. I hoped the observers could help defuse the situation peacefully, if that were humanly possible. We spent much of Sunday trying to convince Rockefeller to come to Attica and meet with the observers, then make a public address to the inmates regarding their demands. We failed miserably, for we never counted on the governor of New York State being the murderer he was.

Tom Wicker's wife called before we went in on Sunday to warn him not to go into the yard. "Don't go in there. You've been in three days already. You're a southerner, and it could be dangerous," she told him, but he ignored her warning, and we trooped in.

That morning, for the first time, we were asked to sign liability waivers saying the state was not responsible should anything happen to us. We should have smelled a rat then, because Russell Oswald, New York's commissioner of correctional services, showed us a letter that he wanted to send in to the inmates. One sentence stood out as if it had been neon lit: "Your committee agrees with me that you should surrender, and that we should talk later." We opposed the letter; we thought it would jeopardize our lives. We had not agreed to a surrender, and if the inmates believed we had, they would think we had deserted them. At this point, the state police were firing rubber pellets into the yard. (I was hit once, causing a trickle of blood that wasn't serious.) The shots were reminders that everyone in the yard was in range and vulnerable.

Finally, Oswald agreed not to send in that letter. Then we signed the waivers. By that time, we were down to a handful who were willing to go into D-yard: Wicker, myself, Jones, Eve, reporters Rudy Garcia and Dick Edwards, and a new arrival, Minister Franklin Florence. Among those who turned tail and refused to enter D-yard was state senator John Dunne, who would later become a member of the attorney general's Civil Rights Division during the Bush administration.

Although we didn't know it, this would be our last trip into D-yard. Down a long tunnel, into an empty yard, through the connecting cross of Times Square, and finally, into D-yard.

We were outraged when we found out from the inmates who were escorting us that the commissioner had betrayed us and sent in the letter. One of the inmates said some of the prisoners wanted to kill us. I was standing right behind Tom Wicker and watched the back of his neck turn, very slowly, a deep beet red. As scared as I had ever been, I wanted to run as fast as I could back to the safety of the prison officials.

In my mind, I prepared to have my throat cut. I intellectualized that it wouldn't hurt much; it would be over quickly. But if I ran, I would always be remembered as a coward. I thought it was all going to end here, for me, in the Attica yard. And I understood why we had been made to sign the waivers. Oswald wanted us to be killed, for then the authorities would have a perfect excuse for going in, guns blazing. If we were killed, with the state cleared of all liability, they could retake the yard. Why else make us sign releases at this point? But their plan didn't work.

I decided not to run and steeled myself against whatever was to come. They took us into D-yard two by two, with Wicker in the third group and me in the fourth. When I was taken through, I looked quickly to see whether there was any blood on the ground and was relieved to see none. I joined Wicker and the others at the command table. Big Black Smith told the men that the observers had not approved the letter and that Oswald had lied. The men applauded, and we each got a chance to speak, thus stopping any hotheads in the group from slitting our throats.

When I spoke—and I've gotten lots of flak on this—I told the inmates that I had been informed by members of the Black Panther party that they had been in touch with the embassy of an unnamed foreign country—North Vietnam—which had agreed to grant asylum to all prisoners who were released. Although I knew the state would never let them go, I thought it was good to give the men hope and even offered to take their names. Later on, the McKay Commission, which investigated the Attica massacre, Tom Wicker, and some others were critical of me for doing this, saying I had raised false hopes. I thought at the time that gaining confidence for the observers was the most important thing.

Wicker had been talking to some of the guards who had been held as hostages. "Governor, come in here or we're dead men," one said, sending a message to the governor. Another, Sgt. Edward Cunningham, who was killed in the final shootout, said that Rockefeller "must give [the inmates] clemency from criminal prosecution. . . . Anything else other than this is just as good as dropping dead."

Commissioner Oswald contacted Rockefeller that night and asked him to come to the prison to talk to the observers. He suggested that Rockefeller make an announcement to the inmates over the loudspeaker. The governor refused. We observers saw that time was fast running out. There was a doomed feeling hanging over the prison. I went back to the motel to sleep.

Bloody Monday, the Final Day

When I arrived back at Attica at about 9:00 A.M., I was not allowed inside. I heard the drone of helicopters and moments later smelled the pungent Mace-like gas. People began to cry. I heard very faint *pop-pop-pop* sounds, the sound of shooting, of double-O buckshot and dumdum bullets entering human flesh. Until that moment, I somehow had never believed that the rebellion would end in bloodshed. I felt it would be worked out, that the two sides would come to some agreement. As I heard the guns, I felt totally impotent. I couldn't do a damn thing.

In ten minutes, a prison official came out and said, "It's all over. We've retaken the yard." Nine corrections officers were dead, their throats slit, he said. The onslaught had been ordered because the inmates were cutting the throats of the hostages, he added.

Naively, I believed what he had said about the cut throats. He was in there; I was outside. I didn't know that what he said was all a lie. I was interviewed by reporters and said it should never have happened, that the governor should have made an appearance and spoken to the inmates—through a megaphone from the safety of the catwalk over the yard if he was unwilling to go into D-yard itself. I was crying.

There was no excuse for what happened that morning at Attica. The troops that retook the yard included state police, sheriff's deputies in bright orange raincoats, and corrections officers; they used rifles, shotguns, and sidearms. They blasted away, even at people lying on the ground, overcome by the gas. You can see this carnage on film, since some of the rifles were equipped with motion picture cameras. They shot indiscriminately at anyone who moved, and the bodies of those who were killed were simply torn apart by state-issued ammunition.

An eighteen-minute amateur videotape of the massacre shows hostages with prisoners holding knives to their throats. Then you can see tear gas everywhere and hear an amplified voice saying: "Surrender peacefully. You will not be harmed." Then you hear rifle shots and automatic gunfire, and you see the dead and dying on the catwalk over the prison yard.

When the assault began, the unlucky guards who thought they were being rescued stood up. And were shot down. They were dressed in prison garb, and they were simply mowed down by their own side. At the front gate, as the state forces charged the prison, the troopers and deputies were yelling, "Save me a nigger!" I heard it all over the place. They were out for blood.

Later that day, I was eager to leave this horrifying scene as fast as possible and asked Lotte to pick me up after she checked out of the motel. Carrying our luggage, we walked down the street in front of the prison. Suddenly, a car rushed toward us, trying to hit us. We managed to jump behind a tree. Years later, during an unrelated criminal trial, I met the state trooper who was driving that car. He said that he was sorry he had scared us, but his fury at me overtook him. He didn't think he would have gone through with it, but he wasn't certain. I wasn't, either.

1973
Assessing Attica

Two years later, I was seated at a dinner party next to Mary Rockefeller, the governor's daughter. She turned to me and asked why I had called her father a murderer. I told her that his coming to Attica could have saved those lives. She said, "But he might have been killed if he had gone in the yard."

Commissioner Oswald had gone into the yard, and he didn't die. But I told her, "Your father didn't have to go in the yard." He had only been asked to get on a bullhorn where the prisoners could see him, in an area controlled by the state troopers, on top of Times Square or at a window in the stewards' room, where we observers met. If he had backed the proposals and promised they would be put into effect, I believe that would have ended the Attica uprising.

To this day, I believe Rockefeller was a murderer. Everything must have welled up in him, including racism—since D-yard was pretty much controlled by blacks and Latinos—and injured pride, since the inmates had embarrassed him, had dared to take hostages, had flouted his authority, and had hurt his hopes of becoming president.

The tragedy at Attica did serve a purpose, though. Since those five monstrous days in 1971, any prison rebellions that have occurred have not escalated into full-scale massacres. Public outcry over Attica and an awareness that the entire situation was badly managed have changed the way prison uprisings are handled. Although there have been several prison takeovers during the last two decades, including those in Arizona, New Jersey, Florida, Georgia, New York, and Illinois, never has any person in authority ordered a retaking of an institution by force. For this alone, the deaths at Attica were not in vain.

But the small creature comfort gains made after Attica are today seriously threatened. Prisons are dangerously overpopulated. And, of course, the racism I saw at Attica is evident in all prisons because the majority of inmates are black or members of another minority, while corrections officers, outside of the large cities, are generally white. Racial hatred is always present in prisons; so is the potential for another Attica. To make it worse, a Supreme Court decision recently made it next to impossible for injured inmates to sue guards, thus virtually giving prison officials carte blanche to brutalize their charges.

In the end, we must believe the prisoners. Their purpose was not to take over a New York State prison yard. What they wanted was to be heard, to be treated as human beings and not humiliated, degraded, and harassed by the racist guards.

Attica also taught us the lesson of Rockefeller. During the crisis, his cowardly indecision and inability to act destroyed him as a viable political figure. President Nixon was behind him all the way, incidentally. Within twenty-four hours after the massacre, Nixon came out with a public statement in support of the murders ordered by Rockefeller. Nine of the governor's own guards died by his order. By his command, state officials told the Big Lie, that guards died because their throats had been cut by prisoners.

On Tuesday, September 14, the Monroe County medical examiner reported that all of the guards died from bullet wounds. There were no throats cut at Attica. All the killing was the work of officials of the state of New York. Only the authorities had the guns and the bullets. Rockefeller had murdered his own people. In addition, half the inmates and hostages were shot in the back and appeared to be lying down when they were shot, according to Dr. Michael Baden, then New York City chief medical examiner and one of the forensic experts who came to Attica to determine just how the hostages had died.

When I spoke at SUNY Buffalo the day after the massacre, I talked about the Big Lie. I also said that if the authorities had wanted to immobilize the inmates, they only had to use gas. They did not have to shoot to kill. Attica did not have to happen. In tears, I said, "The real murderers wore uniforms, the real murderers had state-issued weapons and ammunition, the real murderers had names, not numbers."

I believed then, as I believe now even more strongly, that sometimes violent events like this are necessary to dramatize certain situations and that there was a point to it all. Sometimes the human spirit can't take any more, and then you have what the world calls violence. In this country, much good has come out of violence, such as the ending of slavery and the partial enfranchisement of black people. I am not a pacifist of any sort, either religious or philosophical, and I agree with Rap Brown that sometimes "violence is necessary."

As a result of the uprising, some improvements were made in the daily lives of inmates at Attica. Many of the proposals set forth in the twenty-eight points have been realized both at Attica and elsewhere in New York State. Today Attica is one of the few prisons that permit conjugal visits. After Attica there was a greater public understanding about what really goes on in a prison. So prisons improved a bit, and inmates are now treated in a slightly more humane fashion. But our punitive incarceration system is still simply awful.

Compare our system to Holland's, where all individuals who are convicted enter prison with indeterminate sentences. If they

act appropriately, follow the rules, and show signs of improve-
ment, they are deemed rehabilitated and are released, no matter
what they've done. In the United States, we have no real rehabili-
tation, only vengeance and retribution. Our prisons are often brutal, bestial places where the guards who run them end up as
brutes and beasts themselves.

1976
Murder Charges

Four years later, I was back in Buffalo. By this time, Lotte and
I were divorced, and I had remarried. My second wife, Margaret
Ratner, was a young attorney with whom I had fallen deeply in
love while we worked together on a case in St. Croix in 1973.
Margie and I, along with former attorney general Ramsey Clark,
were in Buffalo to defend the two Attica inmates who had been
charged with murdering Officer William Quinn. After the massacre, when the Attica indictments came down, all but one were
against prisoners; a single state trooper was charged with brutality
but was never convicted. Although thirty-nine people had been
killed by law enforcement agents, the key indictments were for
Quinn's murder.

The murder trial began in early 1975 and ended on a snowy
day in April. Margie and I defended a nineteen-year-old named
John Hill, a man of Italian and Tuscaroran ancestry, whose Indian
name was Dacajawiah. He asked us to represent him because of
my work in several Philadelphia cases involving members of the
Iroquois Confederacy. Ramsey represented another nineteen-
year-old, Charles Pernasalice, whom everyone called Charlie Joe.

During the trial I remember an incident when one of the prospective jurors Margie was questioning answered her with the
words "No, sir." I remember Margie standing there and saying,
"It's not sir, it's madam."

At the time of this trial, New York State had one death-penalty statute remaining on the books: For the crime of murdering a
law enforcement agent, the punishment was death. Shortly after
the trial, a ruling by the court of appeals invalidated this statute.
But when we first represented Johnny Hill and Charlie Joe Pernasalice in 1975, they were facing death sentences if convicted.

We knew that the evidence against Johnny was heavier than
that against Charlie Joe and that the case against him would be
more difficult. Johnny was half Mohawk, half Italian, and bigger

and more visible than Charlie Joe. We expected that some witnesses would testify that Johnny had struck Quinn with a club during the melee at Times Square. Moreover, the state had procured inmate witnesses who were willing to perjure themselves for anticipated favors.

What really happened at Times Square on September 8 is that twenty or more inmates pulled and banged on a gate, the gate gave way because of a defective locking system, and the insurrection began. Of course, the reason a supposedly tough prison gate would give way so easily has to do with the shoddy way the institution was constructed and maintained. And with capitalism's eternal quest to make a few bucks on the side. The prison, dedicated by FDR in 1931, was supposed to be the last word in penal institutions, but it had quickly deteriorated due to overcrowding and lack of satisfactory maintenance.

That prison gate was supposed to be held in place by a steel rod that went about six inches into both the floor and ceiling. But the rod was too short. To save money, someone welded on a foot-long extension and as a result, this crucially placed gate proved flimsy. When inmates started banging on it, it gave, and as they pushed through, they beat the three guards there with broomsticks and baseball bats. Basically, Johnny and Charlie Joe were indicted to represent all the inmates who had taken a whack at the guards. The state needed some scapegoats, and who better than two Native Americans?

The trial of Johnny and Charlie Joe was a political trial, very emotional and passionate, recalling the monumental tragedy which had taken place four years earlier. Ramsey, Margie, and I were supported by the Attica Defense Committee, made up of volunteer attorneys and others.

Together we shared a suite with Ramsey at the downtown Statler-Hilton, which we called the Stalin-Hitler—always looking for comic relief when in a tense situation. We had a bedroom, Ramsey had a bedroom, and we shared a connecting sitting room. Margie and I always went out to dinner, but Ramsey would often stay in and cook his food over a Sterno can at night. He lived like a monk. We would ask him to join us, but he would usually get a can of beans and cook it in the room. That's the spartan way he lived. Only when his wife, Georgia, visited did he dine out.

After spending Monday to Friday as defense attorneys on a death-penalty murder case, the three of us would unwind on the weekend trip back to New York City by being as silly as possible.

When I insisted, each weekend, that we take the toll-free Fifty-ninth Street Queensboro Bridge into the city from La Guardia Airport, Ramsey said I was loony and had an obsession with that bridge. I told him my reason—I don't like to pay tolls, because I don't like to give the government money if I don't have to—but he continued to kid me about being in love with the Fifty-ninth Street Bridge.

Although we gave it our best shot, the trial had a tragic outcome for Johnny; he was convicted and got twenty to life. Charlie Joe, however, was found guilty not of murder but of the lesser charge of attempted assault in the second degree. Ramsey has always said that Johnny's was a more difficult case and that's why only he was found guilty of murder. Maybe it was because there were more witnesses against him and he was a larger, more sinister looking man than Charlie Joe. I am not really certain.

That was one of the few times in my career that I felt truly dejected. The *Buffalo Evening News* ran a picture of me and Ramsey peering out a window of the Erie County Jail, looking very sad. Although it was April, it was snowing, and flakes were swirling around the window. Johnny and Charlie Joe had just been taken back to the jail; Ramsey and I were there to see them and were feeling quite blue.

Charlie was released the following week and never went back in. Johnny remained in prison for about four years, until the next governor of New York, Hugh Carey, after an investigation which revealed the unfair manner in which the Attica prosecutions had been handled, commuted the sentences of all the Attica inmates who had been convicted, thus making everyone immediately eligible for parole. Johnny was passed over the first time, but the next time he came before the board, he was released. The Attica prosecutions were over.

I had begun work on Johnny's appeal, but he was released before anything really happened. I was tied up in too many other cases, so Johnny asked Ramsey to take over the appeal. Ramsey agreed and worked with Ed Koren, a lawyer with the ACLU's prison project. They both put in a tremendous amount of work, but then a very sad thing happened. They argued the case before the court of appeals, and the argument went very well. In the meantime, Johnny had been released when his sentence was commuted by Governor Carey. But he became involved in a fracas in Greenwich Village's Washington Square Park and, afraid that it would affect his freedom, disappeared. When he was scheduled to appear in court, we had no idea where he was.

According to New York law, if a defendant fails to appear, he loses his right to appeal, so the court's decision was never written. Not long after, Ramsey was in an elevator at the court of appeals building in Albany on another matter when one of the judges said to him, "You know, you would have won that case."

I was enormously upset and disappointed because the court of appeals decision would have shown the essential unfairness of the murder trial. And, most important, it would have cleared Johnny's record—unless, of course, he was tried again and convicted, which was extremely unlikely. To me, it was terribly unfortunate that the aborted decision overturning the conviction of John Hill for the murder of Officer Quinn was never made public.

Johnny and I have remained good friends; he lives in the Washington, D.C., area, and I see him whenever he comes to town. He is closely involved with Native American affairs and frequently appears at demonstrations on behalf of his people. Charlie Joe is married, has two children, and, I believe, owns and lives on a sailboat in the Caribbean.

I have never quite recovered from Attica. For a long time afterward, I was filled with hate. I hated the public officials who allowed the massacre to happen. I hated their coldness, their inhumanity. What I saw and heard at Attica added to my experiences in Chicago and crystallized my political thinking. While I learned in Chicago that the government is dirty and corrupt and will utilize any means to prevent dissent, Attica showed me that the government can also be heartless and will even sacrifice the lives of its own to save face and protect the status quo.

Attica maimed many people. Devastated by the lies the state told about how the hostages were killed, Arthur Eve practically had a breakdown afterward. In addition to lying about throats being cut, officials had said Big Black cut off an officer's testicles and stuck them in his victim's mouth. Eve repeated some of these things, just as I did, and when he found out they weren't true, he unraveled a little. He could not comprehend that people would deliberately lie that way. He was more naive than I, being younger and not having had the experience of the Chicago trial.

Civil Suit

The Attica inmates fought for twenty years for public recognition of what occurred on September 13, 1971. With the help of Elizabeth Fink and several other dedicated volunteer attorneys, the inmates maintained a civil suit for damages against New York State. The original defendants in the suit included the estate of Governor Rockefeller as well as Corrections Commissioner Russell Oswald, state police major John Monahan, Attica warden Vincent Mancusi, and Deputy Warden Karl Pfeil. The Rockefeller attorneys successfully obtained an order of dismissal against the late governor's estate, but the other defendants eventually came to trial, twenty years after the massacre.

In late 1991, the trial revealed some of the terrible truths about Attica. Scores of witnesses, including members of the National Guard, testified about the barbarities that took place after Attica was retaken by the authorities. Jerry "the Jew" Rosenberg related how Deputy Warden Pfeil watched him being beaten, then yelled, "Kill the Jew bastard," and hit Rosenberg across the head with a chain. Big Black said he had to lie naked on a table with a football under his chin for hours, threatened with death if he dropped the ball; while he lay there, he was burned on his chest with cigarettes and hot bullet casings and beaten on his testicles. Another prisoner told of running a gauntlet of corrections officers who hit him with batons as he ran, naked, over ground strewn with broken glass. Others testified about being left to lie in their own blood, of being urinated upon by guards, of being beaten until their bones broke or they became paralyzed.

Former state senator John Dunne testified that on that final morning he was shocked and horrified: "I said, 'I'm seeing something I should not be seeing. I want it to stop.' " What Dunne saw, what we all knew, was man's inhumanity to man, so common in our prisons. We know that inmates are often routinely beaten and abused by corrections officers who neither understand nor want to recognize that their charges, although convicted felons, are still human beings.

The Attica civil suit charged that the four officials—Oswald, Monahan, Mancusi, and Pfeil—used more force than necessary to overtake the prison, allowed guards to brutalize inmates afterward, and failed to provide the medical care they knew would be needed as a result of the violent takeover.

The jury found for the prisoners, agreeing that the punishment given inmates after the takeover was cruel and unusual and included extreme physical abuse and other forms of retribution. It also found that only two doctors were on the scene to care for the dying and the injured and there was virtually no blood supply. On the claim of overseeing brutality against inmates, however, the jurors found only Deputy Warden Pfeil liable. They deadlocked on blaming Warden Mancusi, Corrections Commissioner Oswald, and state police Major Monahan.

One juror, a teacher, distraught at this last decision, told a newspaper reporter afterward that justice had not been done. "I can't go back to my classroom and teach justice," she said. I understand what she meant. Attica was a war with unequal sides: One side had guns and public support, while the other had only fear and loathing from both the public and the authorities.

Today things are much the same. Attica is still overcrowded. The prison population remains 80 percent minority, and the guards are still almost 100 percent white. The harassment of inmates by corrections officers continues.

Attica, like Chicago, changed me immeasurably. Although the tragedy saddened me, it did not depress me. I have never been one to throw up my hands in defeat, and more than ever, I was determined to fight. Attica stimulated me to action. I grew stronger, harder, more resolved in my beliefs and goals. I would go wherever people's lives and civil rights were in danger. I headed for Wounded Knee.

CHAPTER THIRTEEN

Wounded Knee

---

*I shall not be there. I shall rise and pass. Bury my heart
at Wounded Knee.*

AIM

In 1968, A GROUP OF NATIVE AMERICAN LEADERS CREATED THE AMERI-
can Indian Movement (AIM), their goal being to improve their
people's bleak, impoverished lives. AIM undertook a series of
dramatic demonstrations, including a 1969 occupation of the former federal prison on San Francisco Bay's Alcatraz Island and,
three years later, the takeover of the Bureau of Indian Affairs (BIA)
building in Washington, D.C.

I first became involved with AIM through a case in Philadelphia in 1972. A group of high steel workers, members of the Iroquois Confederacy, were sitting on a fire escape at the Colonial
Hotel, where they lived, watching a movie being shot in the street
below. Somehow the mattress they were sitting on accidentally
fell into the street. Two of Philadelphia police chief Frank Rizzo's
officers ran up the fire escape, guns drawn, and began firing.
When the smoke cleared, one man, an Onondaga named Leroy
Shenandoah, had been killed, and several other Native Americans had been wounded. It was ironic that only a few years earlier
Shenandoah, a soldier at the time, had represented the army in
President Kennedy's funeral cortege.

The Philadelphia police tried to cover up their brutality by
charging the four wounded Native Americans with resisting ar-

234

rest and inciting to riot. Oren Lyons, a chief of the Onondagas, asked me to represent one of the men. I appeared for the defense at a preliminary hearing but was unable to represent them at the trial because I had another case.

During the trial it was revealed that the cameraman who had been shooting the movie had turned his camera upward and caught the police running up the fire escape. When this film was shown in court and it became clear that the police had been guilty of criminal action, the real villains were revealed. Since it was obvious that the defendants were innocent, they were acquitted. When, after the trial, Police Chief Rizzo was elected mayor of Philadelphia, it proved to me once again that the public has a great tolerance for criminality by public officials when their crimes are committed against minorities.

Five years after its inception, AIM was a well-organized militant group that the FBI believed represented a threat to the U.S. government. As a result, it set out to destroy the group. By then, the Bureau had already crushed the Black Panthers and other militants and activists, using pernicious tactics that were first uncovered in the mid-1970s and have since been thoroughly documented. The actions taken by the FBI and other police groups "to protect national security" by destroying dissident organizations and individuals have always been part of the American government and for all I know may be a part of all governments.

The FBI focused considerable resources on AIM, which it described in a report as "one of the most violent and extremist-oriented organizations yet encountered by the United States. . . ." The report hypothesized links between AIM and "radical terrorist and extremist groups, both foreign and domestic."

While I don't believe at all that AIM threatened national security, I do agree that the Native American people were a threat to the Establishment. First, they were romantic figures whose history has always attracted white Americans: kids play at being Indians; museums feature Native American history and folklore. My own attitude toward Indians was born in the innocence of childhood and nurtured by Saturday afternoon matinees and feverish games of cowboys and Indians.

The entire saga of Indian history in the United States is so alluring that much of the country is named after its indigenous people: rivers, cities, towns, mountains—even manufactured goods, like cars. All of this meant that AIM, unlike other political groups such as the Black Panthers or the Nation of Islam, had great romantic appeal to white Americans and the potential for gaining their support.

Second, Native Americans have claimed a large geographic portion of this country, including some of the land's richest mineral deposits. Corporate America, with its vested interests in these wealthy deposits, stands to lose enormously if the Indians ever regain even a fraction of their homelands. And regaining homelands and autonomy for Native Americans is what the American Indian Movement was all about.

First Siege

The massacre at Wounded Knee occurred when three hundred Minnecojou Lakota were slaughtered by the Hotchkiss machine guns of the U.S. Seventh Cavalry four days after Christmas, 1890. The attitude displayed in 1890 by cavalry leader Maj. Samuel Whitside and his horse soldiers prevailed for more than eighty years. Whitside just didn't give a damn about Indians, and neither did the U.S. government.

Black Elk, a survivor of that massacre, wrote:

> I did not know then how much was ended. When I look back now from this high hill of my old age, I can still see the butchered women and children lying heaped and scattered all along the crooked gulch as plain as when I saw them with eyes still young. And I can see that something else died there in the bloody mud. . . . A people's dream died there.

From the 1700s through today, America's indigenous people have been stripped of their culture, land, and ability to survive. Native Americans lost millions of acres that the U.S. government originally promised they could retain, including valuable lands containing mineral deposits.

Second Siege

To commemorate the 1890 massacre and to publicize the plight of Native Americans who lived—poor, underfed, unemployed, and unhealthy—on reservations throughout the West, what came to be called the Second Siege of Wounded Knee was organized. During the winter of 1972–73, hundreds of Oglala Sioux, plus Native Americans from other tribes and nations, came to Wounded Knee, a dot on the Pine Ridge Reservation in South Dakota.

The situation on the Pine Ridge Reservation was already tense because of the occurrence of a plethora of unsolved murders of Native Americans and a melee between whites and Native Americans at the county courthouse in nearby Custer. In addition, many reservation residents were dissatisfied with Dick Wilson, the tribal leader handpicked by the BIA. Long-simmering feuds between different factions of Native Americans on the reservation were ignited by the Gestapo tactics employed by Dick Wilson's squads. He organized the "goon squads"—so-called Guardians of the Oglala Nation—to roam the reservation and keep "order." But the bullies and toughs created hell on earth for the reservation's residents.

This was the situation at Wounded Knee when AIM came in at the request of the Oglala Sioux Civil Rights Organization, a group that wanted to protest Wilson's reign of terror as well as other grievances against the U.S. government. Hundreds of Native Americans took over the tiny community to protest continuing injustices perpetrated by the goons and by the BIA in the name of the United States.

The U.S. government already had a military presence at Wounded Knee because it was a federal reservation, but after AIM became involved, the government augmented its forces with an army: FBI agents, federal marshals, state troopers, BIA police, even units of the army and air force. The government's eventual use of military force in this domestic situation was a gross violation of the law.

I became involved when my old friend Chief Lyons and Pedro Bissonnette, a leader of the traditional Indians at Pine Ridge, both called me. "The leadership would like you to come out," Pedro said. I flew at once to Rapid City, South Dakota, where I was met by a group of Native Americans who drove me to Wounded Knee. Before we could enter the embattled hamlet, our panel truck was stopped by the FBI, and we were forced to wait for hours in the vehicle. But since I was there as a lawyer, the Bureau eventually opened up the roadblock and allowed us in. We passed a little stream where I saw my first real tepee; then I noticed burned and wrecked cars that had been placed by AIM members on either side of the stream as their improvised roadblock. I was appalled at my initial view of Wounded Knee: St. Mary's Church, the Wounded Knee Trading Post, all the other buildings, were dilapidated and desolate.

Inside the church, which was used as a central meeting place, I met Russell Means, Dennis Banks, and other AIM leaders. They and the leaders of the Oglala Sioux Civil Rights Organization were holding Wounded Knee, refusing to allow anyone not affiliated with AIM in or out. At issue were the demands of the Native Americans and the refusal of the U.S. government to honor those demands.

The government wanted AIM off the reservation so things could get back to normal. But the Native Americans had several demands: public hearings on the 1868 Fort Laramie Treaty between the United States and the Oglala Sioux; an extensive probe of the BIA; and indictments of Dick Wilson and the goons who had committed serious crimes against reservation dwellers.

The government would not give in to any of these demands and surrounded Wounded Knee with armed forces which threatened to come in shooting if the Native Americans didn't give up, return the reservation to normal, and eject the outsiders—members of AIM. The situation reminded me of Attica. I thought the whole time I was there, For God's sake, I hope this doesn't turn into a bloodbath. I hope they hold back and negotiate.

Initially, the government made an offer to end the siege. But it refused the Native Americans' suggestion that both sides should withdraw. The government refused to withdraw its presence from the reservation. Instead, it would allow the Native Americans to stack their guns and leave Wounded Knee, thus ending the siege. No arrests would be made at that time, according to the government, but there was the possibility of indictments later. I thought it was a bad settlement and said so. I didn't think the Native Americans should give in so easily.

John Echo Hawk, an Indian from the Native American Legal Defense Fund (NALDF), disagreed with me and shouted, "The deaths of my brothers and sisters will be on your head." He added, "We made our point, and we've been here a week, so now we can get out with no one being hurt."

I said to Russell Means, "Of course, it's more dangerous to stay and not take this easy way out. But on the other hand, what the hell did you do this for, anyway?" Russell said they had occupied Wounded Knee to make a political point; they wanted to draw America's attention to the plight of Native Americans all over the country.

"Walking out," I said, "the time is lost. You've only been here a week." So, on March 5, Russell burned the government's proposal in front of television cameras that were there to record the historic siege. John Echo Hawk, with his more conservative approach, left the Knee in a huff.

I did not believe the political point had been made; the occupation had not gone on long enough to galvanize the country. I was hopeful the siege would continue, that the political issues would be clarified to the public and that negotiations would continue with no one being injured. But, of course, I had my doubts: John Echo Hawk had made me feel very uneasy. He was a Native American, and for that reason alone he probably knew more than I did. I was a white middle-class lawyer who had just walked into this situation. Did I have a right to tell Russell Means that I thought the government's offer was a bad deal?

I hoped John Echo Hawk wasn't right and that my political judgment was correct, because Wounded Knee, at that moment, was a tinderbox and there was real danger in continuing the occupation. Anything could have happened; the place was surrounded by FBI SWAT teams and other military groups.

I didn't change my opinion, and Russell and the others agreed and didn't give up. In the long run, the danger had to be secondary to the political protest.

I stayed at Wounded Knee, off and on, for much of the duration of the negotiations, living in a nearby building, the infirmary. The infirmary was part of the trading post that was owned by a couple, the Gildersleeves, a white man with a Native American wife. They remained unharmed during the occupation. I came up with a plan to ensure there could never be any accusations that the Indians had taken them hostage. On behalf of AIM, I offered the Gildersleeves an option to buy their trading post for the astronomical price of $5 million. The couple agreed, of course, since the place was only worth about $100,000, and they signed an option form I typed up. They had nothing to lose by signing, and it probably made them feel less afraid, since they could then view themselves as negotiating with the enemy rather than being at its mercy.

In the midst of negotiations, Ramon Roubideaux, a lawyer who was the chief mediator for the Indians, left because he couldn't take the tension and was racked with nerves. As he walked out, he said to me, "You take over." For the moment, I was the chief negotiator.

At that time, about 250 FBI agents, the largest concentration of agents in the United States, were camped out at Wounded Knee. The government used one of its standard tactics: To justify having the FBI take over an area, the Bureau portrays the residents of that area as lawless desperadoes. (In 1993, the rationale for destroying the Branch Davidians in Waco, Texas, was much the same.)

The negotiations between the Indians and the government were fruitless, endless discussions. Stanley Pottinger, the assistant attorney general from Washington, Martin Walsh of the Federal Mediation Service, Russell Means, Dennis Banks, other leaders, and I went every morning to the tepee and first smoked a pipe of birchbark tobacco. Then we talked. But nothing was resolved, so after some days I went home because I had cases in New York and couldn't stay in Wounded Knee forever.

A week or so later, Pedro Bissonnette called me again, and I returned to the Knee on March 9, accompanied by Dave Dellinger. We went through the same ritual of getting in; then, suddenly, on March 10, the government lifted the roadblocks. It appeared that the feds were going to let everyone walk out and the siege would end without anyone getting hurt. This was premature, as it turned out, but at the time, all of us—Native Americans, lawyers, and supporters—were delighted with what seemed to be a good resolution. We planned an honoring ceremony and feast as a tribute to the leaders of the siege: Russell, Dennis, Stanley Holder, Carter Camp, and Milo Goings, who had been shot in the leg and was the first casualty of the occupation.

For the feast, word went out to butcher a heifer. I watched a youth take aim with his rifle, fire, and then saw the animal drop. What happened then is kind of amazing: None of the Native Americans there knew how to butcher the heifer. They were so far removed from their heritage that they no longer knew how to cull meat from the land. Many of them had been raised in the city and were not schooled in the old ways; Russell Means, for example, had been an accountant in Cleveland; Vernon Bellecourt, a hairdresser in Minneapolis.

A white CBS cameraman stepped forward, said, "I know how to do this," and butchered the animal. While the meat was being roasted at an open fire, we went up the hill to pay our respects at the common grave of those who had been butchered by the U.S. Cavalry eighty-three years earlier.

At the first Wounded Knee incident, Big Foot's small band of Minnecojou Sioux had been shot in the back as they fled from the cavalry. Because of a blizzard, they remained unburied for days, then were thrown into a common grave, marked by a small stone containing the names of some of the dead.

Russell, Dennis, I, and the others walked by the grave and placed our hands on the stone. Amazingly, I felt the stone move ever so slightly, and as it did, I looked up on the hill beyond and saw a young Indian, maybe fifteen years old, seated bareback on a horse. Although it was cold, he was naked from the waist up, with a red bandanna around his forehead and a rifle in one hand, the butt end on the horse's neck; he held his other hand in the air, as if in greeting. I was so affected, feeling the stone move, seeing the young boy who epitomized all of my old romantic ideas. There was a timelessness to it; he could have been a ghost from 1890.

After the march, we ate the wonderful meat that had been grilled over an open fire and then sat on into the evening around the fire. Later that night, believing the Wounded Knee confrontation was over for good, I packed up and again went home. But the very next day, government postal inspectors tried to enter Wounded Knee, and a group of Native Americans detained them, thinking they were there to spy for the U.S. government. Then a van driven by a Native American was chased by the FBI, and an agent was shot in the hand. The cease-fire had fallen apart.

The Wounded Knee siege continued and WKLDOC ("wickledoc"), the Wounded Knee Legal Defense/Offense Committee, comprised of paralegals and lawyers, came in to work on behalf of the Native Americans. Finally, seventy-one days after it had begun, the Second Siege ended, not with a bang but a whimper. By May, the press had lost much interest in Wounded Knee as had the public, some of the Native American leaders were off raising money, and, tired, cold, hungry, and depressed by the death of a young leader, Buddy Lamont, the remaining Native Americans at Wounded Knee marched out of the hamlet.

The U.S. government did not honor a single demand the Native Indians had put forth. The 1868 treaty was not discussed. The BIA was not investigated. Although Dick Wilson and his goons were not indicted, several hundred Native Americans were brought up on federal charges.

The Leadership Trial

Shortly after the end of the Second Siege, indictments were handed down against Native American leaders Russell Means, Dennis Banks, Clyde Bellecourt, Carter Camp, Leonard Crow Dog, Stan Holder, and Pedro Bissonnette for conspiracy to illegally occupy Wounded Knee and assorted other crimes.

Russell Means and Dennis Banks were tried separately from the others, and some of the latter were never prosecuted. To my great sorrow, Pedro Bissonnette was assassinated in October 1973 by one of Dick Wilson's goons because of his role in the Oglala Sioux Civil Rights Organization. Pedro's murderer, like most of those responsible for the killings on the reservation, was never found.

The trial of Russell and Dennis, called the Leadership Trial, began on January 8, 1974, in St. Paul, Minnesota, and lasted an incredibly long eight and a half months. I represented Russell, working with a defense team that included Kenneth Tilsen, Mark Lane, Larry Leventhal, and Douglas Hall.

To me, this trial had everything: significance, drama, and political meaning. At Wounded Knee, I had developed a kinship with Russell, Dennis, and company and had become totally caught up in the Indian world. Every time I took a case which revolved around a cause in which I believed, my zeal was absolute. This time it was the Native Americans.

The trial was held before South Dakota chief U.S. district court judge Fred Nichol, a man whom I came to respect very much by the time it was over. The prosecution's team leader, Assistant U.S. Attorney R. W. Hurd, was quite inept and was also severely handicapped by the fact that federal agencies—specifically, the FBI and U.S. marshals—would not provide him with relevant wiretapping data and other information. This was an excellent illustration of the degree of paranoia and mistrust among the authoritarian guardians of American security. Often they won't help each other out if it means revealing trade secrets.

The prosecution took more than six months, presenting a long string of witnesses who claimed to have knowledge of Russell and Dennis as evil, criminal renegades; as it turned out, a majority of this testimony was perjured.

The defense was relatively quick, because our main point was that Russell and Dennis were political prisoners. One of our most important defense witnesses was Dee Brown, author of *Bury My Heart at Wounded Knee,* who established the historical significance of the 1973 occupation of Wounded Knee by tying it in politically and spiritually with the 1890 incident. We cited the 1868 Fort Laramie Treaty, which had guaranteed the Oglala Sioux their land, without interference, "as long as the rivers shall flow . . . as long as the grass shall grow." This treaty was a negotiated settlement between the Sioux and the United States which gave the Sioux half of what would eventually become the state of South Dakota and a small section of North Dakota as well.

Marlon Brando

I met Marlon for the first time at this trial. Born in Omaha, Nebraska, he has an affinity for Native Americans and has donated vehicles and bail money and supported their causes for many years. One evening, I joined Marlon and his girlfriend in their hotel room. He told me he had come to St. Paul to watch the Leadership Trial because he was planning a movie about Wounded Knee and wanted to see me in action. "I'm a method actor, and I have to see the subject that I'm playing in his native habitat," he said. Of course, I was very flattered. He had a script by writer Abby Mann, author of *Judgment at Nuremberg* and many other works. Columbia Pictures was supposed to produce the film, but the project fell through. Today Oliver Stone is thinking of reviving it.

Marlon and I became friends—as much as it's possible to be friends with him—and have worked together, over the years, on many political issues. Marlon is aloof, reclusive, and retiring. He loathes public appearances so much that he is no longer accessible to people in the movement, or anyone else for that matter. But with all his quirks, I liked him very much when we first met and still do.

Marlon always told me he wanted to play a lawyer, and he finally did in a wonderful film about South Africa, *Dry White Season.* Throughout the film, he wore his glasses on top of his head, as I always do. After I saw it, I told him, "You stole my trademark," and he replied with a broad smile, "It's not copyrighted."

Mark Lane

Throughout the Leadership Trial, I commuted back and forth to New York. Margie and I lived in her fifth-floor walkup on Perry Street in Greenwich Village. One weekend, I was due in at 8:00 P.M. on a flight from St. Paul, and Margie was expecting me. Ken Tilsen, a defense lawyer on our team, called her and said, "Sit down. I have some news: Bill is in jail."

The judge had thrown Mark Lane and me into the Ramsey County pokey for contempt. During court that day, he heard someone laugh, thought it was the Native Americans sitting in the audience, and ordered the marshals to throw them out. Within seconds, eight marshals were lying unconscious on the courtroom floor. They had tried to oust the AIM heavies who were seated in the first two rows.

I rushed up to the bench and yelled at the judge: "You brought this on us. They didn't laugh! You should have had a hearing!" Then, protesting the removal of the Indians who had fought with the marshals, I yelled, "Take me also!" Of course, it was courtroom theatrics talking; I did not really want to go to jail, particularly on a Friday afternoon. Judge Nichol was so disgusted with me that he actually pushed me hard, in the chest, to force me away from the bench. Mark Lane—always hungry for publicity—ran over and shouted, "Take me, too!" The judge held us both in contempt, and the two of us spent the night in the Ramsey County Jail.

As it turned out, I enjoyed that Friday night in jail. As I usually do, I made the best of it and found the experience exhilarating and not at all frightening. Margie, who had flown out as soon as she heard, came to me directly from the airport and loaned me her toothbrush. She also promised to try to get me out, but I was reconciled to spending the entire weekend in custody. The only reading materials in my cell were some comic books and the Bible, so I stayed up all night and read the Bible. My love for the Bible, which I often quote in court, stems from a college course I took, "The Bible as Living Literature," taught by Alexander Witherspoon, a wonderful Yale professor. That night in jail, I read through all my favorite parts, like St. Paul's Epistles and, of course, the Song of Songs: "Thy two breasts are like two young roes that are twins, which feed among the lilies."

Margie drew up a writ of habeas corpus and got me and Lane released the next morning. When she appeared before the judge, she promised that, if we were released, we would not talk to the press. Judge Nichol actually borrowed another judge's car, drove with Margie to the jail, picked us up, and took us to where we were staying. Then he went home to his apartment, which was directly across from the courthouse. When he looked out of his window a few minutes later, he almost had apoplexy: Lane and I were busy talking to the press and posing for television cameras. I saw no conflict, because it was Margie who had promised him we wouldn't talk to the press; I certainly never made that promise. But whatever I said to the press about the situation, I was not at all hard on the judge.

In a way, I was a bit sorry Margie got Lane released from jail. He had dropped the case he was working on, the murder prosecution of a Native American, and joined the team on the Leadership Trial because he thought the publicity would be more intense there. Over time, Lane's desire for personal publicity had become a sickness, as it can with anyone. Many lawyers have their problems with the malady also, and I am no stranger to the feeling: You always want to be in the media, no matter what gets you there. It's a strong urge, but I had learned my lesson years before when *Esquire* magazine wanted me to pose for a Richard Avedon cover in which I'd be held in the arms of a giant wooden cat. I almost agreed until Lotte made me realize that it would be completely undignified and had nothing to do with law or any of my political beliefs—only with my ego.

Charlie Garry was house counsel for cult leader Jim Jones's Peoples Temple in San Francisco, but Mark Lane sort of forced his way in there also. Garry was absolutely convinced that Lane was morally responsible, in part, for the mass suicides of some nine hundred followers of Jones in 1978 in Jonestown, Guyana. Months before the deaths, Jones had called me for some legal advice and had invited me and my family to Jonestown, but my instincts told me to turn him down.

Jim Jones was losing it mentally toward the end, and Garry told me that he felt that Lane had a lot to do with feeding Jones's paranoia. "They're going to come and kill you," Lane would tell Jones. When the suicides actually occurred, Lane and Garry were locked in a building, under guard, convinced they were about to be murdered. Garry told me that Lane persuaded the guard to let them go by saying, "There will be no one left to tell your story unless some of us are freed."

As they ran out through the jungle, Lane said to Garry, "You shouldn't have eaten that sandwich. It was poisoned." Fortunately, it wasn't, but Garry always held a grudge against Lane after that for not at least warning him that the sandwich brought by their guard might be lethal.

Summation

At the Leadership Trial, my summation was dramatic and emotional. The night before I was to sum up, I was desperate. Here was a historic criminal trial, one of the longest in American history, maybe the longest. I was going to be the last voice for the defense—and I had no idea how to end. I had planned to refer to the trials of Socrates and Jesus, both of whom were obviously much more than common criminals but were tried as such. I would compare Russell and Dennis to these two and to others who had been prosecuted as lawbreakers but whose actions arose out of powerful spiritual or political convictions.

In desperation, I sought help from Meridel LeSueur, a wonderful midwestern writer and the mother-in-law of my cocounsel Ken Tilsen. "I've just got to have something to end up with that's brilliant, eloquent, and moving," I said. Meridel quickly solved my problem: "Go to the St. Paul Library and get out Stephen Vincent Benét's poem 'American Names.' " I rushed to the library and found "American Names" in a Benét anthology. The book's foreword explained that Benét became an expatriate because he was horrified at what had been done to the American Indians. When I read the poem, I understood why Meridel had suggested it.

The summation in St. Paul was, I think, as good a closing as I have ever done. I was so emotionally involved that I gave it everything I had. The Second Siege of Wounded Knee was the result of the terrible circumstances in which so many American Indians lived, I said. "The confrontation was an attempt to secure some reason for remaining alive—some hope so that Indian children wouldn't have the highest suicide rate in the nation."

I concluded with the last six lines of Benét's moving poem:

> I shall not rest quiet in Montparnasse.
> I shall not lie easy at Winchelsea.
> You may bury my body in Sussex grass,
> You may bury my tongue at Champmedy.
> I shall not be there. I shall rise and pass.
> Bury my heart at Wounded Knee.

I was crying when I finished, and there wasn't a sound in the room. Then there was a hesitant ripple of applause, the judge rapped his gavel, and that was it.

During jury deliberations, one juror became ill, and the judge inquired whether both sides would accept eleven jurors. The defense agreed at once, but the government refused. The judge was furious. The nine-month trial had cost millions of dollars, and the government would not agree to an eleven-member panel because they believed that the stricken juror, an elderly white woman, was on their side! (In reality, she was not and had already voted to acquit Russell and Dennis of the conspiracy charge, the most serious in the indictment.)

Because of the government's lack of cooperation, Judge Nichol angrily dismissed the charges against Russell and Dennis in order to avoid a mistrial. His harsh words for the prosecution and the FBI reminded us all, once again, how devious and vindictive the government could be. And the judge showed how radical a change he had undergone during this trial: "Although it hurts me deeply, I am forced to the conclusion that the prosecution in this trial had something other than attaining justice foremost in its mind. . . . The waters of justice have been polluted, and dismissal, I believe, is the appropriate cure for the pollution in this case."

In reaching his decision, the judge summarized all of the government's acts of misconduct that had taken place before and during the trial. These included illegal eavesdropping, subornation of perjury, mishandling of the files, and withholding of evidence. Perhaps the most egregious malfeasance was the prosecution's efforts to hide the fact that one of its key witnesses, who was being shepherded by the FBI, had raped a young high school girl in a nearby Wisconsin town while he was awaiting his court appearance. Mark Lane had done a superb job investigating this matter, and I must give him the enormous credit he deserves.

It was a wonderful victory, which I mistakenly thought meant that we were on the brink of a real turnaround in America. I felt that if a federal judge could be convinced, after some months of listening to all the facts about AIM and the FBI, that injustice had been done, the cleansing process in America had begun.

Of course, I was wrong. What happened in that courtroom in St. Paul was an aberration. It has happened much too infrequently in the years since—to me, to others—but I still seek it whenever I enter a courtroom to defend a client. It's called justice.

Shootout at Pine Ridge

A year after the Leadership Trial, two years after the end of the Second Siege, the atmosphere of bitterness, hatred, and fear at the Pine Ridge Reservation was kept alive by the FBI's continuous harassment of the residents and the goons' strong-arm methods. Pine Ridge between 1973 and 1975 was a war zone. Scores of Native Americans died, and no one was ever held accountable for their murders. It was only after two FBI agents were killed there that the outside world noticed that people were dying on that reservation. Only when their own died did the U.S. government care. Dead Indians meant nothing.

On June 26, 1975, FBI agents Jack Coler—a Colorado SWAT member—and Ronald Williams had driven swiftly and unannounced toward an AIM encampment, known as "Tent City," on the Jumping Bull Compound on the Pine Ridge Reservation. Their ostensible assignment was to arrest Jimmy Eagle, a youth who was charged with stealing a pair of boots, but their real mission was to keep tabs on AIM leaders: A map was found on Coler's body that pinpointed the locations of AIM leaders' homes.

As Coler and Williams raced up the hill, the occupants of Tent City felt that they were under attack; both sides began shooting, but it is unknown who shot first. During the shoot-out, the two agents and a Native American, Joe Stuntz, were killed.

Four men, Robert E. Robideau, Darelle Dean Butler, Jimmy Eagle, and Leonard Peltier, were eventually indicted for the murder of the agents. No one was ever charged with the murder of Joe Stuntz. The government eventually dismissed the charges against the youngest of the four, Jimmy Eagle, and Peltier fled to Canada. The two remaining defendants, Bob Robideau and Dino Butler, were tried on charges of aiding and abetting in the murder of the two agents. John C. Lowe, Bruce Ellison, Jack Schwartz, and Margie and I represented them. In addition to the lawyers, the defense team included Stewart Albert and Judy Klavir, who had also been members of the defense team at the Chicago Conspiracy Trial.

Trial at Cedar Rapids

The trial of Butler and Robideau was moved to Cedar Rapids, Iowa, because of anti-Indian prejudice in the Dakotas. Chief U.S. district judge Edward J. McManus presided. For about a month before the trial began on June 7, the FBI had spread rumors in the small city that AIM members were going to go on a rampage, murdering police, a cop a day. In order to skew the trial and sway the jury, several federal agencies participated in this fear campaign, including the Office of the U.S. Attorney, the Office of the U.S. Marshal, and the Justice Department. As a result, the police in Cedar Rapids were completely paranoid. They truly believed that Armageddon was about to come down upon their heads.

Despite the government's attempts to roil the waters, the trial began quietly, and the Native Americans who attended were orderly and civil. Even the Iowa National Guard cooperated by lending some large tents to house the many Indian visitors who were expected to attend the proceedings.

During this trial, I appeared more disheveled than usual. The air in Cedar Rapids was so permeated with oatmeal dust from the Purina plant that my two suits were perpetually covered with a grayish powder. I spent time with Marlon Brando again; he had come to observe the trial. He would stand outside the courthouse at lunchtime with Dick Gregory. The townspeople never expected to see a movie star like Marlon Brando in Cedar Rapids. They would come up to him excitedly to shake his hand. Marlon was very supportive and affable with me and everyone else during his time in Cedar Rapids. On July 7, I turned fifty-seven, and he threw a party for me at the defense team's rented house, complete with a huge cake and a chorus of "For he's a jolly good fellow." He even led the singing.

Our defense of Butler and Robideau was based on the premise that the FBI had acted unethically and immorally and had caused much of the trouble on the reservation, including the deaths of its own agents. The prosecution's witnesses were liars and phonies; at the last minute they decided not to use one, Myrtle Poor Bear, an emotionally disturbed woman, probably because they knew the defense would destroy her testimony.

Our witnesses were called mainly to establish FBI malfeasance, especially the Iago-like tactics of an FBI agent named David Price, who had been the partner of one of the slain agents, Ronald Williams. We accused Price and the FBI of deliberately suborning perjury and of using witnesses on the stand who were willing to lie. It was a strategy long familiar to those of us who worked on political cases in the 1960s and 1970s. The FBI used convicted criminals—or those who were about to be convicted—who were willing to say just about anything to secure reduced sentences; or they used terrified young people who could be frightened into repeating whatever the Bureau suggested they say.

Our most important witness was Sen. Frank Church, head of the Senate's Select Committee to Study Governmental Operations with Respect to Intelligence Activities, known as the Church Committee. He testified that as part of its program known by the acronym COINTELPRO, the FBI had spread disinformation about certain organizations, including AIM. As a result of Senator Church's testimony, we were able to subpoena FBI director Clarence Kelley as a witness. I believe that this was the first time a director of the Bureau had ever testified in a criminal trial.

When I had Kelley on the stand, I tried to show that the rumors about AIM members planning to kill police officers had been planted by the FBI. I showed Kelley telegrams and cablegrams sent from Washington, under his name, to all federal and state law enforcement officers in South Dakota. These messages stated that AIM was going to fake accidents on the highways in South Dakota; then, when police turned up to investigate, AIM members were going to ambush and murder the officers.

Kelley denied ever seeing or authorizing these telegrams. In fact, he said he understood that AIM was a perfectly valid civil rights organization and one of the few that had the express approval of the FBI, certainly the approval of its director. I attempted to prove that most FBI agents subscribe to the cynical premise of Civil War general Philip H. Sheridan—"The only good Indians I ever saw were dead"—but had no success, as Kelley denied any negative attitudes toward Native Americans.

In the end, the campaign of lies and misinformation backfired, because the people of Cedar Rapids, including the jury, eventually stopped believing the federal government when they realized that the reports about AIM members killing police were totally unfounded.

When I questioned Kelley about COINTELPRO, he said the program had ended in 1971. Kelley actually damaged the prosecution and helped the defense because he lost his cool while he was testifying and made it clear that he thought the lives of two FBI agents were more important than the lives of anyone else, especially Native Americans. However, he did admit that all people had the right to defend themselves when attacked.

The jury deliberated for five days and found Robideau and Butler not guilty. We all burst into tears and cheers. We had secured acquittals for two Native Americans on charges of murdering a pair of FBI agents. Although the town and the judge were against us at the beginning, by the end of the trial they had seen the inherent unfairness of the government's treatment of the Indians and the unfairness of the case against them.

When the not-guilty verdicts were announced, FBI agents in the courtroom sobbed in frustration, which, I must say, I enjoyed. I was glad they could feel what it was like to fight and lose. I thought, For once, you're on the receiving end.

Leonard Peltier

The acquittals of Butler and Robideau and the dismissal of charges against Jimmy Eagle were bad news for Leonard Peltier, the fourth man charged with murdering the FBI agents. If he was not convicted, the deaths of those agents would remain unavenged. The Justice Department pursued Peltier relentlessly. According to FBI memoranda secured through Freedom of Information Act requests, the FBI held at least six conferences in the months before Peltier's trial to determine how it could help the prosecution get a conviction.

Peltier, an Ojibwa Sioux with long black hair and a bushy mustache, was extradited in 1976 from Vancouver, where he had fled after he was indicted for the FBI agent murders. He was extradited on the basis of fraudulent affidavits signed by a "witness," Myrtle Poor Bear. Although she signed the affidavits, this woman was not present on the reservation when the two FBI agents died. The Bureau now candidly admits that these affidavits were fake. However, no one has ever been penalized for this.

Leonard Peltier was tried in Fargo, North Dakota, despite documentation that the judge, U.S. District Court judge Paul Benson, was thought to be notoriously anti-Indian. A later decision of his in an unrelated case was reversed on appeal because of a racial slur he made during his charge to the jury. I was unable to represent Leonard because I was on another murder case at the time, so another New York lawyer, Elliot Taikeff, was selected to lead a defense team that included John Lowe and Bruce Ellison. Taikeff turned out to be the wrong man for the job.

From what I have read in the trial transcript, Judge Benson ruled against the defense almost every time. Many of his rulings were the exact opposite of rulings made by Judge McManus in the Cedar Rapids trial of Butler and Robideau. McManus had ruled that certain autopsy pictures could not be shown to a jury because they were too inflammatory; Benson allowed the autopsy pictures in. McManus had ruled that pictures of the agents graduating from the FBI Academy would prejudice the jury; Benson allowed them in.

In many ways, it was like the Chicago trial: The judge misinterpreted the rules of evidence whenever he could so as to ensure a conviction, and the prosecution faked all kinds of evidence to make sure the defendant was found guilty. Leonard Peltier was framed by the FBI. They menaced and coerced witnesses and threw the law books out the window, just as they did in Chicago.

But unlike Chicago, the government won. Leonard was convicted on two counts of first-degree murder. He has been incarcerated ever since, an all-American political prisoner.

Peltier's Appeals

Leonard Peltier has appealed three times since his conviction, steadfastly maintaining his innocence, consistently contending that the ballistics evidence against him was fabricated just like Myrtle Poor Bear's affidavits. The U.S. government has long since conceded that it no longer considers Leonard the killer of agents Coler and Williams but believes he only aided and abetted those who did kill them. Despite this belief, Leonard has not been given a new trial.

I have represented Leonard in appeals and hearings since his original conviction. After he was convicted, attorneys Michael Tigar and John Privitera filed an FOIA request on his behalf. As a result, we received thousands and thousands of pages the defense had never seen before from FBI files—known in Bureau jargon as RESMURS—although many files are still being withheld.

Leonard's conviction had been based almost entirely on the strength of one lie: that a .223 shell casing supposedly found in the open trunk of agent Jack Coler's car matched an AR-15 rifle falsely attributed to Leonard. But the files we obtained revealed that the prosecution hid a report showing that this weapon could not possibly have fired the fatal shots because it had a different firing pin. This information came to light long after Leonard's first unsuccessful appeal.

When we learned of this suppressed report, we asked Judge Benson to grant Leonard an evidentiary hearing. Quite predictably, he refused. We then appealed to the Eighth Circuit in St. Louis to order Judge Benson to conduct such a hearing.

At the time, I was working on another case and arrived in St. Louis at nine-thirty on the night before the oral argument. I was met by Tigar, Privitera, and Ellison, who were up to date on everything. In Eighth Circuit hearings, you are only allowed twenty minutes, so you must take advantage of every second. The judges can sabotage you by asking delaying questions and taking up all your time. So it was essential that I be up to date on the case, know everything, and prepare a well-planned strategy.

That night, as I walked around my room, changing, showering, brushing my teeth, and putting on my pajamas, the other lawyers followed me in and out of the bathroom, hammering facts into me. I listened carefully and then concluded that the Eighth Circuit judges would almost certainly rule against Leonard, as they had in the past. I decided to really give it to them. I would let these judges know how I felt about the great injustice being done to Leonard. Everyone agreed with this adversarial strategy, based on our impressions of the judges who would be on the bench the next morning and their previous adverse decision in regard to Peltier.

I planned what I would say: "This is a disgrace, and you people have minced around this forever. It's high time you did something." On that note, we all went to bed.

The next morning, I went into court casually, glasses on top of my head, tie askew, since I didn't really care what kind of impression I made. But as soon as I walked into the courtroom and saw those judges, I had the feeling that they wanted to listen, that they were interested in Leonard, that they were not dead set against us. I immediately smoothed down my hair, straightened my tie, fixed my glasses, and spoke as politely as I've ever done in a courtroom. Within seconds, I changed my attitude and the thrust of the argument, and as it turned out, I did the right thing. The judges were listening, and they ordered a new hearing.

The hearing took place a few months later, on October 1, 1984, in Bismarck, North Dakota. FBI ballistics expert Evan Hodge was the only witness. At Leonard's trial, Hodge had testified that the crucial .223 casing had been ejected from the AR-15 attributed (falsely) to Leonard. But Hodge had also written the report exonerating that very rifle, the report that had been hidden from the defense team. The prosecution had further misled the original trial jury by stating that only one AR-15 rifle was at the compound when in reality there were three.

Although Hodge's testimony did nothing to dispel the import of his withheld report, predictably, Judge Benson still refused to grant Leonard a new trial.

We returned to the Eighth Circuit. On October 15, 1985, I argued before a three-judge panel that Benson was wrong in finding that the Peltier jury would not have acquitted him had it known of Hodge's suppressed report. The government, in order to diminish the effect of the Hodge report, now took the position that it didn't know who shot the agents, that Peltier was merely an aider and abettor and not the cold-blooded executioner of Coler and Williams it had previously made him out to be. Therefore, it didn't matter at all whether the casing was ejected from his weapon.

Almost a year later, the Eighth Circuit ruled against us. But anyone reading its long opinion—except for the very last sentence, which denied a new trial—would have concluded that we had won. The ruling stated that the FBI had "withheld evidence . . . favorable to Peltier" which "cast a strong doubt on the government's case." Had this evidence not been wrongfully suppressed, "there is a possibility that a jury would have acquitted Leonard Peltier."

In deciding not to grant a new trial to Leonard, I believe that these judges violated their oaths of office. Had the victims been grocery store clerks or gas station attendants, they would have swiftly ordered a new trial. But because the victims were FBI agents and not ordinary citizens, they simply could not bring themselves to do the right thing.

The degree of their unexpressed shame at their failure to follow the law was shown in a letter written several years later by Judge Gerald Heaney, author of the circuit's unfavorable opinion, to Sen. Daniel Inouye, chair of the Committee on Indian Affairs. In this letter, Heaney recommended that Peltier's sentence be commuted. He wrote that a commutation would begin "the healing process" in the government's stormy relationship with Native Americans and that "the FBI was equally to blame for the shootout and that the entire responsibility can't be placed on Peltier."

Despite support from American politicians—more than fifty members of Congress filed a legal brief siding with Leonard's appeal, stating that his case demonstrated "a clear abuse of the investigative process by the FBI"—as well as from international groups and religious figures, the U.S. Supreme Court declined to review Leonard's case. Undoubtedly, it, too, does not want to offend the Bureau.

Leonard Peltier most recently appealed in November 1992 with Ramsey Clark as his main attorney. By this time, I think Leonard needed a new voice to speak for him. I've been arguing unsuccessfully for Leonard for the past seventeen years; we needed fresh blood.

On July 7, 1993, my seventy-fourth birthday, the Eighth Circuit again denied Leonard's appeal. Despite the clear finding of the 1985 panel of the same court that the government altered its premise that Leonard had cold-bloodedly murdered the agents, the opinion, written by a visiting judge from Washington, D.C., insisted that this was not true. By some convoluted process of reasoning, the court rejected the earlier finding that the government's theory at trial "was that Peltier killed the two FBI agents at point-blank range with the Wichita AR-15." The court held "that Peltier either personally committed the murders or aided and abetted their commission." Once again, another trio of federal judges had bowed to the FBI's might and made a mockery of their oaths of office.

I have no doubt that at some point, sooner, I hope, rather than later, Leonard Peltier will gain his freedom. Often referred to as the American Sakharov, his worldwide supporters include Amnesty International, the World Council of Churches, Archbishop Desmond M. Tutu of South Africa, and the late archbishop of Canterbury. I believe the political ramifications of continuing his imprisonment will eventually convince even the hardheads in the government to commute his two life sentences.

If Leonard had been granted a new trial, it would have been relatively simple for the defense to demonstrate that if Butler and Robideau were acquitted, Leonard should also be exonerated. There was basically no difference in the evidence presented against the three men, with the exception of the now thoroughly discredited testimony about the .223 casing. Any jury hearing Leonard's case again would have had to take very seriously the fact that the government lied, the FBI lied, and the ballistics evidence was falsified. His case is a classic example of a total miscarriage of justice and a symbol of this government's cruel and base treatment of our indigenous people. I am thoroughly ashamed that in the name of law my country is holding hostage a Native American for whom the prison gates should have opened long ago.

In May 1993, I wrote to Hillary Rodham Clinton in response to a rather terse letter she had sent to one of Leonard's new lawyers, Eric Seitz, who had requested a presidential review of the case. She wrote to Seitz that her husband had no power to interfere in an ongoing criminal case. In my letter to Mrs. Clinton, I criticized her for her cold response to Seitz's reasonable letter and informed her that she was quite incorrect about limits on presidential interference in criminal cases. She should have recalled former President Bush's pardon of the indicted Caspar Weinberger.

Some weeks later, one of Mrs. Clinton's aides called me and said her boss apologized for the tone of her letter. This was followed by a note from her appointments secretary: "I know that [Mrs. Clinton] would want me to convey her appreciation for your thoughtfulness, along with her best wishes. Thank you for your letter. Your patience and understanding are deeply appreciated." I guess she thought she had received an invitation to a lawn party rather than a desperate appeal for a man's life.

I only hope that I live long enough to see Leonard free.

After Wounded Knee

In the decades since the Second Siege, the government has never really let up on its pressure against Native Americans, and along with other WKLDOC attorneys, I've continued to work on cases involving Indians.

AIM has had its ups and downs, splitting into factions and subgroups. Today it is a national movement rather than an organization, with no real meetings or leaders. But there are many Native Americans working actively for various Indian causes and concerns. Russell Means suffered through many arrests and legal battles and continues to be an outspoken advocate for his people. From his home base in South Dakota, he has traveled around the country to act in several films, including *The Last of the Mohicans,* in which he played the character Chingakgook. John Trudell had a strong supporting role in *Thunderheart,* the movie version of the murder of Anna Mae Aquash, an outspoken activist on the Pine Ridge Reservation. Floyd Westerman, another alumnus of Wounded Knee, was in *Dances with Wolves* and *The Doors.* It was Floyd who remarked that AIM has now become AIMA (American Indian Movement Actors), because Native Americans are so much in demand for acting roles.

Dennis Banks today organizes freedom runs all over the country to publicize the heritage of Native Americans. He fought off extradition to South Dakota in the late 1970s while he was living in California. He was wanted for sentencing for his role in the Custer Courthouse melee that took place just before the Second Siege. (On February 6, 1973, a group of Native Americans, including Banks, entered the Custer Courthouse to meet with officials to protest the murder of a young Indian by white hoodlums. A fight between Indians and police that began outside the building spread rapidly, and the courthouse was burned down. Dennis Banks was indicted later that year for his alleged involvement in the riot.)

A movement to prevent his extradition was led by Marlon Brando, Jane Fonda, myself, and many others. We convinced then governor of California Jerry Brown not to send Dennis back to South Dakota, and he became a professor at the University of California at Davis, teaching Native American history and culture.

In 1982, conservative Republican George Deukmajian succeeded Brown as governor, having run on a platform which included a promise to return Dennis to the tender mercies of South Dakota. To avoid extradition, Dennis fled with his family to New York State, where they sought shelter on the Onondaga Reservation. Dennis also made a formal request for sanctuary to New York's governor Mario Cuomo. Cuomo turned him down, saying that while no law enforcement agents would be allowed to enter the reservation because of its sovereign status, Dennis would be arrested if he left there. Truthfully, I don't think any governor has the power to give sanctuary to a fugitive from another state.

After about a year on the Onondaga Reservation, Dennis grew tired of being cooped up and decided to surrender to the authorities in South Dakota. I made the legal arrangements and went there and waited for him at the Rapid City Airport. Of course, the South Dakota authorities were also there. To our surprise, Dennis arrived in a car, escorted by a long caravan of vehicles. He gave himself up, and I accompanied him to Custer for a bail hearing; we were turned down, though, because Dennis had jumped bail a decade earlier.

Later, during a long sentencing hearing, many people spoke on Dennis's behalf, including some of his students and author Alice Walker. Walker testified about the work Dennis had done at the University of California, including encouraging minority students to attend college and to graduate. Dennis received one to three years and served a year.

Reunion

Twenty years after the siege of Wounded Knee, in February 1993, I took Margie and our daughters, Sarah and Emily, there for a reunion. We landed in Rapid City, South Dakota, and headed for the Alex Johnson Hotel. The hotel, built the same year that Mt. Rushmore was sculpted, is filled with Indian art, including a picture of Mr. Johnson, dressed in full Indian regalia, wearing a war bonnet. When we arrived, the girls and Margie went up to their rooms while I headed for the large mezzanine reserved for the reunion.

Stepping into that room made me feel as if I were walking backward in my own footsteps. Everyone was twenty years older, but to me they all looked the same. These were people with whom I had shared a most momentous time in my life, and I felt enormous affection for them. Of course, I hugged everyone. All around me I heard cries of "Bill! Over here!" Everywhere I turned, I saw old friends. Then there was a small ceremony in which I received plaques honoring the Center for Constitutional Rights for its participation at Wounded Knee and for successfully representing two Native American women who faced the death penalty when they were charged with murders twenty years ago.

One woman, Rita Silk Nauni, had just returned to her native Oklahoma after a confrontation with her abusive husband in L.A. When she arrived at the Oklahoma City Airport, she didn't even have taxi fare, so she and her young son began walking. A police car pulled up, and when the officers, a man and a woman, started toward her, Rita was convinced they were going to take her son away and give him to her husband. In sheer panic, she ripped the female officer's gun from its holster and shot and killed the other officer. The Center for Constitutional Rights became involved in Rita's case and, through a series of legal maneuvers, was able to get her released from prison. It is a miracle that she did not get electrocuted. My only appearance in the case, in an Oklahoma city court, resulted in my being held in contempt for protesting the judge's refusal to let me speak on her behalf.

I looked around the reunion and eventually found Russell; Dennis was not there. Russell had gotten a little older, with the aura now of a famous movie star. He also is about to produce his own films. I talked to most of the lawyers who had worked on Wounded Knee cases, including Ken Tilsen, Larry Leventhal, Bruce Ellison, Terry Gilbert, and Joe Beeler. I found myself happy to be alive, glad I had made it through these last two decades so I could experience this wonderful reunion.

The following morning, we all traveled by bus to Porcupine, several miles from Wounded Knee. There we ate breakfast and then set out on a nine-mile march to the Knee. We divided into four groups so we could approach it from the four directions of the universe, east, west, south, and north. The entire nine-mile hike was uphill, and I became totally winded after a while, so I rode in a car. Margie, Sarah, and Emily walked all the way. I was in the first car, so I could keep the march in view; it was beautiful. Two miles before our destination, I got out of the car because I just had to march into the Knee.

As we got up on top of the last hill, I could see Wounded Knee, or what was left of it, and it was a tremendous kick. I remembered walking in on a different road, but much the same way, twenty years earlier. We marched to an area just outside the common grave of hundreds of Native Americans, and the ceremony began. Sarah and Emily were quiet, and then Emmy asked if I would go with her to the gravesite. We went into the graveyard together, and I saw the stone which I had remembered as being much bigger. "Put your hand on it," I told Emmy, and she did. I placed my hand on it, also, and again felt it move, ever so slightly.

Later, when Russell asked me to speak, I joked, at first, and said that twenty years had taken its toll on me, so I had to duck in and out of a car along the way. But I was glad that I had arrived here finally. It was very moving for me to be here. "I came here for my children," I said.

Sarah was sixteen then; Emily, fourteen. Margie and I felt it was probably the last time we would take them with us to such an event; they had reached the age where they wanted to be with their own friends, not us. In my speech, I talked a lot about Emily and Sarah and how I hoped this trip had meaning for them. I think it did.

Later, I spoke with Russell, who said, pointing out over the view, "You know, there was a half-track over there. There were FBI agents over there." He re-created the whole picture of the surrounding forces.

I asked, "Russell, does this take you back, too, to when we first met?"

"It certainly does," he said. "My life is sort of different now."

He told me that when he played Chingakgook, he had objected about the breechcloth he wore because, as he told the director, it was much too small. I asked, "Russell, was that because of the size of your tomahawk?" He laughed. The breechcloth simply was not historically correct, but the director didn't care and told Russell, "When you're producing your own films, you can wear any size breechcloth you want, but while I'm the director here, you wear that one." That remark, Russell told me, confirmed his desire to become a producer himself.

After the speeches, after the ceremony, pipes were lit. When I was handed the pipe, I turned it around to the four directions; then I puffed and passed it on. I said, "All my relations," which means "this is for everyone," reflecting the Native American belief that everything, no matter how insignificant, is part of the cycle of life.

Then we all went back to Porcupine.

CHAPTER FOURTEEN

Fallout

---

*Kunstler goes to the brink of saying something for which
we could indict him, but he never goes over the line.*

Margie

BETWEEN 1966 AND 1976, MY OWN PERSPECTIVE AND LANDSCAPE
changed as radically as America's. My mother and father died,
and my brother, Michael, slid into a deep depression after his son
committed suicide. I divorced, remarried, and began a new family.

I first met Margie in 1968 when she was a law student working to defend Columbia University students. Under the guidance
of Students for a Democratic Society, they had taken over some
buildings on the Columbia campus to protest the university's policy concerning the surrounding black community. We met a second time in Manhattan Criminal Court, where I engaged Margie in
a conversation about how I had smoked a joint in a ski lift over the
weekend. She later confessed that she thought I was an old fart
trying to impress her. She was right.

I didn't see much of her for the next two years. Then, when I
needed help on a murder case—I represented defendants charged
with the machine-gun murders of eight people at Fountain Valley,
David Rockefeller's plush Virgin Islands resort—I saw Margie and
her then husband, progressive lawyer Michael Ratner, who now
works for the Center for Constitutional Rights. When I asked if
either of them wanted to work on the case with me, Margie volunteered. Although she denies that her decision had anything to do

with me, I don't believe her. I like to think she was as attracted to me as I was to her. In the Virgin Islands, we worked together on our case daily, and what began as physical attraction grew into a deep and abiding love.

My first marriage had been falling apart for a long time. Lotte is a very smart woman, and I'd been entranced with her since we met as youngsters. Everything had been fine at home until I became wrapped up in the civil rights movement. Although Lotte was also involved, I really threw myself into it, floating around the South, constantly traveling. Because I was often away from home, Lotte and I had less and less contact and gradually lost a certain degree of intimacy. We had married when Lotte was only seventeen, before she had a chance to attend college, and I think she regretted that. She also wasn't too pleased with being stuck at home taking care of two children while I ran around the country doing exciting work. Add to these differences and our loss of intimacy the fact that we always had twin beds. They were pushed close together, but there was a table in between, so in order to start anything, I had to crawl out of my bed and into hers.

I was also influenced by the many sexual encounters I had with other women during my travels. These young women pursued me, most likely because I was something of a celebrity, and the more well known I became, the more aggressive the women got. For someone with my vanity and ego, it was very gratifying. How could I resist?

In the beginning, I had mixed feelings and a bit of guilt, but after a while, I began to see these other women as a natural part of life. I viewed myself as a glamorous movement figure, part of the counterculture. People in the movement encouraged women to sleep with me. I remember once when a civil rights leader walked into a room, pointed to a young woman, and said, "You're to go with Kunstler tonight." It was certainly not the right way to treat women, but we all did it.

I was middle-aged, in that dangerous decade between fifty and sixty, and suddenly I found that young women desired me. It made me feel youthful and wanted and wonderful. It had nothing to do with being unhappy in my marriage, because I wasn't. But I was at that age where you have to prove to yourself that you've still got it, that you can still get it up. In many male lives comes this moment of crisis when you think: I'm losing my hair. I'm losing my teeth. I've got varicose veins. I'm never going to be the same as I was at twenty-five or thirty. I have all sorts of worries about money and everything under the sun. Yet out there is a fantasy world that for a moment makes you forget all of it. You can be twenty-five again.

My work was demanding and sometimes frightening, and I was very often lonely. So I formed many alliances, both one-night stands and relationships that endured a bit longer, as I made return trips to the same city or town. These were not love affairs, only physical encounters that eased my loneliness and made me feel young and vital. It's no wonder, though, that I didn't feel very warm toward Lotte when I returned home.

Over the years, Lotte had lost some of her glamour and appeal to me. When I would return home to Westchester from my travels, she was there, not to be my concubine but as wife and mother, doing the dishes, cooking food, or taking care of the children. I saw these other women only in connection with romance and sex. They were beautiful fantasies who would be in my bed at night and gone the next morning. I never saw them peeling vegetables or cleaning the stove.

I am certain that Lotte had some inkling of my relationships with other women, but she never said anything, and she never demanded a divorce. I don't think she ever did want a divorce, but she must have been very angry and disgusted with my childish behavior. So with less sexual intimacy between us and more wrangling, I would start to think, Gee, it was great last night with so-and-so down there in Birmingham. At home, I had to deal with the real world of mortgage, kids, and all the rest of it. I loved Lotte, primarily because she was the mother of my children and a very good person, and I was determined not to leave. But our relationship never recovered.

What finally broke up my marriage was falling in love with Margie. The situation was irresistible: the tropical Virgin Islands, working together for a year on a challenging case, an extremely attractive woman, and a highly susceptible man. Initially, I appreciated her as a lawyer, then as a woman. I've always been attracted to faces like hers: mysterious and exotic. I fell for her without reservation, and over the years my feelings for her have, if anything, increased fivefold.

In 1973, just before the Wounded Knee trials, I moved out of the home I shared with Lotte. Shortly after that, we were divorced. The worst thing I did to Lotte occurred the day before I moved out. We had a long talk, and she confronted me about every infidelity. I admitted to it all. Then she asked me if I had learned anything. Without thinking, I said, "Yes. I've learned that I am not going to do the same thing to Margie." In retrospect, that was a cruel statement, and I'm very sorry I said it.

While I was doing the Wounded Knee trials out West and after Margie had separated from her husband, we saw each other on weekends. At first, we each had separate apartments, because she wanted me to figure out how I really felt; then we lived together. Finally, we made the commitment and decided to marry. On October 6, 1975, we drove to Judge Bruce Wright's chambers on lower Broadway in Manhattan, parked at a fifteen-minute meter, ran inside, got married, and ran out.

We have been together now nearly twenty years. I am still very much in love with Margie. We have a powerful relationship because we are very different. She is restrained and doesn't like publicity, while I am as outgoing as can be. Emily once said to Margie, "You're an introvert, and he's an extrovert." I think it is that difference that gives a great deal of strength to our marriage.

Looking back, I realize those one-night stands thirty years ago were not really very much fun; they were actually quite empty. I muttered the same things in a different pair of ears every night— all the things you say when you're in a state of high sexual tension, like "I love you" or "You're beautiful." Today I can't conceive of saying those things to anyone but Margie. They would seem so tawdry. And that's an amazing change from the way I lived during the sixties.

Although I'm in my mid-seventies, I don't feel old; I feel just as I was. But I have a relationship with Margie that is the relationship of my life, and that is very satisfying. Of course, we have our ups and downs. Nothing is placid with two people like us. She's enormously bright and can fly off the handle the same way I do, and we both have low boiling points. But the deep love is there for me, always, as I think it is for her.

My Parents' Deaths

All through my early adult years, even into my forties, my parents and my brother and sister were very important to me. Then the deaths began, and, as I guess it is with everyone, I began to feel my own mortality. My mother died in 1966 while I was trying the Washington, D.C., school desegregation case. I was forty-seven. She had always said she would never move from the nine-room apartment on Central Park West, but my father decided it was too big for the two of them, so he had signed a lease for a smaller place. The day they were to leave, just as the moving van pulled up to the building, my mother lay down on her bed quietly and died. It was a great shock because she had not been ill.

One of our family jokes is that hers is the only funeral ever held in a Santini moving van. It's good that we could joke about it afterward, but at the time we certainly couldn't.

I didn't cry when she died, although I was always closer to her than to my father. After she died, my father, then in his eighties and still active, still working, spent all his time with his girlfriend, Iris Fish. They went to museums and theaters and did all the things my parents had never done. My parents had rarely gone anywhere. My father would say, "It's too much for your mother," and she would say, "It's too much for your father." But with Iris Fish nothing was too much, and he did it all. (Later, we all came to realize that his relationship with Iris Fish may have antedated my mother's death.)

One year after my mother died, my father collapsed with his hand on the front door, on his way out. He had always had a heart problem, but he took his nitroglycerine and had seemed fine. After he collapsed, we took him to St. Luke's Hospital, and they put him to bed. He was not critical, the doctors said. However, the next morning, I was at an ACLU board meeting when Mary called to tell me our father had died.

I rushed to St. Luke's and ran into his room. He was lying on the bed with his chest all blue, probably from the doctors pounding on it to try to revive him. For some reason, I believed I could wake him up, even though I had been told he was dead, so I grabbed him and yelled, "You son of a bitch, wake up! You can't leave us now!" I kept shaking him, trying to make him live. Several doctors and nurses ran in and tore me away. I just didn't want him to go. I absolutely couldn't accept it.

My father's death meant that I was next in line. All the grief for my mother that I hadn't expressed came out when my father died, and I cried uncontrollably for months, in cars, at home, on the street, everywhere. It took a long time before I could get myself under control.

Michael

My brother died in 1984. He was only sixty-three. A drastic change had begun eight years earlier when his son, Billy, committed suicide. Michael changed then from a charming, ebullient man to a totally withdrawn human being. Billy was named, like me, after my paternal grandfather. He had always been a strange little boy. Although I certainly don't claim to understand if there is a relationship between how he was as a young child and what happened later, I can remember that he was not like other children. Whenever our families got together on holidays, Billy would always cling to Michael.

Years later, after Billy graduated from college, Michael set him up in a foreign-car business in Stamford, Connecticut. Then Billy fell in love and took his girlfriend to Europe, where the relationship must have deteriorated, because they each returned separately. A short time after he came home, without his girlfriend, Billy killed himself by putting a hose from his car's exhaust pipe into the car window.

Michael knew Billy's romantic problems were at the root of his suicide, but he could never stop blaming himself, for he and Billy had had breakfast together on the morning of his death. I often said to Michael, "You were not responsible in any way for this," but I got nowhere.

Much as I loved my brother, much as I felt for him, I began to dread seeing him. Although I knew he was breaking apart internally, I couldn't help him. One of my major faults is that I'm too impatient with people to be a really good listener. I'm not very sympathetic, and I get bored with people who complain or agonize over their problems, as Michael was doing—as he was entitled to do. My way of dealing with emotional trauma has always been to avoid and deny.

Avoiding was made easy for me because in 1976, when Billy died, I was already living in New York City, and Michael was still in Westchester. During the years between Billy's suicide and Michael's own death in 1984, I was busy with my own life and very involved with my new family: Sarah was born on November 5, 1976; Emily, on June 24, 1978. Michael and I saw each other infrequently during this period.

To this day, I'm sorry I wasn't of more help to Michael. He needed someone to listen to him, and I just couldn't do it. He spent his last years busy with a dozen different projects, all of them attempts to fill up the terrible hole in his gut. He finally killed himself, too, although it wasn't an actual suicide. Michael had heart trouble and was supposed to undergo open-heart surgery. He kept delaying it until he finally died. He was still a young man, and I believe he purposely avoided having the surgery. Also, he died after a strenuous turn on his exercise bike, something that he was not supposed to do because of his heart problem.

Michael has been gone for almost a decade, and I really miss him. I also miss my mother and father, my grandparents—and the wonderful, secure, and very happy childhood they provided for me on Manhattan's Upper West Side, some seventy years ago.

Fallout

At the same time that my family life was undergoing radical changes, my work life continued along the path I had started during the early sixties. I continued to take on political cases, a large number of which resulted directly from the government's illegal and intrusive attempts to destroy dissent by individuals and organizations.

As the 1960s became the 1970s, whatever idealism remained in the movement was destroyed. Some people became disillusioned or discouraged by losses or burnout and turned away from the movement, seeking answers in spiritualism, materialism, alternative lifestyles, and dozens of other pursuits. Others remained active at least through the mid-1970s, even though it was not an easy time. There continued to be much violence and many deaths. The fallout from the sixties was intense.

The later years of the movement were marked also by chronic infighting and divisiveness. Many conflicts began as misunderstandings which then grew into feuds, the flames fanned by the FBI. By the early 1970s, the counterculture and antiwar and Black Power movements had been seriously weakened by the FBI, but I was busier than ever. Although the number of willing lawyers had dropped sharply from its sixties peak, I continued defending political and counterculture activists against the numerous criminal charges that were brought against them by the government and various law enforcement agencies. Because the old charges of breaching the peace weren't doing the trick, the authorities began raising the ante. As a result, Stokely Carmichael was charged with insurrection in Georgia, a capital offense, and Rap Brown faced riot charges in Maryland.

The government did not succeed in its efforts to destroy the movement, though, despite what we later found out were mammoth efforts, both expensive and extensive. There were some individuals, like the Berrigans and Dave Dellinger, whose voices simply could not be stilled. I continued to do the work that was meaningful to me, filled with the same passions I had felt in the South and in Chicago, determined not to rest until each client who came to me received as much justice as I could wrest from the system.

COINTELPRO

The nadir of the FBI's evil was COINTELPRO, a counterintelligence program designed to subvert and destroy all dissent, especially the civil rights, antiwar, and Black Power movements. For years after the sixties ended, my legal work consisted of trying to counter the effects of this project. COINTELPRO was in full operation between 1956 and 1971, although COINTELPRO-type methods continued to be used for many years afterward—and may still be in practice today. The first such program was created to investigate the Communist party-U.S.A. in this country, but ended up targeting individuals who had nothing at all to do with the party, like Dr. Martin Luther King Jr. In 1968, a New Left COINTELPRO was begun after the student takeover of the Columbia University campus.

COINTELPRO—with techniques that ranged from petty to degrading to deadly—was the dirtiest sort of program, one that all sixties radicals believed existed but couldn't prove. Respecting no one's privacy or constitutional rights, the program wiretapped people and created provocative anonymous letters. It used break-ins, the IRS, informants, and other devices to cause dissension between rival political groups and to discredit and harass movement leaders and supporters.

The program was used only against groups that demanded either a fundamental change in the country's attitudes, a return of land, or the unity of minority people. The FBI tolerated groups like the United Jewish Appeal, the Urban League, and the National Organization for Women. But it infiltrated and attempted to subvert every single civil rights and political organization, both peaceful and militant, including Dr. King's SCLC, SNCC, SDS, NAACP, the Nation of Islam, and the Black Panther party.

COINTELPRO broke up marriages—the union of Stokely Carmichael and Miriam Makeba never recovered from a campaign of vicious letters, created by COINTELPRO—and caused many deaths. Actress Jean Seberg, who was married to novelist Romain Gary, was a contributor to the Black Panther party. As documented in the Church Committee Report, gossip columnist Joyce Haber ran an item in 1971, planted by COINTELPRO, claiming that the baby Seberg was expecting had been fathered by prominent Black Panther David Hilliard. Seberg went into premature labor and miscarried three days later. Her emotional reaction was evident in that, after the miscarriage, she placed the fetus in a glass coffin so that the press could see that it was a white baby. Seberg killed herself in 1979. Her husband committed suicide a year later.

COINTELPRO Targets Blacks

In 1967, COINTELPRO set up Black Nationalist and Racial Intelligence Investigation sections. In March 1968, a month before Martin King was assassinated, Hoover sent a memo to FBI operatives stating that the Bureau's goal was to prevent the rise of a black messiah who could "unify and electrify" the movement. Names mentioned were Martin King, Stokely Carmichael, and Elijah Muhammad, the head of the Nation of Islam. Late in 1968, the Bureau gave orders to cripple the Black Panther party.

The Bureau also kept what it called the Black Extremists List, which included almost every black individual who was active in civil rights, whether they were Black Panthers or members of the Southern Christian Leadership Conference. (This particular program was the forerunner of the now-well-documented *Frühmenschen*—which means primitive man in German—an FBI policy uncovered in 1982 which unjustifiably targets black officials, both elected and appointed.)

In 1970 and 1971, the FBI stepped up counterintelligence against the Black Panthers, creating a rift between Huey Newton, Eldridge Cleaver, and Bobby Seale, turning factions within the party against each other, and wrecking the group's reputation.

Huey Newton, a founder of the Panthers, was a physically beautiful human being with a superior intelligence that enabled him to earn a Ph.D. while he was in prison. Initially, he had been looked up to by fellow Panthers as a god. When he was imprisoned in 1966, blacks gained strength from rallying around the "Free Huey!" movement. Eventually, however, Huey became nothing more than a target for police and FBI agents. Like Adam Powell, Rap Brown, and so many other black activists, his entire adult life was consumed by fighting legal battles. Huey had serious drug and emotional problems and ended up an addict. Although he died in a drug-related street fight, I am certain that neither he nor the countless other black leaders who died young would have done so without the invidious interference of the FBI.

From 1963 until his death in 1968, Martin Luther King was the focus of an intense program to destroy him as a leader of the civil rights movement, according to the Church Committee Report. Wiretaps, informants, lies, and rumors designed to discredit him, and, after he received the Nobel Peace Prize, a concerted effort to undermine him internationally, were some of the tactics used to bring him down.

Finally, in 1969, the Bureau took credit for the assassination of Malcolm X, labeling the 1965 murder the result of its successful stimulation of the feud between Malcolm and his former spiritual leader, Elijah Muhammad.

The Church Committee

COINTELPRO remained a secret for years until an FBI office in Media, Pennsylvania, was broken into on March 8, 1971, by persons unknown, who then sent papers stamped COINTELPRO to Carl Stern, an NBC reporter. When he asked J. Edgar Hoover what the word meant, Hoover denied any knowledge of it. After NBC filed a Freedom of Information Act lawsuit, the FBI capitulated and admitted to the existence of a counterintelligence operation that it claimed had been created to investigate certain dangerous people and organizations within the United States.

After COINTELPRO's existence was uncovered, the U.S. Senate formed a committee to investigate it, headed by Sen. Frank Church of Idaho. The Church Committee Report, issued in 1974, revealed that the program was not counterintelligence at all, but rather covert action against domestic organizations. It had violated the constitutional rights of hundreds of thousands of Americans and, as the report said, "went beyond the collection of intelligence to secret action designed to 'disrupt' and 'neutralize' target groups and individuals."

The report stated that when the FBI formed its New Left COINTELPRO, since it didn't know exactly what the New Left was, it had undercover agents infiltrate dozens of groups of antiwar activists, free-love advocates, pot-smoking hippies, and rebellious college students to find out what was going on.

Tale after tale of the FBI's criminal actions fill the seven volumes of the report. It placed blame for much of COINTELPRO on the administrations of both Kennedy and Johnson and concluded that they were well aware of the FBI's attempts to discredit Martin King and were therefore responsible for these nefarious FBI activities. The report also revealed that the Nixon administration was deeply involved in COINTELPRO.

According to the report, "Between 1940 and 1973, two agencies of the federal government—the CIA and the FBI—covertly and illegally opened and photographed first class letter mail within the United States." There were twelve mail-opening programs during those years; in just one of those programs, *215,000* pieces of mail were opened and photographed. In New York City, the mail-opening program ran from 1953 until 1973, and some copies of letters remain on file today. Those whose mail was opened include Linus Pauling, Edward Albee, John Steinbeck, SNCC, and SDS.

Finally, the Church Committee recommended that an oversight panel be created to ensure that this type of truly un-American activity was never again allowed to happen. Such a committee was formed, but I believe that the FBI still continues to use COINTELPRO-type methods to violate people's rights.

The actions against the counterculture by the FBI during the sixties were real. We were not paranoid. We did not imagine these things. They really happened. "The Bureau's self-imposed role as protector of the existing political and social order blurred the line between targeting criminal activity and constitutionally protected acts and advocacy," the Church Committee Report stated.

With COINTELPRO, nothing was off limits. In fact, when William C. Sullivan, FBI assistant director for domestic intelligence since 1961 and the head of COINTELPRO, testified before the Church Committee in 1975, he said: "No holds were barred. . . . This is a rough, tough business."

After Sullivan testified, Hoover fired him and locked him out of his office. Sullivan then returned to his native New Hampshire. The day after the house committee investigating the assassinations of Martin Luther King and President Kennedy unsuccessfully attempted to subpoena Sullivan, he was killed in what has been described as a hunting accident. The son of the local sheriff had mistaken him for a white-tailed deer.

After a national magazine retained me to investigate Sullivan's death, I discovered that he had been wearing a red and black mackinaw when he was killed, with nothing white showing. I have no doubt that he was murdered in retaliation for his perfidy before the Church Committee and to prevent him from testifying about the murders of King and Kennedy.

After years spent trying to deal with the effects of COINTEL-PRO, my rage at the FBI's almost unimaginable evil remains undiminished because I believe that it succeeded in many of its horrifying goals, given the deaths of Martin King, Malcolm X, and other sixties leaders.

But I also believe that, on a larger scale, the program failed to deter us and was unable to stop the political and social progress of the sixties. The effects of that era extended beyond individuals and groups, and real changes in our political and social structure took place. The decade of the sixties was a demarcation line, and we can never go back.

Disband the FBI

Since I have represented many clients whose lives were affected by the FBI, I am certain I have an enormous file in the Bureau, but I certainly would never pay the money it requires to copy it. I don't really care what's in it. I have seen some of Jerry Rubin's file, which is many thousands of pages long, and read what one agent said about me: "Kunstler goes to the brink of saying something for which we could indict him, but he never goes over the line."

Probably because I was a lawyer who represented activists rather than an activist myself, the government hounded and harassed me more subtly than they did my friends in the movement, like Rap, Stokely, or Abbie Hoffman. For me, there were small annoyances. The FBI has unsuccessfully tried an assortment of minor tricks to tarnish my reputation and damage my legal career. For example, right after Attica, in 1971, I received frequent calls from someone who appeared to be involving me in an imaginary plot to assassinate Governor Rockefeller. He'd say, "We're all ready, Bill. Just give the word." I realized I was being set up and that if a shot rang out over the governor's mansion, I'd be implicated. I also believed the calls were being taped, so I decided to publicize them by calling a press conference.

The next thing I knew, the state police wanted to put a recording device on my phone to intercept future calls. They brought in a big machine with a blinking red eye and put it in my bedroom. Of course, I never received any more calls, so after a month, I asked them to remove the machine. Today I proceed on the assumption that my phone is tapped. If I really want to discuss something important, I use a public phone or talk on the street.

Over the years, agents have broken into my office, stolen my Rolodex, and taken my personal IRS and divorce files. A homing device once was put on the car of my friend Stewart Albert, an unindicted coconspirator in the Chicago case, and his wife, Judy Klavir. We recovered $20,000 from the FBI for that because we had the device, marked with Bureau serial no. 107, in our possession. The Bureau admitted ownership of the device but later stole our lawyer's office safe where it had been stored.

Many years ago, I lost my address book while I was on an airplane. In 1979, when I learned from Julian Bond that his unlisted telephone number had been discovered by the FBI in "Bill Kunstler's address book," I wrote to the Bureau and demanded that it be returned. The FBI claimed that after I inadvertently left the book on the plane, whoever found it turned it in to one of its resident agencies. Instead of sending it back to me, however, it was Xeroxed and sent to every FBI office in the country.

In addition to this petty harassment, the IRS audits me virtually every year, and I have neither the time nor the energy to litigate what are obviously not random audits. To me, this is all part of the price I pay for being a gadfly. The Bureau no longer has a domestic counterintelligence program (at least that's what it says), but it keeps close tabs on people like me, who it believes represent a threat to national security. It's all done in the tradition of Joe McCarthy and J. Edgar Hoover. (Ironically, Hoover and I have something in common. In 1970, the University of Notre Dame made me an honorary fellow one year after Hoover had received the same honor.)

Since the FBI uses taxpayer dollars to fund its extreme and ridiculous investigations of anyone who expresses dissenting opinions, even resorting to crime—including theft, encouragement to murder, subornation of perjury, and manipulation of the judicial process—to achieve its ends, I have always advocated its disbanding. Before 1919, this country didn't have centralized police; it's the type of agency that invites corruption, like the Soviet equivalent, the KGB. Except for its laboratory and a centralized data computer, we don't need a federal law enforcement agency.

The FBI relies on shibboleths, makes many errors, and tries to overwhelm juries rather than prove facts to them. In fact, FBI agents take a special course on how to testify in court in order to influence jurors. One of my stock questions to FBI agents on the stand is: "You are taught how to influence juries, aren't you?"

"We have a course," they will answer. "The course teaches us not to influence but to testify so that jurors can understand what we're saying." Like St. George slaying the dragon, FBI agents have no scruples about how they do it as long as they get the bad guys. I would also eliminate the Central Intelligence Agency (CIA), because it is about the same as the FBI, perhaps worse. Now that the Cold War is over, perhaps the time has come to give some serious thought to saving the taxpayers the enormous annual appropriations made to these agencies.

JoAnn Little

During the mid-1970s, although I continued to represent political activists, I began to expand my work to represent clients whose cases were political in some other way, such as the case of JoAnn Little in 1975. She was a young black woman who had been picked up for stealing a television set and some clothing in North Carolina. She was required to remain in jail while awaiting trial because she couldn't raise bail. The white jailer, who was the sheriff's brother, entered her cell one night and tried to force her to perform oral sex on him. JoAnn somehow got hold of an ice pick, stabbed him to death, and then escaped.

She was soon caught and indicted for first-degree murder, a death-penalty charge. Her lawyers were Morris Dees, head of the energetic and effective Southern Poverty Law Center, and North Carolina attorney Jerry Paul. The trial was to be held in Raleigh before Judge Hamilton Hobgood. When the judge forced Dees out of the case, I agreed to join in JoAnn's defense. But when I appeared before Judge Hobgood, he would not allow me into the case, perhaps because he knew of my aggressive reputation. I was angry and told him I was sorry that North Carolina's justice had not improved since I had first represented clients there in 1961. For that remark, he threw me in the clink for a day. When I was released, I announced publicly that Judge Hobgood wanted JoAnn convicted "by any means necessary, in violation of his oath as well as the Constitution."

Many years later, I ran into Judge Hobgood, now retired, as he walked into the North Carolina Bar Association's annual convention in Asheville. I said, "Hi, Judge, remember me?"

He took one look at me and said, "I should have put you away for life."

"I'm glad you don't have the power anymore," I replied, but there seemed to be some humor in this interchange.

JoAnn Little became a cause célèbre because she had killed in self-defense while being sexually assaulted. Women all over the country raised bail money for her, and eventually she was acquitted of the murder charge. Because she had escaped from prison, she still owed North Carolina some time, but she took off and left the state.

One day, I received a call that JoAnn had been picked up, accompanied by an armed man, after a high-speed chase in Brooklyn. I went running to court to represent her. Because she was only a passenger in the car, there were no charges against her, but the North Carolina authorities now knew where she was. When they tried to extradite her to serve the time she owed, I represented her in *People ex rel. Little v. Ciuros,* which became a leading case on extradition. New York's highest court indicated there might be some situations where it would grant relief, but we ultimately lost. I had argued that if JoAnn was returned to North Carolina, she might be seriously hurt or even killed by the prison guards there because of her acquittal in the murder case. She finally had to return to serve out her term, but because of the publicity surrounding her case, she escaped any harm. After her term was over, JoAnn moved to New York and now lives in Brooklyn, where she works at a local hospital.

Joanne Chesimard

Two years after JoAnn Little was first arrested, I became involved in a serious political case when Joanne Chesimard (now Assata Shakur), a revolutionary, poet, and member of the Black Panther party, was charged with involvement in the murder of a New Jersey state trooper. During a 1977 shoot-out on the New Jersey Turnpike, the trooper and a member of the Panther party, Zayd Shakur, had been killed. Sundiata Acoli, a Black Panther, had been driving; Joanne had been in the front passenger seat and Shakur in the back.

Assata's was a political prosecution. Any time a black person is charged with a crime against a white law enforcement officer, I consider it political. I accepted the case when Evelyn Williams, Assata's aunt, called me in. I worked with New Jersey attorney Stuart Ball and New York lawyer Laurence Stern; Stern and I commuted together every day to New Brunswick, New Jersey, in the ancient Saab my nephew Billy had rebuilt for me.

Although I found Assata beautiful as well as political, intelligent, articulate, and a joy to represent, our relationship started off badly. She had complained about her basement cell in the all-male Middlesex County Jail because she was watched constantly, the lights were always on, and she had no windows, natural light, fresh air, or view of the outside world. She had been confined in the basement because the authorities claimed they had no women's facility.

Without consulting Assata, I told the press that her quarters were adequate. I had not yet spoken with her and, in my attempt to get along with the sheriff, decided to tell the press that everything was fine. I learned a hard lesson then, that you don't discuss anything concerning a client's well-being, particularly one in captivity, unless you talk to him or her first. When she read my comments in the next day's paper, Assata hit the roof. I thought that would be the end of our relationship. She was furious, and rightfully so. I realized she was totally justified in the way she felt, that I had done an indescribably stupid and demeaning thing to her. It was a most valuable lesson.

Assata's was going to be a very rough case, so I had tried to create an aura about myself—of congeniality with the sheriff and the other authorities—so that the trial would not be completely rancorous. I knew that because a state trooper had been killed and the defendant was a Black Panther, the authorities would be out for blood. The state police in New Jersey were so much like storm-troopers that their commandant, Col. Clinton Pagano, would not permit a single one of them to talk to us at all, even to say as much as good morning.

In attempting to be congenial with the sheriff, I had forgotten an essential lesson: The sheriff is an enemy, as are the prosecutor, judge, and other authorities. They don't have the same interests as a defense lawyer and his client; their agenda is always at odds with the defendant's.

Once I got over the hurdle of those statements to the press, everything was fine between me and Assata, and the trial proceeded. The surviving state trooper, who had run away when the shooting started, later tried to regain his colleagues' respect by testifying that Assata had held a gun on him. Since she was seriously wounded in the right shoulder during the shoot-out, we tried to prove that she could not have been holding a weapon when she herself was shot. Our expert, pathologist Dr. David

Spain, testified that the bullet could not have entered Assata's shoulder the way it did if she was holding a gun. According to Spain, Assata was shot while sitting in a noncombative position in the car and did not participate in the shoot-out.

But my argument was not strong enough, and there apparently were secret pressures on the jury; Assata was convicted. Later, I found out some of the shenanigans that went on among the supposedly sequestered jurors. A law enforcement agent told me that a member of the New Jersey State Assembly had gone to the hotel where the jury was sequestered and had talked to them about the necessity to convict. Another juror slipped out of the motel to get some whiskey, was stopped by sheriff's deputies, and was then later returned by them. When I publicized this and sought a mistrial in 1977, this juror sued me for defamation of character. Rather than subject myself to a civil trial in New Jersey, where I was bound to lose, I publicly apologized and paid him a small settlement.

I was starting to work on Assata's appeal when I heard that her friends had done far better for her than her lawyers. Assata was liberated from the Prison for Women in Clinton, New Jersey, by a number of individuals who believed that she had been unjustly convicted. She eventually made her way to Havana, where she still lives and where Margie and I visited her in July 1992. Margie and I had gone to Havana as part of a delegation sent by the US + Cuba Medical Project to deliver pediatric antibiotics to the Cuban Red Cross. After we arrived, I called Assata. I had not seen her in years, not since I had last visited her at Clinton after her conviction. The three of us had a wonderful reunion, and I cherish her last words to me. She praised me for my work and asked me to continue helping other African Americans who are subjected to political prosecution. I assured her that I would.

The Brinks Robbery

The fallout from the sixties continued for many years. Some of my clients had been charged as a result of their activities during that period. Some of my other involvements occurred because of my intimate connection with the movement.

One night in October 1981, my telephone rang at two in the morning. "Will you accept a collect call from somebody in a correctional facility?" At first, I assumed it was a client, but when I heard it was a young woman whose name I did not recognize, I refused to accept the call. I went back to sleep, and a few hours later, the phone rang again. It was the same caller, and this time she said, "Please tell Leonard." When I heard those words, I immediately knew the caller was Kathy Boudin, Leonard Boudin's daughter and a member of the Weather Underground. She had just been arrested in connection with what came to be known as the Brinks Robbery.

On October 21, 1981, in Rockland County, just north of New York City, a group had attempted to rob a Brinks armored truck of $1.6 million. During the ensuing shoot-out, a guard and two police officers were killed. Kathy Boudin, Judith A. Clark, Samuel Brown, and David J. Gilbert, all members of the Weather Underground, were arrested shortly after the confrontation.

The first time Kathy called me that night, she had used an alias. She didn't want anyone to know her identity, as she had been underground for more than a decade, since the Greenwich Village town-house explosion in 1970. The second time she called, I woke Margie up, and then we called Leonard. Early the next morning, Margie and I, Leonard and his wife, Jean, and his partner, Victor Rabinowitz, drove up to the Rockland County Jail where Kathy was being held. We all went in to see her, and after we finished talking, she asked if we could pick up her child, then a little more than a year old, from the baby-sitter's. We returned to New York, and while Leonard, Jean, and I waited at the West End Tavern, a Columbia University hangout, Margie went around the corner and got the baby, Chesa.

At one point, right after the arrests, I was asked to make a statement to the media about the Brinks case. Trying my best to downplay the political aspects of the robbery, I said, "What are you all getting so excited about? This is a garden-variety robbery. Because these are radicals and there are whites and blacks together, you're making a big deal of it. This is nothing more than a regular robbery."

To a certain extent, what happened next mirrored my experience with Joanne Chesimard. I made my statement to the press because I thought I was doing the right thing for the defendants. But when I met with them later, in prison, they were furious. To them, the Brinks robbery was a revolutionary act because it was the first time since abolitionist John Brown attacked the federal arsenal at Harpers Ferry, Virginia, that whites and blacks had physically fought together on the same side as an integrated unit.

I realized that I should have consulted with the defendants before I spoke to the press.

Leonard did not ask me to represent Kathy, but instead asked Len Weinglass, my cocounsel in Chicago, to take on her defense. Perhaps Leonard wanted to handle the defense from the sidelines and thought that Len would be more amenable to such a relationship. Or maybe he thought Len's easygoing style would be more helpful to his daughter than my flamboyant one. Perhaps Leonard believed the caricature of me which persisted for many years, that I was all bluster and not lawyerlike. Many people, to my despair, believed it. Later, I did represent another person connected with this case, Anthony N. LaBorde, whose charges were eventually dismissed because of lack of evidence.

Len did a good job with Kathy's case, and after much legal maneuvering, she pleaded guilty to a single count—and was sentenced to twenty years. She is currently serving her term in New York's Bedford Hills Correctional Facility, where she has made an enviable record for herself as a writer, instructor of poor and Third World women, and fearsome softball pitcher. Ironically, her brother Michael Boudin—whose suits I helped select when he was a young boy and his father was unavailable—now sits on the prestigious U.S. Court of Appeals for the First Circuit, having been nominated to that position by President Bush.

I was quite disappointed about not representing Kathy, mainly because of my admiration and respect for her father. I had met him years before when, as a neophyte in the area of constitutional law, I needed his assistance with the William Worthy passport case. Leonard had eloquence, charm, and refinement. I often observed him in court and imagined his suit disappearing, replaced by a toga. I fantasized him with a laurel wreath on his head, arguing before the Senate in ancient Rome.

I almost worked with Leonard on one occasion, several years before his daughter's arrest. Philip Berrigan, Elizabeth McAlister, and other antiwar activists were indicted in 1972 by the federal government for conspiring to kidnap Henry Kissinger and hold him hostage until the Vietnam War was ended. Initially, I was one of the lawyers on their defense team but was squeezed out because the others thought that I was much too radical. When I left the lawyers' meeting after I was given my walking papers, I felt as low as I have ever felt. Since I am never one to dwell on the past or on personal problems, this feeling dissipated as soon as my next case came along.

End of an Era

During the sixties, I ran from case to case and never thought much about what was happening. Today I am often asked to analyze that period in history and explain what it meant to our country and whether it has had a lasting effect. Looking back, I realize that the individuals and groups that protested and dissented were all part of one enormous struggle against evil.

The sixties should be an object lesson to us all, I once told my grandson Dan's class at Yale. That particular decade has always been one of overwhelming change in American history. In the 1760s, the struggle began which led to the American Revolution; in the 1860s, a divided citizenry fought the Civil War; and, finally, in the 1960s, the country was nearly torn apart by discord and dissent. These periods are lessons; we must use the techniques and methods of these turbulent decades to achieve our long-range goals.

During the 1960s, organized protest ended the war in Vietnam, destroyed several political careers, including that of President Lyndon Johnson, and ended legally sanctioned segregation in the South. It also changed forever our image of blacks and all minorities, of women, gays, and other disfranchised groups. Inevitably, the decade had its failures and weaknesses, and we are still, years later, fighting many of the same battles. But the sixties was a great beginning, and those who participated in the movement helped bring about changes in the political, social, and economic structure that are very much in evidence today.

During that decade, we made great strides in civil rights, checking the power of government, and all human rights. But we have to keep working not to lose ground and to continue gaining. If we don't fight, evil will win. Those of us, myself included, who believe that the only way to keep government relatively honest is to make sure it knows we're watching also believe we certainly can't trust the government to protect us. This is because the American judiciary, from the Supreme Court on down, and the rest of the system are not friends of the people.

I am not sentimental or nostalgic about the sixties. I still act on my belief that protest, dissent, speaking out, and keeping vigilant is what keeps government from running roughshod over us all. The struggle continues today, although more subtly than in the sixties. That was an exciting, important time. We developed an alternative culture in opposition to the old, moldy status quo. We had a country in motion, happier people, more fun, a generation that went to Woodstock and had a party even while it engaged in a struggle for human rights. But the era was not a party. It was a crusade, and a crusade never ends.

If the sixties taught me anything, from the South in the early years to Chicago in 1969 and after, it is that those with power will never quit, that the Establishment will not rest until it roots out and destroys all opposition. For that reason, those who challenge the Establishment must have the same tenacity.

In *Moby Dick,* Melville's theme of the never-ending conflict between good and evil was personified by the obsessed Captain Ahab's pursuit of the white whale. Like Ahab, the activists of the sixties were devoted, involved, and committed to that eternal war between good and evil. They also believed they could win. They were reinforced by their own exuberance and by the sheer numbers of oppressed people rising up and shouting: Screw you! No more! We want change!

Even though Ahab did not bring down the white whale and ended up sacrificing his life as well as the lives of his crew, the youngest member of the crew, Ishmael, survived and went back to sea. There may be no climactic victories, no perfect green pastures, in the human rights struggles of today and tomorrow, but we must never fail to strive for a beachhead here, a beachhead there. Like Ishmael, we must always go back to sea.

PART FOUR

Politically Incorrect

CHAPTER FIFTEEN

Defending Blacks in a Racist Country

This one's for Larry Davis!

IN THE YEARS SINCE THE ACTIVE POLITICAL MOVEMENT OF THE SIXTIES ended, I have continued to fight against what I view as the evils of our society by representing political clients, minority defendants, and others who I feel need a strong defense. Although I'm often criticized for what I do, sometimes I receive thanks instead of insults. One such happy occasion was a 1985 dinner at which the National Lawyers Guild honored me. After an eloquent speech, the poet June Jordan asked any women in the room whose sons had been represented by me to stand. About thirty black women stood up, each the mother of a son who had, in one way or another, been hurt by the system. I looked at each of them, recalled each son I had defended, and felt very proud.

For more than twenty years my representation of black defendants has been motivated by one of my strongest beliefs: that our society is always racist. No matter what laws are passed or what promises are made, in the halls of justice, the only justice is in the halls, as Lenny Bruce once observed. None of our institutions, including our legal system, deliver on this country's fundamental promise that we are all created equal, especially those of us not born with white skins.

Black people rarely get justice in our courts; so, for me, cases in which defendants are black are political. Naturally, I can't take every one of these cases, so I choose those which are the most difficult, where there is the least chance of an acquittal. You might say I go for the seemingly lost causes. During the 1980s and 1990s, I defended many such clients, most of whom I am still representing because their cases are under appeal. I never give up until I have exhausted every avenue. An acquittal or a Supreme Court decision is the only legal remedy I accept as final.

1981
York and LaBorde

No cause is more predictably lost than when Black Panthers are charged with cop killing. In 1980, two New York City cops, John Scarangella and Richard Rainey, were ambushed as they sat in their patrol car on a Queens street. Scarangella was killed, and Rainey was severely wounded. The two men accused of the assault, James Dixon York (now Bashir Hameed) and Anthony N. LaBorde (Abdul Majid), were former Black Panthers.

I was York's attorney, and black activist attorney C. Vernon Mason, my former law associate, represented LaBorde. Since the defendants were indigent, I was paid the twenty-five dollars an hour the state allots; fortunately, money is not my motivation in these cases. I knew both of these men since they were in the Black Panther party; I knew their families, and LaBorde's wife had been a classmate of my daughter Karin at Tougaloo. Mason and I were assisted by Randolph Scott-McLaughlin and Mark Gombiner, two young, progressive lawyers.

York and LaBorde were tried three times for Scarangella's murder. The first trial resulted in a hung jury. During deliberations in the second trial, one juror had a psychotic episode, so the judge planned to discharge the jury. I wasn't in court when this occurred. I was on my way out of town to give a speech and had left Mark Gombiner in charge. When I checked in with Mark by phone from the airport, he told me the judge was going to declare a mistrial, although the jury, at the time of the disruption, had been 8–4 for acquittal. If the judge changed his mind, didn't discharge the jury, and instead replaced the ill juror, who was white, with the alternate next in line, a black woman, that would probably be good for the defense.

I quickly called the judge, Cornelius O'Brien, and urged him not to declare a mistrial, but it was to no avail. It has always been my opinion that Justice O'Brien saw acquittals as failures for the system and did whatever he could to prevent them.

From this experience, I learned never to leave a case when the jury is out, even if some other matter appears urgent. In reality, out of the hundreds of jury deliberations I've been through, there have been only a very few times when I wasn't there. One time I recall was when I had just been diagnosed with cancer of the bladder, was urinating blood, and my doctor had urged me to get to a hospital. Coincidentally, the cocounsel I left in charge in that case was Mark's twin brother, Robert Gombiner.

Justice O'Brien's decision to abort the second trial resulted in a third trial for York and LaBorde before Acting Supreme Court Justice John Gallagher. Gallagher had a policeman for a brother as well as hundreds of friends who were cops; he was definitely handpicked to ensure convictions. Assigning prosecution-oriented judges to this type of controversial, high-profile case is most common.

While the third York-LaBorde trial was on, in 1986, the U.S. Supreme Court handed down its decision in *Batson v. Kentucky,* which held that it was a violation of the Constitution for a prosecutor to exclude jurors solely on account of race.

Prosecutors and defense attorneys have a certain number of jurors they can dismiss without a stated reason, called peremptory challenges. Jurors can be dismissed because of their expressions, the color of their eyes, or any other subjective reason. In English common law, only the defense had the right to exercise peremptory challenges because of the tendency of most jurors to be pro-prosecution rather than neutral. I always thought it should have continued that way, but over the years our state courts have changed the way peremptories are done. Today the prosecution has the same number of peremptory challenges as the defense.

Now, there is no such thing as a fair jury; an impartial jury is a myth. Each side in a trial wants jurors it believes will be sympathetic to it, so lawyers deliberately set out to select specific jurors. I base my choices of jurors largely on intuition and instinct, always hoping the ones I select have fewer basic antagonisms and will therefore be more likely to vote for acquittal.

In York-LaBorde, the prosecutor struck fourteen of eighteen potential jurors, all young and all black, which seemed to be purposeful discrimination. The only black people chosen for that jury were a few elderly people; younger jurors are generally less conservative and, I believe, would have been more sympathetic to two former Black Panthers. We asked Judge Gallagher to require the prosecution to give its reasons for excluding about 80 percent of the potential jurors who were black.

But the prosecutors replied that they did not have to give reasons, "since these are peremptory challenges," and the judge sustained their response. That judge didn't care at all about our objections; he wanted the prosecution to win. He didn't want young black jurors on that jury any more than he could fly.

At this third trial, York and LaBorde were convicted of murder and sentenced to twenty-five years to life. After we appealed the conviction and lost, we asked the Appellate Division to reconsider the conviction based on the *Batson* issue. When I initially appeared before the panel, I said that Judge Gallagher had been selected to preside over the trial because he was pro-police, and one justice shot back, "Well, you say that all the time."

"Yes, I do, because it's true," I responded.

The presiding judge said, "Let's get on to something else."

Although it was a very hostile all-white bench, we eventually won, a small victory, and on December 16, 1991, the Appellate Division sent the case back to trial court, ruling that the prosecution had apparently violated the Batson Rule.

Judge Gallagher having retired, the matter was assigned, again by some mysterious process, to another pro-prosecution judge, Ralph Sherman, who shocked us by refusing to permit us to cross-examine the prosecutors. They had taken the stand to try to justify their exercise of peremptory challenges against young blacks. This decision by the judge made us realize that we were undoubtedly in for another pro-prosecution decision. Our fears were fully justified when, several months after the hearings, Justice Sherman ruled that the prosecutors had not been guilty of racial discrimination in exercising their peremptories. The Appellate Division, which must decide whether to accept this decision, has not yet ruled.

1981
Lemuel Smith

I am so strongly opposed to the death penalty that I feel committed to taking on any client who, no matter the underlying circumstances, could be sentenced to death if convicted. In 1981, at the request of his mother, I entered the case of Lemuel Smith, a lifer at Green Haven Correctional Facility in upstate New York, who was accused of murdering prison guard Donna Payant.

After Payant was reported missing on May 15, 1981, the twelve towers at Green Haven trembled. When her body turned up the next day, dumped under piles of garbage in a landfill twenty-five miles away, the corrections world was in an uproar. Hers was the first murder of a New York State prison guard since the death of William Quinn at Attica ten years earlier. She was also the first woman guard in the entire country to be killed while on duty. Because of this, the authorities undertook a frenzied investigation and, a short time later, determined that Payant had been lured to the office of the prison's Catholic chaplain, strangled, wrapped in a plastic bag, then thrown into a prison dumpster. They accused Lemuel Smith of the murder.

At the time, New York had one death-penalty statute remaining: An inmate serving a life sentence, who was then convicted of committing a murder, would automatically receive the death penalty.

Lem's mother called me because her son was experienced in the ways of the court and didn't want a public defender. I became quite enthusiastic about winning an acquittal for Lem after an investigation led me to conclude that he had been framed by a corrupt group of drug-dealing prison guards. Perhaps naively, I hoped I could break the wall of silence around Payant's murder.

Lem, thirty-nine at the time, was serving 25-years-to-life sentences for murdering two Albany bookstore owners. Considered a particularly vicious killer, he was extremely unpopular with the guards. From his records, it appeared that he was quite dangerous when not in a controlled atmosphere. However, according to two prison chaplains, who later testified on his behalf, Lem was almost docile when he was under control and taking the appropriate medication. The chaplains were strong supporters of his; the Catholic one testified that he had never heard Lem even raise his voice.

"I took him on as an assistant because of his placid and gentle nature," the chaplain testified in court. Lem allegedly killed Payant in this chaplain's office, but there was never any forensic evidence that the murder actually occurred there. I was and am still convinced that Lemuel didn't have anything to do with Payant's death. First, if he had killed her, he would have had to remove her body from the office, which is in the front part of the prison, then drag it all the way to the rear of the institution, and, finally, place it in a dumpster—all without being seen by anyone. This seemed to be an almost impossible scenario.

I also had evidence that although she was married, Payant had dated some of the other guards; her husband, a prison guard himself, worked at another facility. What really confirmed my idea that Lem had not committed the murder was a call I received from a man claiming to be a Green Haven guard. He said that the night before Payant's murder, she had been drinking with several colleagues at the Thirteenth Tower, an after-hours hangout for prison personnel, when a nude photo of her was passed around. It was a very unflattering rear view, with Payant on her hands and knees. Payant became enraged over the photo and threatened to expose the Green Haven guards' drug business if she didn't get the negative fast, according to my caller.

The Green Haven drug ring was described in detail during Lem's trial in dramatic testimony that might shock those who are unfamiliar with how our prison systems really operate. One of the main prosecution witnesses, guard Martin Rahilly, admitted that he sold drugs inside the walls as well as on the outside. Rahilly, who testified based on the state's promise that he would not be fired despite his illegal activities, is, I believe, a crook and a liar who incriminated Lem in order to save his own skin. The state later reneged on its deal with him, saying that he had not kept his end of the bargain.

A mammoth investigation by New York's inspector general resulted in a comprehensive report about the Green Haven guards' drug ring. They were dealing every drug around on a major scale, including heroin, morphine, cocaine, downers, and uppers. I firmly believe that Payant was murdered by a guard, or group of guards, to prevent her from carrying out her threat to expose their illegal activities. In fact, there was evidence in the case that on the day of her death she had received a mysterious telephone call from a "sergeant," following which she had headed toward the rear of the prison.

The prosecution's case against Lem was mainly their dental expert's testimony that bite marks found on Payant's body were made by Lemuel Smith. We countered that with our own expert, who testified that the marks could not possibly have been made by Lem's mouth. The conflicting testimony of these two dentists was very dramatic. It was enormously damaging to our case that the judge—quite unfairly and improperly—allowed into evidence a photograph of bite marks from another case in which Lem was involved.

I really had no proof that Donna Payant had been murdered

by a guard, or group of guards, but I made the best argument I could. I never found the nude photo, and the anonymous caller never came forward again. The only hard information I had was from one guard who testified that Payant had been having sex with several of his colleagues. But all I could do was raise inferences; I had no smoking gun.

Lem was convicted. After he was sentenced to death by Dutchess County Supreme Court justice Albert M. Rosenblatt, he continued to maintain his innocence. In the courtroom, he said, "I didn't kill Donna Payant. Ask Rahilly who killed her." He turned to the guard, stared at him, and said, "Why don't you tell them the truth, Marty?"

Why, indeed? Rahilly was well connected: His sister was an assistant district attorney, and as a corrections officer, he belonged to a group as tight as any police organization. When any police officer or prison guard is charged with a crime, the ranks close to form a thin blue line with one goal: to protect their own. Better to let a black man, a convicted killer, take the rap. Even if, in this case, the rap was death.

There was a conspiracy of silence among the inmates, too, probably because they were frightened. And some took advantage of the situation by agreeing to testify against Lem in exchange for reduced sentences. Two of them, who were in a room adjacent to the Catholic chaplain's office when the murder allegedly occurred got sweetheart deals for testifying they saw Lem going toward the back of the prison, wheeling a cart.

There was nothing to be done about the conviction, but Ron Kuby, Mark Gombiner, and I appealed the death sentence. In July 1984, I was in Hong Kong, en route to Beijing, when the phone rang at 2:00 A.M., waking me out of a deep sleep. "We won Lemuel!" cried Ron, jubilant. New York state's highest court, the Court of Appeals, by a vote of 4–3, had overturned Lem's death sentence, a ruling that was later upheld by the U.S. Supreme Court.

I was enormously happy that we had saved Lem's life. And that we had eliminated the final death-penalty statute in New York state. Ron, my associate for a decade and now my new partner, had written a brilliant brief, arguing that it was unconstitutional to mandate death without allowing a hearing on mitigating factors. Even though the Supreme Court had previously ruled that states must have alternatives to the death penalty by allowing such hearings, New York nevertheless had a statute that required a lifer convicted of murder to be sentenced to the chair without one.

Ron's brief convinced the Court of Appeals and the U.S. Supreme Court that this statute was invalid, and after this case, New York State had no remaining death-penalty statutes. It was a glorious victory.

Lem had been on death row for more than a year by the time his sentence was overturned and he went back to court to be resentenced. During the proceeding, I berated Judge Rosenblatt for having waited for the Supreme Court ruling before removing Lem from death row. I told the judge he had been callous toward Lem and irresponsible to the taxpayers of the state: "You shirked your responsibility and left to the upper courts the responsibility of deciding whether the death penalty is right or wrong. . . . It was a chance for you, I think, to take the high road, and I don't think you chose it." As we expected, Rosenblatt gave Lem twenty-five to life, the maximum possible sentence.

1985
Darrell Cabey

On a crowded subway train a few days before Christmas, 1984, four black kids aggressively panhandled Bernhard Goetz for five dollars, and he pulled out a gun and shot them. He was immediately hailed as a hero, while the four kids, falsely reported to be armed with sharpened screwdrivers, were labeled as evil wrongdoers. As it turned out, the kids had not been armed, and Goetz was nothing more than a murderous vigilante. What if the kids had been white? I'm certain that Goetz would have been condemned by the same people who so quickly rushed to praise him.

Goetz shot those four youths because he is paranoid and has venomous feelings against black people. As he said publicly, he had been mugged previously and had developed a hatred toward all blacks. In 1986, he was convicted of weapons possession rather than attempted murder because the white public still viewed him as a hero, and he served a reduced sentence of six months.

A year earlier, in 1985, I had been contacted by Shirley Cabey, whose son, Darrell, was one of Goetz's victims. She wanted to sue Goetz because, as a result of the shooting, her son was paralyzed and would never walk again. Also, the Cabey family had incurred enormous medical expenses and needed help to pay the bills. Along with Ron, I brought a $50 million lawsuit and felt confident that we would eventually win because of what Goetz had admitted to police in Concord, New Hampshire, where he fled after the shootings. He told them that, after he shot Darrell and the others, he walked up to Darrell as he lay wounded on the seat of the subway car and said, "You seem to be all right. Here's another." Goetz then shot him again, and it was apparently this second bullet that had severed Darrell's spinal column.

Goetz admitted this when we took his deposition for the Cabey family's lawsuit. I asked, "Did you say these things to Darrell?" and he said, "Yes." When we gave this information to the press, he lost much of his widespread support in the white community. Ron and I have also filed a claim on Darrell's behalf with the Crime Victims Board which is still pending, as is the lawsuit. Meanwhile, our client spends his days in a wheelchair in his family's apartment, watching television, another victim of the cancer of racism.

1985
Wayne Williams

James Baldwin pushed me into the so-called Atlanta Child Murder case, as he had involved me in two New York cases almost twenty years earlier. In his book about the Atlanta case, *The Evidence of Things Unseen,* Jimmy wrote that the man convicted of these killings, Wayne Williams, had taken the fall for the real killers, who had never been charged. Abby Mann, also convinced that Wayne was innocent, dramatized his story in a 1985 CBS television special. After studying the transcripts, I came to agree with Jimmy and Abby and have been working since 1985 to overturn Wayne's conviction.

When Jimmy first approached me to work on Wayne's appeal, I had some misgivings. Although Wayne was black, the victims were twenty-nine black children. Practically no one could understand why I would want to help a convicted child killer. The murdered children were "strangers to safety . . . [because] only the poor watch over the poor," as Jimmy wrote. But after I came to believe that Wayne had been shanghaied, I formed a defense team with Ron, well-known Georgia trial lawyer Bobby Lee Cook, my sometime adversary Alan Dershowitz (who would actually play no role in the case at all), and Lynn Whatley, Wayne's local counsel.

Atlanta's black leaders resisted attempts to reopen the whole sensational and sensitive mess, so I went to Atlanta to convince them to at least remain neutral. Former civil rights activist and Georgia legislator Julian Bond helped me arrange meetings with community leaders, who agreed to a hands-off stance after they viewed our evidence. Mayor Andrew Young, formerly an aide to Dr. King and an old client of mine, had been up in arms against Abby Mann's documentary and had tried unsuccessfully to stop CBS from showing it in Atlanta. Eventually, he and I worked out a truce.

Jimmy Baldwin and I planned to meet in Atlanta in 1985 for a press conference at which we would announce the defense team's filing of the first habeas corpus for Wayne. Ron and I arrived in Atlanta quite late the night before the press conference because our plane had been delayed. I was famished, so we went looking for a meal in the hotel's dining room but found that it was no longer serving dinner. We saw two diners lingering on after their meal; they turned out to be Jimmy Baldwin and a friend of his. Jimmy and I embraced, then I eyed the leftover chicken on his dinner plate. I'm embarrassed to admit this, but I snatched the chicken. I was that hungry. Jimmy, of course, was more than happy to share it with me. We were delighted to see each other and sat and talked for a long time. I didn't know, of course, that it would be the last time our paths would cross. He died two years later.

Wayne Williams's original trial lawyer, Mary Welcome, had not been the right attorney for this case. It was simply too big for her. I like Mary very much, having met her when she was an assistant attorney general in the Virgin Islands, but this was not her case. In addition, important information was withheld from her by the Atlanta Police Department. After Wayne's conviction, local counsel Lynn Whatley, who argued the first appeal, had made contact with a deep throat in the Atlanta Police Department who revealed that members of the Ku Klux Klan had been the real suspects in the child-murder case. Mary Welcome never knew anything about this during the trial.

The police had used wiretaps and undercover police to obtain the information about the Klan, but a decision not to prosecute any Klan members was reportedly made at the top level of state government during a meeting at the home of Georgia governor George Busbee. Many people close to the case informed our legal team that George Bush, then vice president, was one of the high-level officials at that meeting.

The rationale for not arresting Klan suspects was that any prosecution of Klan members would bring on a race war, which probably was a true prognosis, given the tension created by the seemingly never ending discovery of young black bodies. The authorities chose the safer route of finding a black scapegoat and pinning the murders on him.

Wayne Williams was arrested for murdering two young men, but by the time his trial was over, the prosecution had linked him to ten of the child victims. The prosecution had been allowed to flout the law and bring before the jury information about these ten murders. They did this to demonstrate that all the murders—the two adults and the children—had been executed in a similar manner, although they had not. As a result, Wayne was actually, although not officially, on trial for all twenty-nine murders. He was convicted in February 1982 of the murders of the two men. After that, Lee Brown, Atlanta's public safety commissioner—later New York City's police commissioner and, in 1993, appointed as President Clinton's drug czar—moved to close all of the child-murder cases, thus indirectly attributing all the murders to Wayne.

Lynn Whatley won the first appeal of Wayne's conviction but only for a day. Apparently the Georgia Supreme Court had decided to give Wayne a new trial. But, without warning, the court suddenly changed its ruling and affirmed Wayne's conviction.

When I became involved in the case in 1985, our first habeas corpus petition showed, among other things, that police wiretaps had caught some Klan members saying, "Let's go out and get another little kid." A police informant with an eighteen-year record of reliability had infiltrated the Klan and taped many conversations and meetings. He testified at one of our habeas hearings that the chief suspect, a Klan member, had picked out the next victim, a teenaged boy named Lubie Geter, shortly before the youth was killed. So although the police case against the Klan was strong, they never acted on it.

Since that first habeas, along with Wayne's other defense attorneys, I have been involved in several hearings. At one in March 1992, the police informant and a number of other police officers gave testimony that fully supported our position. We are now, in

1994, still awaiting the final arguments. I think Wayne will be vindicated or at least get a new trial. In *The Evidence of Things Unseen,* Jimmy wrote, "It is perfectly possible that Wayne Williams must be added to the list of Atlanta's slaughtered black children." He, too, is a victim.

1986
Larry Davis

When cops are shot, the police want blood, and the public wants revenge—especially when the shooter is black. In 1986, I joined the defense of Larry Davis, who was charged with the attempted murder of six police officers. It was one of my most significant cases because of the blow it struck against racism within the law enforcement and legal systems.

On November 19, 1986, twenty-seven heavily armed police officers, all white except for one Latino, broke down the door of Regina Lewis's Bronx apartment, ostensibly to "talk to" Larry Davis, her brother. Larry was in the apartment when the law broke in but escaped under quite amazing circumstances. The police cornered Larry in a back room, which had barred windows, and blocked the doorway. Armed with a .45 automatic and an ancient shotgun, Larry began firing at his attackers, hitting several of them, who then moved back down the hall away from him. He would never have eluded death or capture except that during the ensuing shoot-out a bullet fired by a policeman hit the lock of a neighboring apartment door and sprang it.

Larry sprinted through a hail of bullets into the next-door apartment and leaped out of an unbarred window into a courtyard. He remained on the run for three weeks, until, on December 6, he surrendered to the FBI. "I was afraid that city cops would kill me," he later said, "so I agreed to turn myself in to the FBI."

Larry, eighteen, claimed that he had been a runner for dirty cops who would keep half the drugs from police drug raids, then hire young blacks or Latinos in Harlem or the South Bronx, like him, to sell the booty for them. But Larry had welshed on this arrangement and was holding out some $40,000 from the cops for whom he worked. Three weeks before the shoot-out, a detective told his mother, "We're going to put a bullet in his head. You raised a lousy bastard." She immediately complained to the Civilian Complaint Review Board of the police department, which must have found some truth in her statement. After an investigation, the detective was disciplined and placed on one-year probation.

Instead of putting him on trial for the police shootings, the Bronx County district attorney decided to try Larry first for the slightly earlier murders of four drug dealers, reasoning that his conviction for those would ensure a similar result in the later case or that a heavy sentence would obviate the necessity for a second trial. In spite of the prosecutors' plans, however, the drug dealer murder trial went well, and Larry was found not guilty of all four murder charges. The jury acquitted, in part, because some of the key witnesses called by the prosecution had rather unsavory reputations and were themselves involved in the drug trade. Moreover, the two prosecutors, William Flack and Brian Wilson, whom Lynne Stewart, my cocounsel, and I referred to as Fred Flintstone and Barney Rubble, were overconfident.

Larry's next trial, in 1988, was the police case. Members of the raiding party testified that none of them had any intention of shooting at Larry the day they broke into Regina's apartment. They also swore that no officer had carried a shotgun that day. But they couldn't explain away a shotgun slug found in the room where Larry was cornered. Our expert, criminologist Dr. Peter De-Forest, said that because of the angle at which the bullet had been fired, it must have been done by someone standing either in the doorway or two feet inside the room. But the police maintained that they never got near the room and were at all times positioned some twenty feet or so down the hallway.

Detective Thomas McCarren, who was badly wounded during the shoot-out, testified that he did not carry a shotgun that day. But he was contradicted when another officer testified that he did have such a weapon.

The best evidence came out during McCarren's cross-examination. He had originally testified that he never fired at Larry because two young children walked across the hall and he was afraid of hitting them. During cross, I said to him, "Detective McCarren, you say that two children came in your way and you didn't fire." Then I asked, "That's a pretty significant thing, isn't it? Did you write it down?"

"Yes, I did," he responded. "When I was in the hospital, my jaw was wired shut, so I could only respond to questions people asked me by writing on a pad. I think all those pads are in a shoebox in one of my closets." My heart sank when I heard this, because I had no idea whether or not he was telling the truth. By law, the defense team was supposed to receive copies of any memoranda written by prosecution witnesses at a criminal trial, but we had not received any copies of Detective McCarren's notes. Taking a chance, I asked, "Can you bring the shoebox in tomorrow?"

The next day, Fred Flintstone Flack walked into court triumphantly bearing the shoebox. It was filled with notebooks and a note, written on a separate piece of paper, which stated: "I couldn't shoot because two children were in the corridor." I was a bit encouraged when I saw that this note had not been written in one of the notebooks. I asked McCarren, "Where did you get that piece of paper? Was that in the shoebox?"

"No, the D.A. gave that to me today," he replied to the dismay and embarrassment of the prosecution. The judge then threw out all of McCarren's testimony about the children in the hall because it was so obviously concocted.

The jury, composed of blacks, whites, and Latinos, acquitted Larry of all of the major charges and found him guilty only of illegal weapons possession.

Larry was also acquitted in his third trial on charges he murdered a Manhattan drug dealer. He lost, however, in his fourth trial for the murder of a Bronx drug dealer in 1991. Convicted on that charge, he is now doing life in a New York State prison. Although I represented Larry in his first two trials, I couldn't do the third because of a prior trial commitment. When it came to the fourth case, Michael Warren, who had done such a fine job for Larry in the third one, wanted my help, but the judge refused, saying that only one lawyer would be appointed. Eventually, though, the judge did allow another assigned attorney into the case. I have agreed to handle Larry's appeal, and the failure of the judge to appoint me to the case will be one of the appeal's points. The appeal is scheduled to be argued in the fall of 1994.

Larry Davis, now Adam Abdul-Hakeem, became a Muslim while in prison. He is a brash, bright young man who, but for this sensational police shoot-out, would undoubtedly never have emerged from the crowd and would most likely have died in the streets of the South Bronx. He has several brothers, all of whom are in prison. Because New York City police officers were wounded during the shoot-out, prison guards beat him up all the time, just on general principle. He's in such bad shape that he's in a wheelchair.

Larry isn't the only one who's been brutalized in connection with his case. In 1989, Ron and I and Stephanie Moore, an attorney for the Center, went to a courthouse in Brooklyn with a group of activist lawyers led by Alton Maddox; Ron and I were the only white people in the courtroom. We were there to show support for C. Vernon Mason, who had been accused of violating an injunction issued to prevent a demonstration. If convicted, Vernon risked disbarment.

We were there all morning, left for lunch, then returned. We were waiting for the judge's decision on a motion to dismiss the charges against Vernon. Shortly after 5:00 P.M. there was some sort of commotion in the back as Vernon was taken into custody and brought down the left side of the courtroom.

Suddenly, with no apparent provocation, the white court officers went berserk, pushing and shoving everyone, including a blind woman. Finally, they got to me. They threw me on my back with my arms behind me, bending my knees up so violently that the left one eventually required surgery. One officer kicked me in the chest, hard, breaking one of my ribs and shouted, "This one's for Larry Davis!" Then they threw me into a cell behind the courtroom along with Al Sharpton, Vernon Mason, Stephanie Moore, Ron, and others.

We were taken by bus to Brooklyn Central Booking. I was put into a large holding cell filled with about twenty black and Latino kids, many of whom were high on drugs. They occupied all the seats in the cell and stared at me—a disheveled, elderly white man—with some hostility as I entered their province. I immediately let them know I was the lawyer for Larry Davis, and that changed their whole attitude. One of the kids said to another: "Get up and give the counselor your seat." After that, it was all friendship and warmth. Then Ron was thrown into the cell, and we busily engaged in giving them free legal advice.

Eventually, we were taken out in chains and loaded into a van that was standing room only. I heard the driver say, "We'll give these people quite a ride." They went tearing through Brooklyn, deliberately hitting every bump and pothole. We were in pretty bad shape when we finally arrived at the precinct where we were to spend the night. I was placed in a cubicle with two other men; Ron was down the corridor, in another cell, exchanging legal advice for cigarettes. I tried to get into a comfortable position on a stone slab of a bunk, with my busted rib beginning to hurt like mad.

In the morning, breakfast was a cold fried egg between two

stale hunks of bread. But life improved quite a bit when a local community relations representative brought us fresh pound cake and hot coffee.

When I was first arrested the day before, a black court officer told me he would gladly testify about what his white colleagues had done in the courtroom. But it was never to be. Ron and I were released, with no charges, in spite of the fact that we had been told that we would be charged with riot, a felony, and a number of other crimes. Had I been convicted of riot, I would have been automatically disbarred.

I submitted a claim against the City of New York because of my injuries but eventually decided not to sue. I wasn't going to ask the system to undo what the system had done. So I have never sued on the matter, even though the injuries I received were substantial. Ron was also badly hurt. I remember seeing him pressed back over the railing in that courtroom, sure that I was going to hear his spine snap. The attack on those of us there to support Vernon Mason had been purely racist. Only the white court officers took part; I didn't see a single black or Latino officer join in. It was, once again, clear proof that racism makes animals out of everyone.

Because of his notoriety, Larry Davis has become articulate, shrewd, and public relations conscious and is working on a movie deal about his life story. To date, a film documentary and a play about him have been produced. A few years ago, while I was speaking at the Five Towns Forum in Nassau County, I noticed that a man in the audience looked very much like me. He wore his hair the same way and had his glasses on top of his head. I said to him, "You look like me." He answered, "I should. I am playing you in the drama about Larry Davis at the Theater for the New City."

1988
Percy Robinson

Contrary to what many believe, most of my cases are low profile and don't get much play in the news. In 1988, for example, Percy Robinson, a black man, was charged with the 1985 murder of an eighty-year-old white woman named Mabel Wayne. The victim was thrown or pushed from her fourth-floor Bronx apartment window during a robbery.

I agreed to defend Percy even though I had known Mabel

Wayne well; she had been a veteran court observer, or VCO, in the Bronx. VCOs are often retired older people who sit in the courthouse all day, every day, watching the proceedings. Mabel, who always called me Sonny, was very smart. She would say, "Well, Sonny, you did this wrong, and you did that wrong." Then she'd list the mistakes I'd made, and she was generally correct. She was so well loved that when she died, she was given a police inspector's funeral, and a street behind the Bronx County Courthouse was named Mabel Wayne Place.

Because of how they felt about Mabel, the police were anxious to find her killer. But they were too eager and made a serious error by relying on the testimony of a woman who, it turned out, was a professional prosecution witness; she was used repeatedly as a courtroom witness by the district attorney's office. During Percy's trial, this woman testified that he confessed to her that he had murdered Mabel Wayne. A second witness, Michael Hardy, also claimed that Percy had admitted the murder while they were both in jail.

I had tried to get as many blacks and Hispanics on Percy's jury as possible, since they understand street life. I also tried to keep whites off, since they are prone to convict blacks, will excuse police brutality against minorities, and tend to believe prosecutors' stories. So it was greatly to our benefit that the jury was composed mainly of blacks and Puerto Ricans.

Hardy, a white man, was a cross-examiner's delight. He had been in and out of jail most of his adult life, told incredible tall tales about himself, and talked much too much. In articles written about him, he had referred to blacks as "spades" and to Hispanics as "greasers." He had spun a few fantasies, too, describing himself as an Israeli soldier during the Yom Kippur War and also as a hit man for the mob. He was so obviously phony that he was a great witness for Percy Robinson. When I cross-examined Hardy, I referred to the article in which he was quoted as calling blacks "spades."

"Didn't you recently say, during an interview, that you referred to blacks as 'spades'?" I asked.

He became very agitated and replied, "No, I didn't say that. Do you want to know what I did say?"

I was in a dilemma. He had put out a challenge, and I had to accept it, but I was unsure of how he would reply. A cardinal rule for trial lawyers is never ask a question of a witness in court unless you are pretty certain of what the reply will be. But I figured that Michael Hardy was so nutty, I would take the risk. "Go ahead," I replied.

He said: "I called them 'niggers.' " It got even better after that, as Hardy became more and more agitated and tried to explain that when he called blacks "niggers," he didn't mean it in a racist way. Finally, he sputtered, "Are you asking me if I'm a racist?"

"No, Mr. Hardy," I said. "You've already answered that question."

That's how this case went to the jury, which was out only a short time, less than a day. Percy was acquitted; the jurors had not believed either witness. They also couldn't understand why a number of fingerprints found on Mabel Wayne's jewelry box were not identified as Percy's if he was supposed to be guilty.

Only after Percy's acquittal did the police department finally check out those prints. The computer turned up a match; the prints belonged to a man who was then doing time in North Carolina. When NYPD detectives went south and confronted this man, he confessed. He had been Mabel Wayne's next-door neighbor and had thrown her out the window when she discovered him looting her apartment.

The NYPD held a press conference to announce how diligent police work had solved this case. No mention was made of the fact that they had first tried to convict an innocent man. I requested a formal apology to Percy Robinson by the D.A. and the police. Of course, they refused. Declining to exonerate Percy publicly was typical of how the police will never admit their shortcomings. Percy had been acquitted of murder, but an acquittal after trial is not an exoneration; it means only that a jury has found reasonable doubt. The police had a duty to make a public announcement about Percy's innocence, but they refused to do so. The real murderer was never tried. He died of AIDS after being extradited to New York.

1989
Alcee Hastings

Over the years, I've defended many black politicians on a variety of charges. Blacks who become elected or appointed officials often become victims of witchhunts, the focus of criminal and other charges, in order to strip them of their power. In 1982, the

FBI's unofficial *Frühmenschen* policy was revealed by an Atlanta lawyer who had worked for the Bureau when he described it as "the routine investigation without probable cause of prominent black elected and appointed officials."

When Florida federal judge Alcee Hastings was impeached by the U.S. Senate in 1989, I became involved through the Center for Constitutional Rights. Alcee was an old friend of mine, a lawyer and former state legislator, who had joined me in defending Ben Chaney back in 1971.

Alcee went on to win election as a state court judge and in 1977 was appointed by President Carter to the federal bench. Alcee had insisted on taking his oath of office in the auditorium of a predominantly black high school rather than in the courthouse, as was customary. During his tenure as judge, he worked on behalf of Haitian refugees and also criticized the policies of President Reagan at every opportunity.

The government placed Alcee under close scrutiny and worked to oust him from the bench. The U.S. Attorney for the Southern District of Florida charged him with fraud, taking bribes, and other misdeeds connected with his sentencing of several organized-crime figures. When he was tried on these charges in 1983, Alcee represented himself and won. Despite his acquittal on all charges, the government obtained articles of impeachment against him from the House of Representatives and scheduled him to be tried by the Senate.

Before any action was taken, though, Ron Kuby, and I filed a federal lawsuit seeking to force the entire Senate to sit as a jury. According to the Constitution, the full Senate is required to try impeachments. The Senate had planned to try Alcee with only a committee of twelve senators. Working with Miami law professor Terrence Anderson and Center attorney Stephanie Moore, we argued that this was unconstitutional. The Constitution states, we argued, that "the Senate shall have the sole Power to try all Impeachments. When sitting for that purpose, they shall be on Oath or Affirmation." But the court ruled that since Alcee's impeachment trial had not yet taken place, our lawsuit was premature.

The Senate promptly appointed a twelve-member committee to hear the evidence, and it recommended that Alcee should be stripped of his judgeship. The full Senate quickly accepted the recommendation. We then filed a new lawsuit, and on September 17, 1992, Judge Stanley Sporkin ruled that based on the Constitution's explicit language, the entire Senate had to sit as a trial jury and that Alcee's impeachment conviction was therefore invalid. The government immediately appealed that ruling, but no decision has yet been made.

A short time after the Sporkin decision, in 1992, Alcee ran for, and was elected to, the House of Representatives from Florida's twenty-third Congressional District. Even if Alcee's case is lost on appeal, he cannot be excluded from his House seat, since the Senate, in its impeachment decision, did not preclude his seeking elective office.

1990
Yusef Salaam

I've been called a sexist pig by a number of women over the years, but when I decided to take the appeal of Yusef Salaam in 1990, one of the youths convicted of raping the Central Park Jogger, more women than ever looked at me with contempt and disdain. Some of the female staff members at the Center for Constitutional Rights, my home away from home, wanted to hang me in effigy, while others just wanted to hang me. I took the case, regardless of what people thought, because Yusef was another in a long line of those who are hated by society; with the odds against him, he needed a good lawyer to stand by him.

The cast of characters in the Central Park Jogger case—young black and Latino defendants and a white victim—indicated to me that the defendants would not get a fair trial. When you have minority males accused of sexually assaulting a white woman, the resulting antagonism goes far beyond the courtroom. Gloria Steinem, in an excellent *New York Times* op-ed piece, suggested that if you reversed the races in certain cases, you'd get very different results. Make the so-called Central Park rapists white and their victim a black woman and the public response would be far different, as would that of the justice system.

Yusef had his rights violated from the beginning. I thought what the authorities did to this fifteen-year-old boy was outrageous. He did not confess either in writing or on videotape, and the only tangible evidence against him was oral admissions that he supposedly made to a detective. While Yusef was kept alone in a precinct room this officer, his mother, aunt, and Big Brother—who happened to be an assistant U.S. attorney—were left cooling their heels downstairs. At his 1990 trial, Yusef, convicted of rape, assault, and several other charges in connection with the attack on the jogger, was sentenced as an adult to five to ten years.

(An interesting note: Two years later, the lead detective in the Central Park Jogger case, Humberto Arroyo, was suspended for pocketing drug money at a 1992 murder scene.)

I appealed Yusef's conviction all the way up to New York's highest court, the Court of Appeals. On December 16, 1993, the court affirmed his conviction, 5–1, rejecting my argument that the police had wrongly isolated him from his family and friends while they elicited his "confession." This confession was the only evidence that connected Yusef to the crime.

In his dissent, which received little attention from the press, Judge Vito Titone said, "[T]here was no justification for the authorities' actions in preventing defendant from gaining access to the helpful counsel of the supportive adults who had gathered to assist him." That was the main point of my argument. The Court of Appeals ruling showed its racial bias. Had Yusef been white, with a middle-class family, his police interrogation would no doubt have been stopped by a knowledgeable parent or available attorney. Instead, his mother, aunt, and Big Brother were kept away from him.

Judge Titone, I was pleased to see, also noted that the police had lied to Yusef during his questioning when they told him, first, that they had taken his fingerprints from the victim's clothing and, second, that he might be released if he answered their questions correctly. The right person—a parent, lawyer, or other responsible adult—might have prevented Yusef from making any statement to the police without an attorney present.

Finally, Judge Titone characterized Yusef's isolation and separation from his family and friends by the authorities as "an undisguised intention to exploit the defendant's youthful vulnerability." It is outrageous that Yusef's questioning occurred the way it did; he was only fifteen, and his constitutional rights were completely ignored. The judicial system of New York State has done to Yusef what some years ago in the South would have been done with a rope or a rifle.

I am not surprised at the Court of Appeals decision, because the court's role is to maintain the social order; keeping Yusef, and as many blacks as possible, in prison is part of the function of the judiciary.

1991
Six Degrees of Separation

Although David Hampton is black, he is not my usual type of client. I jumped at the chance to represent him, though, because his case gave me a break from more serious litigation. David called me a couple of years ago to represent him on misdemeanor charges of harassing playwright John Guare. Guare, who had used David's life story as the basis for his successful and profitable play and movie *Six Degrees of Separation,* claimed that David had requested money and threatened him when he refused to give him any.

David's story is unusual. He came to New York City in 1983, when he was twenty-three, to pursue an acting career but, failing to get a break, used his talent to con some very wealthy people into believing he was Sidney Poitier's son. David was charming. He told one credulous person that Poitier was casting the movie version of *Dream Girls,* then added, "Maybe my father will give you a cameo role." As a result of this mild deception, he managed to elicit food and lodging and some money and clothing. He was very convincing.

He scammed Osborn Elliot, formerly the editor of *Newsweek* and dean of the Columbia School of Journalism, as well as John J. Iselin, the former president of Channel 13, and others. David showed up one night at the Elliots' apartment wearing bloody and torn clothing and said he was a school friend of their children's and that he had been mugged and had all his money stolen. They took him in and helped him out, falling for his Poitier line.

David also tricked several other well-to-do people in New York City. Once the victims of his scams discovered that he wasn't the son of a prominent actor but just a young black kid with nothing, they went to the police, claiming that they had been conned. David was convicted of attempted burglary and served twenty-one months in a state prison near the Canadian border, which seemed to me to be an excessive sentence. Although he had pretended to be someone else, he never took anything that hadn't been given to him. Because he twitted important and influential people that you were not supposed to con, he served almost two years in a maximum security prison for his acts. David confessed publicly and never tried to keep what he had done a secret.

Afterward, the Elliots met John Guare in London and told him the whole story. Guare read clippings about David's scam, and as he told a reporter, "Suddenly, the thing came to me," and he wrote *Six Degrees of Separation*. After David served his time, he came out penniless, so he called Guare, asking for money. At first, Guare said, "We'll talk about it." He was obviously ambivalent. The play had made a fortune for him; then M-G-M had hired him to write a screenplay and had produced a movie version. However, in the end, Guare never gave David a nickel. Maybe he thought he was above it all and that, as an artist, he had no responsibility if he wrote about someone whose life had become public. He began to tape David's phone calls.

"I would strongly advise you that you give me some money or start counting your days," David said during one call that Guare taped. David, arrested and charged with harassment in the spring of 1992, asked Ron and me to represent him. I liked the case because it involved the theater and a clever deception, and was a welcome respite from murder trials. I was also a bit angry that these white liberals would take in a black man when they believed him to be the son of a famous person but kick him out when they discovered he was just an ordinary guy. David had challenged their liberalism, and they had failed the test.

After David's initial call to me, I read *Six Degrees of Separation* and saw that it did parallel his life, as he had told me. Ron and I then went with David to the district attorney's office where a young assistant told us that David was to be charged with extortion, which is a felony, not a misdemeanor. Once again, David had twitted an important person, John Guare, and the Establishment would make him pay.

Ron and I told the assistant that if she charged David with a felony, we would do everything in our power to win. We would tell the press that the D.A.'s office was persecuting this young black man and that, while we could understand charging him with a misdemeanor, a felony charge was outrageous. (The assistant quit the D.A.'s office shortly after that; I think we may have intimidated her.) David was ultimately tried only on two misdemeanor counts, for two of the calls he had made to Guare.

The trial was held before Manhattan Criminal Court judge Plummer Lott. In the very beginning, he called me up to the bench and said, "You know, I was a boy in Jackson, Mississippi, when I first saw you, and I was very impressed by what you did in my hometown." Needless to say, I felt wonderful about meeting my past and seeing that my work with the Freedom Riders back in the 1960s had affected Judge Lott.

The trial was dramatic and fun and gave me a chance to cross-examine Guare. On the stand, he looked like a monkey. He is very bright, but supercilious, and reminds me of so many people in the arts who have no compassion for anyone, care only about their own careers, and regard themselves as above the common herd.

I viewed this as a First Amendment case because the harassment statute cuts into the First Amendment and penalizes certain speech, known as rough speech. One of David's telephone calls was not on tape, and our defense was that Guare's report of what David said was inaccurate. The second call, which had been taped, was played to the jury. We maintained that David used meaningless phrases—like "Kill the umpire!" at a baseball game—when he said to Guare, "Give me some money or start counting your days." There was no question that these were intemperate remarks, but we contended that there was no criminal intent, that David had no intention of doing anything violent to Guare.

The jury acquitted David on the first, untaped, call, a wonderful victory in a small case. But it hung on the second one after deliberating for eleven hours. The D.A. may well try it again, but since David has recently disappeared, it will not come to trial, if ever, until he surfaces.

1991
Kevin McKiever

When Kevin McKiever was arrested for killing young Alexis Welsh on Manhattan's Upper West Side, the city was ready to lynch him. She was young, attractive, white, a former Rockette. He was a black homeless man who had been in and out of mental institutions. There was a rush for this man's head, and had I taken this case on my own, I would have been more unpopular than ever. In truth, I took on McKiever's defense because I was asked to do so by the court.

This didn't stop columnist Mike McAlary from skewering me in his column as "a lawyer who is in any given moment the most unpopular man in the city." He wrote about my talking to the press corps in the courthouse about McKiever. "Kunstler remained in a padded chair talking. . . . I guess there is a cause somewhere in a case about a homeless guy who stabs a young woman to death." I am certain that McAlary believed that I belonged in a padded cell rather than a padded chair.

I told the reporters in the press room, "I know it's a case where a lot of people are going to hate the lawyers and hate the defendant. A lot of people will say, 'This is a no-good murdering son of a bitch. You shouldn't take the case.' "

One reporter responded, "He is a no-good murdering son of a bitch." I answered, "Alleged no-good murdering son of a bitch." They asked me why I took the case. "Because he was the only pariah around."

The forensic evidence against McKiever turned out to be very weak. A palm print found on the murder weapon didn't belong to him or to anyone else known to the police who may have had contact with it. There also wasn't a drop of the victim's blood on McKiever or on his clothing. He had only been arrested, apparently, because he was the likeliest suspect—a ragged, homeless man—near the scene of the murder when it occurred.

But a trial seemed fruitless, since, as time passed, Kevin McKiever clearly became more and more insane. We asked the judge to order a psychiatric examination to determine whether he was competent to stand trial. During the proceedings, many of Kevin's psychotic fantasies were revealed, including his notion that I had sodomized him when he was eleven years old.

When this was discussed in court, the judge, totally deadpan, said, "It's funny, Mr. Kunstler. I didn't know you and Mr. McKiever went back that far."

Eventually, the judge ruled that Kevin was not competent to stand trial and sent him to a psychiatric center. After only six months of observation and treatment, he was declared competent to stand trial and was discharged. His mental condition immediately deteriorated once more. When he next appeared in court, the trial judge quickly committed him to another psychiatric institution for further evaluation. Recently he was again declared competent, with trial set for late 1994 unless he suffers another relapse.

1992
Marion Barry

I first met Marion Barry many years ago when he was a young field secretary for the Student Nonviolent Coordinating Committee in Jackson, Mississippi. It always seems somewhat unbelievable to me that I end up representing people I knew when they were kids. Suddenly, they're members of Congress, like John

Lewis, or mayors, like Marion Barry. My strong sense of loyalty almost always guarantees that I will gladly represent these old friends when they need a lawyer.

I had followed Marion's career as he entered politics and then was elected D.C.'s mayor. In 1990, he was charged with several crimes, including cocaine possession. He was convicted of that charge, but the jury hung on the other charges. After the trial, the judge in the case, Thomas Penfield Jackson, gave a speech at Harvard Law School during which he criticized the all-black jury and said it had violated its oath of office by not convicting on all the charges.

In 1992, Marion asked me to participate in his appeal. I quickly agreed, since I believed that Marion's case was similar to Alcee's and that he was yet another black official being selectively prosecuted under the *Frühmenschen* policy. Marion had been inveigled by the government into the possession of a controlled substance when it brought a former girlfriend of his to Washington to set him up. Now, Marion was definitely no choir boy and may have used drugs in the past, but the government clearly entrapped him. His ex-girlfriend coaxed him up to her hotel room and fed him cocaine until the police broke in. This sting operation against Marion may have been legal, but it was dirty and immoral. Legality and morality are usually not, in this country, synonymous.

The powerful white Establishment uses federal or state prosecutors to carry out stings like the one that trapped Marion. Not surprisingly, most chief prosecutors are white. For example, in New York state, there is but one black district attorney, Bronx D.A. Robert Johnson, and if he proves too obstreperous, he'll quickly be ousted.

I wrote the section of Marion's appeal brief which accused the court of selective prosecution based on racism. I also accused the trial judge of being a racist. But when the appeal was argued, the three white judges on the appellate court were extremely hostile to my raising the specter of racism, refusing even to admit that prosecutors or judges could be guilty of bigotry. They were like three robed ostriches, heads deep in the sand.

My conviction that the justice system is riddled with racism was supported in April 1991 when New York State's Judicial Commission on Minorities and the Courts issued a report stating that we have a "double-tiered justice system." The report concluded:

There are two justice systems at work in the courts of New York State, one for whites, and a very different one for minorities and the poor. . . . [I]nequality, disparate treatment and injustice remain the hallmarks of our state justice system.

One portion of Marion's appeal was successful in that his sentence was set aside because of technical irregularities, but the trial judge then imposed the same six-month sentence he had originally received, this time on different grounds.

Marion served his time and then, like Alcee, made a dramatic comeback. He was elected to the Washington City Council in 1992. People said, "Well, he's paid his price. Maybe he did a bad thing at one time, but we think he's for our district, and he's a powerful voice, so we voted for him."

1992
Khalil Sumpter

Unlike David Hampton, whose charges were minimal, Khalil Sumpter is more my usual type of client: He had been charged with a double murder. In February 1992, Khalil shot and killed two other black kids at Brooklyn's Thomas Jefferson High School.

Khalil's parents are divorced, but accompanied by their new spouses, they joined forces to support him, came to my office, and asked me to represent him. Before I decided to take Khalil's case, in addition to doubts because his victims were also black, I had many other questions; I knew this case would give me problems. But Khalil was entitled to a good defense. And I saw the school as somewhat the villain because of its negligence in not having metal detectors in place. Thomas Jefferson is part of the larger system which doesn't give a tinker's damn about black people: Keep them off the streets until they're sixteen because that's the law; then get rid of them—to prison, or the cemetery.

Also, if Khalil was sent to prison rather than a youth detention center, he would be somebody's queen before nightfall. He would be forced to become a sex partner and would surely come out a hardened criminal. I thought: If I don't take the case and he's convicted, another young black male's life will be destroyed because of an act which undoubtedly was not venal. I decided to defend him.

My defense would be emotional disturbance; this lowers the crime to manslaughter and makes a big difference insofar as sentence is concerned. Yes, he did it, but he was emotionally disturbed. Khalil had killed because the two other boys had called his house and said they were going to cut his mother. Prior to the killings, one of the victims and Khalil had both been tried for criminal trespass; Khalil was acquitted, but the other youth was convicted and apparently held this against Khalil.

The day after his mother was threatened, Khalil, who was fifteen, got a gun so he could protect her. He assumed that the other youths, Ian Moore and Tyrone Sinkler, also had guns since, in New York's black ghettos, guns, like drugs, are readily available and part of the economic flow. You can buy any gun you want for $300 or less. Guns represent power to powerless people; a gun makes everybody equal. In fact, Sinkler had shot at Khalil the day before the tragedy.

After I decided to take the case, I visited Khalil at the Spofford Juvenile Detention Center in the Bronx. I hugged him, and he kissed me on the cheek. He said, "Thank you, Mr. Kunstler."

I said, "Bill, not Mr. Kunstler. We're partners now." Then I said, as I do to all potential clients, "Don't take me because you've heard my name or because your mother tells you about me. Take me only because you feel confidence in me, that I can represent you well." The meeting was important so that he would have a feeling of camaraderie with his lawyer. I said, "I won't feel bad if you say you don't think you'll get along with me. Or if you'd rather have a black lawyer in here as well."

"No, I want you, Bill," he said. He got that Bill out instead of Mr. Kunstler. I liked him and was glad I had taken him on; taking a case doesn't always mean that I like a defendant. Khalil is a decent kid in terrible trouble that will haunt him probably all of his life. After the visit, his father said to me, "The boy's life is ruined."

I disagreed: "No, it's not ruined, and you must always keep that in mind. He is hurt, but he's not ruined." One act, one event, no matter how awful, cannot ruin a life. A person can always salvage himself.

We tried the case in the summer of 1993, and in July, Khalil was found guilty of manslaughter rather than murder. The jury found that he had shot his victims while he was under "extreme emotional disturbance." On September 7, the judge—a white man who had privately referred to Khalil as "a vicious little bastard"—

sentenced him to the maximum, six and two-thirds to twenty years, despite reports from Spofford that he had been fully rehabilitated. Khalil became just another black cipher caught up in the maw of the criminal justice system. John Russell, his family's lawyer, and I tried unsuccessfully to reverse this unfair sentence. Meanwhile, Khalil is doing very well, pulling down A's in all his subjects at the state juvenile detention center where he is doing his time.

A month after his sentencing, he wrote me a wonderful letter:

I've changed quite a bit and I plan to make a complete 360-degree turnaround to make both you and my parents proud. . . . Thanks for everything. And you're cool for a honky.

How Can You Defend Those People?

Khalil Sumpter was one of those clients who cause people to rush up to me and ask, "How can you defend those people?" To these questioners, I invariably reply, "Why not? What's wrong with these defendants? Are they guilty before being tried? Don't they deserve a good lawyer?"

Since public opinion is not a reliable barometer of anything, I don't take offense at my low approval rating in certain quarters. I know that I am disliked, even despised, by those who hate my clients even before they are tried. I represent outcasts, individuals who are hated for their skin color or religion or political beliefs, people who fight the government. These are exactly the kind of clients I want. My function is not to represent the darlings of society but to represent the damned, those whom society wants to destroy.

Not many lawyers want these clients, and in some ways I can't blame them; they have their careers to consider. I do understand the need for personal security and financial gain that our culture fosters, but somehow I have gotten out of the culture and into the fire. The kind of client I want to represent is exactly whom I do represent. I am satisfied with Yusef Salaam, Larry Davis, and Lemuel Smith. I don't want to be a mouthpiece, paid by the Leona Helmsleys or the Michael Milkens of the world.

Although my career as a radical lawyer began many years ago in Chicago, there are still so many people who can't, or don't, understand why I take certain defendants. Even those I love the most, who love me, my family and friends, sometimes question my choices. For example, Margie didn't want me to represent El Say-yid Nosair, who was charged with the murder of Rabbi Meir Ka-hane in 1990. Margie said that it wasn't really a political case and would put all of us, my teenaged daughters, Emily and Sarah, es-pecially, in danger. But I felt that I couldn't say no to Nosair and live up to my own moral code, so I didn't follow her advice. She was quite right about the danger, however: Shots were fired into our house, paint was thrown at it, protesters picketed, and we were bombarded with more hate mail and death threats than usual. Although I was concerned about the effects on Sarah and Emily, I was not afraid for myself.

Yusef Salaam and clients like him are the source of my strength. I feel compelled to represent them because that is the only way I can fulfill myself. I actually feel most satisfied when almost no one can understand why I'm representing a certain cli-ent. And if I do have doubts, I have to ignore them because I don't have the time to quiver and quake. For me, action is all. So I en-dure my brief moments of uncertainty, but then some source of strength and boldness, or as some have suggested, foolhardiness, takes over, and I act.

I can perhaps explain this with the symbol of Michelangelo's *David.* I often glance at the replica in my office that Margie gave me and draw strength from it. The late art critic Bernard Berenson pointed out to me that Michelangelo's is the only David depicted prior to his killing of Goliath. David is standing there, thinking, like T. S. Eliot's J. Alfred Prufrock, Do I dare? Do I dare? He has the rock in his right hand, the sling over his left shoulder, and he's watching this giant Philistine come down the Galilean hills. He is thinking, If I throw the rock and miss, I am one dead Israelite. If I just wound him, I'm in the same position. But if I hit him and kill him, I've done a great deed for my people and maybe for myself as well.

David is portrayed in that exact moment of hesitation that comes to everyone, the moment when the idea crosses your mind that you might stand up and say something, do something, pre-vent the library from banning the book, stop the injustice or what-ever it happens to be. But as long as it's a thought in your head, no one knows about it; if you don't act, no one will be the wiser.

That's the key to the *David.* David won't be ostracized if he doesn't release the rock in his sling; he's just one of a hundred other Hebrew shepherds on the hills. Since there's no personal urgency, he's in that finite moment when he must make a fateful decision, one that no one will be aware of until it's made, one that no one will criticize him for not making.

It is a moment that occurs often in my life. Every time I decide to take on a Larry Davis or a Yusef Salaam, I make a choice. While I'm hardly comparing myself to David, my choice is whether to take on the giant or to let it slide. No one will know. When I choose, I choose what I believe is the right thing, despite the odds against it. Over the years, my David moments have come more frequently. Do I dare? Do I dare? I usually do when I can take on the system or when I believe that a certain defendant won't get a fair trial. So while the prevailing notion is that I never turn a case down, that's not at all true. I have to choose from among countless desperate phone calls and letters. If a crime is political, I take the case; if the defendant belongs to an oppressed group, I take it. And if the defendant is a friend, I always try to come through.

I also occasionally take private cases for a fee, but I won't take a case that goes against my political grain. I was asked to represent Frank LoCascio, John Gotti's codefendant in his 1992 trial, but I turned it down. It was not my kind of case, and LoCascio certainly had the resources to find another lawyer. This doesn't mean that LoCascio and Gotti got a fair trial—they did not—but only that I felt I should confine myself to the type of client I have been defending over the years.

I would also never represent an individual like Leona Helmsley, who, although she has the same civil rights as anyone, is a rather detestable character with few redeeming qualities. This mogul could well afford a hired gun and did, in fact, eventually hire Alan Dershowitz; a frequent critic of mine, he is not one of my favorite people. I find it reprehensible when a man presents himself as a civil rights attorney, then represents wealthy clients for huge fees.

I thought that Leona's sentence was fair because it wasn't lengthy. The arguments against it—that she was too old, that she was ill—were unconvincing. At the time of her case, I had a client who was dying of cancer in the U.S. Medical Center for Federal Prisoners in Springfield, Missouri, and it took herculean efforts to have him released so that he could die at home. Leona, with her high blood pressure, or whatever ailment she has, fainted in court to try to avoid prison. She also claimed that she couldn't do time because she had to keep her hand on her elderly husband's chest at night and whack him if he stopped breathing. Even though I don't like to see anyone go to jail, it was probably good for the republic for her to do some time. After all, Leona is the woman who said, "Only the little people pay taxes."

One of the strongest arguments put forth for keeping Leona out of prison was that she had promised to give a fortune to the poor. But that would mean that she was buying her way out of jail. Donald Trump tried that unsuccessfully with Mike Tyson; he promised to donate $1 million to charity so Mike wouldn't have to do time for his rape conviction, but no one wanted his money. One wealthy crook, Wall Street wheeler-dealer Michael Milken, bought his way out of prison, not with money but with information; he became a government witness and gave evidence about other Wall Street defendants in exchange for a reduced sentence.

So, no, I wouldn't represent Helmsley or LoCascio; I defend misfits who don't have clout. Some are in high-profile cases; some are not. I take on as many as I can, the majority at no fee. They take up enormous amounts of time because the appeals go on for years and years. The only time a case is really over is when a client is acquitted, and because I'm defending so many lost causes, that doesn't happen too often.

Risking Contempt

Whether it's Lemuel Smith or Wayne Williams, when I decide to represent a defendant, I do everything humanly possible for my client. If I have to go all out and risk contempt charges, I do. I don't care what the critics say when I take on these lost causes. Because if I'm going to be sensitive about disapproval from a columnist like Mike McAlary or a lawyer like Alan Dershowitz, who once called me the David Duke of the legal profession, I should have been a real estate salesman. Actually, criticism makes me feel that I'm doing exactly the right thing.

If I win a case, I'm lucky. If I alleviate punishment, I'm also lucky, for the odds are always against a defense attorney, particularly one with my type of cases. But I don't want accolades for what I do. Lawyers should be treated no differently than any other cog trying to make the wheels of justice turn a little more smoothly. Of course, sometimes a few spokes get bent or broken. And, on occasion, we reinvent that wheel. The important thing is to keep going; there's always another case waiting.

CHAPTER SIXTEEN

The Despised Muslim

Please don't represent Salameh!

I TAKE TO HEART HARRY TRUMAN'S DICTUM "IF YOU CAN'T STAND THE heat, get out of the kitchen." I pay a steep price for what I do, some might think a ridiculously steep price, but it's my life, and I'm willing to pay it. Sometimes I lose friends; sometimes I bring down the wrath of my family on my head. But I always do what I believe is correct, based on the standards I've developed over the last thirty years.

Many of the beliefs and values that split the country in 1969 still divide us; there still exists a perpetual war between "them" and "us," between the good guys and the bad guys, the inner city and the suburbs. We are a nation divided, torn apart by hatred, fear, and poverty. I see my work as one small attempt to end the factionalism, heal the wounds, and move society toward dispensing justice, real justice, to everyone.

In recent years, I have taken on many Muslim clients and have earned myself even more hatred and disapproval than for my representation of black defendants. Today Muslims are the most hated group in the country; the moment a Muslim is accused of a crime, the specter of terrorism is raised, and everyone panics.

I don't think I have ever felt as detested as when I joined the defense team of El Sayyid Nosair, a Muslim who was charged with the 1990 murder of Rabbi Meir Kahane, founder of the militant Jewish Defense League (JDL) and Israel's anti-Arab Kach party. Although many people disagreed with Kahane's politics, early in his career, his rallying cry of "never again"—Jews should never again accept anti-Semitism and Gestapo-type barbarism without resisting and fighting back—was hailed by many Jews. Because I am Jewish, the criticism against me for defending Nosair was particularly vehement.

At the time, I was already described in the press as "the lawyer everyone loves to hate." One reporter wrote, "When Kunstler wins, everyone loses," and another, that I was possibly the most despised lawyer in the country. This, of course, did not bother me. It was a tribute to my work.

But I do think twice when confronted with a case which I know will cause me and my family enormous unease, and so I gave careful consideration before I finally decided to represent Nosair. It was a good decision; he needed a particularly strong defense. He was the focus of exceptional hatred, and practically everyone assumed he was guilty as charged.

So why do I take on these outcasts, like Nosair, when I know I'll get such opposition from almost everyone? There's no doubt that I enjoy the public attention connected with these kinds of cases. My pleasure in the limelight, according to Margie, is caused by my wanting everyone to love me; in lieu of love, I look for public attention. But I think love is too strong a term. In fact, I wouldn't like it if everyone loved me. Being opposed keeps me sharp. But I do want to be liked and feel very hurt when I'm not. I admit that I want universal respect: People may not agree with what I do, but they can respect me for doing it.

My main reason for taking these unpopular cases, however, is that these people deserve the best defense possible. Since they are often indigent and can't afford to hire hotshot defense attorneys who charge high fees, they end up with public defenders. I believe defendants like Nosair do better with me than they would with public defenders, who, while well-meaning, are often young and relatively inexperienced. So I take the cases.

1991
Nosair

I entered the case of El Sayyid Nosair in part to show my support for the Arab struggle for self-determination. Among people of color, it was not an alienating decision, but among fellow Jews, the white middle class, and many of my colleagues at the bar, it was considered a major defection.

The case was actually quite dangerous to me and my family; telephone and mail death threats increased, and our house was besieged with picketers and assorted other harassments. In the South, during the sixties, I could leave the conflicts behind and come home. But the Nosair case was right in my own backyard, and I didn't like that one bit. Margie was understandably very upset.

When the Jewish Defense Organization (JDO) picketed my house to express their support for Kahane and their anger at me for defending Nosair, I sent letters to my neighbors apologizing for the inconvenience and asking them to bear with it. I ended with "Please forgive me and remember that, just like a trip to the dentist, it will feel so good when the JDO is finished." My neighbors proved to be very supportive.

Up to this point, Nosair is the client who gave me the most personal and professional trouble. Margie, other lawyers, friends, all urged me not to defend him. The question I was most often asked (which I am always asked about controversial clients) was: Do you think he's guilty? Then: Why did you take the case?

Do I think Nosair was guilty? Who knows? He always maintained his innocence. I'm not inside his head, and I wasn't at the scene of the murder. But I deeply believe in Nosair's right to a defense, whether he was innocent or guilty. I think it's ethically correct to defend someone who I believe is guilty. Otherwise, only the innocent would have lawyers.

Sometimes an aggressive defense attorney is virtually all that stands between a defendant and the enormous power of the state. Defense lawyers keep prosecutors honest (to a certain extent) or, at the very least, accountable. We protect people's rights and inject some compassion into a process that is often mechanical, grinding, and deadly. We also try to keep the law relatively free of deception. After all, it is no better than the rest of society; sometimes it's worse. When the full power of the state comes down on a defendant, he needs an advocate to guide him through the complex legal system and save him from prison, death, or whatever fate awaits him.

If we win, maybe it's because we use the system's contradictions to manipulate it. Or because we're extremely aggressive and use the Constitution itself to challenge the prosecution's case. Sometimes we're just plain lucky.

One of my most important tools is public relations. Ever since the Chicago Conspiracy Trial, I have held press conferences and am always available to the media so that I can humanize my clients after they have been thoroughly demonized by the prosecution. It is essential to the defense that the public realize a defendant is a human being, a person, just like everyone else. And while I cannot deny that I do enjoy the limelight, I court publicity to benefit clients, not myself.

Taking a case before the court of public opinion is done frequently by both defense and prosecution. Recently, in the case of O.J. Simpson, the prosecution began to document its charges against the lionized former football star before a secret grand jury and, at the same time, present to the public, by calculated, anonymous leaks to the media. By doing this, it seriously inhibited the presumption of innocence to which every defendant is entitled. I doubt if you could find anyone who has not been influenced by the prosecution's "revelations" of evidence allegedly linking Simpson to the murders, some of which have already been discredited.

To counter prosecutors trying defendants in the court of public opinion before they actually go to trial, defense attorneys must use the same forum but in a different manner. We have to counter a presumption of guilt with a presumption of innocence.

Since winning a case depends in part on a jury's perception of who a defendant is and since jurors are members of the public, the public must truly comprehend a defendant's humanity—that he is not a devil or evil incarnate, but a man or woman, like you and me, with a job, a family, problems, and emotions. So I hold press conferences, give interviews to newspaper reporters, and go on television talk shows to ensure that the public recognize that my clients are people. I did this with Nosair, and I believed it helped enormously. I rely greatly on public relations in my most difficult cases, for example, in the defense of Colin Ferguson, accused of shooting and killing several people on the Long Island Railroad, and in the representation of defendants in the alleged Islamic conspiracy to bomb several locations in New York City.

When I first took on Nosair, I believed he was guilty, so I suggested an insanity defense. In the hospital, though, unable to speak because of a bullet wound to his throat inflicted by a postal inspector on the night of Kahane's murder, he had written: "I am innocent." It was the refrain he uttered from the moment he arrived in Bellevue Hospital's prison ward, shot and under arrest, until the very end, and it was what he told me when we first met: "I am innocent." A review of the evidence revealed that the case was triable. Rather than a hopeless open-and-shut case, the evidence made me believe that Nosair had a good chance of being acquitted at trial. Along with my cocounsel, Michael Warren and Shanara Gilbert, I withdrew the insanity plea and went straight on reasonable doubt, which turned out to be the right move.

In preparing Nosair's defense, I followed the procedure that I use in most of my cases. I used discovery material—like police and forensic reports—to help me decide how best to proceed at trial. I read all of the witnesses' statements, interviewed the defendant at length, then researched all the applicable law. Michael, Shanara, and I filed a number of motions. For example, we sought to determine whether searches of Nosair's home were overbroad. We also moved for hearings to determine whether statements taken from him at the hospital while he was sedated comported with Fourth Amendment standards and whether his arrest had been made without probable cause. Normally, we don't expect to win most of these motions, given most judges' proclivity to believe the testimony of police officers, but they do serve to give us some insight into the prosecutor's analysis of the case.

During trial, the prosecutors from the Manhattan district attorney's office presented a case with serious weaknesses. For example, although several people testified that they had seen Nosair near Kahane when the rabbi was killed, a videotape made by a Kahane supporter moments before the assassination showed that not a single one of these "eyewitnesses" was standing where they said they were when the shooting occurred. During deliberations, the jury several times requested that the videotape be played back for them frame by frame.

The prosecution's case also contained several inconsistencies that were never fully explained. First, no autopsy was done on Kahane. Dr. Charles Hirsch, New York City's medical examiner, decided on his own, with no input from the family, that an Orthodox Jew would not have countenanced an autopsy. This was most unusual, for even when a victim is an Orthodox Jew, an autopsy is done if it's a murder case. Officials will sometimes even countermand a family's insistence that no autopsy be performed. For example, when Yankel Rosenbaum, a scholar and Orthodox Jew from Australia, was fatally stabbed in Crown Heights in 1989, an autopsy was performed against his family's wishes.

Second, after Kahane was shot, a crazy Jewish doctor jumped into the ambulance with the rabbi and prevented EMS personnel from intubating him, a procedure that might have saved his life.

According to an EMS report, this doctor also twisted Kahane's neck "horribly."

There were other unexplained details. Unmarked bullets were found that did not match the gun found next to Nosair. A witness at the trial said he saw shots coming from a gun with a black barrel. Someone stuck a black gun in the back of one of the EMS people, but it could not have been Nosair, because he was no longer at the scene. Also, his gun was silver.

At one point, I learned of a conflict between Rabbi Kahane and some of his followers over funds allegedly missing from his two yeshiva accounts in a Brooklyn bank. My defense of Nosair was based on the fact that no one had actually seen him kill Kahane and no evidence directly linked him to the murder. I also planned to put forth the theory that Rabbi Kahane had been killed by one of his own followers because of financial problems within the Kach party. But New York State Supreme Court justice Alvin Schlesinger did not permit me and my cocounsel to bring this information into evidence or to question witnesses about this subject. We were convinced that the judge was trying his best to cripple our defense.

On the other hand, he was fair when he charged the jury before they began deliberations. He said, "You can't speculate [about evidence]. You can decide there wasn't enough evidence." We stressed to the jury that there was no direct evidence proving that Nosair had killed Kahane. On December 21, 1991, the jury acquitted Nosair of murder but convicted him on lesser charges of gun possession, assault, and coercion. His acquittal, which shocked many people who had already judged him guilty, came about because the Manhattan D.A.'s office had failed to prove beyond a reasonable doubt that he had committed the murder.

Despite the many mysteries that lingered around Kahane's death, the not-guilty verdict was a thrilling victory. A few weeks later, on January 29, 1992, Nosair was sentenced on the lesser charges in a tension-filled chamber in the courthouse at 100 Center Street. The lower Manhattan streets were clogged with Jews and Arabs whose animosity toward each other was palpable. The two groups expressed such bitterness and malice that I was reminded of the dogs and hoses of Bull Connor's Birmingham. It all came back to me as I walked up the steps of the courthouse between the two groups of bearded, dark-haired Semites, ranting at each other. The Arabs carried signs that said Zionism Is Racism and Justice for Nosair, while the Jews held yellow and black placards that read Kahane Lives.

Inside, two dozen armed court officers stood at attention around the courtroom in a solid line blocking the well of the chamber in which sat defendant, judge, lawyers, and prosecutors. Bags and briefcases were checked for weapons. Those Arabs and Jews who were allowed into the chamber sat behind the rows of reporters. The defense attorneys and Nosair, wearing his traditional tunic and kufi, or cap, sat on the right side of the courtroom, with Arab supporters filling the rows behind us. Prosecutors Mary Ann Wirth and William Greenbaum sat on the left of the chamber, with Kahane supporters crowded into the rows behind them.

Given a chance to speak before the judge pronounced sentence, Nosair precipitated chaos when he said, "I'm innocent. All of what is happening to me is based on the fact I'm an Arab Muslim. I want to extend my condolences to the family and friends of Kahane." One Jew cried out, "That's an insult!" Another shouted, "Death to Nosair!" As these two men were removed from the courtroom, Nosair said that he invited the family of Kahane to come and talk to him. Another Jew shouted, "You pig!" He, too, was removed. The Arab supporters—quiet, rigid, disciplined—had obviously been ordered to sit tight.

Judge Schlesinger was clearly angry that Nosair had been acquitted on the murder charge. Although he said, "The one thing that persists is the fairness and vitality of our system of law. . . . We are a nation of laws, not men," it was pure rhetoric, with not an ounce of truth. He then attacked one of the basic tenets of that "fair and vital" system, that a jury decision must be respected, by describing the jury's verdict as "against the overwhelming weight of evidence and . . . devoid of common sense and logic." This reminded me of the English judge who, three hundred years ago, jailed the jury that acquitted William Penn, who would later found Pennsylvania. Penn, a Quaker, was tried for defying a ban against preaching on the streets of London.

Schlesinger continued to denounce Nosair and the jury's acquittal: "I believe the defendant conducted a rape of this country, of our Constitution and of our laws, and of people seeking to exist peacefully together." On the charges of gun possession, coercion, and assault, he sentenced Nosair to the maximum, seven and one-third to twenty-two years.

That night, I spent long hours on the phone with Nosair's wife trying to convince her that all was not lost. We would appeal the convictions, and even if we failed, Nosair would be eligible for parole in five years. Jail time is not all wasted time in a man's life, I told her. Many people who go to prison do endure, and I was convinced that Nosair, with his strong religious faith, was one of them. In prison, he would become the imam, the religious leader, and he would survive. I had no idea that only two years later Nosair would be again indicted for Kahane's murder, this time under a federal statute.

In assessing the murder of Meir Kahane, I'm not at all sure that it was not a blessing; his politics had gone beyond what was at all acceptable, even to many of his supporters. New York State assemblyman Dov Hikind, a staunch Zionist and supporter of Israel, told me once—while we were waiting to appear on a television program—that he thought Kahane had gotten out of control. If Nosair did kill Kahane, it was a political assassination. And political assassination of the right person is not something that I would always describe as wrong.

Defending an individual accused of killing a man such as Kahane can be viewed as a positive act because Kahane's racism and fundamentalism had the potential for interfering with peace negotiations between Arabs and Jews. In a way, his murder may have had a positive effect on peace in the Middle East. Israel did not display great concern about his death. Kahane's Kach party had been banned in Israel in 1988 for being racist and antidemocratic, so there were no tears shed for him there except among his supporters on the far right. I was glad that Rabbi Kahane was not around to sully the historic handshake on September 13, 1993, between Yasir Arafat, chairman of the Palestine Liberation Organization, and Israeli prime minister Yitzhak Rabin.

My feelings on this score were reinforced when, on February 25, 1994, Baruch Goldstein, a Kahane follower, murdered twenty-nine Palestinians while they were at prayer in a West Bank mosque.

1992
General Haq

Gen. Inam Ul-Haq, a retired Pakistani brigadier general, was involved in various international commercial enterprises until he was extradited from West Germany and brought to Philadelphia to stand trial. He was charged with plotting to help Pakistan purchase certain hard metals needed to make nuclear weapons. The general had allegedly tried to purchase metals, through a Canadian agent, from an American company in violation of U.S. laws, which specifically prohibit such transactions. The laws are an attempt to prevent the proliferation of nuclear facilities in certain countries, including Pakistan.

I became involved in the case just after General Haq was extradited. It sounded interesting, and miracle of miracles, there was even a substantial fee—substantial by my standards. Haq had originally been arrested as the result of a long sting operation run by the U.S. Customs Service. Federal agents posed as representatives of the steel manufacturer and officials from the U.S. Commerce Department.

During the general's trial, I kept wondering why the government had kept this very expensive sting going for so many years. I got my answer when I received information about testimony given by Ohio senator John Glenn in July 1990 before the Senate Foreign Relations Committee. He had testified that the U.S. government had, for years, violated all the laws pertaining to the prevention of the creation of nuclear plants in Pakistan. The United States knew that Pakistan had a nuclear facility but was still feeding it with more than $4 billion worth of war matériel. It was clear to me, Senator Glenn, and others that the motive behind this sale of weapons to Pakistan—as we saw in the Iran-Contra affair and similar government scandals—was profit. The government allowed the law to be broken so that American arms companies could make money.

After I was informed about Senator Glenn's testimony, I understood that the government had kept the sting against General Haq operative so it could use him as an example. It could say: "Look what we're doing. We discovered this man trying to acquire a metal used to enrich uranium for the Pakistani nuclear facility, and we prosecuted him as hard as we could. We do prosecute individuals like Haq. We really are trying to ensure that there is a nonproliferation of nuclear materials and facilities in certain countries."

Glenn accused the administration of violating several federal statutes. President Bush was committing crimes using his powers, and my Pakistani general was the fall guy.

U.S. district judge James Giles, a man who remembered me from my civil rights work in his hometown of Lynchburg, Virginia, gave us a very fair trial, knocking out one of the two charges. But General Haq was convicted of the other, issuing a false certificate in furtherance of a conspiracy to defraud the United States. Judge Giles was quite brave and just. When the government asked for a ten-year jail sentence plus a fine of half a million dollars, he refused.

"A ten-thousand-dollar fine is enough. No jail," said the judge. "The defendant Haq has already served many months in pretrial detention, and he has a health problem. I also think he was dangled like a fish on a line." The sentencing and the judge's words were published in the *Philadelphia Inquirer,* which was great for the general because he sent the article to Pakistan to let his countrymen understand that he wasn't a venal criminal.

During the trial, the general had been tremendously depressed. He was a man who had served thirty years in the Pakistani army, had retired early as a protest against his country's failure to institute democracy rather than a military dictatorship, and who, at the age of sixty-three, was faced with the possibility of a long jail term. But when the judge made his wonderful statement, I felt Haq throw back his shoulders and regain his military bearing. His eyes lit up, and he revived. I felt good for him.

Judge Giles's words were very important to me, and I think he did himself proud with his decision. By noting the government's culpability, by not mouthing formula words of support for the federal structure that ran his court and paid his salary, Judge Giles had won my heart. If a federal judge could publicly state that a defendant was "dangled like a fish on a line" by the government, then my fast-declining faith in federal judges was restored, at least for the moment.

February 26, 1993
World Trade Center Bombing

On February 26, 1993, in the middle of a busy workday, a twelve-hundred-pound bomb exploded in one of the basement parking garages of Manhattan's World Trade Center (WTC), killing six people and injuring at least a thousand. The 110-story structure, the tallest in New York City, is a graphic symbol of American capitalism. I was in South Dakota at the twentieth reunion of the Second Siege of Wounded Knee, when I heard about the bombing and that it had supposedly been carried out by terrorists. One of my first thoughts was that I would, inevitably, somehow become involved. Others agreed, and more than a few people said to me, "There's your next case, Bill."

March 2, 1993
El-Jassem

Several days after the World Trade Center bombing, Ron and I appeared in federal court in Brooklyn to request the court to postpone the trial of a client of ours, Khaled Mohammed El-Jassem, described by the government as "a suspected Black September terrorist."

Black September is reportedly the Palestinian group blamed for the deaths of eleven Israeli athletes at the 1972 Munich Olympics. I don't know if it exists today or if it ever existed. Like the Black Liberation Army, Black September is one of those shadowy groups that no one is quite sure exists. If it is real, not something cooked up by a paranoid FBI or CIA hotshot, it supposedly takes its name from September 1971, when King Hussein of Jordan expelled Palestinians from his country.

Our client, El-Jassem, had been indicted almost two decades ago for allegedly placing bombs (which were never exploded) in rented cars outside two Israeli banks in Manhattan and an El Al Airlines freight terminal at Kennedy Airport. He had been free until the authorities suddenly obtained new fingerprint evidence that allegedly linked him to the bombs; he was arrested in Rome in 1991 and was now to be tried. But since his trial was scheduled only days after the catastrophic World Trade Center bombing, which had quickly been linked to Arab terrorists, we argued that El-Jassem would not get a fair trial.

Judge Jack B. Weinstein, a law school classmate of mine and, I once thought, a fair judge, turned down our request to have the trial postponed, and it went on as scheduled.

At the time of El-Jassem's arrest in Rome, he was a forty-five-year-old high-ranking administrative official of the Palestine Liberation Organization. After he was brought to this country, his wife called and asked me to represent him. I took the case because, obviously, a Palestinian accused of terrorism starts off with many prejudices against him and would need a strong defense.

El-Jassem had been indicted in both the Eastern and Southern Districts of New York. The Eastern District's assistant U.S. attorney, Charles E. Rose, noted for his antiterrorist work and a man with whom I've crossed swords many times, asked me to try the case in the Eastern District. He wanted the case so much he could taste it. "You know me. I'll be fair, and we've worked together before," Rose said. These prosecutors really love to take on the bad guys.

El-Jassem had no preference, so I opted for the Eastern District. Rose had been relatively decent with me on a number of politically charged cases, and because the federal courthouse is in Brooklyn and I always travel by subway to Brooklyn, it would be cheaper and easier for me to try the case there.

The prosecution claimed that El-Jassem had planted the bombs in order to assassinate Israeli prime minister Golda Meir during a 1973 visit to New York City. Although El-Jassem was linked to at least one of the bombs by fingerprints, it seemed passing strange to me that this "match" had not been discovered for almost twenty years. During the trial, which lasted only three days, no one could explain this oddity. After the match was supposedly made, the FBI obtained a warrant for a man named Khalid Duhham Al-Jawari, who was linked to Black September. Using that warrant, they arrested my client, El-Jassem, even though he denied that he was Al-Jawari. The government, however, had located a photograph of El-Jassem on a 1973 immigration form issued to someone named Al-Jawari.

El-Jassem never had a chance. Tried only days after the WTC bombing, he faced a jury terrified by the specter of domestic terrorism. As his trial began, the first WTC arrests were made, and all those charged were Muslim, adding to the prejudiced beliefs about Muslims already held by many New Yorkers. Judge Weinstein made only a perfunctory effort to question jurors about their feelings, but I remain certain that no panel selected right on the heels of the WTC tragedy could possibly have been fair to this man. El-Jassem was convicted, after a three-day trial and only three hours of jury deliberations, of planting the three unexploded car bombs.

Judge Weinstein sentenced him to three consecutive terms of ten years despite the fact that he was now a husband and father and quite different from the person he had been twenty years earlier—if indeed they had the right man. I have no doubt that the sentence imposed was the result of the judge's own prejudices rather than any sense of justice.

Incidentally, during the trial, the FBI claimed that it was impossible to transfer a fingerprint from one place to another. Months later, a number of New York state troopers were convicted of doing just that in order to criminalize innocent defendants. So much for the Bureau's denials.

Ibrahim El-Gabrowny

After I had been contacted by a couple of defendants in the World Trade Center bombing, Margie made it clear that she did not want me to become involved. I didn't need these cases, she said; they were dangerous to our family and made her fearful and uneasy. Initially, I took the client who I thought Margie might be more reconciled to than any other, Ibrahim El-Gabrowny. I was well acquainted with him because, as a relative of Nosair's, he had been an active member of his defense team. Although he was arrested right after the bombing, Ibrahim was only charged with obstruction of justice; he had allegedly interfered with federal agents who attempted to search his apartment in connection with the case.

Margie had been fearful that I would defend Mohammad Salameh, the man charged with renting the Ryder van that was supposedly used to deliver the bomb to the World Trade Center. I received calls from my two oldest daughters, Jane and Karin, who both said, "Please don't represent Salameh!"

Even though I completely understood the concerns expressed by my family, I was quite shocked by the attitude I saw displayed at the 1993 National Lawyers Guild dinner by the many friends who came up to me and said, "Don't get involved with Salameh." If this was the viewpoint of liberal lawyers, what must be the attitude of those people who are not so liberal?

I agree that bombing the World Trade Center was crazy, and I don't condone it. I can, however, understand why someone would want to bomb it for political reasons, for the building is a monument to American corporate structure and capitalism. I regret, as I suppose the bombers also regret, that people died in the process.

After I agreed to defend El-Gabrowny on his minor charges, someone called in a death threat against me to the police department, a rather unusual move, since most death threats I receive are made directly to my office. Our local precinct took the risk seriously and assigned a detective to make sure I didn't get bumped off; needless to say, my family was most unhappy about the threat.

Despite the attempts to frighten me and my family, despite

the possibility that someone might actually harm me, I felt strongly that I must make my stand. Even though some cases are dangerous and will anger people, it's important to become involved in them. Those are the chances my family has to take with me. If I were going to be timid and refuse to take a case because some nut might do something terrible, then I wouldn't be practicing law anymore. And I wouldn't be me anymore.

Of course, Ron believes I am never afraid and loves to tell tall stories about my alleged lack of fear. But I am not fearless and have had my heart in my throat many times. I'm fairly careful and do everything in my power to keep the danger level as low as possible. I keep the office locked, watch where I go, don't walk alone into cul de sacs, and try to have people around me all the time. So, no, I don't take chances. But there are not too many things that can frighten me overmuch, which is probably the reason I can take cases other people are afraid of.

Margie is used to it; she understands what my life is, and I really commend her. She takes it all into consideration and doesn't raise a terrific storm. She quickly became reconciled to the idea of my representing El-Gabrowny and handled it well. Although she hardly sees eye to eye with fundamentalists of any religious stripe and particularly those who denigrate women, she gradually accepted my involvement in this case—including the other defendants that I came to represent some months later.

Ibrahim El-Gabrowny is an intelligent, helpful, and likable man. A civil engineer with a bachelor's degree from the University of the Suez Canal, he is a general contractor, married with six children. He is a devout Muslim, president of his mosque in Brooklyn, and is well liked in the Islamic community.

During Nosair's trial, he worked with me and the other lawyers and on a few occasions saved us from being roughed up. Ibrahim saw to it that I was escorted from the courthouse and driven home in a waiting car. When Kahane supporters surged toward me threateningly in the corridor of the courthouse, Ibrahim ordered Muslims to interpose themselves between me and the Kahanites. He also arranged for Muslim supporters of Nosair from Jersey and Brooklyn to attend the trial. It was El-Gabrowny who kept tight order among his people in the courtroom the day Nosair was sentenced, as he had done throughout the trial.

After the WTC bombing, Ibrahim's wife and brother asked me to become involved when he was charged with obstruction of justice. He was indicted separately from all the others who were accused of the WTC bombing. When I visited him in jail, he expressed concerns about legal fees, but I told him not to worry, that money didn't matter. I felt strongly that I had to defend him because of my feelings of loyalty. Plus, I saw nothing linking him to the WTC bombing, not even worthwhile innuendos. And, at any rate, you can't run the Constitution on innuendos.

The government initially became interested in Ibrahim because Mohammad Salameh had given Ibrahim's apartment as his address on his driver's license. To me, it is perfectly natural and a typical act of friendship to allow a friend to use your address for a driver's license. People do it all the time.

Ibrahim was arrested six days after the bombing. When he asked to use the bathroom, he was not given access to a sink because the authorities intended to examine his hands for evidence of contact with explosives. Ibrahim told me that since he could not use the sink, after he urinated, he flushed, then washed his hands in the clean water. The authorities spread a ridiculous story that he had erased incriminating evidence from his hands by washing in his own urine.

As a religious Muslim, he must wash after all bodily functions, and this was during Ramadan, the most holy period in the Islamic calendar. Since it is clear that he had obviously washed his hands during the six days between the bombing and his arrest, the government could have had only one motive in spreading this ridiculous story: to portray him negatively in the public's mind in order to further its depiction of an evil Islamic conspiracy comprised of weird people who would wash in their own urine. Another reason for the story was to furnish a basis on which the court could deny him bail.

Ibrahim's bail hearing was held before district judge Richard Owen, as prosecution-oriented as they come. The government pushed for no bail, citing the hand washing, Ibrahim's address on Salameh's license, and most damaging, fake Nicaraguan passports for Nosair and his family that were found in his possession. The government inferred that if Ibrahim had these passports, he was planning to help Nosair escape from the Attica Correctional Facility, where he was serving his sentence. Now, while I believe Nosair was unfairly sentenced, I wouldn't urge anyone to break him out. And I seriously doubt that a levelheaded individual like Ibrahim would plan anything as foolhardy as that.

Ibrahim had been arrested on March 4, 1993, the same day as

some of the men accused of bombing the World Trade Center. At his arraignment a few days later, his case was, by random selection, assigned to Judge Michael Mukasey and that of the WTC suspects, to Judge Kevin Duffy, a far more experienced jurist.

In June, ten Muslims were apprehended at a Queens warehouse and accused of a monster conspiracy to blow up the Holland Tunnel, the FBI building, and the United Nations, among other targets, kill public officials, and overthrow the governments of the United States and Egypt. Because the authorities were anxious to have Judge Mukasey, an ardent Zionist, try the conspiracy case, they threw El-Gabrowny into that mix by alleging that he had had some connections with several of those defendants and that he was a conspirator. As a result, the government had the judge it wanted for the far more serious case.

Prior to the new charges, Ron had been going from mosque to mosque in order to acquaint their members with their legal rights in case the FBI sought to investigate them. We even prepared a primer detailing what they could legally do if agents sought to question them. During one of his visits, Ron met Siddig Ibrahim Siddig Ali, a Sudanese who spoke perfect English. Later, when Siddig was arrested and charged with the monster conspiracy, he asked that we come to see him at the Metropolitan Correctional Center (MCC), the federal detention facility in lower Manhattan.

When I visited Siddig, he told me that the government's confidential informant, Emad Salem, had maliciously sought to entrap him and others into saying and doing things that would bring them afoul of the law. I was very taken with Siddig; Margie saw him interviewed over Cable News Network (CNN) and was impressed also. Siddig did not appear to be a single-minded, zealous fundamentalist. He had a good sense of humor and a stable family life and was well spoken and handsome. He understood the political nature of the case against him and seemed eager to fight back on both the legal and political fronts. He impressed me, and I decided to represent him.

On July 15, Siddig and nine others were arraigned as suspected terrorists in what Ron and I call "the plot to bomb everything and kill everybody." At the arraignment, where Ron and I represented Siddig, it was disclosed that the government had received permission to bug the telephones of Siddig and one other defendant under the seldom-used Foreign Intelligence Surveillance Act (FISA). This statute is supposed to be used only in cases where a foreign country threatens national security. It also allows the Central Intelligence Agency to act inside the United States, which the agency is not ordinarily authorized to do.

After it was revealed that the entire government case rested on one man, Emad Salem, I told the press that it was a clear case of entrapment. A veteran of the Egyptian army, Salem claimed that he had pretended to be a conspirator and had taped conversations with the others concerning their alleged conspiracy and bomb making.

In the weeks and months after the arrest of the ten Muslims in Queens, even more flamboyant charges were added by the government, and five more individuals, including El Sayyid Nosair, swelled the number of defendants. It all reminded me of the Perils of Pauline: a new trauma, a new charge, almost every week. It never ended. The authorities churned out one ridiculous allegation after another against these men so that they would be viewed by the public as the worst possible villains before they were even tried. The authorities' manipulation of the media and the public continued through the summer, fall, and winter of 1993–94. Hardly a day passed without a story that contained some new twist and crime the government claimed had been planned by the indicted men. Months before their trial was to begin, almost everyone was already convinced of their guilt.

Conspiracy

In August, the authorities linked the WTC bombing with the "plot to bomb everything." In order to simplify the enormous, confusing, and complicated conspiracy, the government accused two men of being the linchpins that connected the different parts of the giant conspiracy.

The first man, El Sayyid Nosair, was a perfect choice for the government; he was already a familiar figure. He was charged with conspiring to bomb the WTC and to overthrow the government through terrorist bombings. Inmates close to Nosair were offered payoffs and reduced sentences to testify that they had overheard him plotting with Salameh and Mahmud Abouhalima, WTC defendants who had visited him in prison.

In December, Nosair was again indicted for the murder of Rabbi Kahane, this time under RICO, the federal Racketeer Influenced and Corrupt Organizations Act. Bringing the indictment against Nosair under a federal statute eliminated the possibility of double jeopardy—trying an individual twice for the same crime.

Because Judge Mukasey refused to appoint Michael Warren, co-counsel on Nosair's state murder trial and his choice to defend him against the new federal charges, Nosair was forced to proceed with a lawyer appointed by the court.

The second human link, Sheikh Omar Abdel Rahman, was also indicted in August. The fifty-six-year-old blind religious leader had been a familiar figure to the public ever since the WTC bombing in June. The government had continually and publicly speculated that the sheikh was at the heart of the alleged conspiracy. Finally, it charged him with directing both the WTC bombing and the conspiracy. The sheikh's fiery preachings, in which he had denounced the secular Egyptian government and allegedly urged jihad, or holy war, were regarded by the United States and Egypt as the ideological basis of terrorist acts committed by Islamic revolutionaries in both countries. When he was arraigned, the sheikh denied that he inspired terrorism, led a conspiracy in this country, or directed the WTC bombing.

I believe that Nosair was indicted because Atty. Gen. Janet Reno capitulated to enormous pressure from the Jewish community to remedy the jury's acquittal in his state trial. I think Reno also gave in to political pressure when she indicted the sheikh, since there is absolutely no hard evidence of his involvement in any conspiracy or plot.

The sheikh first retained Harry Batchelder, who promised to represent him without fee. When Batchelder changed his mind over financial issues, the sheikh turned to Ron and me. We visited him at the federal correctional institution in Otisville, New York, where he was being held. Ron and I believed that the only reason for the sheikh's indictment was to prevent his deportation to Egypt. We were certain that Egyptian president Hosni Mubarak had persuaded the U.S. government to bring the charges to ensure that Sheikh Rahman would remain in this country. Mubarak definitely did not want him in Egypt, rallying support against his government.

After we agreed to represent the sheikh, Judge Mukasey cited a potential conflict of interest. In November, he ruled that we could not represent the three defendants because Siddig Ali and Ibrahim El-Gabrowny were charged with committing criminal acts, while the sheikh was charged with directing the acts. Their defenses would conflict, Mukasey said, and gave us a few days to make our "choice." Ron and I wanted to continue representing all three, since we felt that a united defense, as in the Chicago Conspiracy Trial, would be the most effective way to destroy the government's case. We refused to make the "choice" put before us, viewing it as the government's attempt to divide the defendants and weaken their defense.

And despite Mukasey's warnings about conflict of interest, all three defendants wanted us to continue defending them. But in the end, as it often does, the court prevailed. We were removed from the sheikh's case, and he was assigned a public defender. But the religious leader refused the court-appointed attorney and told Judge Mukasey that if he couldn't have us, he would represent himself. This response reminded me of Bobby Seale's ordeal in Chicago: a defendant not allowed to have the counsel of his choice, then choosing to represent himself.

Since Chicago, many court rulings have reiterated the Sixth Amendment right of a criminal defendant to "assistance of counsel for his defense." The Constitution gives a defendant the right to choose his own counsel and also the right to represent himself. In *United States v. Seale,* the U.S. Seventh Circuit Court in 1972 condemned Judge Hoffman's failure in Chicago to make sufficient inquiry into Bobby Seale's objections to proceed to trial without counsel of his choice.

The Seventh Circuit stated: "If the Sixth Amendment right to the effective assistance of counsel means anything, it certainly means that it is the actual choice of the defendant which deserves consideration."

By refusing to allow Sheikh Rahman his counsel of choice, Judge Mukasey had violated the Constitution. In my opinion, his action, which did violence to our Bill of Rights and our justice system, was just as reprehensible as, although quite different from, violence done by terrorists.

At the same time, Assistant U.S. Attorney Andrew McCarthy moved to have Ron and me disqualified from representing any of the defendants. Mukasey refused to do so, either because he felt it would look bad to deny them their counsel of choice as well, or he couldn't figure a colorable reason to bounce us.

During the various legal proceedings in the weeks and months before these defendants were to be brought to trial on September 19, 1994, Judge Mukasey ordered both defense and prosecution not to discuss the case in the media. This resulted in a rather ironic occurrence. During a television interview, I recounted that Ron and I had evidence that Emad Salem, the government's confidential informer, was himself involved in the

WTC bombing. Not only had he confessed to the crime during a conversation with an FBI agent that he had secretly recorded—as defense attorneys, we were given copies of transcripts of these and other conversations—but he was hospitalized less than three hours after the blast with a middle-ear attack. We had information that Salem was prone to these attacks when exposed to shots or explosions; he had suffered a similar attack when he fired a rifle on a practice range without wearing earplugs.

James Fox, the head of FBI operations in New York, was also questioned in the same television interview. He denied what I had said by contending, in effect, that I was all wet. When asked if the FBI could have prevented the WTC bombing based on information it had received from the informer, Salem, Fox denied that the Bureau had received any advance information.

After the interview was aired, Assistant U.S. Attorney McCarthy wrote to Judge Mukasey, complaining about the comments I had made. A day after Mukasey received the letter, on December 10, 1993, Fox was suspended for commenting publicly about the case. McCarthy was, of course, peeved that his letter had led to Fox's suspension and said that the letter had been written to point out *my* comments, not those of the FBI boss. I was more than pleased with the outcome: My big mouth had indirectly brought about the downfall of an FBI chief!

At the end of December, Judge Mukasey said he would consider severing from the trial the murder of Rabbi Kahane as well as the alleged plot to kill Mubarak because he was uncertain what the murder and the plot had to do with sedition against the United States.

On January 18, 1994, we filed motions asking for the Kahane and Mubarak sections of the case to be severed. The hearing was held on January 24, and, months later, the judge denied the motion, undoubtedly because the government was relying on the shock value at the trial of these changes.

The World Trade Center Bombing Trial

On September 14, 1993, Ahmad M. Ajaj, Nidal Ayyad, Mohammad Salameh, and Mahmud Abouhalima went on trial in federal court in Manhattan for bombing the World Trade Center. The prosecution re-created the bombing and tried to link each of the men to it. But the defense contended that the men had not been accurately identified, that there was reasonable doubt that these were in fact the individuals who had planted the bomb. The defense also contended that the government was trying Islam, the religion and culture of these men, in addition to the men themselves.

One of the supports of the government's cases was a gas station attendant who said that he had serviced the yellow Ryder truck—which was alleged to have contained the WTC bomb—the night before the explosion. He was supposed to come into the courtroom and point out two of the defendants who, he had told the authorities, had been in the vehicle that evening. However, he startled everyone by identifying two of the jurors as the men he had seen.

In March 1994, all four Trade Center defendants were convicted of the bombing. The jury, after hearing mainly circumstantial evidence during the five-month trial, deliberated for only four full days and found the defendants guilty on all counts. Following their convictions, they asked Ron and me to handle their sentencing. They felt, with considerable justification, that their trial attorneys had shortchanged them. However, the trial judge refused to permit us to do so, citing a mythical conflict of interest. He sent the four to a prison hundreds of miles away from New York prior to their sentencing, an unprecedented act, and then imposed 240-year terms of imprisonment, all while preventing them from being represented by counsel of their choice.

Full Circle

As I waited for the conspiracy trial to begin, I felt that I had come full circle. In Chicago, a quarter of a century before, I had defended seven men against conspiracy charges. In New York, in 1994, I was once again representing defendants on conspiracy charges. And although this may be difficult to believe today, for those who don't remember or who weren't born yet, in 1969, the Chicago defendants were despised by many people because of their beliefs, values, and lifestyles.

And, as in Chicago, the government still used the same tired old tactics to eliminate or discredit individuals and groups that it feared or hated—in this case, Muslims. It created monsters, larger-than-life evil figures, then manipulated their images in the media. In December 1993, a prosecutor in the conspiracy case misled a federal judge into believing that he possessed incriminating tape-recorded conversations between two of the defendants when these recordings did not exist. And the government itself, at about the same time, admitted that highly prejudicial, and untrue, leaks to the media by anonymous federal agents were "cowardice in anonymity" and "reprehensible."

In the World Trade Center bombing trial, the prosecutor had played a videotape of an explosion found in the possession of one of the defendants without informing the jury that the bombing scene was taken from a Hollywood feature film.

By the end of the government's campaign to depict the Islamic defendants as worse than anything, even Nazis, the public was more than willing to accept an unjust trial.

Like Chicago, this was a political case, and the defense of the fifteen alleged conspirators had to be political; the case could not be won on legalities. I would conduct the defense by putting the government on trial, just as we did in Chicago.* To that end, I spoke out during 1993 and 1994, urging supporters of the fifteen defendants to build a defense committee. I told them to make certain that the defendants did not feel alone; I suggested that organizers work in their communities to create backing for the defendants. During the trial, the courtroom would have to be filled with supporters at all times. People would have to raise money and press their case in the media.

The U.S. government had put Islam on trial. My job was to defend the practitioners of this misunderstood religion, who, like any people who are different, are ostracized, feared, and persecuted.

---

*On June 24, 1994, Ron and I received a one-sentence letter from Siddig Ali, discharging us as his counsel. He is now working for the government and, because he will likely be a witness against El-Gabrowny, our original client, we may have a conflict of interest and be forced by the government to leave the case.

CHAPTER SEVENTEEN

Lost Causes

Even an unsavory character is not to be imprisoned except on definite proof of crime.

Many of the cases I'VE HANDLED OVER THE LAST TWENTY-FIVE years could be called "lost causes" because the defendants, often out of synch with mainstream society, stood very little chance of being acquitted and were, in the words of Clarence Darrow, "life's damned." They may be members of a minority or another oppressed group. They may have radical political views. They may have committed other crimes. They may be hated by almost everyone.

Throughout our history, we have had government-manufactured villains, such as Communists, terrorists, labor-union leaders, mobsters, black militants, Islamic fundamentalists, or whatever group was out of favor at the time. In order to support official terrorism, like the shooting down of union members and Black Panthers or the beating of antiwar and civil rights demonstrators, the government makes its enemies into monsters so that it can get away with murder and the public says no more than "What does it matter? They were only criminal syndicalists or union people or organized-crime figures or terrorists."

In the past, for example, striking union workers were considered enemies of the people because a labor union on strike was committing a crime called criminal syndicalism. At different times throughout our history, our enemies have been anarchists, pacifists, Japanese-Americans, or suffragettes. Today our enemies of choice are alleged terrorists, particularly those with Arabic names. But organized-crime figures run a close second.

Ironically, some groups that were yesterday's villains are today's heroes. Who would have imagined, for example, when we fought Japan during World War II—and even imprisoned Japanese Americans in concentration camps in this country—that today we would seek Japan's business and its money?

Members of unpopular groups should not be thrown to the lions; someone needs to stand up for them. I always remember what Pastor Martin Niemoeller said:

> In Germany, they came first for the Communists and I didn't speak up because I wasn't a Communist . . . the Jews . . . the trade unionists . . . the Catholics. . . . Then they came for me, and by that time no one was left to speak up.

Organized Crime

My relationships with some organized-crime figures have baffled both friends and foes, but these are no different from any of my other cases, because mob figures often serve as scapegoats for the government and quickly become everyone's favorite bad guys. This country has a long tradition of bias against Italian-Americans, and we love making villains out of individuals who are linked to organized crime. Defendants accused of such ties are almost always discriminated against, almost always assumed to be guilty. In America, if your last name ends in a vowel, you're immediately suspect. Many of the great civil liberties decisions have arisen from cases in which the defendant's last name ended in a vowel, as Justice Felix Frankfurter once said. So that when I represent an organized-crime figure, it is usually on a civil rights issue.

The ACLU also takes some organized-crime cases because of the prejudice against these defendants. I remember hearing about a meeting years ago in Apalachin, New York, between Vito Genovese and other well-known organized-crime figures. The house where the meeting took place was surrounded by state troopers who were watching to see what was going to happen. The wife of one of the men at the meeting saw the troopers and told her husband. The mobsters ran out of the house and across the fields but were caught and arrested on trumped-up charges. Osmond Fraenkel, then general counsel to the ACLU, investigated, determined that these arrests were unfounded, and moved to vacate the ensuing convictions. When a federal appellate court agreed with him, one of the judges wrote, "In America, we still respect the dignity of the individual and even an unsavory character is not to be imprisoned except on definite proof of crime." Unfortunately, this is a concept often ignored by our legal system.

Organized-crime figures fascinate me, in part because they are complicated people who live and operate under intricate and somewhat enigmatic rules and regulations. In their adherence to the institutional rules of the church, marriage, and the family, they exhibit a morality which is difficult to reconcile with other aspects of their lives.

Also, I must confess to a slight romantic attraction to the folk-hero quality I see in them—the result of a lifetime of reading crime stories, as well as the attraction I always feel to danger. Although organized-crime figures are part of the capitalist system, they also rip off the system. I view them as banditos, renegades, which appeals to me whether they're renegades in the Old West or here on New York's Mulberry Street.

I am attracted also to their paternalism and to their power. I'm certainly not immune to power. I remember that Martin King and I once went to Bobby Kennedy's office in the Justice Department to persuade him to offer more protection to civil rights workers in the Deep South. As I looked at his children's drawings tacked up on a wall behind Bobby, I sensed the enormity of his power and felt its immense allure.

The Don of New England

My introduction to the world of organized crime came in the late 1970s, when I represented Raymond Patriarca, who was then known as the "Don of New England." The moment we met, although Patriarca was elderly and quite ill, I was instantly aware that he was well named; I was in the presence of a patriarch, a Godfather. People would come into the room and ask him for favors, which he would either grant, deny, or refer to someone else. I suspect there was not much difference between Patriarca and King Henry VIII. One ran a country, one ran a so-called family, and monarchs both, they existed on goodwill, favors done, tribute exacted, and fear.

Patriarca had requested my help on a civil rights case. The

Providence Journal had sued the FBI, under the Freedom of Information Act, for the release of tape recordings intercepted by the Bureau in a 1966 tax evasion case, *United States v. Taglianetti,* and suppressed on constitutional grounds. Although Patriarca was not involved in that case, his voice had been recorded on some of the tapes. The FBI still had the tapes, and the newspaper intended to print transcripts of them.

The FBI had only halfheartedly opposed the newspaper's lawsuit because it really wanted the tapes made public. Along with Harris Berson, a Providence lawyer, I intervened for Patriarca, contending that illegally obtained tapes should not be publicly disclosed. The court sustained us, a victory for Patriarca's civil rights; his rights, after all, are entitled to protection by the Constitution, just like yours and mine.

Later, after the victory in the Taglianetti tapes case, Margie and I were invited to a celebration party at Ruggiero's on Grand Street in New York City's Little Italy. Our hosts, looking for all the world as if they came from central casting, were very gracious. Margie was the only woman at our table; our hosts' wives and girlfriends sat at a separate table.

When the wine came, someone said, "Let the counselor give the toast." I stood up but didn't quite know what to say, so, without thinking, I raised my glass and said the first words that came into my head: "Here's to crime."

There was absolute silence at the table. When I sat down, Margie whispered in my ear, "You've said exactly the wrong thing. That was a terrible toast. It's a great insult." The meal continued, and I put it out of my mind. (This toast came back to me, many years later, when I met John Gotti in a Brooklyn courthouse.)

Joe Bonnano

I was once asked by my old friend Charlie Garry to represent his client Joe Bonnano. Charlie was on another case, and Joe, reportedly once the head of the Bonnano crime family, had been subpoenaed to appear as a witness in a case in New York City. The heads of the so-called five families of organized crime were being tried on charges of leading a mammoth illegal conspiracy in what was called "the Commission Case." At that time, Joe was an old and very sick man who lived in Tucson, Arizona, with one of his daughters.

Rudolph Giuliani, now mayor of New York City, and Michael Chertoff, then Giuliani's assistant and now U.S. attorney for New Jersey, had brought the case against the five families. Joe was subpoenaed to testify about what he had written in a book he had coauthored about his life two decades back. Since it was a certainty that Joe would be jailed for contempt rather than agree to testify, he had clearly been subpoenaed only for his publicity value.

Because he was elderly, with a weak heart, and not allowed to travel, the trial judge, Richard Owen, held a hearing in Tucson. I attended it at Charlie Garry's request, but I was also quite interested in the legendary Joe Bonnano. It was a break for me from my usual serious cases because the only charge against Joe was failure to obey a subpoena. I went to Tucson, met Joe, and rather liked him; we got along famously. He had an aura about him. He was a relic of a remote, romantic New York and reminded me of my own grandfather, Pa Moe.

Part of Joe's hearing was held in a hospital because the old bandito was really quite ill. It was painfully obvious that Judge Owen intensely disliked Joe, so all his rulings were pro-prosecution. I did my best, was quite outspoken, and was almost held in contempt. When the judge became furious at something I said, which I can no longer recall, he said, "One more remark like that and you'll be in the clink." I subsided, but at least he knew how I felt.

In the end, the judge disregarded medical testimony about Joe's heart condition and ordered him to come to New York. Joe refused and was sentenced to do time in the federal prison hospital at Springfield, Missouri. He served the time, and that was the end of it.

John Gotti

In 1987, I was in U.S. District Court in Brooklyn when a modern-day bandito, John Gotti, walked up to me and introduced himself. "I just wanted to say, do you remember that crazy toast you gave at that dinner down at Ruggiero's?" he asked.

"I've never forgotten it. My wife thought it was awful," I answered.

"Awful! We thought it was wonderful!" Gotti said. "You know, I was one of the guys around that table. After you and the missus left, we all laughed our heads off."

"I'm glad to hear that, because my wife thought that it probably was a grave insult."

"No," Gotti said, smiling. "It was the funniest thing we'd heard in a long time."

After that initial meeting, I saw Gotti in court many times and visited him in jail during his 1992 trial for racketeering under the federal RICO statute. Gotti is a very likable man, charming and urbane, handsome, dignified looking, and dressed to the nines. At the trial, columnist Cindy Adams, who was sitting with Anthony Quinn, asked me what I thought of the whole thing. I said, "I think he ought to get a civic award. If what the government says is true, he got rid of nineteen hoods at no expense to the taxpayer." My daughter, Emily, was with me that day and was thrilled when Gotti waved at us.

Although many people have asked why I represented John Gotti, the truth is that I never really did in the traditional sense. I simply filed a petition for him on a civil rights matter. At the government's request, the trial judge, I. Leo Glasser, who considers himself a civil libertarian, had refused to allow Gotti and his codefendant, Frank LoCascio, to be represented by their counsel of choice. My motion contended that their Sixth Amendment rights had been violated, that they should be allowed to have the lawyers of their choice represent them.

Bruce Cutler had successfully represented John in three previous trials. Determined to eliminate Cutler, the government successfully moved to disqualify him, claiming he was house counsel to Gotti and that the prosecutors intended to call him as a witness. John's second choice, lawyer James Larossa, was also made ineligible to represent him by the same device. But the prosecution never actually called either man to testify. On the first day of trial, the court, at the government's behest and for the same reasons, also removed LoCascio's lawyer, George Santangelo.

My petition to restore Gotti's and LoCascio's lawyers was denied. I had not really expected to win because the federal court of appeals seldom grants these petitions, but I felt it was necessary to bring to the public's attention that these defendants were not allowed to have their counsel of choice. Later, after Gotti and LoCascio were convicted, I made an unsuccessful motion to set aside their convictions on the grounds that the judge had wrongly excused a black woman juror on the eve of deliberations.

What was important to me in John Gotti's case is what is always important: the chance to demonstrate that in its prosecutions of certain people the government will willfully violate the Constitution. In John's case, it went all out.

Half of what I do is to educate the public, and this case gave me a great opportunity. The public had been indoctrinated with the idea that the government was Sir Galahad and John Gotti was the worst creature who ever walked the face of the earth. Neither is true. Maybe I've lost all perspective on what's good and what's bad, but I don't regard John as the most evil criminal in our history. The very government that attacked him was the same one that cost us many thousands of American and Vietnamese lives in the Vietnam War.

If what the government said was true and Gotti was a bandit, then he was no different from bandits all over the world. Of course, murder is against the law no matter who the victim is. But to designate Gotti the archcriminal, to say that people who participate in the internecine warfare that goes on between members of crime families are worse than anyone else—even worse killers than the president, at whose behest hundreds of thousands were killed in the Gulf War, even worse than a government which conducted radiation experiments on unsuspecting human guinea pigs, even worse than the corporations that made Dalkon Shields, thalidomide, and DES—is hype, overkill, and quite simply a lie.

Even if every claim the government made about John was true, it was still not acceptable to make him into a cipher who could be treated differently from everyone else. We cannot follow different laws for different people. In Robert Bolt's play *A Man for All Seasons,* Henry VIII asks his Lord Chancellor Thomas More to ignore the law and legitimize his divorce so he can remarry. When More's son-in-law Roper urges him to go along with Henry and change the law, More replies, "The law, Roper, the law. I know what's legal, not what's right. And I'll stick to what's legal." If the law is altered for one person, it becomes totally bland and loses its meaning. And that is exactly what was done to Gotti and LoCascio by not allowing them to be defended by the lawyers they had chosen.

In addition, John's fifteen-month preventive detention before trial, combined with a sequestered and anonymous trial jury, gave the public the impression that this was a most dangerous defendant. There have been anonymous juries and sequestered juries before but rarely both at the same time. During this trial, the government threw the Constitution to the winds. It tried to convict him by hook or by crook—I think, by crook.

I did not charge a fee for filing the petitions for Gotti and LoCascio because I felt that I was representing the Bill of Rights and the Constitution rather than the individuals. I also did not want anyone to say, "Kunstler's like all the rest. He wants the money, so he takes a Mafioso case." I didn't want to be one of their hired hands; it would hurt my credibility and make me the same as other lawyers who take cases for fees rather than principle. I don't criticize them for the way they run their professional lives; I just prefer my way.

On several occasions, I attempted to advise John, but he rejected my suggestions. Bruce Cutler is a street fighter and was therefore the perfect lawyer for John. After the court removed Cutler as well as James Larossa, I recommended that John represent himself. At that point, he knew the government had tapes of him talking with his cronies, knew Salvatore "Bull" Gravano was going to testify against him, and knew he had nothing to lose. I thought having him conduct his own cross-examination of Gravano would have been an enormous bit of theater.

What Bobby Seale did in Chicago taught me the importance of a defendant's actions in the courtroom. It's very powerful when a defendant tells the jury directly that he is being treated unfairly. There is really no way the court can penalize a defendant who does this except, of course, to hold him in contempt or take some other action just as useless. I wanted John to stand before the jury, the way Bobby Seale had done twenty-five years ago, and say: "I've been deprived of my lawyer. I've been deprived of my constitutional right to have my counsel of choice."

But unlike many sixties activists who loved being involved in the legal process, John Gotti, like most people, is dependent on lawyers to do his legal work. During the Chicago trial—which is still my benchmark for measuring legal strategies—the defendants used a far more dynamic approach. Of course, they didn't have as much to lose as John. Ultimately, they succeeded, though, whereas he failed. This kind of action requires a defendant with the courage to be political, which John is not. He spoke out about his rights only when the jury was out of the courtroom.

After Gotti was convicted of murder and racketeering, I visited him and offered some further recommendations for legal strategy with regard to his sentencing. I suggested that Bruce Cutler conduct the sentencing hearing because I didn't believe the judge would have the nerve to throw Cutler out for that small part of the trial. It was a certainty that John would receive the maximum sentence, and I felt that having Cutler as his lawyer then would have dramatically demonstrated how the court had kept him out when it counted. But John ignored this suggestion, too.

During my later visits to John at Metropolitan Correctional Center, if I had anything meaningful to say, I wrote it, because I don't trust prison waiting rooms. He would either nod or write an answer. I am very careful about being taped, much more so than he was. The tapes that convicted him showed that either John didn't care what he said and where he said it or didn't understand the capabilities of electronic eavesdropping—which I find difficult to believe. I was actually shocked by what was on those tapes, for anyone with knowledge of state-of-the-art intercept equipment knows you can't get away from microphones by going into a hallway.

While there is a long history of the government tampering with jurors, as occurred in the Chicago conspiracy case, there was no hard evidence that John Gotti tampered with the jury during any of his trials. Therefore, there was no valid reason for sequestering the jury during his last trial. Since sequestered jurors are in the custody of the Department of Justice and dependent on it for food, shelter, and other comforts, they immediately feel they're being protected against the defendant, which, of course, prejudices them. At the same time, John was held in jail on the grounds that he was too dangerous to be allowed out, creating another bias against him.

U.S. Attorney Andrew Maloney went even further when he summed up to the jury and did the unforgivable. He said, "If you let him go, if you acquit John Gotti, you won't be safe on the streets." That statement was a complete violation of the constitutional rights of the defendant. To give jurors a personal involvement in a conviction, to pander to their fears, is a cardinal sin. Although Gotti's conviction was eventually affirmed, the appellate court called Mr. Maloney's remark "totally inappropriate," "indefensible," and "an intolerable attempt . . . to instill fear of the defendants." If a defense attorney had ever uttered an equivalent diatribe, he would quickly be looking for bail money.

There was considerable government hanky-panky with the jury during this trial. First, the court eliminated a black juror, juror no. 3, referring to her as "combative," which, in my lexicon, after fifty years of watching black-white relationships, means "uppity."

After the trial, she called me because she knew I had been Dr.

King's lawyer and told me that the foreperson had been visited secretly in the middle of the night by U.S. marshals. The marshals then removed from juror no. 3's drawer in the jury room—a drawer that she shared with the foreperson—a note that she had written about signaling between one FBI agent in the audience and another who was a witness. (She said she saw one agent adjust his tie and thought it meant he was signaling the witness. The agent who had adjusted his tie said that he did it only to let the witness know that *his* tie was untied. What baloney!)

According to juror no. 3, the marshals then planted her note in a bag of clothes that she sent home via her husband to be cleaned. As a result, the judge accused her of sending a message out. Juror no. 3 swore to me that she never removed the note from her drawer in the jury room and never sent it out. Why would she? It was meaningless to anyone on the outside.

Instead of ordering a hearing on this situation, the judge dismissed juror no. 3. In her place, he put in alternate no. 3, who, it turned out, had lied on her jury questionnaire. She had kept to herself the tidbit that her husband was a former FBI agent.

After the trial, I also received a call from juror no. 10. He, too, was black. He was removed from the jury the day before deliberations began, and he told me that he had been ejected for no reason.

Another caller, juror no. 12, told me that alternate no. 3 (the woman whose husband was an ex-FBI agent) had told the other jurors, long before deliberations began, that she believed Gotti was guilty. Finally, at least two jurors, including alternate no. 3, were allowed to go home during the trial, breaking sequestration. Since the judge would not grant a hearing on this matter, we will never know why any of these shenanigans occurred.

While this appears somewhat convoluted, it is exactly how the government operates if it desperately wants to win a case. I learned that lesson in Chicago, and from watching the illegal contact during the Gotti trial, I can see it still holds true today. As the Church Committee Report revealed almost twenty years ago, federal law enforcement will go to any extremes to make its case.

After John was convicted, I made a motion to set aside the verdicts because of jury tampering and other irregularities. I argued before Judge Glasser that one juror had been improperly dismissed, two others improperly retained, and two allowed out of their hotel rooms in violation of sequestration; that the jury was unduly pressured to convict Gotti; and that some of the jurors

showed pretrial prejudice against the defendants. "It was a violation of the defendants' Fifth and Sixth Amendment rights," I said.

Assistant U.S. Attorney John Gleeson, arguing against my
motion, said, "Mr. Kunstler has presented a lot of smoke here."

"Judge, where there's a lot of smoke there may be some fire,
and you ought to have a hearing," I said. I was fairly certain that
Glasser would not have the courage to hold a hearing on these
matters, but I was making a record for the appellate lawyers to use
later when they appealed John's conviction. As I expected,
Glasser denied my motion. To my great surprise, Gotti's distin-
guished appellate team did not include these juror issues in its
brief. Predictably, the appeal was lost, and the Supreme Court has
just refused to grant a review.

When I discuss John Gotti's constitutional rights, my intention is not that he be given special privileges. What I wanted for
him is what I want for every single American citizen in a court of
law: a level playing field.

If it is argued that this country is better off without people
like John Gotti, it would also do better without many corporate
presidents, without the Milkens and their kind. The Gottis of the
world always get the worst, while the Milkens get the best because
they're the golden boys who break the law for the right people and
with the right goals: making money and maintaining the Establishment.

The manner in which John Gotti was prosecuted and tried
violated the Constitution and as a result hurt the American people—whose Constitution it is. That they don't realize it is only too
sad.

Dancing Cops and Hell's Angels

For the last fifteen years my practice has consisted of an assortment of mismatched, hard-to-categorize cases, all difficult,
fascinating, and anti-Establishment. I have even represented
some very unusual clients—for me—including a white cop and a
group of Hell's Angels.

Ray O'Prey's New York Police Department gold detective
shield now hangs on my office wall. He was once the leader of a
troupe of dancing cops. When Sarah was attending the Little Red
Schoolhouse in the 1980s, she participated in a dance recital at
the Felt Forum. It was called the Event of the Year and was orga-

nized by choreographer-dancer Jacques d'Amboise. It featured all kinds of entertainers, including Judy Collins, Mary Tyler Moore, and O'Prey's jazz-dancing cops.

The night of the benefit, Ray said to me, "I need your help. The department thinks I'm gay or whatever, even though I have a wife and three kids, and it's hounding me." The NYPD has a terrible record of persecuting its members who have histrionic talents; for example, for years they've been after one officer who is a clown in his spare time. Ray said the brass didn't want his troupe to dance in uniform, but, of course, the whole point of the group was that they performed in NYPD uniforms. Ray's group of twenty men and women went on as scheduled and became the hit of the show.

I represented Ray when his bosses tried to get him on every offense possible: that he didn't hear a radio call while he was training two rookies; that he parked his motorcycle on police department property; that he took sick leave when he wasn't ill. I got him through most of these hearings successfully, but at one point the brass retaliated by taking away his gun and assigning him to handle desk-appearance tickets in the basement of One Police Plaza. Ray, a detective with twenty-six years on the job, was obviously overqualified for this sort of work, so I brought a federal suit against Police Commissioner Ben Ward. In *O'Prey v. Ward,* I sued for money damages and a return to regular duty for Ray.

In court, we went before my friend for many years Judge Kenneth Conboy, a former deputy police commissioner. Despite his police affiliation, he forced a reasonable settlement: Ray retired at full pension and received a good amount of money. Before he moved to Maui, Hawaii, where he has since opened Ray's Orchids, he mounted his gold shield on a plaque which was inscribed: "To William Moses Kunstler, honor to a good man." I treasure that shield because it reminds me that injustice can be directed at anyone, that I must remember not to make assumptions about people, even cops.

But it seems that I'm no more immune to making assumptions than the next guy, as can be seen by an encounter I had with the Hell's Angels in Toledo, Ohio. I had always believed that the Hell's Angels were racist and anti-Semitic, but as it turned out, I was the prejudiced one.

I was called into this case by Gary Wolf, who told me, "There are only three Jewish Hell's Angels in the history of the club. I'm one of them." Gary and Ron met at a restaurant in Cleveland

Heights, Ohio, where everyone eats lox and bagels, corned beef sandwiches, and matzo ball soup. Gary asked us to enter a very serious case, with death-sentence possibilities. Although I wanted to work with the other lawyers involved—including Ohio lawyers Terry Gilbert and Ralph Buss—I didn't think I would get along with the Angels themselves. I had heard too many bad things about them. In the end, I agreed because it was a potential death-penalty case. I would also be paid a reasonable fee.

It was also a personal challenge. While it's easy for me to justify defending oppressed minorities no matter what they're accused of, I have a hard time feeling the same way about neo-Nazis, Ku Klux Klanners, or skinheads. None of these groups are my usual bag, and they generally don't seek me out. The Angels held some interest, though, because they are depicted by some as evil incarnate; in that sense, their rights often are violated. Like the Mafia, they are portrayed as the bad guys. And they are racist, but in a rather cartoonish way. For example, one member of the Cleveland chapter, Nazi Dave, swore that having met me, he would have Lenin's face tattooed on his left shoulder to match the Hitler tattoo on his right one.

While we worked on the case, Ron and I lived in an Econo-Lodge just outside Toledo. We spent quite a lot of time with the Angels and never heard a racist, sexist, or anti-Semitic remark from any of them. Not even a single joke. Perhaps they were on their best behavior, but still, I never heard anything.

Our client, an Asian Hell's Angel named Stephen Yee, had been charged, along with several other Angels, with a mistaken-identity murder. The government theorized that the victim, who was shot and killed while driving a yellow van, had been mistaken by our guys for a member of the Outlaws, a rival biker group. During the trial, DNA evidence was introduced, and there were conflicting interpretations of it, but in the end everyone was convicted, including our client. We introduced evidence about prosecutorial misconduct and other illegal actions by the government, but to no avail.

After the defendants were convicted and sentenced to long prison terms, we participated in a joint appeal for all the convicted defendants, but almost a year after oral argument, the three-judge court affirmed the convictions.

Brando's Tragedy

Marlon Brando, one of the great acting geniuses of all time, could be called the king of lost causes. He has chopped away at his own resources of brilliant talent with the twin blades of emotional problems and family disturbances. At this point, he should be nothing less than the grand old man of American films. Instead, his is a reclusive, problem-filled life. It turned tragic several years ago when his oldest son killed his daughter's lover, the father of her unborn son.

My friendship with Marlon began during the Wounded Knee Leadership Trial and has lasted for twenty years. Truthfully, though, I always expected tragedy to hit him in one way or another. Although we have always kept in touch, I never realized how lonely he was until he called me one day in February 1990. Ron took the call because I was out of town. Ron and Marlon chatted for quite a while; then Marlon left a message for me to call him. He called again over the next few days, saying he really needed to talk to me, but he gave Ron no idea what he wanted.

I returned home and called Marlon back. He asked me to see him, but I couldn't, I said, because I had just come back after being away for several days and had some obligations to attend to. Ron overheard this conversation and ran into my office, making flapping motions with his arms until I realized that he wanted to go in my place. I suggested to Marlon that Ron go out instead of me, and he agreed. I still had no idea what he wanted.

Ron was picked up at the L.A. airport and driven to Mulholland Drive, where Marlon lives on a hilltop. Marlon's house, whose former owner was eccentric billionaire Howard Hughes, has an unassuming exterior, with a security phone and gate, then a long driveway alongside a wall that is totally covered with foliage. Unless you knew exactly what you were looking for, you wouldn't be able to see that there was a house in there. The one-story dwelling is rather modest, with a lovely garden. Ron spent a night there, sleeping in the TV room, which, only months later, would be the scene of the homicide.

Ron and Marlon talked for twelve hours straight, from morning till night. A stunningly beautiful Japanese woman, Marlon's companion, made sushi and sashimi for the two men. She speaks several languages, holds advanced degrees from a number of Japanese institutions, and is an heiress worth millions, according to Ron.

Although Marlon had a few substantive legal questions, most of the conversation was quite general, and Ron had a sense that he just wanted company, someone to talk with. This is a man who has lived his later life as a complete recluse, in part because he absolutely cannot step outside his home without being mobbed by reporters. Consequently, he spends as much time at his home in Tahiti as possible.

Marlon talked about a Jewish couple who had taken him in as a young boy, the Jewish Defense League and Zionism, the Sikhs, the FBI, and his relationship to the American Indian Movement. It was, according to Ron, the sort of free-ranging discussion one would have as a student with lots of time and few responsibilities. The next morning, they spent two hours figuring out how to work a new coffee machine; then Marlon made breakfast. Afterward, he called a cab to take Ron to the airport. Apparently, while Marlon's first choice was me, he was quite satisfied with Ron.

Three months after Ron's visit, Marlon called me again, but this time it was the middle of the night. It was serious business: a family killing. Marlon phoned me at 2:00 A.M. on May 16, 1990 and said, "Christian just shot Dag, and I've been trying to revive him by mouth-to-mouth resuscitation, but it hasn't worked. Can you come out tomorrow?" I said I would be on the first available plane.

Marlon's oldest son, Christian, had shot Dag Drollet, the lover of Marlon's daughter Cheyenne and father of his first grandchild, with a .45 automatic. The police had just arrived, and Marlon asked me what he should say. "Don't talk to the police and don't let Christian talk to the police," I advised.

Ron and I flew to California that night, but before we left, we had more press calls than we have ever received on any single case. It was a frenzy. I issued a short statement; then we headed for the airport and arrived in L.A. very early in the morning. Miko, one of Marlon's nine children and now Michael Jackson's bodyguard, drove us to a hotel where we met with Marlon. The next day, we went out to the house to see him again. He was absolutely devastated; his sense of sorrow was just overwhelming. Cheyenne was there, completely broken up and refusing to talk to any of us. In the TV room where Ron had slept, the gold-brown carpet was stained with blood.

Christian was in custody, and we planned to appear in court that morning, enter a plea of not guilty, and ask for bail. The prosecutor sought a brief adjournment of several days, a request that was granted over our strenuous objections. We returned to New York and three days later came back to Los Angeles for the bail hearing. We had told Marlon to get as many people as possible involved in the hearing, have a bail bondsman stand by, and get his pal and next-door neighbor Jack Nicholson to sign an affidavit saying that Christian would be a good bail risk and that he had known him since he was a kid. I also suggested that Marlon himself attend the hearing.

When we got to the courthouse, we met the local counsel we had retained, Dan Stormer, and discovered that Marlon was parked in a limo a block away. I walked to his car and told him to get to the courthouse pronto. In court, I thought things would go our way. Marlon had come through with an affidavit from Jack Nicholson; a bail bondsman was standing by. Marlon was there with his third wife, Sarita, Cheyenne's mother. (Sarita appeared with Marlon as his young Polynesian love in *Mutiny on the Bounty*.)

The scene in that court was truly mad. Photographers and cameras are freely allowed into California courtrooms, so that the flashbulbs, klieg lights, and whirring of the power drives made it chaotic. Photographers motioned us out of the way or told us to move closer—get out of the shot, get into the shot. It was an unbelievable circus, press from all over the world—*Paris Match,* German, Dutch, Italian, and many other foreign media, as well as their American counterparts. Of course, Marlon was the focus, and they snapped his picture endlessly.

I had heard that the judge, municipal judge Rosemary Shumsky, was very reasonable. In trying to get her to set bail for Christian, I described the killing of Dag as "a tragic accident, a confrontation over an alleged attack on Mr. Brando's daughter Cheyenne by the deceased, and a confrontation and accidental discharge of a firearm." But my argument failed, and the judge abruptly denied bail. Outside the courthouse, Marlon stood on the steps and made a brief, very conciliatory statement.

When my turn came, I denounced the judge's decision, saying, "I think that this was an outrageous decision and that she misused her power . . . sitting up there like a toad and not taking a single note and then saying there is no basis for bail." I heard later that Marlon thought I had gone much too far, that my remarks could hurt Christian in some way. My approach is always to attack the system, and despite Marlon's opinion, I believe it is an approach that works.

I told Marlon I would take necessary steps to appeal the no-bail decision; then I returned to New York. About a week later, as I was about to fly to L.A. to play a bit part in Oliver Stone's *The Doors,* I received a call from California lawyer Robert Shapiro, who said Marlon had asked him to become involved in the case. I got the impression that Shapiro was a wheeler-dealer, in with the movie crowd, and not really a trial lawyer. His clients include O.J. Simpson, Vince Coleman, and Darryl Strawberry.

When Margie and I arrived in L.A., Miko met us at the airport and took us back to Marlon's house. After some small talk, Marlon said to me, "I'd like to see you alone for a moment.

"I've found the bullet. I've found the bullet," he said after we went into the bedroom, and he showed it to me. Apparently he had crawled naked on his hands and knees around the television room, pressing his body against the rug, and had located the bullet, which the police had missed.

"What should I do? Should I throw it off the hill here?" he asked.

"No, give it to the police," was my advice. He showed me the bloodstained couch that he had removed from the living room and put into a shed. He told me that when the shooting occurred, he heard a shot, walked into the TV room, and saw Drollet lying on the couch. He gave him CPR, but it didn't have any effect. For some reason, he then picked up the television remote-control unit and placed it on the body. Later on, the police mistakenly assumed that Christian had shot Drollet while he was watching television.

The spot where Marlon found the bullet backed up Christian's story that he and Drollet had been fighting when the gun went off. It did not support the prosecution's theory that Drollet had been shot while he was lying down, watching television. Earlier I had suggested to Marlon that we arrange with former New York City medical examiner Michael Baden to do the autopsy on Drollet. Baden's report also backed up Christian's story that Drollet and he had been fighting when the fatal shot was fired.

Marlon had genuinely loved Dag. He absolutely loves children and babies. When Ron was there, Cheyenne had talked to Marlon from France about some sort of medical problem she had. He was very concerned about her and talked to the doctors and took care of her problems long distance.

Marlon was apparently unaware that Drollet had been beating Cheyenne on a regular basis. He beat her in Tahiti, in California, before she became pregnant, while she was pregnant. From what I understand, Marlon only found this out after Drollet's death. When I was at Marlon's house this time, I mentioned the beatings to him, and Sarita said, "Yes, that happened also in Tahiti." Marlon was very surprised and upset that this information had been kept from him.

Cheyenne's beatings would be the basis of a good, strong defense, I thought. The night of the shooting, Christian and Cheyenne had gone out to supper while Drollet stayed home. She told her half brother about the beatings; then they returned home. Christian had had a few drinks with his meal, and there was a fight between Christian and Drollet. Christian owned several guns, including a .45, which went off during the fight. Dr. Baden had told me that it was a perfectly feasible explanation, given the trajectory of the bullet and where Marlon found it.

As I left Marlon's house that night, Robert Shapiro was coming up in the limo with Baden. Based on what I could see then, the worst that could happen to Christian would be a manslaughter conviction. If Baden testified that Drollet was standing up when he was shot—if Christian testified they had been fighting—then it was not cold-blooded murder but a somewhat inebriated brother fighting to avenge the violence done to his half sister. I felt the case should go to trial.

During the next few days, I didn't spend any time with Marlon because I was doing my small part in *The Doors*. When I returned to New York, Shapiro called and told me that he would be in command of the situation from now on. Marlon didn't call me; he has not called me since.

Eventually, Shapiro worked out a deal, and Christian pleaded guilty to manslaughter in the first degree, for which he received ten years, a sentence he is now serving. Later on, Marlon must have had serious doubts about the legal course he had chosen. He tried to have Christian's guilty plea withdrawn and his sentence vacated, but he was unsuccessful.

Marlon made an error, in my opinion, by going for the plea bargain. Christian had not committed premeditated murder, and even if he had been found guilty at trial, he would not have received a sentence stiffer than the ten years he did get. Had he gone to trial, he might have been acquitted, or he might have received a shorter sentence. I thought that considering the situation, the gamble was well worth taking.

Marlon opted for Shapiro, a negotiator, the type of lawyer who works things out. The usual unintelligent approach in these cases is to assume that the best way is to utilize the lawyers who play the system's game. Of course, I think it's the worst way. But to run to the fixers of the world, the lawyers who have connections, is always wrong. It rarely works.

Marlon was also motivated, in part, by his aversion to publicity; a plea instead of a trial meant less time in the public eye. In many ways, this seemed to me to be unfeeling behavior on Marlon's part toward his son.

Moreover, on some fundamental level, Marlon approached the tragedy as a fair-minded person who felt that there should be some consequences for his son's actions. He didn't feel that Christian should just walk away scot-free even if we could obtain an acquittal. Getting Christian off would not have sat well with Marlon's very finely honed sense of right and wrong in the universe.

I am not comfortable criticizing Marlon, though, because I love and respect him for what he's done as an actor and as an activist. But as a lawyer I believe he did the wrong thing. For Christian's sake, I resent that Marlon did not call a meeting of a group of lawyers so that options could be discussed. That would have been the most intelligent way to handle this kind of tragedy. Marlon could have gotten input, a consensus, but he went the plea-bargain route, and Christian got slammed.

I imagine it is very difficult to be the son of Marlon Brando. You see *Last Tango in Paris,* and think, Hey, that's Dad up there. You can never be as attractive, successful, wealthy, or virile as your father. Christian was actually doing well, though, and worked at landscaping, welding, and a bit of acting, backed, I have heard, by a $100,000 trust fund set up for him by his father.

Marlon did a fairly good job of shielding his children from the publicity and hysteria surrounding the Brando name. But because of the force of his personality, his children could not have remained completely undamaged. I have been exposed to a wide variety of people, many charismatic, potent, and powerful. But Marlon Brando exudes more implicit power than any other human being I have ever met. Whatever he says and does is so hypnotic that it requires a tremendous effort of will to remain thoughtful, objective, and reasonable when you're in his presence. When he talks, it's almost as if one is compelled to look at him, listen to him, and agree with him. I'm quite certain that Marlon's particular brand of power cannot be explained rationally. And as a result of this personal magnetism, he has become accustomed to getting anything he wants.

Marlon lives a strange life, however. For example, he will throw away all his mail without even glancing at a single piece. He is somewhat out of this world, in orbit somewhere where reality can't reach him. Unfortunately, his allure and glamour have forced this withdrawal on him and turned him into a reclusive man who trusts very few people. On the whole, it's very difficult to judge him, to understand his motives, because he's so withdrawn that you never really get to know him.

His is a strange saga. I know he had long and bitter domestic difficulties with his first wife, Anna Kashfi, over Christian, which may have scarred that boy beyond recognition. Over the years, I have heard about problems that Marlon had with some of his children. For example, he would never keep a sharp knife in his house. I remember once I was trying to cut a piece of meat and asked, "Where's the carving knife?"

Marlon said, "There are none, just butter knives."

I believe he feared that Cheyenne would use a sharp knife inappropriately. Despite his greatness, and he is great, I cannot say that Marlon Brando, as the head of a family, is someone who should be emulated.

Prosecutors and Judges

During the last ten years, with the courts going sour, leaning farther and farther to the right, with Neanderthals being elevated to the federal judiciary, it's more urgent than ever that we defense lawyers use every weapon we have. Part of our weaponry is using the media, so I try, whenever I can, to teach lawyers who are on the correct side, what we euphemistically refer to as the Left, to do that. The odds are so stacked against the defense that one always must fight fire with fire, a concept now recognized by the American Bar Association insofar as access to the media is concerned.

The system is terribly corrupt. Crimes are committed in the name of "justice" by prosecutors and judges who themselves are never punished. I remember first coming to this conclusion when I read an Illinois case, *Miller v. Pate*. In the late 1960s, a drifter was indicted for the rape and murder of a young girl even though the only hard evidence against him was a pair of his undershorts that had been found stained with a red substance. After a chemist testified at Miller's trial that the substance was the same blood type as the victim's and different from Miller's, the defendant was convicted and sentenced to death.

It was later discovered that the prosecutor had these shorts dipped into red paint and that the chemist had lied on the stand. Although the U.S. Supreme Court reversed Miller's conviction, neither the prosecutor nor the chemist was ever accused of any crime. When I read that case, it became clear to me that if those two, who were clearly guilty of attempted murder, remained unpenalized, the system would virtually never punish anyone on the prosecution side for committing such heinous acts—and it just about never has.

Over the years, this thought was substantiated time and time again. A good example occurred in 1988 when Ron and I attempted to block the extradition to India of two young Sikhs accused of committing a number of crimes in that country. Our adversary was Special Assistant U.S. Attorney Judy Russell. During the proceedings, she and the magistrate hearing the case received five anonymous death-threat letters. Because of these threats, courtroom security was intensified: Rooftop sharpshooters were in position around the building; the defendants' arms and legs were shackled; and several Sikh spectators were subjected to humiliating searches.

We discovered, to the shock of everyone in that courtroom, especially the magistrate, that Russell had concocted and mailed the threatening letters herself. Instead of being punished, she was permitted to commit herself briefly to a psychiatric hospital; one year later, she pleaded not guilty because of temporary insanity and was acquitted of all charges. For all I know, she may be practicing law today. If any defense lawyer had committed these acts, it's a safe bet he or she would be disbarred and serving a long sentence.

No matter what they do to obtain convictions, prosecutors are not punished. Neither are judges. I discussed this before an audience composed mainly of judges at a 1993 conference organized by the New York Supreme Court Justices' Association. After several speakers praised themselves and their colleagues, I stood up and made remarks that shocked them:

> I've listened to all of you tonight, and what I've heard is
> a lot of misinformation. I heard one judge say the
> judiciary is the only branch that really defends the

Constitution. Another said that all the judges work hard and are sincere and don't let their personal ideologies get into it. That is all so much hogwash. I don't believe it, and I don't want my silence at those remarks to be interpreted as agreeing with any of this poppycock.

Their mouths were hanging open as I continued:

Judges are creatures of the Establishment. They do what's politically correct for them. The worst of them are mean-spirited, racist bastards. As for defending the Constitution, they probably violate it more than any other branch of government.

A collective gasp came from the audience. I went on, giving a pertinent example. Journalist Jack Newfield had written a vicious and unprincipled article about a judge whom I happen to like, Laura Safer-Espinoza. Newfield had originally been scheduled to be on the panel that night but had been scratched by the program's organizers because of this column.

You want to talk about defending the Constitution. Look what you did to Jack Newfield. You disinvited the guy for exercising his First Amendment rights. I didn't like what he wrote, either, and thought it was a bunch of lies, but we should have had him here to pin him to the wall.

After my speech, I was surrounded by a passel of judges who said, "Well, you've certainly got guts," and other similar remarks. I loved it; it was a chance to kick the Establishment in the ass, an opportunity I rarely pass up. And by making my comments before a group of judges, I had a rare opportunity to accuse them directly of their failure to uphold the Constitution, their selfish interest in furthering their own careers above any concern for the justice system, their racism, and finally, their lack of fitness to be judges.

On a more positive note, the composition of the U.S. Supreme Court has changed dramatically in the last few years, and I now have some hopes for a weakening of the majority's antiliberal polarization. The appointment of Ruth Bader Ginsberg may help in this regard, and as I write this, Justice Harry Blackmun is still on the bench, although he has recently announced his retirement.

He is a great favorite of mine, having written, among many other significant opinions, the majority opinion in *Roe v. Wade*. A couple of years ago, I wrote Justice Blackmun, asking him to spend an hour with me, Arthur Kinoy, and Morty Stavis so we could acknowledge and show our appreciation of his growing liberalism and ask his opinion about how progressive lawyers should best spend their time.

Blackmun wrote back that he was unable to meet with us because he was too busy. But he added these words of encouragement:

> I share your expressed concern about our attitude toward
> the Bill of Rights. The year [1992] has been difficult, but
> my basic optimism has not been completely dispelled.
> The pendulum has a way of swinging. . . . May the three
> of you not let flagging spirits drag you down. This is a
> time to keep chins up.

I was thrilled with this response; like me, Blackmun was clearly an optimist as well as a true lover of the Bill of Rights.

Blackmun and I have met several times over the years. Once, on a plane in 1970, he walked over to me and said, "Can I sit with you? I'm Harry Blackmun." As we talked, I suggested that he get out from the shadow of Justice Burger, that being called a Minnesota Twin was not the best thing in the world. We spoke about a common acquaintance and good friend of Blackmun's, Miles Lord, a former federal judge in Minnesota, who was then under attack for ordering a mining company to cease polluting Lake Superior. When our plane landed and we went our separate ways, I gave Blackmun an enormous hug.

This happened right in front of Judge Florence Kelley, a New York family court judge, who looked as if she were going to go through the floor at the sight of a Supreme Court justice and Bill Kunstler locked in each other's arms. Years later, I read in Bob Woodward's book *The Brethren* that when he returned to Washington, Blackmun told his law clerks about the incident and was quite excited about being embraced by a radical lawyer.

In 1992, I attended a lecture Blackmun gave at New York University, and when he saw me, he called out, "Bill!" We embraced again. When I argued the first flag-burning case in 1989, he was on the bench, of course, and his grandchildren were in the audience. My daughters Emily and Sarah were in the audience, too. In the cafeteria, Blackmun waved us over to sit with them, but I didn't go because I didn't think it would be seemly, and most important, I didn't want to lose his vote.

As I hoped, Justice Blackmun voted for our side in both flag cases. He is not a flaming liberal, though, and sometimes goes along with some bad decisions. But he's the very best we've got. In his dissent against the restrictive and regressive *Webster v. Missouri* decision, which limited reproductive rights, he accurately described the mood of the Supreme Court at that time: "I'm afraid a chill wind blows from this Court."

When I heard that Justice Blackmun was stepping down, I immediately composed a sonnet, "On the Retirement of Justice Harry Blackmun." It ends, "His was the lonely but enlightened voice / That punishment by death should never be. / There's little that we owe to Nixon's reign, / But naming Harry may reduce the stain."

Gay Rights

Time slips by; I get older and grayer but continue to fight.

In early 1993, Paul O'Dwyer, a young lawyer and member of the Irish Lesbian and Gay Organization (ILGO), asked Ron and me to file a lawsuit to stop the St. Patrick's Day Parade because, as happens every year, groups of gays and lesbians were not allowed to march under their own banners. The other Paul O'Dwyer, an older, better-known lawyer (no relation), told me that even though he agreed with ILGO, he would not join the lawsuit because stopping the St. Patrick's Day Parade went against his Irish grain. (Paul O'Dwyer and I go way back: My grandfather was his physician when Paul came here in 1920 from Ireland.)

Shortly before the parade was to take place, Manhattan federal judge Kevin T. Duffy sustained a claim by the parade's organizer, the New York County Board of the Ancient Order of Hibernians, that since it was a religious event, it could exclude any groups it wanted to. I felt strongly that everyone should be allowed to march in an important New York City event like the St. Patrick's Day Parade and that the Catholic Church's doctrines should not be permitted to control its makeup.

Because the doctrine of separation of church and state mandates that city streets, personnel, and funds cannot be used for a religious event, I suggested that we file a church-and-state-separation suit. "If you get us plaintiffs, just ordinary people who live in

New York City, we'll file the suit to stop the parade," I told Paul.

He rounded up four willing plaintiffs who charged that by claiming it was a religious event, the parade's organizers violated separation of church and state if the event utilized city funds and personnel. I didn't want to stop the parade, but I didn't want the organizers to get away with misrepresenting it as a religious event, either.

The organizer's members change their point of view each year, according to their needs. The year before, after ILGO filed suit to be allowed to march, the Ancient Order of Hibernians said the parade was a civic event; anyone could apply to march, but there were sixty groups ahead of ILGO, which had to wait its turn. Another federal judge ruled that this was fair and dismissed the ILGO suit, and the gays and lesbians didn't march in 1992.

In 1993, the organizers knew if they continued to claim it was a civic event, it would fall under the Human Rights Law of the city of New York, which had already determined that the gay and lesbian groups should be allowed to march. So the organizers changed their tune and now insisted that the parade was religious.

I have always had an affinity for the Irish, probably because of their long struggle to be free of the British. I have been a student of Irish history for years and write occasionally for the *Echo,* an Irish newspaper. Framed in my living room is a replica of the Irish Republican Declaration of Independence, which I love passionately.

One of my few heroes is the Irish patriot Sean MacBride, whom I was thrilled to meet when he visited this country and stayed at the home of Michael Ratner. In 1988, when MacBride died, I was privileged to write his obituary. MacBride, the founder of Amnesty International, and Linus Pauling are the only two persons in history who received both the Nobel Peace Prize and the Lenin Peace Prize. During his lifetime, MacBride was briefly the foreign minister of Ireland and, while attending law school in Dublin, chief of staff of the underground Irish Republican Army (IRA). He was a very great man.

Margaret Kelly Michaels

Undoubtedly, many people who read about my involvement in the Margaret Kelly Michaels case saw it as another example of my increasing senility, since I have always said I wouldn't get involved in alleged child-abuse cases. But I entered this case because of my love for Morty Stavis and my sense of duty to him. Morty's sudden, accident-related death on December 17, 1992, deprived us of one of the most brilliant lawyers of our time. The president of the Center for Constitutional Rights as well as one of its original founders, Morty was my friend and perennial lawyer. When George Stavis, one of Morty's sons, asked me to argue Michaels's appeal for him, I felt that I owed it to Morty to do so.

The case began when a young woman was accused of sexually molesting dozens of toddlers at the Maplewood, New Jersey, nursery school where she worked as a teacher. In April 1988, Michaels was convicted of 115 counts of child sexual abuse and sentenced to forty-seven years in prison.

Along with Robert Rosenthal, I argued the appeal in early 1993, and Michaels's convictions were unanimously reversed by New Jersey's appellate division. This reversal was the result of Morty's hard work as well as that of three young lawyers—Daniel Williams, Daniel Finneran, and Rosenthal. Morty was the architect of the argument, but his assistants did enormous amounts of research and legwork. The reversal was a tribute to Morty's determination and brilliance, and when it took place a month or so after oral argument, I knew that his spirit was somewhere rejoicing.

Michaels's case had been like the Salem witch trials. Panic and hysteria took over and caused excesses that destroyed due process. Panic does strange things to people, as happened in the cases growing out of the World Trade Center bombings. Panic leads to fear, and fear leads to injustice, as we saw with the World War II imprisonment of Japanese-Americans. In this case, because everyone was so horrified by the accusations against Michaels, judges, prosecutors, and parents all believed she had to be convicted, regardless of the evidence, regardless of what really happened.

When the New Jersey appeals court reversed her convictions because of monumental procedural errors, the Michaels case was sent back to the trial court. Her trial had been unfair: Defense experts were not allowed to question the children, and state investigators grossly manipulated three- and four-year-old witnesses, who were permitted to testify on closed-circuit TV rather than in the courtroom.

The state, goaded by the alleged victims' parents, wanted to retry Michaels and appealed to the New Jersey Supreme Court to obtain permission for the children to testify. Now in their early teens, they would have been asked to attest to what supposedly happened to them more than eight years ago. The court has just ruled unanimously in Michaels's favor, and her long ordeal is finally at an end.

Sol Wachtler

When the chief judge of New York, Sol Wachtler, was charged with harassing and threatening his former lover, Joy Silverman, a wealthy Republican socialite with connections at the highest levels of government, I was especially interested in the way the FBI arrested him. Michael Chertoff, the U.S. attorney in New Jersey and a Bush appointee, exploited the situation to get as much publicity as possible out of it. My initial feeling about Wachtler's arrest on November 7, 1992, was not so much sympathy for him but dislike of Chertoff and his tactics.

Wachtler's daughter Lauren, a lawyer with whom I had worked briefly on a civil matter some years ago, called me. "My father is suicidal, terribly depressed," she said. I offered to visit Wachtler in his Long Island home, but that never came to pass. Later, I wrote an article about his case for the *Amsterdam News* and sent a copy to Lauren for her father. The article described the preferential treatment given by Chertoff's office to Special Assistant U.S. Attorney Judy Russell (the prosecutor who mailed bogus threatening letters during the Sikh extradition case and was allowed to go unpunished) and compared it to Chertoff's overkill on the Wachtler case.

Lauren told me the article had a positive effect on her father. "You know, it really buoyed his spirits. I would love you to handle his case," Lauren said. But, as I told Lauren, a progressive attorney like me would not be the best person to defend her father. Furthermore, since Sol Wachtler was wealthy, with enormous resources and considerable connections, he was not at all my kind of defendant. Although, to some extent, the manner of his arrest could be seen as a violation of his civil rights, I was very certain he would do much better with another lawyer.

What Wachtler did to Joy Silverman was inexcusable, but I do understand it. He had a love affair, was knocked out of the box by a younger man, and fell apart emotionally. It happens all the time, often with violence involved. While I couldn't excuse Wachtler's conduct, I saw his arrest—the large contingent of agents used to "capture" him, an electronic bracelet to monitor his movements, house confinement, an indictment on five major counts—as extremely excessive. The man had been destroyed, his life was in ruins, a Greek tragedy. The hoopla surrounding his arrest had been unnecessary and done solely so Chertoff could feed his own ambition. After Wachtler pleaded guilty and was sentenced to eighteen months in prison, I began to write to him on a more or less regular basis. The letter from him I prize the most concluded: "You might be interested in knowing that amongst me and my fellow prisoners, you are a folk hero."

Tie Me Up! Tie Me Down!

In 1990, when the Motion Picture Association of America (MPAA) gave the Spanish film *Tie Me Up! Tie Me Down!* an X-rating, the film's distributor, Miramax Films, decided to fight. Miramax's position was that *Tie Me Up!* should not have been X-rated. This rating leads people to assume that a film is pornographic, and as a result, many theaters won't run it, and potential audiences are lost.

When I first appeared for Miramax before an MPAA appeals board, I pointed out that Marlon Brando's classic *Last Tango in Paris, Midnight Cowboy,* and many other highly regarded films were X-rated—but that was years before the X-rating was expropriated by pornographic films. Today an X-rating means pornography, I argued. But I was unable to convince a majority of the board's members to change the rating.

I then filed a petition in a New York court seeking an order to overturn the MPAA's decision. Floyd Abrams, a leading First Amendment lawyer, represented the MPAA. The judge, Charles Ramos, seemed sympathetic to our point of view as I presented excerpts from several films that are rated R, even though they contain sexual scenes far more graphic than those in *Tie Me Up! Tie Me Down!*

I didn't think we would win. But never, in my most optimistic mood, did I think that even though we would lose, we would actually end up victorious.

Judge Ramos's decision stated that this type of petition didn't apply here. But he simply couldn't understand why there was no MPAA rating between R and X and why the association hadn't copyrighted the latter designation. There were worthwhile films, he said, that deserved a different rating. In the face of this judicial scolding, MPAA gave up the X-rating and came out with a new copyrighted designation—NC:17, which means not for children under seventeen.

Rock Against Racism

The most recent of my six arguments before the Supreme Court (the first three were in the late 1960s and early 1970s) took place in 1989 and 1990, pitting me against the Establishment as I tried to defend the Bill of Rights.

For years I had obtained permits for the Rock Against Racism (RAR) concerts held every spring at the band shell in Central Park. RAR was founded by Dana Beal, an old client of mine who had succeeded Abbie Hoffman as head of the Yippies. Each time I obtained the permit, I had difficulty, since the City didn't really want the concert. The affair always attracted long-haired freaks to the band shell, which was near the high-rise and high-priced apartment buildings on Fifth Avenue and Central Park West. The concert sponsors would always be offered other sites outside the park, but they preferred the band-shell area because it was small, didn't need a large crowd to fill it up, and was especially suitable for the concert.

For the previous eight years, the city had permitted the concert to be held at the band shell. However, as the result of complaints about excessive noise from writer Isaac Asimov and several other Central Park West residents, the city passed an ordinance that would require any amplified event to use a City-approved company to provide and operate all sound equipment. That way, it could control the sound level.

This seemed clearly unconstitutional, a violation of a First Amendment activity, like requiring a newspaper to hire a City agent to run its printing press. A number of RAR attorneys filed suit, a federal judge ruled against them, but upon appeal his decision was reversed. The City then turned to the U.S. Supreme Court for help.

I argued the case for RAR in 1989 before the high court in what turned out to be quite a relaxed Supreme Court argument. The proceeding was almost humorous, because, as it progressed, several justices reminisced about the music they had listened to during their college days. Justice Antonin Scalia went into a long discussion of the music he enjoyed as a Princeton student. Justice Thurgood Marshall, who almost never participated in oral argument, interrupted my argument to ask, "Rock music has to be loud, doesn't it?" I assured him that it did.

Despite the conviviality, I lost. The justices eventually ruled, 6–3, that it was constitutional for New York City to force its sound mixer on anyone using Central Park as long as that individual did not interfere with the substance of the music, only its volume.

Flag Burning

I was proud to stand before the U.S. Supreme Court in 1989 and 1990 and argue that the First Amendment gives us the right to burn our flag as a protest, just as it allows us to say what we please.

The solution to racist, hate-filled speech from Klan members, white supremacists, and the like is more speech, not repression of it. That's why we should have the right to burn the flag—which is symbolic speech. If the flag stands for anything, it stands for that right. That is why, on August 22, 1984, a young man named Gregory Lee Johnson burned an American flag outside the Republican National Convention in Dallas to protest Reagan administration policies. Convicted under Texas law of desecrating a "venerated object," Johnson was sentenced to a year in jail and a $2,000 fine. After a series of appeals by ACLU attorneys, Texas's highest court ruled that Johnson's conviction was unconstitutional. The state appealed the ruling to the U.S. Supreme Court, which heard the case, *Texas v. Johnson,* on March 21, 1989.

David Cole, a brilliant young Center lawyer, wrote the brief, and I argued it. My method was to use precedents, many of which had been written by the justices themselves. I made my point, that the person who burned the flag did not intend to do anything other than exercise his right to free speech.

In response to a question from Chief Justice Rehnquist, I argued:

> Can you say you can't force [people] to salute the flag or
> pledge allegiance to the flag, but can you then say we
> can force them *not* to show other means of disrespect for
> the flag, other means of protest over the flag by saying
> you can't burn the flag? I think they're the same, in all
> due deference.

When Rehnquist looked quizzical, I added, "I don't know if I've convinced you. . . ."

He replied, "Well, you may have convinced others."

To me, this was one of my most important cases because it went to the heart of the First Amendment. I told the court:

> To hear things or to see things that we hate tests the First
> Amendment more than seeing or hearing things that we
> like. It wasn't designed for things we like. They never
> needed a First Amendment for that. This amendment
> was designed so that the things we hate can have a place
> in the marketplace of ideas and can have an area where
> protest can find itself.

We won, but by a narrow margin, 5–4. In his majority opinion, Justice William Brennan wrote, "We do not consecrate the flag by punishing its desecration, for in doing so we dilute the freedom that this cherished symbol represents." And in Rehnquist's anguished dissent, he cited as authority the national anthem and the patriotic poems "Concord Hymn" and "Barbara Fritchie."

When the court's decision was released, it caused a furor. President Bush called for a constitutional amendment to overturn the court's ruling. Congress responded by quickly enacting a federal statute banning flag burning, the Flag Protection Act of 1989. A number of young people, including Gregory Johnson, decided to test the new statute as soon as it became effective. On that day, they burned flags on the steps of the U.S. Capitol and outside the Seattle post office and were promptly arrested. David Cole and I argued in federal courts in Washington and Seattle that under the Supreme Court ruling in *Texas v. Johnson,* the new law was clearly invalid. The judges agreed with us, and the two cases were then consolidated for argument in the Supreme Court.

Since, unlike the lower tribunals, the high court did not permit split arguments, only one of us could present our case. David Cole said to me, "You argued the first one; let me argue the second one." I desperately wanted to do this myself. I thought that if I didn't make the argument, it would look peculiar. I was the older lawyer and didn't want to sit second seat.

"David," I said, "let's figure out a way to decide who should do the argument. I think I ought to do it. You think you ought to do it, and there are strengths on both sides."

Ultimately, I suggested that we leave it up to our clients, and David agreed. There were eight originally, four in Washington and four in Seattle, until the charges against Johnson were dismissed simply because the government disliked the symbolic value of his involvement in the case. The seven remaining defendants were all young, and I was certain that they would vote for David. I would feel hurt, but I was prepared to accept their decision. To my surprise, they voted in my favor, 4–3.

I was totally exhilarated, and David took it very well. I tried to make up for this decision by including many references to David during the argument. When the argument was over, unlike my usual self, I ducked away from the cameras and the reporters, leaving them to David.

Ever since, I have thought about whether I should I have been gracious and said to David, "You go ahead and argue it." I guess I should have done the generous thing and backed down. But the truth is that, psychologically, I couldn't do it. The public associated me with the case, and I couldn't accept being second seat to a much younger man who had been out of law school only a few years. I also thought that he would have lots of time to argue before the high court, while, at seventy-three, I didn't see myself with many more opportunities. When I told David that, his response was: "Well, you never know." Which, of course, is true.

This was a clear example of my good angel fighting my bad one. The bad angel won out, as I knew he would.

I argued the case on May 14, 1990, telling the justices that burning the flag was exactly the type of speech the First Amendment is designed to protect, adding that the new statute was quite illegal and unconstitutional. If flag burning is symbolic expression, any efforts to prevent it violate the First Amendment, I said. "Respect for the flag must be voluntary. Once people are compelled to respect the flag, it's meaningless," I said during my thirty minutes, the time allotted to each side.

David's brief on this case was again brilliant, and we won with the same close vote, 5–4. The federal statute was invalidated. We then sweated out the proposed constitutional amendment that would have undone both cases, making it a crime to burn the flag; happily, the amendment idea quickly died. In 1992, the state of Texas asked the Supreme Court to reconsider its 1989 and 1990 rulings, but the request was denied.

"And, in the end," as humorist P. J. O'Rourke wrote in *Parliament of Whores,* "the most interesting thing about the great flag-burning debate . . . would be how quickly that debate evaporated."

(Prior to these cases, the last time I had worked on a Supreme Court case was in 1976 in *Banks v. Holder.* I met Arthur Banks, a black actor, in 1974 while he was serving five years in federal prison in Terre Haute, Indiana, for resisting the draft. Five years, the maximum sentence for avoiding the draft, was generally given only to blacks, while whites were dealt with far less harshly. While he was in prison, Banks led a demonstration to the warden's office for better prison conditions. After the demonstration, the prison goon squad entered his cell and beat him up. He was accused of kicking a guard in the testicles and indicted for assaulting a federal corrections officer.

When I was speaking at an Indianapolis high school, I was asked by Banks's girlfriend to represent him. I agreed and, along with a young Indianapolis lawyer who was in the state legislature, appeared in court for the defendant. But federal judge Gale Holder refused to allow me in because of my political views. After I filed a petition for a writ of mandamus with the U.S. Court of Appeals for the Seventh Circuit, the judge was overruled, and I was ordered into the case. In 1976, Margie and I, determined to get Banks, who had been transferred to a federal prison in Sandstone, Minnesota, released while the legal wrangling was going on. We filed a petition of habeas corpus with federal judge Miles Lord, who held a hearing and freed Banks immediately.

In the meantime, Judge Holder, supported by thirty Establishment Indiana lawyers, appealed to the U.S. Supreme Court for permission to appeal the Seventh Circuit's decision. The petition was granted. Morty Stavis and Margie and I worked on the brief, and Morty made the argument before the high court because it would have been difficult for me to argue on behalf of myself.

We won the Supreme Court argument when the justices dismissed Judge Holder's petition as "improvidently granted," which left the Seventh Circuit opinion in effect. I was to be allowed to legally represent Banks. Happily, the government decided not to try him on the assault charges, and he was never returned to prison. Today he is pursuing his acting career in California.

Robert Nelson Drew: Saving a Life

Since 1984, along with Ron, I have been deeply involved in trying to prevent the execution of inmate Robert Nelson Drew. Bobby, found guilty of committing a 1983 murder in Houston, Texas, was scheduled to be executed in October 1993.

After Bobby was convicted of the murder, his codefendant had confessed to it: "I alone committed the murder. . . . Robert Drew did not assist me." Also, a key eyewitness recanted his statement. But neither the courts in Texas nor the federal courts would reverse Bobby's conviction.

The state and federal courts refused to intervene because Texas has a "thirty-day rule," which states that new evidence of innocence uncovered more than thirty days after sentencing cannot be used to set aside a conviction. This completely unfair law was upheld by the U.S. Supreme Court on January 25, 1993, with Justices Blackmun, Stevens, and Souter dissenting.

The new evidence in Bobby's case didn't surface until 101 days after he was sentenced. When Justice Blackmun dissented from the high court's sustaining of Texas's thirty-day rule in another case, he wrote: "The execution of a person who can show that he is innocent comes perilously close to simple murder."

Bobby's death warrant had been signed by Judge Charles Hearn, a born-again Christian, who embellished his signature with a cartoon of a happy face: "Please note that the order sets your execution date for October 14, 1993." This was followed by the judge's signature and the smiling cartoon. Our client felt the cartoon was an outrageous mockery and asked us to file a motion for a new trial; we did, but were unsuccessful. To charges of insensitivity and inappropriateness, the judge responded, "I'm a happy person," adding that he always added a smiling face to his signature—even if it was on an execution order.

It seemed that Bobby's execution was a certainty, and on October 13, Ron and I traveled to Texas, since Bobby had requested us to bear witness to his death. We visited him at Ellis Unit I of the Texas Department of Corrections in Huntsville, which housed some 373 men awaiting extermination. A day earlier, an Austin judge had refused to block the execution. Ron and I, along with George Longnecker, one of Bobby's most dedicated supporters, spent three hours with the condemned man. Although he was understandably tense and nervous, he managed to joke. "I love Jesus," he said, "but I prefer not to see him this week."

Our meeting with Bobby Drew ended at precisely 4:15 P.M., when three burly guards arrived to take him to the Walls Unit. There, we were told, he would later be strapped to a gurney, and a tube would be inserted into his vein. At 12:01 A.M., a signal would be given, and a mixture of three deadly chemical substances would begin to flow into his body. We were told that it would take about five minutes for all of his vital signs to disappear, following which he would be pronounced dead. George Longnecker had arranged with a local mortuary for the cremation of the body and intended to take the ashes to Bobby's native Vermont and scatter them over one of his favorite lakes.

When we left the prison, we were very depressed. Ron and I planned to return to the Walls Unit at 11:30 P.M. to witness Bobby's execution. But shortly after we arrived at our motel, we heard the incredible news that a Texas appellate court had issued a stay! It was so close to the execution that Bobby had already eaten his last meal of six fish sandwiches, six cheeseburgers, a double order of french fries, chocolate ice cream, and a cold soda.

He was quickly returned to Ellis Unit I, and we spoke to him later that night. He had always believed he would be saved, he said, and chided us for not having faith. For the moment at least, Bobby's ordeal was over.

Six months later, the stay was overturned. At 12:22 A.M., on August 2, 1994, Bobby was executed. Ron was with him when he died. No court ever heard his new evidence.

There is a deeper issue, however: America's continuing pre-occupation with the death penalty, which, experience has shown, does not deter murder or other capital crimes. With more than two hundred executions since the Supreme Court opened the floodgates in 1976 and with death-row occupants now numbering more than twenty-six hundred and steadily increasing, we have become the world's charnel house. We stand alone among the Western nations, the others having abolished capital punishment as both inhumane and counterproductive. Our nearest rival in putting people to death is South Africa, and it is far behind. We have permitted the spirit of vengeance to overwhelm and stifle our humanity. Every person we execute negates our illusory image that we are a compassionate and merciful society.

Although the U.S. Supreme Court has never held that the death penalty is "cruel and unusual" and thus violative of the

Eighth Amendment, Justice Blackmun recently stated in an agonized dissent:

> From this day forward, I no longer shall tinker with the
> machinery of death. . . . I believe that the death penalty,
> as currently administered, is unconstitutional. Even the
> most sophisticated death penalty schemes are unable to
> prevent human error from condemning the innocent.
> Innocent persons have been executed . . . and will
> continue to be executed under our death penalty
> scheme. Perhaps one day this court will develop
> procedural rules or verbal formulas that actually will
> provide consistency, fairness, and reliability in a
> capital-sentencing scheme. I am not optimistic that such
> a day will come.

When I read these words, I sent him a button which someone
had given me. It read: "We kill people to teach people it is wrong
to kill people." He wrote back, "I enjoyed the button and shall
keep it among my many artifacts here."

Politically Incorrect

I am committed to taking somewhat politically incorrect
cases in part because, over the years, my perception of good and
evil has changed drastically. I cannot regard someone like John
Gotti as more evil than someone in George Bush's position. This
doesn't mean John is a Sunday school principal; he engaged in
very rough business, much of it illegal, violent, and deadly, for all
I know. But on the other hand, he didn't commit the many inde-
cencies that some officials get away with. These people also violate the penal code—Oliver North and Caspar Weinberger, for
example—but they are not punished. Sometimes they even
become heroes and candidates for public office.

What's worse—organized crime or corporate crime? The
crimes committed by Michael Milken affected hundreds of busi-
nesses and thousands of employees who lost their livelihoods,
homes, health, perhaps even their lives because of his manipulations. His punishment for this was three years in jail, and he was
allowed to keep half a billion dollars. Many people would will-
ingly do three years in jail for that amount of money.

What about the effects of the malfeasance of the savings and loan executives on the rest of us? Don't American corporate heads commit crimes? I can't really judge organized crime as any worse than many so-called legitimate people. Sometimes the government behaves worse than any individual. Leonard Peltier has been imprisoned for eighteen years by the government, which has long since admitted it fabricated and hid evidence and suborned perjury in order to convict him. Is that not worse than what Gotti did? What about the corporations whose profit-making goals result in serious harm to others? For example, when Nestlé's corporation peddled its baby formula in Third World countries, it spread lies about nutrition in order to convince women to substitute its formula for nursing.

Americans have to stop accepting at face value the lies and misinformation we are fed by corporations, the government, and the rest of the Establishment. Descartes said, "The first precept was never to accept a thing as true until I knew it as such without a single doubt." We must not believe anything until we are satisfied that it is true. Since many people don't have enough information and don't want to bother to get it, I feel a responsibility to try to provide that information, at least in my area of expertise. Because once they have the facts, people do wake up. Watergate woke us up. So did the Iran-Contra affair.

Of course, after a while, the details fade. William Safire once quipped that Watergate would quickly be forgotten because in America "it's always darkest before the yawn."

But I refuse to become cynical, and I remain a cautious optimist; that's why I keep fighting. Whether a defendant is black, brown, white, straight, gay, Arab, or Jew, if it's a political case, I'm there.

Minorities need stronger advocates than whites. And the rich have resources that the poor can't even imagine. Thus, I define capital punishment this way: Those without capital get punished. As Third World people become the majority in this country early in the next century, they will continue their struggle to attain the promise of the Bill of Rights—and lawyers like me will be there to help them.

In recent years, the Bill of Rights, virtually destroyed by the decisions of the Supreme Court majority during the Reagan-Bush era, has nearly ceased to exist for most of the people in this country. Maybe it exists for the middle class and the rich, but it doesn't for most of my clients. We lawyers who call ourselves progressive must find a way to change this both within and outside the courtroom.

We used to look to the federal courts for our salvation, but Reagan and Bush filled these courts with ideologues who are fundamentally antilibertarian. An example is the appointment of Clarence Thomas, a man to the far right of Ghengis Khan. Today we must take our battles back to the state courts, try to win with the juries, and hope that Congress will continue to overrule some of the most egregious Supreme Court decisions, as they did with the passage of the Civil Rights Act of 1991. And we must keep fighting and strive for a better day.

CHAPTER EIGHTEEN

The Fire This Time

People, we best make ourselves ready.

THE COP WAS JUSTIFIABLY EXECUTED, I TOLD THE CROWD AT A RALLY twenty-seven years ago in Oakland, California. John Gleason, a Plainfield, New Jersey, policeman, had been stomped to death by an enraged crowd of blacks earlier that year during an offshoot of the so-called Newark riots.

Since then, and before then, a civil war has been fought in this country. That war has gone on for generations. At this point, I believe that some form of a revolution appears to be inevitable. While I think that violence is wrong, sometimes it is the most effective method of dramatizing grievances and perhaps the only way to force the public to pay attention. James Baldwin called it *The Fire Next Time*—the holocaust that will occur when black people finally act out their rage.

Back in 1967 the Plainfield cop had ignored orders, entered a black ward, and during a confrontation, shot a youth, Bobby Lee Williams, twice in the stomach. When Williams fell, Gleason, with the crowd closing in on him, ran for his life. When his cap fell to the ground, he stopped to pick it up, a fatal mistake. His pursuers trampled him to death.

My comment about Officer Gleason's death was criticized sharply. While it might appear insensitive, it reflects my conviction that certain acts of violence are inextricably related to the awful turmoil, mainly across racial lines, that plagues our society. The cancer of white racism will eventually destroy us if we can't eradicate it or at least arrest its metastasis.

The reaction of New Jersey officialdom to the policeman's death shows graphically how this disease permeates our nation. Bobby Lee Williams, who eventually recovered from his wounds, was tried for a variety of crimes, and I represented him, along with William Bender, a Center for Constitutional Rights lawyer. Although Bobby was found guilty of only a minor infraction and received a light sentence, that he was tried at all indicates the community's need to condemn the black victim and avenge the white policeman. George Merritt, the man convicted of Officer Gleason's "murder," was ultimately exonerated when Morty Stavis discovered that the state police had hidden from the defense a key identification witness's contradiction of his own trial testimony.

The Great Emancipator

To relieve our collective consciences, we whites have constructed one illusion after another to convince ourselves that we are not racists. Even Abraham Lincoln, "the Great Emancipator," often referred to blacks as "niggers" and attempted to rid America of them. He developed a plan to "colonize people of African descent" in the South American Republic of New Granada, now Colombia. In August 1862, he called a number of free blacks to the White House and told them about his plan, adding, "You are yet far removed from being placed on an equality with the white race." White blood was being shed unjustifiably in the Civil War on behalf of black people, Lincoln told his visitors. "There will never be peace in this country unless you get out."

Noah Pittman, whose brother had invented a form of shorthand, was at the meeting and recorded it. His notes mention that some of the blacks cried out, "Shame! Shame!" when Lincoln spoke those words. The next day, Frederick Douglass called him a "sublime racist."

When Lincoln's White House audience was unenthusiastic about his preposterous plan, he then arranged for the newly recognized Republic of Haiti to receive American blacks shipped to its Ile à Vache (Cow Island). Of the first four hundred sent, many died of tropical diseases or were murdered by Haitians. After the few survivors were returned to America, Lincoln reluctantly abandoned his colonization idea.

In 1964, I visited the great American writer Carl Sandburg at his home in Flat Rock, North Carolina, while I was working on a civil rights case in nearby Charlotte. I had first read about Lincoln's forced emigration schemes in Sandburg's monumental Lincoln biography *The War Years*. "Mr. Sandburg," I asked him, "how do you square this plan with your love of Lincoln?"

"It was just an aberration," Sandburg said. "The first half of 1862 was a very low point in the war, and Lincoln despaired of ending the bloodshed. He was so upset by the great numbers of people dying that he thought if he could only get rid of the blacks, the conflict would go away."

I took Sandburg at his word, but after I learned more about Lincoln, I came to realize that "the Great Emancipator" had indeed been "a sublime racist." Even the Emancipation Proclamation, which was not issued until the end of his second year in office, was billed by Lincoln as "a fit and necessary war measure" rather than a humanitarian act. It liberated no slaves, as it only affected those in the Confederate states while keeping in bondage those in areas loyal to the Union. When Gen. David Hunter, the Union commander at Fort Sumter, received news of the proclamation, he freed all the slaves at the retaken fort. But Lincoln countermanded Hunter's order, saying, "They are slaves. They remain slaves."

Lincoln's assassination made possible the ten glorious years of the Reconstruction period that followed the Civil War. Had Lincoln lived, he would have almost certainly implemented his 10 percent plan. If 10 percent of those in any seceded state who had voted in 1860 (white males only) pledged allegiance to the federal government, Lincoln's plan provided for that state to be welcomed back into the Union with no restrictions.

Andrew Johnson, Lincoln's successor, didn't have the political clout to push the measure through. But Lincoln most certainly would have, and there would never have been a Reconstruction era during which enormous numbers of ex-slaves were absorbed, at least temporarily, into the mainstream.

In many ways, John Wilkes Booth saved the humanitarian gains of the Civil War by assassinating Lincoln, quite the opposite of what he had intended. No historian will advance this theory, and, of course, the great mass of people who visit the Lincoln Memorial would not want to accept it. But as Thucydides once wrote, "History is words without meaning." Amen!

Recently, the hardly radical *New York Times* acknowledged the extent of our black-white dichotomy. Probing the 1993 murders of tourists in Miami, a *Times* editorial drew attention to the racism of a Florida sheriff who had commented publicly that a tourist—who was white—was the first person slain in his county that year. He ignored the black resident who had been killed there only three weeks earlier. The editorial said the sheriff's remark was "a slip of the tongue, perhaps, but revealing nonetheless."

What this newspaper so belatedly noticed, blacks have known for centuries. Most of their leaders who dared to raise the issue have been persecuted, assassinated, or both. We have only to recall the criminalization of Marcus Garvey's "Back to Africa" movement, the hounding of W. E. B. Du Bois and Paul Robeson, the vilification of Martin King and Malcolm X, and their subsequent murders.

Malcolm X

When Spike Lee made his film biography of Malcolm X and cast me as the racist judge who put Malcolm away, I had a difficult time speaking my lines. It was the real Malcolm I saw standing before me, not Denzel Washington, an actor. Finally, I forced myself to think about prison's positive effects on Malcolm—that's where he found Islam and changed his life—and was able to pronounce sentence without choking.

Malcolm and I first became acquainted in 1960, but it was some time before I finally understood his political message. We met when I invited him to appear on my WMCA radio show *Pro and Con*. Its format consisted of two guests debating a controversial issue, and Malcolm was so interesting and articulate, no matter whom he was debating, that he appeared on the show several times. During his first appearance, Malcolm discussed the question "Is Black Supremacy the Answer?" with the Reverend William M. James, pastor of the Metropolitan Community Methodist Church in Harlem.

I liked Malcolm instantly, even though I had been as wrong about him as I had been about Martin King before we met. While I expected Martin to be saintlike, which he surely wasn't, I thought Malcolm would be a fire-eater, burning with hatred, with no sense of humor. He was actually quite the opposite, a warm, responsive human being, not at all as he was depicted by the media.

From 1960 to 1965, I ran into Malcolm on radio programs, speakers' platforms, and airplanes. He was quite wonderful, and I came to care for him very much. Once Lotte, who was then active in civil rights, asked Malcolm if he would give an interview to the *Patent Trader,* a small Westchester weekly that could hardly have had many black readers. Malcolm sat and talked good-naturedly for four hours to the reporter, a paraplegic with multiple sclerosis named Gil Joel, who used one toe to type his notes.

While Malcolm probably had no idea of the true extent of J. Edgar Hoover's villainy toward him and other black leaders, he certainly understood that the white Establishment would fight to the death to maintain its power and assets. When Malcolm, early in his career, referred to whites as "devils," he was portraying them as enemies of black people. He spent most of his public life trying to convince his black audiences that they had to resist the white avalanche "by any means necessary." A failure to resist, he often said, was part of a residual slave mentality. I completely agreed with him.

After he made his Hajj to Mecca, Malcolm became even more dangerous to the Establishment. He then understood that he needed to include everyone, not only his black sisters and brothers, in the struggle against oppression. It was then that the FBI redoubled its efforts to provoke violence between him and Elijah Muhammad. The FBI succeeded. Breaking from Muhammad in a rift that would lead to his downfall, Malcolm formed his own Organization of Afro-American Unity (OAAU).

On February 14, 1965, former SNCC staffer Mike Thelwell and I met Malcolm in a New York airport. He looked haggard and tired, very unlike his usual impeccable self. He was untidy and unshaven, his suit wrinkled, as if he had been up all night. He seemed very nervous, the only time I ever saw him when he wasn't consummately in control.

Malcolm told us that his situation was desperate. He felt threatened by various forces, the FBI and the Nation of Islam. "I'm going to be dead," he kept saying. He was extremely agitated, and when we tried to reassure him, he wearily replied, "I know what I'm talking about." I remember saying, somewhat naively, "Well, it can't be that bad. Nobody can do anything to you."

At some point during the conversation, Malcolm took me aside and said, "I have had a conversation with Dr. King. He talked about how we might amalgamate, work together, that he would do the South and I would do the North and we would try to have some sort of a unified command." Malcolm said he and Martin had talked about warring against poverty and racism and everything else that hurt blacks and kept them down. Despite his exhaustion and nervousness, he was quite excited about the possibility of uniting with Martin.

I remember this conversation well because of the horrors that followed. That same night, Malcolm's home in East Elmhurst, Queens, was firebombed. On Thursday, certain of his impending death, he told a reporter, "I live like a man who's already dead." Three days after that, he was assassinated.

On Sunday, February 21, he had arrived at the Audubon Ballroom to prepare for his weekly speech to OAAU members. He had given orders that no one in the room be searched for weapons as they entered, so as Benjamin X Goodman made warm-up remarks, he scanned the audience for members of the Fruit of Islam (FOI), the security force of the New York mosque. Goodman didn't see any FOI members, so he finished his remarks and introduced Malcolm.

Malcolm strode vigorously to the plywood lectern at center stage. Just as he began his greeting, "Salaam Aleikum, brothers and sisters," a five-man death squad went into a well-rehearsed plan. A man in the rear shouted, "Nigger, what are you doing with your hand in my pocket?" Malcolm called out to the audience, "Hold it! Take it easy!" Another man, who had been seated in the first row, emptied both barrels of a sawed-off shotgun into Malcolm. Betty Shabazz, Malcolm's wife, screamed, "They're killing my husband! They're killing my husband!" and threw their children to the floor. Two more assassins rushed to the stage and fired ten more shots into Malcolm's downed body as another accomplice in the rear threw a smoke bomb.

Malcolm was most likely dead before he hit the floor. Still, Gene Roberts, an undercover cop who acted as his bodyguard, tried mouth-to-mouth resuscitation. It was no use. Malcolm X was declared dead by a Columbia Presbyterian Hospital physician at 3:30 P.M. from "multiple shotgun slugs and bullet wounds of the chest, heart and aorta."

Strangely, a uniformed NYPD officer had been stationed in the hospital's emergency room before the assassination. And although there were no cops visible in the Audubon Ballroom that afternoon, two officers present in the building, hidden from public view, were in radio contact with the cop in the emergency room.

Perhaps nothing is more revealing than the FBI's formal announcement after Malcolm's assassination that it would play no role in the inquiry into the murder. Although the Bureau had devoted thousands of hours to investigating Malcolm, Elijah Muhammad, and the Nation of Islam, it instructed its New York office "not to furnish the NYPD with any information developed without prior Bureau clearance. . . . This appears to be a murder case, basically a problem of the NYPD, and the FBI should not become involved."

We now know from revelations of the Church Committee in the mid-1970s and subsequent investigations into Malcolm's assassination that his death was indirectly caused by the FBI. In 1969, four years after Malcolm's assassination, the FBI took credit for it and called it the result of its successful stimulation of the feud between Malcolm and Elijah Muhammad. The FBI had worked hard to exacerbate the difficulties between Muhammad and Malcolm and had also created problems where none existed. Malcolm had been followed, watched, wiretapped, and hounded by the FBI for years before his death. FBI agents didn't actually pull the trigger that awful day, but they figuratively loaded the guns and placed them in the hands of the assassins.

On the Saturday after Malcolm was murdered, I crowded into Harlem's Faith Temple of the Church of God in Christ along with hundreds of others as thousands more stood in the streets outside, grieving. I heard Ossie Davis eulogize Malcolm as "our manhood, our living black manhood.

"He was a prince—our black shining prince—who did not hesitate to die because he loved us so."

Malcolm's Assassins

After Malcolm was killed, I was asked by the family of Talmadge Hayer to defend him. Hayer had been arrested at the scene after being shot by one of Malcolm's followers. I refused because of my relationship with Malcolm, but now I wish that I had accepted. Because of what I subsequently learned about Malcolm's assassination, that is one case I am sorry I turned down.

Hayer was tried in 1966 for the murder of Malcolm X, along with Thomas 15X Johnson and Norman 3X Butler, now Khalil Islam and Muhammad Abdul Aziz, respectively. After first denying his own involvement, Hayer then admitted his guilt but insisted that neither Johnson nor Butler had had anything to do with Malcolm's murder. He testified that four other men, whose names he refused to disclose, were the ones who had planned and committed the murder with him.

I was at the trial as an observer when Hayer testified, and it appeared to me that when he took the stand on behalf of Johnson and Butler, he may have hurt them badly. Refusing to give up the other four names made it appear as if he were lying in order to save Johnson and Butler, since his own guilt was so clear. During his summation, the prosecutor emphasized this point, and when the jury convicted all three men, it was obvious that it had not believed Hayer at all.

In September 1971, during the Attica uprising, I met Hayer, who had changed his name to Mujahid Abdul Halim; he was in charge of the Muslim inmates who were guarding the hostages. He told me that he felt guilty about letting Butler and Johnson rot in jail for something they had not done. But he still refused to reveal the names of the other assassins. "I'm between a rock and a hard place," he told me.

Finally, in 1977, during a talk with me and Nurridin Faiz, an Islamic cleric, Hayer finally gave up the names: Benjamin Thomas, Leon Davis, Wilbur Kinley, and William X Bradley. Hayer said all of the assassins belonged to the Newark Mosque No. 25. During a series of prison visits, he revealed all the details of the assassination and then signed a lengthy affidavit affirming what he had told me.

Acting New York County Supreme Court justice Harold I. Rothwax, determined not to rock the boat, ruled that this affidavit was not enough to reopen the case, even though Hayer had named and described the four men and given their last known addresses as well as information about their backgrounds. An investigation might well have determined the truth. But the FBI, aware of its part in Malcolm's assassination, desperately wanted the truth kept under wraps, probably forever.

An additional factor was that Malcolm's widow did not want the case reopened, undoubtedly because she didn't want to relive those awful moments when she watched her husband die under a hail of bullets. Louis Stokes, then head of the Black Caucus in the U.S. House of Representatives, told me that Malcolm's murder had not been included in the investigations undertaken by the House Select Committee on Assassination because of Betty Shabazz's objections. The caucus, he added, would not support any attempt by me to reopen the case unless she changed her mind.

Frustrated, there was not much I could do except publicize the names Hayer had given me. I named them during an appearance on the *Dick Cavett Show* in 1993. And I provided Spike Lee with documentation about them. After he read the material I gave him, Spike adopted Hayer's version of who really killed Malcolm and listed the four names in the credits of his film *Malcolm X.*

By now, Butler and Johnson have been released from prison, but their names have never been cleared. Although on a work release program, Hayer is still an inmate.

Comes the Revolution

Malcolm is just one example, albeit a noteworthy one, of the lopping off of black leadership. Yet, despite what happened to him, King, Garvey, Powell, and so many others, the struggle for freedom and equality continues, muted in one era, thunderous in another. Its goal, as described by Frederick Douglass during the Civil War, is the "full and complete adoption" of blacks "into the great national family of America."

The L.A. rebellion in 1993—in reaction to the Rodney King verdicts—was a small indication of the type of revolution that I believe is inevitable. The uprisings in Watts and Newark and other cities thirty years ago were also an indication. The rage and frustration will erupt, Baldwin wrote in *The Fire Next Time,* and we will reap the whirlwind. America will only wake up when it's burning up. Burn, baby, burn!

I watched the Rodney King verdicts come in on my television screen, sitting in the living room of my old Federal house, thinking how, 140 years ago, it had been used as a stop on the Underground Railroad. The Rodney King case, in which the venue was changed to ensure that the white cops who beat him would be cleared, showed us what could be unleashed in the fire next time. Rodney King brought it home once again: No matter what the cops do, even if you have it on tape, they will not be convicted.

I could imagine what that white middle-class jury was thinking when they acquitted the four police officers: "Listen, Rodney King is black. He was probably at fault in some way. If we vote against these officers, what are the police in our community going to do to us? They're not going to watch our house anymore, they're not going to help our kids cross the street, and they may even frame us for something. Where best does our future lie?"

I think, unbeknownst to them, their future holds many more L.A.s, not merely a few long, hot summers but serious, dangerous revolts. The L.A. uprising had a positive effect because it forced federal indictments against the cops who had beaten Rodney King, no small thing. And even though the two policemen who were found guilty of federal charges of violating King's civil rights received light sentences, at least someone was held responsible. Also, in April 1994, a federal civil jury awarded King millions of dollars in compensatory damages but denied him punitive damages.

Too many Americans don't comprehend the rage in the black inner-city dweller. My current defense of Colin Ferguson, a black man charged with murdering six people and wounding nineteen on the Long Island Railroad on December 7, 1993, is based on that "black rage." I first heard the term a generation ago in a book bearing that title written by two black psychiatrists, William H. Crier and Price M. Cobbs.

> People bear all they can and, if required, bear even more. But if they are black in present day America they have been asked to shoulder too much. . . . Turning from their tormenters, they are filled with rage.

Ferguson's rage was a catalyst for violence resulting from a preexisting mental illness, most likely schizophrenia. It was a mental condition no different from the battered-wife syndrome, posttraumatic stress disorder, or the child-abuse-accommodation syndrome in that, in conjunction with mental illness, it gave rise to terrible acts of violence. Ferguson, from a wealthy Jamaican family, had attended private school, enjoyed many luxuries, and was never able to adjust to the white racism that he found when he came to this country. He never developed the defense mechanisms that American-born blacks are forced to learn. (Although in April 1994 Ron and I were barred from talking to the press about Ferguson, which we had been doing in order to humanize him to the general public, the court has lifted the gag order, and we can once again freely speak for and about our client.)

I feel strongly that it is essential that white Americans begin to understand black rage and take it seriously. Read the newspapers: The revolution may already have begun. As Baldwin wrote in warning to his brothers and sisters: "A dreadful day is upon us, and, as nobody's going to give us any straw . . . people, we best make ourselves ready."

CHAPTER NINETEEN

1994: Kunstler & Kuby

Hey, it's great! Where do I sign?

Attacks Against Defense Attorneys

IN THE LAST DECADE, THE GOVERNMENT HAS LAUNCHED AN ORGANIZED attack against the rights of criminal defendants and their attorneys. In violation of the rights of defendants, we now have anonymous juries, preventive detention, denial of counsel of choice, malicious leaks to the press of prejudicial, often false, material, and fabrication or suppression of evidence.

In the government's vendetta against defense attorneys of a certain stripe—those who represent organized-crime figures, accused terrorists, or other outcasts—it uses a combination of methods. Lawyers are driven out of cases or held in contempt, or they have sanctions imposed against them.

Fee Disclosure

One device, an attempt to force lawyers to report who's paying them if they receive a cash fee of more than $10,000, is a violation of privacy and an intrusion into lawyer-client privilege. The government has secured contempt indictments against lawyers who have refused to disclose the source of funds they receive.

My cocounsel on the Larry Davis cases, Lynne Stewart, was recently under a similar indictment, which could have resulted in her disbarment. When she represented a client in a drug case, the Manhattan district attorney tried to force her to disclose information about her fee. "We want to know where the money came from. The defendant [that Lynne Stewart] represents is the leader of a conspiracy, and if we can show the jury where the money came from to pay her fee, that's part of the proof of the conspiracy," the D.A. said.

Lynne refused to testify before a grand jury and as a result was charged with criminal contempt and refusal to cooperate with a grand jury, a felony. Fortunately, the charges were dismissed by a judge who understood that they had been brought to harass Lynne and would have no real bearing on the case. Since then, however, this decision has been appealed by the D.A. And while her legal problems are pending, Lynne has to endure the uncertainties generated by a possible conviction—which could end her professional career.

Rule 11

One way the government has harassed me and other civil rights attorneys recently is through the use of a Rule 11 sanction. Rule 11 is a newly amended federal rule which provides for sanctions against attorneys who file "frivolous" lawsuits. It has been used primarily against civil rights lawyers. Under a Rule 11 sanction, for example, the Christic Institute, a Catholic civil rights organization, has been saddled with a $1 million fine for its Iran-Contra lawsuit.

I also have been fined as a result of being sanctioned under Rule 11. *In Re Kunstler* had its origins in 1988, when two Native Americans, Timothy Jacobs and Eddie Hatcher, took hostages in a newspaper office in Robeson County, North Carolina, and held them until the governor of the state agreed to investigate drug trafficking by local officials. When Jacobs and Hatcher were indicted by a federal grand jury for hostage taking, I represented Hatcher, and Lewis Pitts, a lawyer for the Christic Institute South, stood up for Jacobs.

Because I was representing Larry Davis at the time, I could not attend the trial of Hatcher and Jacobs, and the presiding judge refused to postpone it. As a result, my client represented himself. We consulted on the telephone each night. Eddie Hatcher did an excellent job and even read a summation that I had written for him. He and Timothy Jacobs were acquitted of all charges.

After the district attorney of Robeson County, Joe Freeman Britt, convened a state grand jury which indicted Hatcher and Jacobs for kidnapping, they had to stand trial again, on state charges, for the same crimes. A defense committee was formed for Hatcher and Jacobs, and its members were harassed on every level. One member of the defense committee, a Native American lawyer who was running for judge against D.A. Britt, was murdered.

On Election Day, because the dead man received the most votes, the candidate who ran second was elected judge: Britt, known for executing more people than any other prosecutor in the country. His office was decorated with a photograph of North Carolina's electric chair.

When I heard about the persecution of the Robeson Defense Committee members, along with Lewis Pitts and Barry Nackell, a law professor at the University of North Carolina, I filed a federal lawsuit against Britt and several other North Carolina officials to stop harassment of committee members. As soon as we filed our complaint, the harassment stopped; we then withdrew the suit.

Six weeks later, lawyers for Britt and the other defendants applied for sanctions against us under Rule 11, claiming that our lawsuit had been "frivolous." The court ordered us to pay $120,000, a monstrous sum for attorneys who work, for the most part, pro bono.

My case was fought by Morty Stavis until his death in 1992. He succeeded in getting our original fine of $120,000 reduced to $43,000. The Committee in Support of Civil Rights Attorneys, a fund-raising group comprised of Spike Lee, Oliver Stone, Ruby Dee, Ossie Davis, Robert De Niro, Brice Marden, the abstract painter, and others, worked to raise money. Ultimately, the Center for Constitutional Rights, with the help of these supporters and others, paid the fine.

Contempt

On December 20, 1991, I received a contempt conviction in connection with my representation of Yusef Salaam, one of the youths convicted of raping and beating a jogger in Central Park. During an appearance for Yusef before Manhattan State Supreme Court judge Thomas B. Galligan, I became furious at the judge. One of the jurors in the rape trial had alleged jury misconduct. He had said that during the trial another juror read news articles about the case to the rest of the panel. When Galligan refused to hold a hearing about this matter, I lost my cool and said, "You have exhibited what your partisanship is. You shouldn't be sitting in court. You are a disgrace to the bench."

Galligan held me in contempt and sentenced me to thirty days in jail or a fine of $250. I refused to pay and intended to go to jail. Apparently a Wall Street lawyer who loves me but who chose to remain anonymous sent Morty Stavis the money for my fine, and I did not have to serve any time. I was most upset. The same thing had been done many times to Martin King; often, when he thought a point would be made if he remained in jail, someone would put up his bail. I was looking forward to spending time in jail and planned to have my teeth cleaned and a physical checkup at state expense. But, mainly, the inequity rankled: The well-to-do can get out of jail, while a poor person, who doesn't have 250 bucks, has to stay in.

My contempt conviction remained on the record, and in April 1992, I appeared before a disciplinary committee of the appellate division to determine how I should be punished. The disciplinary committee—a panel of two lawyers and a layperson—would hear the case, then make a recommendation to the appellate division concerning my punishment.

I enjoyed the hearing immensely. Usually, such hearings are conducted privately to avoid embarrassment to the lawyers facing disciplinary charges. But I went public and invited the public and press to the hearing. The courtroom was full to bursting, with many people standing.

I planned to tell the panel, "I've spent the better part of my life doing what I consider important and constructive work in the law. This type of proceeding against me amounts to deliberate harassment. Characterizing my outburst before Judge Galligan as 'a serious crime' when the misconduct of prosecutors is routinely ignored is unfair and biased."

But my lawyers, Morty and Ron, took the conventional route. Ron most definitely didn't want me disbarred or suspended because then he would have too much work to do. They organized a defense, including testimony from four judges who said I was a good person with a kind heart and the best of intentions. This defense went against my grain. I felt that having judges say that I am a decent man was like begging for mercy. But Morty and Ron did what I would have done had I been the lawyer instead of the client.

The whole episode brought back to me the contempts in the Chicago trial. I remember the furor after they were reversed. Sen. James L. Buckley, a Conservative Republican from New York, was so enraged that my home state of New York had refused to disbar me that he drafted legislation that would have permitted the Justice Department to disbar lawyers and would have removed the disciplining of lawyers from the profession. At the time, 1971, I described Buckley's bill as an attempt to frighten young lawyers away from practicing movement law. In the two decades between Chicago and this recent charge, I have never been convicted of contempt of court, despite some mighty close calls.

Almost a year after my public hearing, in May 1993, the disciplinary committee presented its recommendations. It chose a public reprimand, the least serious of the possible choices. The committee could have recommended that I be censured or disbarred. A reprimand is private, while a censure is public. The layperson on the panel, a woman who displayed an intense antipathy toward me during the hearing, dissented and recommended a censure.

This panel issued an absolutely wonderful statement, which, I must admit, made me feel terrific, along with its recommendation. It said, in part:

> [He] has served long and hard, many times, without
> fees as counsel in difficult and most-times unpopular
> causes. . . . He has devoted the better part of three
> decades in a commendable attempt to insure justice to
> the needy and to preserve the personal liberties of
> oppressed and threatened members of our society. At
> least in part, [his] strenuous efforts have resulted in
> significant improvements in our social and political
> order.

It also noted that I had represented unpopular defendants "zealously and competently" and that I had performed this role as "a credit to [my] profession."

Some months later, the appellate division finally decided what to do with me. Since I expected a reprimand, if anything, I was more than shocked when the court informed me on December 28, 1993, that I was being censured, a more serious and public punishment. This decision to censure me, which agreed with the minority opinion of that woman on the panel who had disliked me intensely, was given without explanation. When I heard about it, I suffered not a moment's unhappiness, though, because I consider the censure a badge of honor. It gives me pleasure to know that even today, a quarter of a century after Chicago, I can still upset the Establishment enough to cause it to put the screws to me. Clearly, the disciplining of anti-Establishment lawyers is part of the price we must pay for the expression of our principles.

Political Lawyers Won't Go Away

While awaiting outcomes in the contempt charge and the Rule 11 sanction, I didn't worry overmuch. If I had worried about everything that came down the pike during my life, I could not have functioned. Through the entire contempt process, I was comforted by the thought that if ever disbarred, I would write full-time on every political and legal subject under the sun and reach a larger audience than I could by practicing law.

But I always knew that wouldn't happen. I didn't think any government agency would have the guts to do it. Also, my offenses have never been monumental. These episodes were just part of the government's pattern of provoking and harassing defense attorneys. The government now understands that the choice of lawyer dictates the mode of defense and that the political lawyer is always a liability for the prosecution. But I am only one of many progressive lawyers; there are quite a number of us who do good work. So, no, no matter how it tries, the government will not eliminate us—as the Third Reich did when it disbarred all of its Jewish attorneys in September 1937.

Criticizing the Government

I've spent a lifetime criticizing our government. I oppose our current system of government, which I view as a tool utilized by the powerful few to control the powerless many. While I have not found a better system, I cannot approve of ours and do not take part in many of its rituals. For example, I never stand for the Pledge of Allegiance, because it is not true; the United States does not provide "justice for all." People don't like this because they want everyone to stand at the altar and worship. I once had a can of beer dumped on my head at Shea Stadium for not standing up during the playing of "The Star-Spangled Banner." During Super Bowl XXV, I agonized when Natalie Cole, a black woman, backed by a black chorus, sang the national anthem, with its hypocritical references to "the land of the free."

Our government compromises where it should be demanding, for example, in the area of federal appointees. Supreme Court nominees have been safe, rather pedestrian, choices. To law professors who write letters to the editor that appointees should be individuals of great scholarship, I say, that's baloney. Appointees should be men and women of great integrity and honor, people who want to uphold the Constitution, not people who want to play it safe within a political system to which they are beholden.

The Supreme Court has, for some years, been an enemy, a predominantly white court representing the power structure. I'd love to see someone like Arthur Kinoy as a member of that bench. But he would never be nominated because he's not safe, he's not mundane, he's not in the government's political mold.

Michael Kaufman, a reporter for the *New York Times,* did a little fantasizing with me over lunch one day as to what Strom Thurmond would ask me if I were nominated. "Mr. Kunstler, when you said, 'Burn, baby, burn,' what did you mean by that?" he would ask.

He'd also ask, "Do you smoke marijuana?"

And I would answer, "I do smoke it, sir, but I don't inhale."

Fear

Despite my being embroiled in controversy and head-on battle with the government time after time, I am not the fearless man that some may think I am. Frequently, I get real scared. During a federal criminal case a couple of years ago, the judge criticized me harshly when I said I hadn't received an important piece of evidence from the U.S. attorney. She said, "I'm going to check your cocounsel. I'm sure he got the document. I'm going to do something about your lack of candor."

For a moment, I was afraid; at the time, I had that one contempt outstanding. I felt a visceral reaction to her threat, a fear that she would make my life miserable or would bias the jury against my client. She acted as if she had me; she would be the judge who finally got Bill Kunstler.

Back at my office, I called my cocounsel, and he hadn't received the evidence, either. So I said to myself, Now, Billy, the little feeling of fear because she's a crazy judge and could make life miserable for you for a year or so—that's something you have to deal with. I decided to go on the offensive. I produced an affidavit and two exhibits, accused the U.S. attorney of defrauding us by withholding evidence, and presented all this to the judge. After she read the documents, she gave me a wan, embarrassed smile. I said, "I want your comments about lack of candor stricken from the record." I don't know if they ever were, but at least I made my point.

Kunstler & Kuby

The first year Ron Kuby worked for me as a law intern, I gave him a beautiful engraved leather address book. Trouble was, I had it engraved "Ronald Quby," because I thought that was his name. When he pointed out the misspelling, I said, "It looks much better spelled Quby. It's how you pronounce it." He laughed. That was in 1982, when I was sixty-three and Ron was twenty-five. He has been with me ever since. Our relationship is based on shared laughter and a similar point of view about politics and the law.

At Cornell Law School, Ron was a brilliant misfit who made Law Review and also worked for Prisoners' Legal Services. When he found that he didn't have time for both, he quit Law Review and realized that his unusual priorities set him apart from his classmates. The work at Prisoners' Legal Services led Ron eventually to a summer internship in my office.

When he called the day before he was to start work, I said, "Come on in. I've got a big job for you. See you at eight-thirty. 'Bye." He called me Mr. Kunstler, and I said, "Bill. Bill. It's always Bill." It took him a while to call me Bill, though, because when he was a kid, I had been one of his heroes.

Ron's first glimpse of me was of a big guy naked from the waist down. I opened the door to him that first morning wearing nothing but a button-down shirt. I offered him coffee and a roll as I scurried around, getting ready for court. Downstairs, in the office, I handed Ron his first job: "Here's a show-cause order. Go down to the Southern District clerk's office and file the order. They're going to assign you a day, and you fill it all in. Then come out to where I am in the Queens courthouse and give it to me immediately. You gotta get it done by eleven in the morning because we're on this trial, these two Black Panthers, and this is very important."

Maybe I shouldn't have, but I added, "Look, if you screw this up, don't come back." I said it in a friendly manner, of course, but clearly I had no time to baby-sit law students if they couldn't do the work. I went to court while Ron did what I had asked him to do. He brought me the papers by 11:00 A.M., and since I had expected nothing less, I didn't praise him.

My goal for anyone who works with me is, simply, to get the job done. That first day, when Ron tried to tell me his travails, I was not interested and turned him right off. It was an important lesson for him, and he learned it well. Today he does what he has to do, and we consult together constantly, but he never complains even when I am at my most irascible, which is far too often.

My habit of delegating work and expecting it to be done right was the butt of a joke that made the rounds years ago when Morty Stavis, Arthur Kinoy, and I were the three heavy honchos at the Center for Constitutional Rights. It went like this: A law student in his first year at the Center shows a brief that he's written to Morty, who reads it and says, "That's terrible, a piece of junk. You gotta redo the whole thing. Let me see it when you're done." The student walks away, crushed. Then he shows it to Arthur, who reads it and says, "It's pretty good. You put your finger on the right issue. Just a few things need to be changed." The student feels a bit better. Then he walks up to me. I leaf through the document and say, "Hey, it's great! Where do I sign?"

That joke is right on the money. I expect a lot from people, but once a job is done, it's over. If you do it well, great. If not, I don't want to hear your complaints or problems. I often yell when someone makes a mistake, which, I admit, is not pleasant, but that's how I function. The people who work with me know that, and they also know I never fire anyone. I let them quit.

The reason I assign work and expect it to get done right is, since I have done tens of thousands of cases—if I count every client, including mass arrests—I can't function if I have to attend to every detail myself. I simply don't have room in my mind for anything outside of my clients. If I give someone a job and it gets done, I'll sign. Just show me where.

Another example of this occurred during Ron's first week, when he accompanied me to court to hear the opening statements at the murder trial of two former Black Panthers. On our way to court, I suddenly and compulsively, as is my way, decided to see if I had my NYU Law Library ID card. When I pulled out the card, it fell down a street grate. Ron gallantly opened the grate and bent down to retrieve the card, but as he did, his pants ripped all the way from the top of his fanny to his crotch. "Nobody will see anything. Don't worry about it. Just keep your coat on," I reassured him. On the train, he was very nervous, so I joked, "Just don't let your pecker flop out during my opening statement."

To me, the important thing was getting to court and getting on with the case. My mind was on my opening, not on Ron's suit. When we got to the courthouse, I went into the courtroom, my only concern making a good opening statement and defending my clients. Ron, on the other hand, found a tailor shop nearby and had his pants sewn before entering the courtroom.

That first summer, Ron wrote a brief on a major case in a very obscure area of law, a remand of the Billy Phillips case which ultimately went to the Supreme Court. Phillips had been a star witness for the Knapp Commission, which investigated police corruption in New York City in the 1970s. After Phillips had been indicted for murdering a prostitute and a pimp in 1968, the Knapp Commission went out of business. Later, evidence turned up showing hanky-panky in Phillips's trial; one of the jurors had applied for a job with the prosecutor, the Manhattan district attorney. I filed a habeas corpus in federal court claiming that Phillips had been framed to discredit the Knapp Commission and offered proof of collusion between the D.A. and the juror. We won, and Phillips's conviction was overturned. But the district attorney eventually appealed the ruling to the Supreme Court, where we lost. The Supreme Court saw nothing wrong with a juror in a murder case applying for a job with the prosecutor and reinstated Phillips's life sentence.

I read Ron's brief on the Phillips case on a Saturday night, and the next morning told him it was one of the best I had ever seen. I asked him to transfer to NYU and work for me instead of returning to Cornell. But Cornell refused to allow him to transfer. Ron worked for me that first summer and at the end considered himself my chattel. I guess he would have done anything for me, and still would. But by now it's mutual.

When he graduated from Cornell the following year, he became my associate and is now my partner. Our practice is chaotic and hectic, and both of us work much too hard. But Ron enjoys it as much as I do. We love the stimulation, the challenge, the excitement of high-profile, difficult cases. To relieve the tension, we laugh a lot, and luckily, many funny things happen in our office. For example, not too long ago I was contacted by a woman from

South Carolina who claimed the FBI had inserted a transmitter into her vagina. "Take it out," I told her. She wasn't very happy with that advice.

I expect Ron will be here always, as long as always is, carrying on the work of Kunstler & Kuby.

Last Words . . . Sort of

I WANT TO END ON A NOTE ABOUT THE FUTURE, WHICH I BELIEVE BELONGS to my children, to all our children. I'm lucky to have four wonderful daughters, Karin and Jane, Emily and Sarah.

When Margie and I first married, she didn't want children. Later on, however, she decided that having a child as part of a committed relationship might be a good idea. I kind of liked the idea, too. What I didn't know then was that having children would keep me young in spirit. With Sarah and Emily around, although I am ancient, I can't act decrepit. I have to show off for them.

Since all four daughters are activists in one way or another, I feel that I've passed on some of my values to them. Right now, Sarah, almost eighteen, is the most active. She was arrested for the first time in 1991 for participating in a takeover of Brooklyn borough president Howard Golden's office to force him to take a public position on a conservative he had appointed to the Board of Education. When I arrived at the precinct where Sarah was being held—in chains—they released her at my request. No charges were filed because she was under sixteen at the time.

For the last two years, Sarah has worked on AIDS and safer-sex education for high school students. In February 1993, she was one of a group who chained themselves to the Board of Education building to protest the board's refusal to give students a voice in policy. Also, in 1993, during a Times Square demonstration against the Gulf War, Sarah was hit over the head by a billy club–wielding cop.

In 1993, she was arrested for the second time for protesting the exclusion of gay and lesbian groups from New York's St. Patrick's Day Parade. When Margie and I rushed to the precinct where Sarah was being held, her arresting officer had a lot of fun with the situation. He said, "Like father, like daughter, I guess."

"That's the worst thing to say. She wants to be an individual on her own," I replied.

"Did I put my foot in it?" asked the cop.

"No, just a few toes," I joked.

Sarah will begin Yale in the fall of 1994. She is the second generation to attend that university, although the third generation has already gone through. Daniel and Jessica, Karin's children, graduated in 1993.

Karin is chief of her section at the New York State attorney general's office and was involved in the civil rights movement in the 1960s. She enrolled at a black college in the South, took part in voter registration during the 1964 Mississippi Freedom Summer, then spent two years in Africa in the Peace Corps. Karin has good instincts, but she can't be as active as she once was, and I don't expect her to be.

Jane, my second daughter, is chief of the department of rehabilitative medicine at St. Joseph Medical Center in Wichita, Kansas. She was arrested several times during the sixties for protesting the Vietnam War. Today she is active in the medical sphere and is president of the Wichita Medical Society. Jane's husband, a very conservative man who is an ophthalmologist, has influenced her to a certain extent. Sometimes, when Jane calls me and says, "Well, George says this, and George says that," playing the devil's advocate, I do my best to hold my own.

My youngest daughter, Emily, sixteen, has the same instincts as her sisters but is not as involved yet. She becomes quite emotional about certain things and clearly has good impulses. Emily does, however, have one arrest under her belt; she joined Sarah in the 1993 St. Patrick's Day Parade protest.

I realize that this book can never really end until I do, and ending is something I have no intention of doing. In 1992, when I carried Louis Nizer, then eighty-nine, up the steps of the Connecticut Supreme Court building to argue a case that he and I had worked on for more than two decades, I realized that a lawyer can really go on forever.

Nizer, who once wrote that "Kunstler, in Yiddish, means magician or artist, a man of wonderful tricks and abilities," was too frail to make it up the steps. I picked him up and carried him. As we slowly climbed up, a reporter asked me, "What are you doing with Mr. Nizer?"

"I'm his seventy-three-year-old law clerk," I replied. Actually, I wasn't in much better shape than Nizer and was afraid I would fall with him in my arms.

Once inside, Nizer argued on behalf of our client, Murray Gold, who had been convicted after four trials of murdering his in-laws. Nizer, attorney Victor Ferrante, and I tried to prove that Gold had been incompetent to stand trial at his fourth trial. We lost in the Supreme Court, but Ferrante and I are still carrying on and trying to get Gold released on parole.

My immediate goals are to defend my clients, to work on eliminating Rule 11, to continue being a thorn in the side of the Establishment, and to finish my book about activist lawyers like Fidel Castro, Ho Chi Minh, and Lenin, who became out-and-out revolutionaries.

For fun, I plan to pursue my burgeoning acting career. I have acted for most of my life, in plays at summer camp, at Yale, and in the army. During the past few years, my small roles in several films have given me great satisfaction. After I was a consultant on a film Oliver Stone may make about Wounded Knee, he hired me to play a lawyer in *The Doors.* I was a consultant on Spike Lee's *Malcolm X* when Spike decided to audition me for the role of the judge who sentenced Malcolm. After my audition, Spike said, "That sounds fine. I'll make you up and make you sound like the most racist judge that ever was." When it came time for me to do my part, I wanted to give Malcolm a suspended sentence, but Spike threatened to cut me from the film if I did, so I dutifully spoke the lines as they were written. The irony of having me play a racist judge added a small extra dash to the film.

At the premiere of *Goodfellas,* director Martin Scorsese told me that I had appeared in his first feature, *Mean Streets,* but I have absolutely no memory of that. He asked me to audition for the role of the lawyer in his remake of *Cape Fear,* and I did, but I lost out to Gregory Peck. I would have loved that part.

I was an extra, an older man out with a young date (played by my daughter Sarah), in *Carlito's Way,* and in late 1993 played myself in *The Paper.* Since I have loved greasepaint and applause all my life, I hope that those directors who find my face and voice interesting will continue to offer me parts.

In whatever future I have left, I will continue to do exactly what I have done since I first entered that bus terminal in Jackson, Mississippi, thirty-three years ago. My father collapsed at the age of eighty-one, on his way to make a house call, and died the next morning. My fantasy death scenario has me slumping down on a courtroom lectern after delivering an impassioned summation in a highly visible criminal trial. Of course, Ron envisions me slumping over *before* the summation so he can push my body aside and say, "Bill would have wanted me to do this. . . ." He jokes that my funeral will be my most well attended press conference ever. And I won't be able to say a word.

But, however it happens, I feel privileged to have lived during crucial periods in this country's history and to have played a small part in some of its more noteworthy events. I have hardly lived a life of quiet desperation. It has been a life whose high points more than compensated for those few that fell below the line, and I could not have wished for more.

I would like to be remembered as someone who did what I wanted to do with my life, who did it with some other end in view than the mere acquisition of tangible, material goods, who had some effect on the lives of people that I touched. And who contributed, in some way or another, to the holding on to whatever rights and liberties are still available to Americans.

If Shakespeare was correct and "What's past is prologue," then there is still much for me to do: cases to be tried, briefs to be written, motions to be drafted, appeals to be argued. I want to go on without a thought that someday I will not. Who knows? I've survived this far. Perhaps I'll always be around, in one form or another.

Index